TOUR de CUBA

Kevin Foster

Cycling Castro's Country

The Tour de Cuba

Book Three

MAY YOU & YOUR LIFE CONTINUE TO BE A Tour de Force!

[illegible] '08

Cycling Castro's Country: The Tour de Cuba

Published in the United States of America by Pisces Publications

For information, address or email...

Pisces Publications
Post Office Box 72
Kaweah Commonwealth,
California (93237)

Website: www.pisces-publications.com

China photos on pages 15, 16, 22 and 23 by Joseph Kugielsky

Back Cover photos by Jean Mayer

All other photos by Kevin Foster

First Edition, First Printing

Hardcover

ISBN 0-9760067-3-1

$30.00

To Jean

My Love, my Life,
Against the world's strife.
My Forever Friend,
Unto the Eternal End...

The true revolutionary is motivated by feelings of love.

Many will call me an adverturer, and I am,
but of a different type who put their lives on the line
to demonstrate their truths.

Ernesto "Che" Guevara

I want to ride my bicycle,
I want to ride my bike.
I want to ride my bicycle,
I want to ride it where I like.

"Bicycle Race," Queen

TOUR de CUBA SPONSORS

As with any great endeavor, you simply cannot achieve your desired goal alone. You need help, and much of it. You need to work with those of like mind in order that all may benefit from the end result.

Therefore, we begin with the most important aspect of any adventure: thanking the appropriate companies and individuals that saw the vision and were willing to sponsor it to the end.

In alphabetical order:

AEROSPOKE (carbon fiber wheels)

ALPINESTARS USA (cycle shoes & gloves)

AVOCET (cycle computer)

CENTERLINE SPORTS (Powerpost seat adjuster)

FASTRAK SYSTEMS (Camelbak water pouch)

INDUSTRIAL STRENGTH EYEWEAR (sunglasses)

INNOVATIVE BICYCLE COMPONENTS (hydraulic brakes)

KLEIN BICYCLES

KOOL FIT AMERICA (therapy lotion)

NEWK BIKE PRODUCTS (bar ends)

NUTRITION FOR LIFE (health products)

PENTAPURE (water filter bottle)

RA ANDO (cycle uniforms)

RESPRO (filter masks)

RETRAKS (bicycle travel bag)

SANDANA HEADGEAR

T-GEAR USA (cut-away seat)

TRI-FLOW (chain lubricant)

ACKNOWLEDGMENTS

As anyone who has ever made the attempt knows full well, writing a book of any size is a lonely, boring, sweat inspired process. At times, trying to fill a blank page can take hours; a full day perhaps. Whereas at other moments the words fly by faster than one can get them on the paper.

Many times I wanted to walk away from the project (and in fact did for awhile). *I'd rather live a grand adventure than write about one*, I thought numerous times, only to return and finish what I had set out to do.

Encouragement goes a long way, whether you're going through the daily mundane exercises that make up one's existence, or living a very public and open life.

To that end, acknowledgment needs to be recognized to those individuals that came into my life and coached me in their own ways to see that this book became a finished reality.

Kelly Culmer. Who never knew what she was dealing with when she chanced upon me. Her delightfully wicked and warped sense of humor could match my own. For me, she excelled as a literary agent, encouraging me to continue writing this book, because she felt there was a need for an adventurous story of this sort about the fabled island nation of Cuba that people of all ages would relate to and one day want to visit for themselves.

Dan DiLandro. An editor's editor. Kelly thought we'd make a good team and she was right. Dan not only did a superb job of handling the first draft of this book (and a bloody mess it was), but became a teacher along the way. He became more excited and involved in reading about the adventure than I was in writing it, which made me want to better myself during the rewrites.

James Chlebda. Bibliophile *extraordinare!* Who loved this story so much, he'd read passages of the manuscript to his dying father, and helped further shape the contents by suggesting I add maps and a question and answer section that only made the book much more useful to future readers.

Richard Fairchild. My sidekick in more ways than one. Another patriotic cyclist who not only maintains my website, but gives numerous suggestions along the way. Like me, Rick is also ignorant of such words as *can't* and *impossible*. He continues to push beyond the limits, and remains an inspiring and one-man cheering section.

Dick Tristao. Mild mannered in life, yet superhuman in graphic design and layout, Dick kept the project focused and on track during the last stages of completion; adding some great ideas of his own along the way and being the calm needed during my neurosis.

And finally, my sincere thanks and gratitude to **The Fans**. Your continued persistence in emailing me wanting more information about traveling throughout Cuba is what finally propelled me to publish this book so that you now have some kind of guide for yourselves.

THEREFORE...let the adventure begin...

PROLOGO

JUNE 10, 1995
DENALI, ALASKA
17,200 FEET

For five days we, along with about seventy-five others, had been trapped in our tents on the icy slopes of Mt McKinley, better known as *Denali, the Great One*. A few days before, three men froze to death in their sleeping bags. The winds continue to howl, battering the tents, trying to rip them apart. The snows piled high, engulfing us. We wondered which force of nature would claim us first.

A French team decided to go for the summit in these suicide conditions, and, shortly thereafter, one of their tents was ripped away by the sheer force of the storm, hurdling 3000 feet down the cliff. And still the winds roared and howled without relenting, never giving us a chance to escape. I lay between my partners in a goose-down coffin.

Someone in our gathering had decided to brave the outside to empty his bowels at a makeshift latrine in the middle of the camp. Within moments, his buttocks froze to the plywood, forcing others to rush out and try to peel him off. I thanked God for my constipation.

We slept to escape, drifting in and out. At this height, there's no rescue. We were totally on our own.

I was now in the second year of a tour called **American Summits** which was my own goal to place a full-scale mountain bike on the highest natural point in each of the 50 united States (from an historical point, our forefathers, in their writings, spelled out our country's name in this manner, to give clearance that States, always being capitalized, shows their sovereignty as a nation unto itself. States rights, but united for strength. There is no reason to change their point of view in my own writings.)-- 49 of which had been completed.

The Tour was for many reasons...

Personally, I had always wanted to see all 50 States. Also, the government was beginning to close down many trails to mountain bikers across the country, and something had to be done to bring attention to that fact.

The Tour would inspire people, young and old, to get outside and exercise, because, "if he can get a bike up McKinley, then I guess I can do that hill in my backyard."

Lastly, my late manager, Charlie Litsky, said I needed a tour of America that would be different, exciting, inspirational and "a first" after my successful 1990 tour of becoming the only person to cycle atop the length of the Great Wall of China.

This was my idea of another first by bicycle-- a feat that nearly everyone I confided in said I'd never be able to pull off. That it would get me, and probably others along with me, killed. But the idea just got stuck in my head-- and I wanted to see it through.

Of course no one told me this would be one of *Denali's* worst climbing seasons in as many years as anyone could remember. From the moment we disembarked in a blizzard at 7500 feet (after which our pilot flipped over upon take off, destroying the plane), to the moment where we now lay, we were pounded by the winds everyday.

At one point, the temperature reached minus 72-degrees below Fahrenheit. The liquid from our nasal passages froze above our upper lips, while the condensation within our hooded masks turned to icicles around our chins. If we didn't keep our breath warm, our lungs would have become lumps of ice. And God help any of us if we had to urinate at the wrong time. In moments, our penises would have turned into popsicles.

No matter what the equipment-- whether it be the goosedown sleeping bags, the Gore-Tex, the fleece clothing, or the layers of other synthetic material we had on us, we just couldn't get warm enough. Bits of ice, like splinters, seemed to run through the blood vessels of our veins.

During the five days of torment, my teammates and I were mostly silent, trying to read whatever books we carried along to clear our minds of the outside conditions, or play mind games, like naming all the capitals of the united States in alphabetical order, then as many countries as we could. None of us bothered much with cooking: Who wanted to go outside to get the snow for melting? We couldn't

This is what happens when one goes walking in minus -72 degrees below zero, Fahrenheit on Alaska's *Denali.*

be sure we would return to safety. We lived on cookies, candy, and trailmix, sleeping more and more to pass the hours. At our altitude, daylight, though clouded by the relentless storm, was always with us. We never once saw darkness. Time stood still.

The $11,000 specially-designed bike for this Tour lay just outside, buried in days' worth of ice and snow. It had become an anchor, and I was ready to toss it off this godforesaken' whore of a mountain as I had done on other State highpoints. To cut it from my life once and for all.

During my drifting in and out, I dreamt and thought about my family, whom I hadn't seen in years. In a few months, my younger brother was getting married. It was to be a reunion of sorts, albeit an uneasy one. My mother had reluctantly come to accept my adventurous lifestyle and world fame. My father was the opposite, having disassociated himself from me in every way possible until I conformed to the standard 9 to 5 lifestyle. My siblings, for the most part, were split down the middle about who I was to the public and what I did for a living.

I thought and dreamt about Jean-- my rock, my best friend, my life. I missed her the most and, during my entrapment, actually cried once, the tears freezing to my face. Part of me knew the summit was lost. Maybe, perhaps, under our own strength, we could reach the top, but not with the bike. I might have been willing to try and die in the attempt, but I couldn't ask that of others. Still, I was optimistic that the storm would clear long enough to give us a chance.

Kevin and bicycle at 17,200-feet of Alaska's *Denali* during the **American Summits** tour, June 10, 1995.

I read my pocket Bible, returning often to the story where Jesus lay in the boat during a great and terrible storm that frightened His disciples to the point where they had to wake up their Master for help. He calmly stood up, raised His hands and said, "Be still" to the winds and the waves. The disciples were amazed, but Jesus just said they could have done it, too... They just lacked faith.

"Be still," I said, somewhat unsteady, huddled under the confounds of my sleeping bag. "In the name of Jesus, be still," I repeated just a bit louder. "Stop the blasted winds!" I shouted, covering my ears. I wanted to run so far and so fast. My hips hurt, my joints throbbed from lack of use. I felt like an old man with bed sores. My three team-mates and I were lined-up in a head to foot position to get the maximum amount of space we could in our three-man tent, plus cram in all the gear we could hold. For hours, for days, we would stare at one another, yet not even know we were doing it. We became unconscious of even falling asleep.

During one of these bouts of escape, I dreamt of warm sunshine and tropical beaches. Hard-bodied, bronzed women with long, flowing hair running naked together. Flesh upon flesh, making love in various places and positions. In the background, I heard Charlie's voice ask, "Where to next, Kev? Where's the next tour going to be?"

I muttered with a smile, "Cuba...Cuba..."

"Kev!...Kevin, get up! C'mon! The storm's let up! We have a chance!" shouted one of my partners, shaking me back into the real world of snow and ice.

And on the sixth day, we went forth from our habitats and stretched, and saw that all was calm around us but for the continued storm, now a thousand feet above.

Before leaving, I grabbed our snow shovel and began digging at a mound I more or less knew where the bike would be. After a few moments, part of a tire and carbon fiber spoke came through. Within the hour the bike was assembled.

Walking a couple hundred feet toward the edge of the 3000 foot cliff, we took some photos of me and the bike for the magazines. The temperature was minus 40-degrees below Fahrenheit, bringing an icy pain to our fingers when left exposed for a few minutes while trying to make the proper lens adjustments. After going through different poses and two rolls of film, I hoped and prayed we would have something to show for our failed summit efforts. We disassembled the bike, strapped it to the framepack and began our descent.

Walking all night back to Base Camp for our return flight to Talkeetna, my face was aglow with the thankfulness to God that I was still alive. My thoughts turned toward Cuba. *Yeah, someplace warm, something not too difficult...*

Although I had deemed myself a failure for not reaching the last State highpoint, my sponsors saw it differently:

"Look at it this way, Kev. We never thought you'd get as high as you did in the first place, and, besides, you can now lay claim to being the only person to have taken a bicycle higher than anyone else on the entire continent of North America," enthused Phyllis McCullough, the perky marketing-public relations manager for my bike sponsor, Klein, and one of my closest confidants throughout the Tour.

"Thanks for the vote of confidence. Now I can think about breaking my own record. In the meantime, let me tell you about my idea for the longest bike tour in the history of Cuba..."

By the time I returned to Talkeetna, I had formulated the plans in my mind and the name...

The Tour de Cuba.

My sponsors were ready to jump onboard once again.

UNO

1

KAWEAH COMMONWEALTH, CALIFORNIA REPUBLIC 1995-1997

You failed! You're a failure! occurred the thought over and over in my head.

You weren't hungry enough! You got lazy! I berated myself, regardless of the compliments and congratulations from my corporate sponsors.

You keep this up and you're going to find yourself back in the 9 to 5 grind. I wallowed in my own self pity.

After 49 successful State summits with the bicycle, having that 50th one end in a failed attempt disturbed me to the point that the other 49 didn't matter. I failed and was a failure. That's all I knew, all I have ever known from family and friends. I needed to redeem myself as quickly as possible. I needed to show the public, and convince myself, that those who supposedly knew me best were wrong.

It was a month upon my return from Alaska, and the end of **American Summits** that I went back into the self-therapy, workaholic routine of laying out the plans for the **Tour de Cuba** with a phone call to the Cuban Interest Office in Washington, DC. Publicly, we may be political enemies, but in private our countries keep an open channel.

Rafael Noriega was the man in charge of Cultural Exchanges between his country and the united States. When I mentioned who I was and what I wanted to do for my next tour, he became very excited.

"Ah! *Si, si!*" his voice raised several octaves. "I remember when you cycled the Great Wall of China. And your recent attempt on Alaska was most impressive."

I thanked him for his kind words, and asked if there would be any problems in finding a host to take care of the logistics while in his country.

"No, I don't see a problem in that," said Rafael in an assured tone. "I will begin with the Ministry of Sport. They would be the best in what you wish to do."

We agreed to plan this next adventure in six months time, beginning at the end of February --perfect weather for a cycling tour-- and time enough to gather the preparations needed for such an undertaking.

My confidant, Jean, was thankful I was going back to work; formulating plans such as the route, reading up on Cuban history, customs and cultures, and trying to learn enough Spanish to keep me out of trouble. So long as I kept busy, I would stop using her as a soundingboard and a shoulder to cry on over being a miserable failure.

Since meeting one another at the end of 1992 in our little town of 480 Souls, she has always been straight-forward tough with me, never allowing me to get too far down the abyss of depression.

"I don't have time for your theatrics," she'd say very plain and matter-of-fact. "Now get back to work."

"I want some sympathy!" I'd yell. "You should comfort me in soothing words of love and appreciation."

"You didn't fail. You came back alive. Appreciate that," she answered in an icy-cold tone, adding, "You know I care about you. It doesn't need to be said."

I would throw up my arms, looking Heavenward, and walk away in frustration, knowing she was right, yet never admitting it to her. She's been the best part of my life, and knows me better than anyone alive. She's the Scorpion to my Pisces. The concrete that keeps me from floating too far off to La-La Land.

During the planning process, I knew the State Department had up-to-date information on every country in the world. When I called to ask about Cuba, I was met with the first real blockade of the embargo since growing up with it all my natural-born life.

"And why do you want information on Cuba?" demanded the woman on the other end, refusing to give me her name when I asked for it.

"I'm planning on spending a couple of months there," I casually answered back.

"Are you a government employee, college student or with some type of religious organization?"

"Not that I can recall," I answered.

"Are you married to a Cuban exile who is now a U.S. citizen?"

I sighed at the question. The embargo has many wide loopholes-- which is normal when trying to adhere to (ridiculous) codes that Congress tries to pass off as law.

"No. Just an adventurer, going as a representative of our country in peace and friendship."

"Don't you know there's an embargo going on?!" She screamed through the phone, making me pull back the receiver.

"Oh, really?" I stated coldly. "I hadn't noticed. Tell me, how's the plan working? Are we making the Cubans suffer enough for all the problems they're causing us?"

"What's your name?" she demanded. "We're going to arrest you."

I laughed. I couldn't help myself. It just came out. "Before or after?" How I wished we were face to face.

"You know it's against the law to go to Cuba or any other country we say is off limits."

"Yes. So much for being free," I volleyed. "Listen clear, dear. I'm an American. I go where I want, when I want. You going to arrest me for doing my job? For going as a representative of my country in peace and friendship? How's that going to look to the media?"

There was a moment's pause as she decided to change course. "If something happens to you down there, we're not responsible. You'll rot in their jails."

"Thank you for those comforting words of warning."

"You can't spend more than one hundred dollars per day, and the only souvenirs you can bring back with you are those of educational value," she stated in an ice-cold tone.

"Wouldn't sampling the country's excellent rum and cohiba cigars be of educational value?"

"I'm going to enjoy seeing you behind bars," she hissed

"So would alot of other government employees. You've done your job. Now, send me the requested material."

It was faxed within days to my office.

Preparations over the next several months were going smoothly, which made me nervous. What? None of the usual obstacles getting in my way as they did with China and America? Have you ever noticed whenever you're trying to plan something, whether it be a wedding, a funeral, a lavish party, or a dream, the Devil somehow always manages to be in the details?

A few weeks before I was to go to China, the *Tiananmen Square* massacre broke out. A month before I was to begin **American Summits**, my manager, Charlie, died of a heart attack just as the major contracts were about to be signed, and I had to take on the reins myself. No matter how well I planned these tours out, ol' Scratch always seemed to rear his ugly mug. From experience I knew this **Tour de Cuba** would be no exception.

"Have you heard the news?" asked Jean. Just the tone of her statement made me cringe. "A group called *Brotherhood to the Rescue* sent planes to Havana, and

Getting ready to go to work at the *Badaling* section of the **Great Wall of China**, Summer 1990.

Castro had them shot down."

Balls! *Deja vu* all over again, and just a week before leaving. So close. So miserably, agonizingly close.

I took a deep breath. "Yeah, okay," I muttered into the mouthpiece. "I understand. I'm on it."

Before contacting Rafael in Washington, I paced my living room as reports from CNN were transmitting over the TV. I needed to gather my thoughts. No matter what my feelings were on this delicate matter, I knew from the *Tiananmen Square* massacre experience that the next move would have to be to postpone for at least a year.

"Last time they dumped a virus that killed all our swine in the area," mentioned Rafael, with great excitement filling his voice, raising it several levels.

I sympathized with Rafael. Can a nation allow another to invade their space without a fight? If this were the other way around, and Castro decided to drop a bomb on Miami, what do you think our answer would be to him?

Neither one of us liked the idea of postponement, but there was no choice. It was out of our hands. The politics of the situation were now dictating the moves, and we just had to go with the flow. Of course, there was a good and bad side to all this: the good gave us more time to prepare, the bad left us with a feeling of wait; of being in limbo.

I love a good downhill, but hate riding the stairs.

Secretary of State, Madeleine Albright had a chance to look tough in front of a few hundred thousand Cuban refugees, while Congressman Jesse Helms, the good Christian conservative, gave a rousing speech to keep up with the tradition of hate called the embargo. "...either Castro's gonna leave horizontal or vertical, but one way or the other, he's leaving."

All the fluff sounded wonderful to those who enjoyed hearing such words, but, in reality, it was just a bunch of politicians sounding off on issues that should have been left alone. I find that if a tyrant continues to step on the neck of the oppressed, the slave grows stronger, more resistant, until the tyrant can do nothing more but free the servant thru death, thereby immortalizing the one whom he wanted to crush and make an example of in the first place. In the long run, it's the tyrant who is forgotten during the course of time. This is what happens when we try to take over God's authority, instead of allowing the Lord to do His job, and asking, humbly, "is there's any way in which I can be of service?"

As I grow older and wiser with experience, I realize another year is not that long a period in which to prepare, to focus more clearly the points and goals we wanted to express and achieve during this tour. Like **American Summits**, this **Tour de Cuba** would be another expression of political awareness.

Politicians, government threats, insurmountable and unforeseeable events and obstacles will not keep me from whatever goals I have set for myself. We were going in, and the only way in which we would be stopped was either my government had to arrest me *before* I committed the act, or the Cuban government had to shut their doors.

Oh, what expression can be achieved with the simplicity of a bicycle and the elegance of it's cyclist.

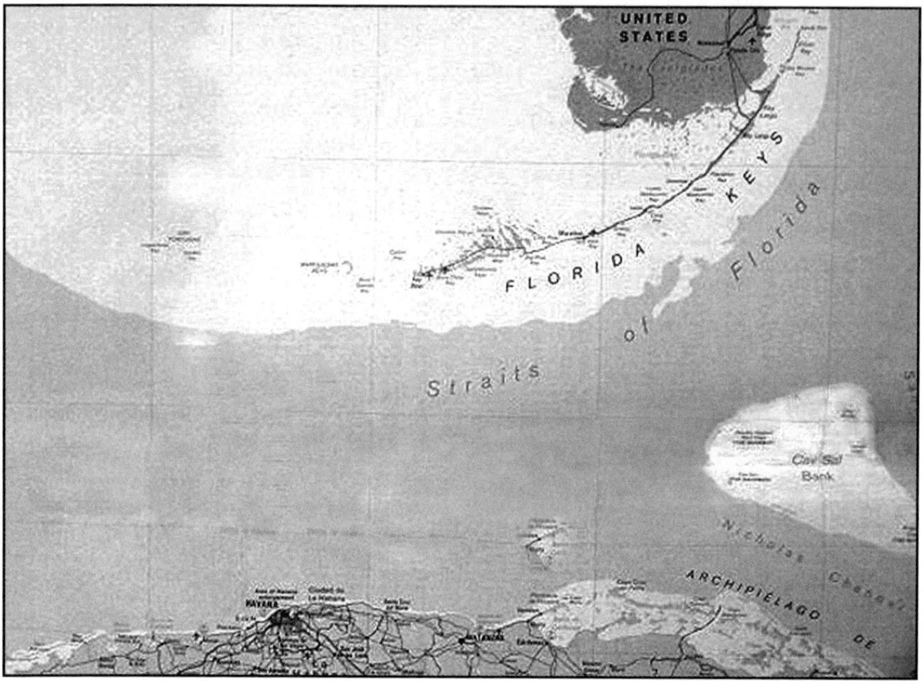

DOS

2

CALIFORNIA to CUBA
NOVEMBER 8-10, 1997

Going to sunny Cuba isn't exactly as easy as, say, taking the "red-eye" to New York. For one thing, most of us Americans can't go the direct approach unless we have a special visa from the Cuban government, as I had, or special permission from the US government, as I didn't have.

"Because you have a Cuban visa, you can fly out of Miami on *Mexicana* Airlines," assured Noriega. It sounded simple enough, but then reality set in, along with its various forms of complications.

I was just one American out of the annual 60,000 going to the sunny, embargoed island. Visa or not, I would be following the rules as outlined by the State Department strictly forbidding direct flights to Cuba. Yeah, I could fly out of Miami, but it wasn't going to be a straight shot.

"The plane leaves every Friday afternoon to Havana by way of Mexico, or on Saturdays by way of the Bahamas," said a spunky woman named, appropriately enough, Mercy, who would teach me the value of her name, with a dash of patience thrown in for good measure. "Of course, your weight's going to be a problem. The airline only allows sixty-six pounds per person, and they won't budge on that."

"What happens once the limit's crossed?" I asked.

"Then you'll have to pay $2.75 per pound after that."

"Mercy, c'mon," I begged. "The bike's my job. It's part of my equipment. I shouldn't be penalized like this. Cut me some slack."

There was a moment's hesitation as she began to calculate some figures and try another maneuver. "Okay," she piped, "I can let the bike go on the wheelchair rate, which is a flat thirty-five dollars. That won't cut into your sixty-six pounds."

Finally, I was seeing some light at the end of this tunnel; a ray of hope. I was nearly ready to sign up until two things stopped me: budget and connecting flight.

Since my first major Tour, I've always had to scramble for the dollars, because the cycling industry's tunnel vision of spending their entire budgets on their thoroughbred racers leaves nothing for the group I represent-- recreational cyclists.

Getting all the equipment I need to do the job has never been a problem, and in many cases, I've had to turn stuff down, but trying to extract funds from these overweight corporate "cyclists" is like trying to bang loose day-old mud from an obsolete bottom brake. Too much pounding often leads to damage. Therefore, I go outside the industry for my funding, and even then, I must be creative, and make sure my budget is as low as I can possibly get it.

Millionaire adventurers are a fantasy.

My budget for this Tour was strict for all the miscellaneous and unforeseeable expenses: monthly house bills when I'm away (you think the water, electric and phone companies would be understanding if I told them I wouldn't be around for a couple of months); caring for my little *Lhasa Apso* girls, *Hanzhu* and *Jia Tu*; fuel to drive to Los Angeles and then storage for the vehicle; overnight stay at a hotel; food; plane fare; $100 roundtrip ticket for the bike (cyclists are penalized, so face it); the cost of the Tour while in the country ($1000 max); and so much for bribes and favors along the route of the Tour (it happens in every country, with the US being the most expensive). The total cost I figured for this **Tour de Cuba** would be a tight $5000.

The other problem went hand-in-hand with the budget: the connecting flight to Miami.

Because we were now into the winter months, it seemed like everyone was flying south, which meant the airlines could soar their prices to stratospheric levels. I was looking at a $700 ticket just to get across the country-- not to mention the $450 roundtrip ticket to Havana.

Still, I was able to keep the 66 pounds that didn't include the "wheelchair" bike, thanks to Mercy's maneuvering. Before signing on with *Mexicana*, I placed a call to *Cubana* Airlines in Toronto, and found their weight limitations to be 44 pounds per person, with a $2.50 charge per pound over that amount. I was ready to go south.

"I have you down traveling with a wheelchair," mentioned Mercy, as she tallied up the price. "Remember to bring your special visa from the State Department, or else you'll have trouble getting on."

Mercy said that last statement so routine matter-of-fact, I nearly missed it.

"Excuse me? You mean my visa from the Cuban government?"

"No, your visa from the American government giving you permission to travel to Cuba. Immigration won't let you through the gate without it."

I began to curse under my breath, and my mind raced for another solution. "What if I flew out of Mexico?"

"You could, but then I'd have no control over the weight limit, and if the Mexican government needed the cargo space, they could tell the passengers to leave their bags behind, and just go with a carry-on."

I was doomed and in check, but not yet check mated. Mercy would hold a seat for me no longer than 24 hours. It was now up to God and prayer to see what the next move was going to be. I began to scan my map of North America for any and all possible routes to Cuba.

Giving this matter some careful thought, I came to the unorthodox conclusion that if I wanted to go south, I had to head north, because let's face it, no one wants to fly north in the wintertime, just as who really wants to fly south during the summer? The airlines proved me right when it was revealed I could go roundtrip from Los Angeles to Toronto for $200, plus, of course, the added $100 for the bike.

Excited, I informed Mercy of the plan, to which she casually answered, "But *Mexicana* doesn't fly out of Canada."

I cursed again. I was back in check mode with *Cubana's* unyielding 44-pound weight limitation. And no way were they going to let the bike pass as a wheelchair... I had to resort to drastic measures, contacting the man in charge, Carlos Rivera, who could waive the weight or do pretty much as he pleased in that department.

"No, I won't waive the weight," he announced with all the power and authority given to him. "But I will double the amount to eighty-eight pounds." After that the per pound charges would begin to add up.

I began to plead. "Mr Rivera, through this bike tour, I'm trying to show the ridiculousness of the embargo and unite our two countries. Could you not make an exception in this case and waive the weight?"

"No," he stated calmly and matter-of-fact. "I will double the weight. That is all I will do."

I began to rub my throbbing temple with the phone, and kept a calm breathing cadence. "Would you put that eighty-eight pound rate in writing?"

"It is not necessary."

Somehow, experience has taught me that you just can't trust what people tell you. But being diplomatic, I replied, "Mr Rivera, how can I be sure that the people at the ticket counter will know what was discussed between us when I go to board the plane?"

"Do not worry. I will send them a letter." And that was how it was settled between us.

I bit my lower lip to restrain myself from going ballistic with Rivera as my soundingboard, but not so with Noriega in DC, as I vented my anger.

"What's going on here, Rafael?! Isn't this supposed to be a tour between our two countries in peace and friendship? Why should I be sticking my neck out if I'm not getting any cooperation from your side?"

"Well, you know, *Kebin*, it is out of my hands," he casually remarked.

I was ready to walk away from the entire Tour, except that everything was in place with the sponsors and media, so I set my ego aside and went forward as planned.

As far as making the actual arrangements to fly out of Toronto, that presented its own set of problems. I couldn't deal directly with the airline, because I didn't have a Canadian credit card, and you can't use an American one because of the embargo, which meant I had to go through a middle-man, a ticket agent. Strangely, the longer you wish to stay in Cuba, the more the cost of the ticket. Two weeks is $300, four weeks is $450, and so on up to eight weeks, the maximum. My stay in Cuba would be for a total of six weeks, and *Cubana* only flies on Sundays, so the timing between connecting flights had to be precise.

All the negotiations were over with, all the time planning and training were behind as I glanced out the window at the layer of cotton-candy clouds below, listening to a *concerto* by Bach over TWA's speaker system. The days were becoming shorter, the weather colder. We were headed north.

I continued to listen to the music, trying to relax. It reminded me of those long ago days when my ritual was to play Bach at breakfast, during the cycling tour of the Great Wall. If it weren't for that Tour and the worldwide attention it brought, I would have no name, no reputation of being the first to do the seemingly impossible. I wouldn't be on my way to Havana for the longest cycling tour in the history of Cuba. I would perhaps still be in a factory, seeing the best years of my life fade away to old age and uselessness.

I often ask people when they confront me with their dreams, "Do you want it bad enough?" and the usual reply is an enthusiastic YES! "How bad? Bad enough to do it for free? Bad enough to die for it?" At this point many of these people look at me strangely; some even back away as though they were dealing with a psycho. Who knows? Maybe to some extent they are. **The Great Wall of China Tour** was my first major dream to come true, and even though I knew there were many people in the world that thought the same way I did-- even some who were prepared to steal the dream from me once it broke out in the news-- I knew the one who was the hungriest, the one who was prepared to die for it, would succeed. That's one of the reasons why I achieved the seemingly impossible: While others bickered over money and position, I did the tour for nothing more than the supplies that were donated to me, and, upon completion some 2000 miles later, had staggered the world's imagination that a high school-educated ghetto kid can make good on what he says he'll do.

I felt utterly blessed and thankful to God for giving me my health and allowing me to continue what I was able to do-- no matter how insignificant it may have seemed to the world at the moment. I was on my way to another adventure, new experiences, and lifelong memories...

My brief, overnight stay in Canada was at an end as I stood in line with many others for the southbound trip to Havana. I set up a relay system with a bud

What goes down, must come up. *Badaling*, China.

of mine in Toronto to contact Jean. She may find it difficult to actually formulate and say the words, "I love you. I care for you," but knowing that she does, I couldn't leave her stranded without word from me for six weeks if it was at all possible to reach her by some means. Because of the embargo, telephone contact between the United States and Cuba was forbidden, but that didn't stop us from redirecting our calls via Canada.

As I reached the front counter to pick up my ticket from the travel agent, my gut was acting up-- the worry over the weight restrictions resurfaced. What about the bike, I wondered? What about the Beast?

"You're only allowed twenty kilos," smiled the young lady at the counter, when I placed my bike bag on the weight scale. My gut gave a slight twist.

"Yes, I understand," I answered politely. "Carlos Rivera doubled the weight for me. Is there a note or letter of some kind explaining the situation?"

As she looked through her piles of paperwork, my heart raced a bit from it's regular beat. She began to unknowingly shake her head as the pile of forms became lower.

"I'm sorry," she said, "I see nothing from Mr Rivera."

I asked to see the man in charge, and was pointed in the direction of a stout fellow in a *Cubana* uniform, who spoke some English.

I explained who I was, and asked if Carlos Rivera left a note of any kind doubling the weight.

The man glanced at his desk quickly. "No note." He returned to handling other complaints.

Other people began to crowd around us, thrusting tickets into the man's face for his stamp of approval to board the plane to Havana. Desperation on my part began

Another day's victory on *Badaling's* Great Wall!

to set in, forming beads of sweat along my forehead. I really do hate being right about my lack of trust in people, and now I had to be pushy. There was no way I could miss that plane, and I wasn't about to leave the bike behind, or pay whatever the per pound price would be.

"*Senor, por favor!*" I yelled through the crowd, meeting him face-to-face. "Call Mr Rivera, please!"

He pressed his lips tight; his eyes narrow with hate. He yelled something in Spanish, and made the call.

While he was doing this, I quickly searched my briefcase for the document I sent to Rivera about the agreement on the double weight. Rivera wasn't in apparently as the *Cubana* official quickly turned to me and said a bit more sternly, "There is nothing."

I handed him a copy of the fax I sent to his boss a week before. He grabbed it out of my hand with such force, I thought the paper would rent in two. He scanned the document.

"Mr Rivera promised me the weight. C'mon, you have the authority to let me pass."

He placed his signature on the paper, cursing under his breath, and gave it to one of his assistants. He allowed me through the gate. For the time being the problem had been solved, but Rivera told me when we spoke that I would have to deal with *Cubana* in Havana on the weight for the return flight... Just one problem at a time, that's all I ask.

The Toronto-Havana five hour flight was billed as a *no-frills excursion*; the travel agent wasn't kidding. For one, Cuba's fleet of planes were from the leftover days of the Soviet Union. None of the creature comforts, found on Western planes I was accustomed to, existed: no in-flight film or piped-in music, the air conditioning rattled to where nuts and bolts shook loose; one of them dropping close to my lap, and the food service was reduced -- literally -- to peanuts. The young American woman beside me sat bolt upright, her knuckles going white by the firm grasp she had on the torn, polyester armrests.

Thankfully, there was the ever-present rum and assorted beverages to keep us going. The passengers, especially the young woman, loosened up to where if this party plane were to go down, we would ditch without feeling the pain, laughing all the way to our deaths.

By the mid-way point of our flight, there was a smoke-filled, alcohol-induced gathering in the tail section, headed by a group of female Cuban-Canadians. It grew louder and more raucous with each passing hour.

"Hey, honey!" yelled out a brown-skinned buxom lass, her braided hair flowing about her shoulders. "You no like to have fun with us?"

I tried to avoid the question by pretending I was dozing off, but that didn't stop her and another girlfriend from coming down the aisle.

"Why you sit here by yourself?" She took the unoccupied seat next to me, the American woman giving it up long ago to join the party group in the back. Her lighter-skinned girlfriend sat on my other side.

"Bad habit of mine I never broke myself of," I deadpanned, as they laughed uproariously, nearly spilling their drinks into my lap.

"Hey, you funny," laughed the whiskey-voiced, light-skinned woman. "I like you. You're cute. Can I kiss you?"

Before I had the chance to answer the question, her girlfriend chimed in, "Hey, what you mean? I saw him first, I get to kiss him first."

"I think I need a drink," I diverted, not wanting to be in the middle of a cat fight. They thought this was a good idea, and called out to one of the flight attendants, who emerged with a cart of bottled beverages.

Rarely am I stunned by beauty, but as the flight attendant approached us, I was speechless. Her skin was the color of smooth milk chocolate, her features petite, her soft hair braided and pulled back, her eyes like that of a doe and her lips soft and moist that made her perfect white teeth sparkle. I instinctively looked at her hands and immediately noticed a wedding ring-- thank God. I think I would've dropped to my knees and asked her to marry me. Forget the language barrier, we'll deal with that as time goes on. If this is what the majority of Cuban women were going to look like, I was a dead man.

She gave a slight smile and asked what I would like to drink. I was so captivated by her dark, piercing eyes I couldn't speak; couldn't form the words I wanted to say, as thoughts of my naked body clinging to hers formed in my mind and groin.

"Oh, honey, I see we gonna have a good time," laughed the light-skinned redhead, placing her hand near my raised lap. "Where you staying in *Habana?*"

I shifted in my seat as my two loudmouthed companions ordered a rum and coke for me-- more rum than coke, the better to loosen me up faster. Fortunately, if I can stay with the same brand of drink throughout the party, I have no problems holding my own. It's just when I begin mixing that I find myself in danger of losing control. And that, I knew, would be a mistake with my new found felines, who went from me to the group in the back.

Our first stop was the beach resort of *Varadero*. As we began our descent into the island nation, I could see from my window, lush tropical jungles, beautiful sandy beaches, and the crystal clear waters of the Caribbean.

Upon exiting, the heat hit us all at once. We broke into a sweat, shedding our jackets and rolling up our long-sleeved shirts. It was late afternoon, supposedly the coolest part of the day, and it was mid-November. I wondered what I was in for, and just how bad the humidity would be.

Our layover was for a half-hour. The party group continued their festivities. I viewed some of the tourist items-- the assorted T-shirts saying *Cuba*, or *Havana,* or *Che Guevara*, the popular Revolutionary war hero and personal friend of Castro's. During the six weeks of my stay, a day would not go by that I wouldn't see Che's face looming at me from billboards, posters, T-shirts, stamps, coins, paper currency, and anything else the Cubans could think of putting his face on.

Dead heros are very popular in Cuba.

Once again we were back in the air. The party group continued, fully uninhibited, as the stewardesses tried to keep their noise to a reasonable level, trying hard not to laugh or smile or join them in the moment. A flight to Cuba is not a subdued, smokeless one. If you ever decide to go to the jewel of the Caribbean, be prepared with a party mindset from the moment you enter the plane to the time you step off upon your return flight home. Cubans revel in their festivities. To them the joy of life is an artform.

Upon arriving at the Havana terminal, the mood of the party group took on a different mode, as evidenced by the presence of the military. They became unusually silent, holding themselves upright in a most serious manner, as we made our way to the immigration booths.

I donned my stars and stripes jacket, and my two girlfriends from the plane became quite solemn. "*Senor*, no wear jacket in here. Very bad. Military no like."

"Well, they're just going to have to get used to it," I answered, refusing to be pushed because I happened to be wearing my country's colors.

One of the more inebriated male partiers beside me asked, "Where you from?"

"United States."

"Ah," his eyes lit up, and arms spread wide open, "*Americano!* We love *Americanos*," he announced, loud enough for everyone in the room to hear.

The light-skinned girl told him to shush, while the buxom lass had a more unconventional way to keep her friend quiet by grabbing the back of his head, pulling him into her enormous breasts. Would've worked for me, but he pushed the jugs away, protesting even louder, "No! I say what I want! I am no Cuban citizen!"

People began to give him a wide berth as he staggered toward me in a drunken state. The armed guards held their rifles tight, ready to use them. I kept my stand and my cool, my eyes all over the room, marking in my mind exactly where the guards were, and ready to drop to the floor if they attempted to position themselves in a firing mode. I silently prayed for words of wisdom.

Slurring his words, he pressed himself into me, "Listen, my friend, I love America. America good country, but I live in Canada for nine years now, and am citizen, so I can say fuck Fidel--"

"Sh, Luis! You crazy? You want to get shot?" said the braided, buxom beauty through apprehensive eyes.

"No! I still say *fuck Castro*," he announced in a loud, drunken-brave voice, so that no one could mistake hearing him. The guards were ready to kill this midget-- in self-defense, of course.

"He make this country poor. He take from the people. And I can say all I want, and speak freely, because I Canadian citizen, and have family here, so I canno' be thrown out."

"But then you place your family in danger, *amigo*," I stated calmly. "And that is not wise."

He was quiet for a moment, then patted my chest. "Yes, you are right, my friend, you are right." Coming closer as though he wanted to kiss me, he stood on his tiptoes and whispered, "But I still say fuck Castro, and I hope someone kills him soon."

He clapped his hands together and let out a laugh, going off to rest his head on the breasts of his buxom girlfriend, who announced to no one in particular, "Oh, I *lobe* this man. *I lobe him!*"

In a Communist country, the military and police are suspicious of all foreigners, so it takes twice as long to get through the line. Of course, being the "colorful" person that I am, it seemed to take longer for me to get through customs, while an elderly man waited just behind the barrier with a cardboard sign with my name on it.

I watched him show his sign to various males who would shake their head while heading out the doors. A Japanese-Canadian whom I never met or spoken with during the flight, asked him, "You're looking for Kevin Foster? That's him right there," he pointed with assurance. I keep forgetting I'm well-known to a specific group of people.

Motioning to him that I acknowledged his presence, he quickly came over to see about speeding up the process, speaking with the officer who was examining every inch of my American passport. Words were exchanged in Spanish-- probably something to the effect that I was here by the invitation of the government, and an escort was waiting just outside. Whatever was said, the examination process was quickly completed; the military man tore off the top section of the visa and allowed me to officially enter the country. In Cuba, they don't stamp united States passports, because they don't want Americans getting into trouble with their government. Very patriotic of them.

My next stop was to the baggage claim area to pick up the oversized bike bag. There, I was met by two other men, one of them introducing himself as Alberto, a representative from the Sports Ministry.

"How do you do, Mr Foster. Allow me to be the first to welcome you to our country." We shook hands all around, and they helped me with my bags.

Outside, it was already night. The stench of sewage mixed with humidity and stale body odor hit the nostrils instantly. The place swarmed with people of all ages who were jockeying for position. One young man won out for the honour of carrying my bags to the jeep, oblivious to my protests. Since Castro reluctantly legalized the US dollar in 1993 (after Mother Russia had said no more $5 billion a year), the country has operated on three different money systems: the Cuban National *peso* at a ratio of 1:1 that foreigners other than American and Canadian are obliged to use, but that the Cubans don't want, and the regular Cuban *peso* being the other in which Cubans are paid for their labor, and which they *really* don't want. The rate, at 23-to-1, is so unfair that Cubans are trying to find any means in which to earn the valuable American dollars from the tourists-- even if it means forcing their labor upon them. There's not much you can do about it but go along and pay the dollar tip.

Once we were settled in the jeep, Alberto asked where I would be staying.

"Hasn't that been arranged?"

"No, not to my knowledge," replied Alberto.

"During the last two years of our correspondence, wasn't I clear enough that my host would take care of all the arrangements once I was in Cuba?"

"We will take care of all travel and security, yes, but to my understanding, accommodations were not included."

"When is the meeting supposed to take place?"

"I am not sure," answered Alberto. "Mr Palaez is a very busy man. Perhaps it will be sometime tomorrow."

Before leaving the united States, Noriega had informed me that I would be meeting with Jose Palaez, the president of the Cycling Federation in Cuba and the vice-president of International Cycling. A top man in Castro's inner circle, so I was told-- but now it looked as though some of the plans were being altered, and I was going to have to foot part of the bill until the matter was cleared up. From experience, I expected this and brought enough US dollars to cover myself in such a crisis. I was going to be here for six weeks, and I needed enough to survive on.

"Do you know of an inexpensive place where I can spend the night?"

"Yes, I believe so," Alberto answered most diplomatically, as he shifted uncomfortably in his seat, trying to avoid any eye contact with me.

He said something to his driver, who drove us to one motel that was completely full, and then to the *Hotel Morro*. The rooms were $24US per night-- for a king-size lumpy bed; old, musty-smelling, stained carpeting that you wouldn't dare walk on in your bare feet; a color TV that worked-- sometimes; a noisy air-conditioner; hanging electric wires; some wooden furniture; a tiled bathroom with a lidless toilet bowl complete with tissue; and a cold water running sink and shower. The three-and-four-inch roaches were uninvited guests and not included in the overall price. I was back in familiar ghetto living conditions from my youth. I had come full circle.

With Alberto of the Sports Ministry after helping to extend my visa.

Before leaving me for the night, Alberto announced that he would be calling in the morning to arrange an afternoon meeting between myself and Mr Palaez. Once alone in my dreary room, I sat on the edge of the squeaky bed and flicked on the TV, switching between the CNN News station and the English-speaking HBO channel. I wanted some noise, but most of all I wanted company-- no matter how artificial it was. *Salsa* music played outside, with Spanish-speaking voices filtering through the second-story window. Cars honked their horns, speeding past the hotel situated a block from the ocean. I felt very alone and depressed in the world.

As I began to formulate some of the questions that would be asked and what my answers were going to be, my entire gut was telling me that all was not going to be right once that meeting took place. I opened my briefcase to extract the map of the route and other notes to study. A plan B would need to be formulated-- and soon -- because one thing was for sure: Under no circumstances short of being physically thrown out by Castro himself, would I leave this country as a tail-between-my-legs failure. I was here to do a job and get it done as best I could.

Point-to-point, lighthouse-to-lighthouse, one end of the island to the other, there would be a **Tour de Cuba**, or there would be headlines of a different nature.

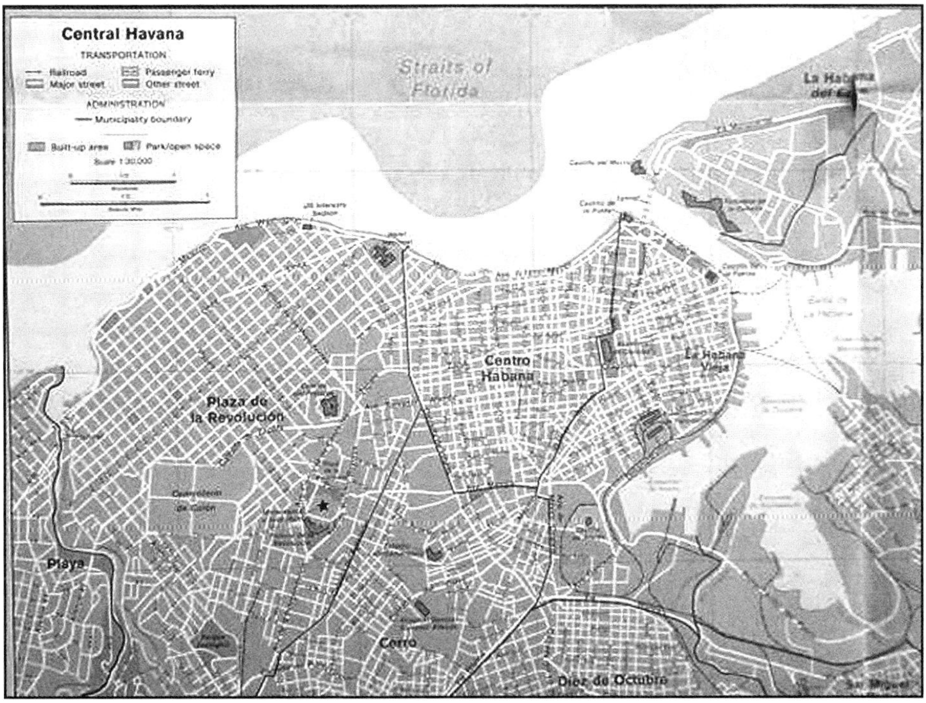

TRES

3

HAVANA, CUBA
NOVEMBER 11, 1997

For a moment I didn't know where I was, as I laid in bed listening to the rattle and hum of the antiquated air conditioner. Sounds of conversation and laughter filtered through the open window; female voices outside my door could be heard echoing from the hallway.

I glanced at my watch. At 10am it was already a warm 80-degrees and climbing. I crawled out of bed, splashed cold water on my face, got dressed, and headed out the door with my camera for my first glimpse of Havana during the day. I hoped the smells and sights would be somewhat better than last night.

Not a chance.

Although there was something giddy and intoxicatingly illegal about being in Cuba, the effect soon wore off. The utter filth and poverty brought me back to a hard-hitting reality. The *Hotel Morro*, with all its faults in comparison to our Western hotels, was, in reality, the oasis in an area of bombed-out piles of rubble that people were actually expected to live in and call home sweet home. Aside from the paint job these buildings from the '20s and '30s badly needed, many of them didn't have windows, while others were just decaying-- falling apart piece by piece, the rubble spilling onto the sidewalks and streets as passersby simply walked over or around them.

A large number of stray dogs was also evident. Scraggly and thin to the point that one could see their ribs outline their torn and bloodied skin. They roamed where they liked, defecating the streets of the city. It became an obstacle course for people just to get from one point to another. The bitches, with their numerous tits hanging to the ground, didn't seem to have enough in them to produce one more litter. I wondered why the Cuban government didn't have some kind of agenda in place to either destroy the majority of these creatures-- and some of them would surely find that a welcome relief--or simply have a spay and neuter program.

I thought of my own girls, *Hanzhu* and *Jia Tu*, a mother-daughter pair of *Lhasa Apsos*, and how blessed they were for having the care and pampering they received. Just to look at these animals made you hurt, but then, the majority of Cubans live no better off than a step above. They have shelter and a way to acquire food, at least.

Smog was another problem I noticed throughout my time on the island nation. The 40-year-old trucks vomited huge clouds of thick, black fumes that would make a cyclist choke and momentarily blind when the steaming grit hit you in the face. You could avoid them if there was time, but often you simply had to lower your head, hold your breath and go head-on until you could reach clear skies again. During the Tour, there wasn't a day that went by I didn't choke from the fumes, and needed to wear my sponsor's face mask in order to breathe. Cuba may be called the jewel of the Caribbean, but this was definitely a paradox in Paradise.

The Market Square, sitting almost directly across the street from the *Hotel Morro*, was a large slab of blacktop about the size of a football field where people with the properly licensed government papers were allowed to sell their handicrafts to passing tourists that walked the *Malecon*, the main road in Havana that followed the Caribbean coast.

During these morning hours, venturing forth from my cocoon, the Square was already half-full with booths of knitted clothing, wooden sculptures, books about the history of Cuba and its dead heroes, food vendors that served the country's popular pork sandwiches and *refresca*, touristy toys and knick-knacks that either said *Cuba* or *Che*, and the most popular sightseeing attraction, the painters that laid their untold hours of creations on the sidewalks beside the filth.

Taxis and private cars-- many of them fairly newer than their '50s counterparts-- lined the streets. Judging from their looks, they at least appeared to be from the '70s and '80s. The ones I liked the best were Russian and actually smaller than the old VW Beetle. They were the most economical, getting about 50 miles to the gallon, which is great when fuel goes for $3.00US per. I didn't think anything that tiny could be comfortable, but I fell in love with them so much, I had wished I could take one home with me, just to scoot around town.

From my removed vantage point of the *Hotel Morro's* courtyard, I could take in the entire colorful scene: the hustle and bustle of the vendors and artists that were selling their wares to passersby, hustlers trying to make any dollars they could, private

Part of Havana under reconstruction.

and public cab drivers buzzing about the Square and the *Malecon*, the *crescendo* of voices of all different dialects speaking the same language of buying and selling... It was a festive, upbeat environment. Then I entered the zone, and was immediately swarmed upon by *Cubanos*.

"Hey, Mista, got some nice *cohibas* for you. Very good price."

"No...no smoke."

"Bes' cigars in all of Cuba. Very good price."

"No smoke."

"You buy for friends as gifts."

"Can't."

"Why?"

"*Americano*."

"Ah, *si, Americano*. Where from?"

"California."

And then they would tell me they had family in Florida, Texas, New York, or California. Rarely would I hear of any other States mentioned. Many of them told me how their brother or sister had left the country without so much as a letter, postcard or phone call in years-- as though they had just disappeared from life altogether.

Then, of course, knowing you were an American, and presuming you, like all Americans, were rich, they began offering other products and services, the second most popular being women...

"Hey, Mista, got nice woman for you. Very good."

"No."

"*Si!* Any kind woman you want. Do anything for you. Make you happy. I show you, you like!"

During my morning experience at the Market Square, I spent a good deal of time along the sidewalk where the painters displayed their work. I became acquainted with a couple of the artists named Ernesto and Luis.

Ernesto, a middle-aged man with an expanding mid-section and a personality to match, had been painting most of his life, selling on the sidewalk or to some of the art galleries in Havana. But, as he pointed out, "It is more expensive to buy me there than it is to buy from me here."

After a couple hours of surveying the merchandise, I returned to the *Morro,* where I approached the front desk. The only reply was that there were no messages.

As I was about to have lunch in the Hotel's restaurant, a middle-aged woman of average height, dressed in a T-shirt with a long, thinly-veiled psychedelic '60s frock, topped by a felt hat, and fitted with open-toed sandals, entered the foyer. She wore narrow, octogon-shaped glasses, and her auburn hair flowed to the shoulder, as well as from her armpits. Speaking to the desk clerk in such perfect English, I asked where she was from.

"Berkeley," she replied with a smile. "And you?"

"Near Sequoia National Park."

"Same state. Small world."

Her name was Patricia. She'd already been at the Hotel for a week of a one-month stay, learning how to speak Spanish at the University of Havana through the *Global Exchange* program. In fact, there were a group of Americans in the class that were staying at the Hotel, some of whom I had seen last night in the foyer when passing through on my way to checking in.

"I was about to have lunch," I mentioned to Patricia. "Would you care to join me?"

The invitation would be a chance to pick her brain on the ins and outs of getting around Havana on *pesos*-- where to convert my dollars, for instance, and other bargains that would allow me to extend my money. Without word from my host, after all, I had no idea how long I was going to be stuck in town.

"Thanks," she smiled, "I already bought my lunch at the market, but I'll be happy to join you."

While Patty lunched on raw vegetables she had gathered from the market and bought with *pesos*, I ordered a large plate of rice and beans.

"*Congris*," said Patty when the waitress left to fill the order. "There are separate words for rice and beans, and if spoken that way, you'd get a plate of each. But if you want the two mixed together, you'd say *congris*."

I repeated the word several times to myself, as I knew throughout the Tour, *congris* would be one dish I'd be ordering quite often.

"What made you come to Cuba?" I asked while waiting.

"I came here about twenty years ago when our country was allowing Americans to travel for a short period before closing the doors again. I fell in love with the country and the people. Now that there's a loophole allowing us to travel to

Cuba through the arts and education program, I decided to return."

Ordering a couple of cold cans of American Coca-Colas, I laughed when they arrived. "So much for an embargo, huh?"

"You can find almost anything American," mentioned Patty, munching on a green-leafed stalk. "All the major companies bring their products in through their Latin American affiliates. Just a few doors down, there's the local PanAmerican store where you can find Pepsi, 7-Up, frozen foods like pizza and pasta, Kerns fruit juices, Levi jeans, Hersey's chocolates, Microsoft and Sony products... anything American."

I made mental notes of all she was saying.

"About a quarter-mile east of us is the *Habana Club* where every liquor and most junk food is served. It's totally American, but only the rich can afford the hot dogs, hamburgers, french fries and banana splits, because it's all flown in daily from Miami."

"I noticed we get CNN and HBO."

She nodded her head knowingly while sipping her Coke. "Yeah, Cuba can pick up Miami easy via satellite. We're on the same one-ten volt current, and videos are NTSC."

Nearly jumping out of my seat from all the exciting information Patty was bestowing upon me, I edged closer, and asked the all-too important question, "Where can I change some of my dollars into *pesos*?"

She gave a shrug and answered, "At the Marketplace. But don't do more than ten at a time. If you know where to look, you could live a week off that. Just up the street is a pizza place and a group of food vendors that you can buy from in *pesos*. But places like the PanAmerican store and the *Habana Club* are in dollars."

By the time my plate of *congris* arrived, Patty had finished her simple lunch of raw vegetables. Now the tables were turned for information.

"So, what brings you to Cuba? What group are you with?" she asked.

The *congris* was very good and satisfying upon first taste. "Actually, I'm not with any group," I stated matter-of-factly. "I'm here to do the longest bicycle tour in the history of Cuba. To bring peace and friendship between our two countries through the press coverage, if possible."

"Oh," she said with a weary look, her eyes narrowing. "So that's your job? Riding a bike and doing these kinds of tours for money?" She sipped her Coke, continuing to look through me with steely, judgmental eyes. Just the tone of her statement and the near death quiet made me feel like a whore.

"Does not Jesus command us to love thy neighbor as thyself? Is that not one of the most important commandments?"

"Excuse me?" she blinked, shaking herself back into the present world.

"A shrewd lawyer turns to his Creator, and asks, 'Master, who is my neighbor,' to which the Lord replies, 'The one whom ye hate the most.'"

I waited a moment for Patty to grasp what I was trying to say before continuing. "For whatever reasons why you're here or I'm here, the end results are the same... we want to see the embargo end, because we love our neighbor."

"And you think riding a bicycle through this country will help?"

"I don't know. I'm here and I have a job to do."

Patty's look of contempt and silence spoke volumes-- loud and clear. I knew there was nothing I could do or say that would find favor in her sight so I continued with my views, hoping to reach her in some way.

"This embargo has been going on since the year I was born. Should we not try to show love and kindness to our supposed enemy? Perhaps that would get us further?"

Patty's contemptible look turned into laughter. "Castro needs to leave before this country can turn itself around."

"Perhaps, but that's not going to happen. Forty years ago the people wanted Castro and his Communist-Socialist state, therefore they must now accept their fate until Providence changes it."

Patty kept shifting in her padded seat at the uncomfortable turn of the conversation, but since I was on a roll, I felt compelled to continue.

"Haven't we tried enough times to kill Fidel and failed? Each time we do, the people rally behind him, because Cubans have a fighting spirit. The more we try to starve them, the more they hang on. To be able to show love and mercy would make us look better in the eyes of the world, and show that one nation should never interfere in another country's politics. I mean, if we can do business with slave-labored China and Ho Chi Minh's Vietnam, then why not have commerce with Cuba?"

She drank the last of her Coke, gathered her things and stood up. "Well, I have a lecture to attend tonight. You have your views, but I think you're missing the point. Anyway, good luck with whatever it is you're trying to do."

Alone in the restaurant, the *congris* began to taste dry and cold, as the loneliness set in once again. Patty just didn't understand the laws of God and nature. She was a product of liberal, media-manipulated thinking. One of the masses, while I was forever locked in the minority.

Back in my room, I placed a call to Cable News Network's office, as I had told the staff at the company's Atlanta, Georgia headquarters I would, who in turn, sent word ahead to Havana of when I'd be arriving.

"Yes, this is Lucia Newman," sounded the very suave and sophisticated voice when introductions were made. You can always tell those who've had a primo education, and those from the other side of the tracks. It shows in the voice, dress, walk-- every general and detailed mannerism. Right down to the manicured (or greasy) fingernails.

"Why exactly are you down here?" asked Havana's head bureau chief. "What's this Tour all about?"

I'm always nervous around reporters, whether it be in person or on the phone. I've been in the spotlight long enough now to know that anything I say can and will be used against me in a court of media.

"This *Tour de Cuba* is for peace and friendship," I stated. "Enough with this embargo. It's ridiculous and has to end. And Captain America is here to bring attention to that fact."

"Captain America, huh?" she said dryly.

"You'll understand once we meet."

"Have you been in the country long?" Oh so formal.

"Long enough to enjoy a cold Coca-Cola." I quipped. "But I'm still looking for a McDonald's."

The Havana cemetery, like all others throughout the nation, bury their people above ground.

"So am I. When you find one, let me know," she replied, without missing a beat.

"It's a date," I shot back. The ice between us was broken, and I couldn't wait to meet her.

"There's time Friday afternoon to do an interview. How does that sound to you?"

"Fine. No problem," I nodded to myself.

"Come by the *Hotel National*. I think the American and Cuban audiences will find your story quite interesting."

Lucia could go round-for-round with me and be quite witty. I imagined her to be somewhat of a devil-may-care under that perfect, Vassar charm of hers, and was looking forward to our meeting.

As the afternoon hours passed with still no word from Alberto, I bounced from the lobby of the Hotel to the outside patio, watching the people mill about at the Marketplace. My mind wandered toward other possibilities of how to pull this Tour off, and I muttered a precise, yet simple prayer to God, "Lord, going back home is not an option, so lead me in the direction in which I am to go."

"*Kebin!* How you today?" asked the scrawny, gigolo handsome, hotel hustler of a bellboy.

"Fine, Humberto. No dollars today?"

"Hey!" he moaned, revealing empty pockets and palms. "No tourists to check in today. No dollars."

"And you like them dollars, *si*?" I smiled.

"*Si!*" he flashed his toothy grin in return, giving me an American, thumbs-up sign. "No like *peso*. *Peso* no good. Can do no thing with it."

"How was it before Castro legalized the dollar?"

"Ah," he moaned, cocking his head to the side and patting his chest. "The police check anytime and if we have even one American dollar, we be thrown in jail for a year or more. It very bad. Now is okay."

"We Americans like to use your *peso*, but you want our godalmighty dollars." I shook my head.

"*Si!*" his eyes lit up with a smile. "We pray for many of your dollars to come to our country."

God bless the Capitalist. By Castro legalizing US currency, more than two billion George Washingtons make their way into the country annually. 1997 was the first year that tourism passed the nation's leading product, sugar.

With my map of Cuba and the daily itinerary of the Tour, I began walking around the neighborhood to think of another plan. I thought about hiring a driver and what the cost involved would be. A quick calculation determined that the total distance of the route beginning in and returning to Havana would be about 4000 kilometers. With fuel at $3.00US per gallon, if we could get one of those Russian micros with a roof rack, they should do at least 50 kilos per gallon, so at 80 gallons I would need at least $240US. But then, could I find a driver that would accompany me for the next few weeks? How much would I have to pay him? There would be our accommodations-- and anything else that could go wrong, such as vehicle breakdowns and other miscellaneous items. Would $1000US cover it all? Sometimes faith can be nerve-wracking, but I really saw no other choice in the matter. I couldn't just sit around and twiddle my thumbs, waiting for my hosts to show up in their good time. I had to do something, even if it did feel as though I were running around with my head cut off. At least, in my mind, I was being productive, and it was becoming a learning experience. Besides, I gathered, if I couldn't hang out on a thousand bucks for six weeks in a Third World country, then I wasn't as experienced as I made myself believe. I had more than enough money, and could figure out a way to acquire additional funds if the emergency arose-- but was there enough time in the schedule to make all the necessary arrangements? At the moment things were not looking in my favor, I thought, making my way back to the Marketplace to exchange $10US into 230 Cuban *pesos*.

Ernesto was still in business, with fewer paintings. I found him sitting under the shade of his oversized umbrella, counting his American booty.

"Looks like you've been having a better day than I have." I took a seat beside him.

"*Si*, my friend, I have done well, and how have you been?"

"Like the bride that's been left at the altar. No word, nothing from my host, and I don't like the feeling."

"Then you must find yourself another groom," he laughed, stuffing the wad of cash into his pocket as tourists continued to pass by and admire his work. "If there's something you like, you let me know. I give you good price," he would call out from time-to-time to the sightseers.

"Funny you should mention another groom, Ernesto," I replied, rolling out the map of his country. His eyes grew big behind his glasses as he studied the route from one end of the island to the other.

"*In-cre-di-bal!* Look at this route! I have lived in Cuba all my life, and you will see more of it than I have."

I spoke of my plan of trying to find someone with a small vehicle that would accompany me, carry my supplies, be my interpreter, and what I could pay for their time.

"Impossible, Kevin, impossible! It would be too expensive. Never work."

"But why? It could."

"The route. It's too long, and you start so far away. You will never find any driver in Havana to go with you. They can make easy a hundred fifty dollars a week just around the city."

"Really?"

Luis, the other artist, who was displaying his work next to Ernesto, agreed. "*Si*. Your idea, no good. Better for you to fly out to *Baracoa*, then find a driver to take you to *Maisi* to start."

That, too, was another plan, for it would only cost about $100US to fly from Havana to the Eastern part of the island. From there, I could continue in my faith walk. But was this what the Lord wanted, or was there something else He had in mind? Whatever the plan, I needed an answer soon, I thought, wandering off, thinking about this new concept.

I came to a Catholic church. A poster hanging on the front door announced the arrival of *Juan Pablo II* in January for the historic first meeting between the Pope and Castro.

Although I was raised Roman Catholic back in Connecticut-- was even an altar boy for a time-- I eventually left to seek God's face and His Will for me. Of course, over the years, I've found that the Church has become little more than a business. Surely, many of the people within the Church are of good and honest character, but the hierarchy leaves much to be desired, and I could never see much difference between the Pope and Castro, except that one dresses in white, while the other prefers to be in black (or military green).

Entering the solemn sanctuary, I came across statues of Mary and Joseph, bringing back memories of my altar boy youth. While I was contemplating my next move in this Cuban game of chess, a church worker appeared from behind, momentarily startling me.

"My name is Angel," he smiled, his hands cupped together in front of him in an *angelic* pose.

We went off into a corner to sit. Once again, I unrolled the map of the route, and explained the turn of events that had led me to this point. Perhaps Angel or someone else in the church knew of someone, a parishioner perhaps, that could accompany me.

Angel took it all in as best he could. He wasn't sure what could be done, but, "I will talk to the father, and see if he knows of someone."

Off he went while I politely waited. Upon his return, his downcast eyes and posture already revealed the answer he was about to say. "I am sorry, my friend, but the father says he can be of no help."

I placed a warm, friendly hand upon his shoulder, and replied, "It's alright, *amigo*. My Father will take care of whatever needs are to be met."

He straightened up with a beaming smile and joy in his eyes. "Ah, *si! Si!* I believe He will. I will pray for you that the journey will be a success."

When someone named Angel wants to pray for you, better that you take the gift and give thanks.

Frustration was beginning to build as I walked the rubble-strewn manured streets of Havana, waving off tobacco hustlers in Nike shoes, American baseball hats, and Michael Jordan apparel.

By early evening, I was mentally, physically, emotionally and spiritually exhausted as I returned to the *Hotel Morro*. I hadn't eaten or drank anything since lunch, and all I felt like doing was collapsing in bed to renew my energy for another strategic round of battle in the morning.

It was close to dinnertime. The outside patio bristled with activity as the Spanish-language American students began filtering out of the bar in laughter and verse, comparing notes on the day's events in class. A rag-tag group made up of people from around the united States, ages ranging from early 20s to mid 60s were taking the Spanish-language class at the University of Havana as basically a cover-up. They could legally travel to Cuba and avoid the hassles of being arrested upon their return to the States. This is another one of the many loopholes you find in the embargo act. No, you can't go to Cuba unless you're on some kind of educational excursion. So, many people take a class in... touring Cuba, for instance. They spend a couple of hours pleasing the politicians back home, then having the rest of the time to do as they wanted. I decided to take the more honest, straight-forward approach, and just go.

As I was about to enter the foyer and head upstairs to my room, one of the "students" -- an elderly gentleman named Adrian who was dressed all in white, smoking a *cohiba* and drinking rum-- called out to me.

I had met him the previous night out on the patio while having dinner, and we shared stories on what the other was doing in Cuba.

During the course of the evening, when other members of the school group joined us, Adrian excused himself for another drink. While he was between the bar and the patio, I noticed a discreet and subtle act of fondling one of the teenage Cuban boys-- children who seemed to hang around the tourist places like bad bar flys waiting to be picked-up. I quickly made a mental note to always be on my guard with the man who dressed in white.

"Kevin, how goes it today? Have you met with your hosts?"

"No," I moaned, hunched over the table. "Not even a phone call, so I'm trying to come up with another plan."

"Maybe you should see our coordinator." Adrian placed an arm around my shoulder. "You're so tense, my boy. Why don't you let me work on you. I have

Ernesto, the artist, displaying his craft along the *Malecon*. Havana, Cuba.

great hands."

"I have no doubt about that," I answered as he guided me toward a group of tables and chairs out on the patio.

"His name's Rodrigo. He speaks perfect English, and knows everyone in Havana. Perhaps he can help in some way."

The Law (there is only one Law, and that derives from God in His Word. What man passes for his law is really code, and the color of Law.) states that faith without works is dead. Meaning, that if you intend to go after a dream, you must have complete and absolute faith. You must train and study and prepare as much as you can. This is the working part. The faith comes in when you begin to take those first baby steps in order to meet the Lord half-way, whereby He can then help you in those times of trouble when you hit a snag. As in the laws of physics, the Laws contained within the Great Lawbook, or Bible, as many of us have come to call it, work whether or not you believe in God.

We all know that God works in mysterious ways, and none of us can think like He does. Nor should we question His methods, which we may deem mad, for the Lord will send our way people that can be of help, like stepping-stones, to get us to our ultimate destination. We must therefore be of an open mind-- cautious, but open to whatever may come our way, whether that next step be from a pedophile, a playboy or a priest. My personal belief is that the Lord wants us, His children, to be of an open mind and understanding heart. To be as He was when He walked the earth nearly 2000 years ago: to be *in* the world, but not of it; to love the sinner (as we are all), but not the sin.

Upon introductions, Adrian joined the rest of the group for an evening lecture, while Rodrigo and I carried ourselves off to a corner of the lobby where I could spread before him the map of the route and explain my plan.

My height-- slender, with round-rimmed glasses, a moustache, and a mop of jet-black hair, Rodrigo did indeed speak excellent English.

He listened intently, and nodded in understanding of what my needs were. "Well, what I think would be best is to find someone that can go with you who knows the roads and can help carry the supplies. This would be the best plan, but unfortunately you're never going to find someone around here, because you only have one thousand dollars."

So I was now back to square one, getting no further than where I was throughout the day, until another man, shorter than Rodrigo and I, happened to walk by. He stopped to view the map out of mild curiosity.

"Ah!" Rodrigo shouted in delight. "You are in luck, Kevin. This is Alfredo, a good friend of mine. If he can't help you, I don't know who could. I trust this man with my life."

So once again, while Rodrigo excused himself, I went over the plan with another player in this game of faith.

Alfredo Rodriquez was the Godsend to my prayers. Nearly a foot shorter than myself and a few years younger. A handsome man with stylish jet-black hair and moustache, he worked as a school recreational coordinator for the 15th municipal district of Havana. He also moonlighted as a bicycle tour guide for foreigners around Cuba and was the man in charge of the bicycles for the group of "students" at the *Hotel Morro.* He knew the ins and outs of his country and the best and most inexpensive way to get the job done, as we went over the plan.

"*Si*, we can do this," he said, so nonchalantly that at first I was in doubt that he even understood what I was contemplating doing.

We carried the conversation from the lobby to my room.

"Alfredo, if we can pull this off, this will be the longest cycling tour in the history of Cuba."

"*Si,* it will be a first, and I want to go, because no one-- no foreigner or Cuban-- has ever done such a tour. It will make me famous in my country."

He understood. But there were still the details...

"How are we going to get out to *Maisi?*"

"We will hitch a ride on a truck going that way."

"We will?"

"*Si.* We do it all the time, all over the country. It will take maybe two, three days. Not cost much. We change some dollars into *pesos* before we leave."

"How much?"

"Hmmm, not more than one hundred. We change more along the way if we need it, but I think we be okay."

Alfredo explained to me that usually he will take a client or a group and begin in Havana. One of the longest tours was going with some people from the capital to *Santiago de Cuba*, toward the East. Then they'd hitch a ride back to their starting point on a truck. The drivers like to make a little extra money; many of them can double and triple their monthly income. In fact, Alfredo explained, in the beginning of that year, he handled all the arrangements through his Cycling Club at the University of Havana-- travel, food, lodgings-- for a group of eight Americans traveling across Cuba for a two week period. He was able to pick up about $100US, which he used to help support his family. Cubans must be inventive in earning dollars if they are to survive in Western comfort in a country with three different legal systems of currency, two of which they hate.

"This tour's going to take at least three weeks. Can you find the time away from work?"

"This no problem, only-- I will no' be paid when I am gone from my job."

"And how much do you earn?"

"Hmmm, a little more than two hundred *pesos* a month, but with my other jobs, I make about eight hundred."

"Alfredo, I can more than pay you for your time. What would you want as a bonus?" He was asking for little more than $40US for his time on tour with me.

With a wave of his hand, he said, "I will do this Tour for nothing because I want to be part of it. Jus' to cover expenses will be enough, but you can pay me what you feel."

His own mountain bike was a 10-year-old, 10-speed, steel-tubed black behemoth that one of his clients left him upon departing from Cuba some years back, a bike he's been using to conduct cycle tours. It was nearly embarrassing when he saw my $20,000, red-white-and-blue, stars-and-stripes, state-of-the-art, prototype creation that took 18 months to build. His eyes lit up when the bike was unveiled. It was lust at first sight.

"We canno' carry all this equipment with us. I have extra side bags you can use--"

"I can't use them."

"Why no'?"

"My bike is not made to hold racks."

"You have an expensive bike that canno' hold bags?" He was obviously wondering what good a bike was if it couldn't carry the weight.

"During my tours, I've always been used to having an entourage with me, someone else carrying the weight."

He shrugged his shoulders. "I can carry the weight, and you take only important things you carry on your back."

So, I was going to be reduced to trashing nearly ninety percent of the weight I brought with me-- though Alfredo said I could leave it at his place. After all these years, I was finally going to do a tour under my own power, sort of, with a companion of one.

Nearly all the points were covered, with the exception of going to his superiors for permission and, of course, the documentation to get through this Tour.

"If Palaez no come through with letter of permission, then we get one from my boss. Although with Palaez it is better, more power. He is well known throughout country, and will be easy for us to go anywhere without problems."

I had no way of contacting Palaez or Alberto, and at this point I didn't care. I was happy; giddy with excitement. Praise God! We were going, Lord! We were really on our way. The Tour was now becoming a very real possibility after these many years of negotiations. Although we would not begin according to the itinerary, we were moving in the right direction.

I generally liked the idea, after all these years and my third major tour, of doing something in peace and friendship between myself, an American, and another individual representing his own country. Regardless of what took place these next few days, I wanted Alfredo along.

"*Cubano-Americano, amigos*, Alfredo," I smiled, extending my hand, which he took in his.

He nodded. "*Si. Americano-Cubano, amigos*."

Unknowingly, this was to be our slogan during the Tour.

CUATRO

4

HAVANA, CUBA
NOVEMBER 12, 1997

I awoke early morning with an excruciating erection. Subconsciously, we have absolutely no control over our thoughts, dreams, and fantasies-- and these resulted in the condition I was experiencing. Reflections of the previous night's encounter with the two young *senoritas* came to mind.

It was about 10pm when I became bored in my room and decided to venture out for a walk along the *Malecon*. When I used to live in New York City, I would often walk the streets at night, alone with my thoughts. It would be time where I could talk to God concerning any immediate problems I was having, listening for an answer. Sometimes, I just wanted to give thanks for His being there, as I was doing yesterday evening. Watching the lights from a cruise ship on the Caribbean's horizon, I was thankful and grateful for Adrian and Rodrigo, and for sending me exactly whom I needed in the form of Alfredo. I felt confident about the back-up plan, but also asked the Great Physician for His healing touch. For renewed energy and to lift the beginning stages of the flu that made my chest feel like concrete.

It was during the quiet of the evening when, out of the corner of my eye, I noticed a pair of young couples approach in slow embraces, enjoying the nearly full moon. They stopped near me, and one of the men asked the time, which I gave him. Getting past the intro stage, he asked if I was interested in buying some cigarettes.

When I declined, he asked where I was from. "Ah, America, very good place."

All four of them couldn't be older than their early 20s, if even that. I watched them as they continued on their way, the girlfriends turning slightly to catch my eye.

I'll say it right now and get it over with... I love the sight of a beautiful woman as I enjoy and appreciate the beauty of a masterpiece creation of art. I lose myself in both. And while some may say I am a womanizer, I tend to keep to myself, spending my life chasing rainbows. But let me state this one final note: the last thing God created was woman. He saved the best, most beautiful creation for last, and I have never found a woman yet that has argued that particular philosophical point with me-- and, ladies, never let your man tell you any different.

As I went back to staring at the horizon, the girls were beginning to return my way, their boyfriends walking off a distance. *Ah,* I thought, *here's where the fun begins.* My second night in Cuba, and already I was being hit upon. This would be something I would eventually have to get used to during my six-week stay, but for my inaugural debut, I was to be baptized with a double whammy, by a pair of bombshells named Isabella and Graza.

Both were petite, scarcely to my shoulder. Isabella was chipmunk cute with short dark hair, dressed in a silky gown, wearing very little make-up. Her girlfriend Graza was just the opposite: long dark hair, fiery eyes, dressed in a short thigh-length skirt and halter top that revealed quite a bit of her well-formed body.

Once we got past the initial awkward stage, the next hurdle was getting past the language barrier-- neither one of us could speak the other's tongue to any great degree. But it didn't take a brain surgeon to know what was happening.

"*Casa,*" asked Isabella.

I pointed across the street. "*Hotel Morro.*"

"Ah, *si, el Morro. Uno*?" She pointed to me.

"*Si, uno,*" I answered. Both girls looked at one another and smiled before turning their attention back to me.

Isabella slid her formed figure next to mine, rubbing her belly into my groin, smiling when she felt the rise. "How long *Habana*?" Her lush lips parted slightly, as she looked up at me with those doe eyes. I wanted to take her in my arms and make love with her right on the *Malecon.*

Joan? Jean who?

It took superhuman strength to pull away from the playful kitten in order to regain control of myself. "*Forty dias.*"

Again, Isabella slid close to me, her hand on my thigh with Graza close behind, her fire eyes lighting up with excitement. There's only so much a virile man can take. Some women like the chase. I was ready to play, pointing to Isabella, asking, "You, *casa*?"

"*Si,*" she answered enthusiastically and we all laughed.

"No, no, no," I said. Pointing to both of them, I continued, "*Uno, dos, tres, casa*?"

At this, Graza's eyes went wide as she looked over toward Isabella. Both turned to me, smiling, "*Si, si.*"

Damn! Now the proverbial ball was back in my court. I had placed a deal on the table, made the offer, and they accepted. But no matter how good the deal was, in reality, it wasn't going to happen. In order to bow out gracefully, I diverted the conversation by pointing to their boyfriends a few hundred yards down the *Malecon*. "*Hombres?*"

"No, no, no," they both exclaimed.

Isabella replied, "We go *casa*," to which I could only shake my head in disappointment and offer them some dollars.

I walked back to my room, more frustrated and more lonely than when I first left it. This is what I get for trying to thank the Lord for His many blessings? I really do hate being tested in this manner, and wondered if the economy was so bad in Cuba; the people so hungry for the American dollars, that they'd pimp and whore themselves in whatever way they knew how for nothing more than to buy decent food and toiletries?

During the following weeks, I was to be faced with every sexual fantasy I have ever had since the age of 12. Of course, at the time, I didn't know this stressful fact. I entered the bathroom to take a forced cold shower. It was one of many I would be experiencing, because in Cuba, it's a luxury to have hot and cold running water. And don't ever let anyone tell you the myths that taking a cold shower or heavy-duty labor and extreme exercise help curb a sexual appetite. They don't. And I have personally proven both theories false over the years.

The pollution in Havana was beginning to get to me, especially after having lived in the mountains for the previous several years. The best thing for me was to get out of the city ASAP in order to regain my voice and clear my sinuses. My energy was wearing down. Despite religiously taking my vitamins, my chest still felt as though a slab of concrete laid upon it. Just before leaving the States, I had come down with a touch of the flu. With the stress of the Tour, and trying to come up with another plan, my health began to deteriorate to where I was coughing up greenish-yellow biles of ooze, and breaking out into a sweat. I needed to renew my energy for the long and arduous cycling journey that lay ahead, or else fail in the attempt. I didn't wish to be stuck in Havana any longer than I had to. I looked upon my plight in an optimistic way, for I knew the Lord had my life in His hands. We would go when He felt I was ready to venture forth, because only He knew the end of my journey. So I rested and relaxed, feeling stronger with each passing moment.

A phone call came to my room. It was Alberto, the man who met me at the airport a couple of days ago.

"What's going on," I asked. "What's happening?"

"I'm terribly sorry for not calling sooner, Mr Foster," stated Alberto diplomatically. "Mr Palaez has been very busy, but wishes to convey that he will meet with you at precisely the noon hour."

"And if Mr Palaez cannot make the meeting for some reason, how will I be able to contact you?" I diplomatically shot back.

"Oh, he will be there," assured Alberto.

Damn! this guy was good at not releasing vital information. I attempted to make another move.

"Alberto, what if something should happen? I don't even have your phone number or any other way to reach you."

"That will not be necessary," answered my host in a calm, authoritative voice. "We will be there."

He was quite busy with other matters, but once again, assured me he and Palaez would meet me at the appointed time. I wasn't buying a word he said.

My only saving grace was Alfredo's commitment to this project. I could count on his hunger and motive. Without him-- whether I liked it or not, whether I wanted to admit it-- I would have to return home a failure. And how would my sponsors feel about that? "...Oh, Kevin has lost his touch. He doesn't have it like he did with China..." I knew I was better than a one Tour life, and I'd been in tougher scraps than this.

When Alfredo showed up at the hotel after his English lesson, we went walking around the marketplace, viewing the different crafts and buying lunch-- mystery meat sandwiches and juice. Unlike the tasty Mexican food one may expect from a Latin country, Cuba's food is bland. They use no spices, no sauces. A pork sandwich is just a piece of meat between a roll or two slices of bread. Very dry, very tasteless.

As we waited for Alberto and Jose Palaez to show up, Alfredo and I went over the bike route again, making a list of the things we would need to do and acquire. He would be dealing with the paperwork, the documents that would need various signatures. When most of the afternoon passed with a repeat no-show, we looked at one another, shrugged it off, and continued on with our plans.

Alberto did remember to call this time to apologize once again and to say that we would all meet at 5pm. Alfredo was more understandable, saying, "that is how the government operates. If we deal on the local level, things go very fast."

Word began to spread throughout the building, between the staff and guests, as to who I was and what I was doing (or about to do) in Cuba. Until I assembled the bike, I was keeping as low a profile as possible, but in the meantime, I began to get to know some of the Spanish language "students" that occupied most of the rooms at the *Morro*. I helped pass out tubes of Tri-Flow lubricant for their dry and rusty chains-- another one of Alfredo's businesses to earn some extra dollars: renting 30-year-old, one-speed bicycles at $1US per day to the foreigners in town.

Since we had time on our hands, Alfredo loaned me one of these Chinese Flying Pigeons, which I hadn't been on since China in 1990. Fortunately, most of Havana, like Cuba, is flat, which helped to keep the dragging chains from falling off. We cycled to the Farmer's Market, an open-air arena crowded with people shopping for their daily food, where mangy stray dogs hang out, hoping for some choice cuts of meat to fall from the tables.

After viewing the various fruits and vegetables, Alfredo and I went next door to a restaurant, a concrete hole-in-the-wall with plastic chairs and tables covered with dirty cloths. Pigs and goats were waiting off to the side to be slaughtered, and the mangy mutts had free rein-- coming and going as they pleased, begging from table to table. There were hoards of flies too numerous to count, and if one were not careful when talking or taking a mouthful of food, one might get more than they bargained for. Alfredo and I ordered plates of *congris*, *yucca* (a boiled vegetable), salad, and beers, all for the expensive price of $2US. After all, we were dining out, and therefore

Taking a truckload of fresh bananas to the marketplace.

one pays for the atmosphere.

No luxury items like paper towels or napkins were present and, upon closer inspection, the utensils were slightly used.

"Do you believe in God?" I asked.

From his relaxed, rocking position, Alfredo nearly toppled over, as beer dribbled down his chin and onto his shirt. After briskly cleaning himself up, he leaned forward, and in a low voice, answered, "No, I don't believe in such nonsense. But I did have a grandmother who carried a crucifix, and prayed and believed in God, so my family had to hide her during the revolution. You couldn't be a Socialist and believe in God, but now the government say it okay to be a Socialist and believe in God." He took a swig of beer, then continued, as though he needed to correct himself for my benefit. "Sometimes, when things go wrong, I look up to the sky and ask, "Why me?'" He laughed and took another swallow of beer. "Why me?"

I smiled. "That's okay, my friend, because He believes in you, and sent you to me. We are going to have some wonderful adventures together, and things will happen that even you won't be able to explain."

Alfredo gave me a quizzical look. Obviously not knowing what to make of my bold statements, he was probably wondering what he was getting himself in to. But I knew he would stay with me to the end: he would be a loyal companion because he was hungry for this *Tour de Cuba*, this shot at fame.

After the Farmer's Market, we cycled to the *Plaza de la Revolution*. A magnificent area of concrete buildings, statues, and open space, much like that of *Tiananmen Square*.

Surrounding the blacktop square, where the people gather to hear Fidel give a couple of speeches a year, lies the building housing the Ministry of Defense. It sports a steel outline likeness of its most popular former Minister of Defense-- the ubiquitous Che Guevara. To the right of it stands a fortress-like building belonging to the Army, and to the left is the National Post Office with the National Theatre of Cuba as its neighbor. Across from the Ministry of Defense is the 20-story People's Tower, where Castro speaks from a podium and where permanently sits the gigantic statue of Josi Marti, another Cuban hero, who fought for Cuba's freedom against the Spanish over a hundred years before, during the War for Independence. Unlike Che, Marti was a president of Cuba, but like the revolutionary, there wouldn't be a day that went by where I wouldn't see some sort of likeness of Marti, on billboards or busts of Josi peering from official government courtyards or in front of people's gardens.

Like the Italians back in my East coast hometown who keep their handsome Virgin Mary statues in their front yards, Josi Marti was Cuba's God, just as Che Guevara was their Jesus Christ. (All Cuban women were considered the Virgin Mary.) If the country ever decided to do its own version of Mount Rushmore, it would consist of Josi, Che, Fidel and Maximo Gomez, another fighter in the War for Independence and a close friend of Marti's.

Aside from Sundays, Cuba has two National holidays where the ordinary working people have the day off from their individual jobs. Parades are given-- May Day on the first of that month, which is a big day in every Communist country; and December 2nd for the Army, because, again, in a Communist country, the military rules.

Since Alfredo lived within a couple of blocks of the *Plaza*, he wanted to take me to his house to meet his family. Heading off onto a side street, we came to an apartment complex that reminded me of any number of Tennessee Williams plays, the most obvious being *A Streetcar Named Desire*. It had a surreal look to it all, and I wondered when I would come upon a Cuban Marlon Brando or witness the children suddenly break out into a song-and-dance number.

We walked the path toward the courtyard, where some people were gathered in smoking and conversation, to the last building in the row. Gazing upward, I could see rows of clothing on lines rising up several layers, displaying their colorful cloth. One tenant could look into another tenant's apartment, or simply call out to them to talk, as some people did. It reminded me of the old country chats neighbors would have over their white picket fences.

Upon entering the second floor home, I was greeted by Alfredo's mother, a petite, cheerful woman who greeted me with a warm smile, and her husband Jerry, an individual of dark features who was the all-around fix-it man for the complex. The only other person in the well-kept, three-bedroom house was Alfredo's blonde-bombshell sister, Dania. Altogether, Alfredo has two brothers and two sisters, and he fits somewhere in between at 34. Alfredo's the only member in his family that can speak English well enough to be understood.

"Come, I show you something," he said after introductions were over.

With the infamous revolutionary hero, Ernesto "Che" Guevara.
Havana, Cuba.

We headed down the narrow hallway to the end, where he shared a bedroom with another brother.

Two large beds occupied most of the room, with clothes, books, bicycle parts, and other miscellaneous items adding to the already cramped quarters. We sat on the beds opposite each other, where he pulled out some American magazines, newspaper articles, and brochures for me to view.

"I have done many tours around Cuba with journalists who then put me in their stories." He beamed with pride. "One time we go to *Bay of Pigs*. Another, from *Santiago* to *Pinar.* I go all over with them as guide, interpreter, mechanic... I also know history of my country and have a degree in geography."

"You are a jack-of-all-trades, my friend," I smiled, as I leafed through one of the sports magazines.

"*Si.* Because we are poor, we must learn to do much, and use what we can."

"This Tour we will be doing is no easy thing," I reminded him. "We will be together all the time for almost a month. We will have to survive on our wits."

He pressed his lips together, and nodded confidently. "*Si*. We will do this and become famous."

The next stop on our loop toward the *Morro* was Alfredo's place of work, nearly a straight half-mile away from the hotel's door-- a huge rotunda sports complex where athletes of all levels train for National and International competition. It has seen its years-- as parts of it were in dire need of being repaired: paint was peeling off the walls, the center grass around the track looked more like a brown weedpatch than the lush green carpet I'd imagined.

Alfredo was sharp to notice my thoughts. "We no' have the proper equipment, and our facilities are poor, but we use what we have, and are fifth in the world in Olympic medals."

And that says a lot about the people's spirit in a country smaller than California with a total population of only 12 million.

Regardless of Alfredo's schedule, he had to check into the office whenever in Havana and view the month's itinerary. While away on Tour, he would have three other co-workers who could fill his workload, as he does for them when they conduct cycling tours. This is how they are all able to earn extra dollars, and work at something that they generally enjoy doing.

As 5 o'clock approached, we headed back to the *Morro* to await, once again, the arrival of Alberto and Jose Palaez. After another half-hour of waiting, we came up empty-handed.

The rule of thumb goes: Shame on you the first time, shame on me the second time. But after that, you must be pretty stupid or incredibly naive.

I think we were both pretty stupid, because we decided to wait a while longer. Alfredo hung out at the hotel bar, watching the basketball game on TV with the other employees, and I decided to check out the corner grocery store. It dealt in American goods for American dollars.

Prices were high. You could get a miniature salt and pepper set for $4US, and nearly anything else you desired, such as Coca-Cola, Pepsi, Carnation canned and powdered milk, teas, spices, ketchup, mustard, frozen pizza, wines, *Asti Spumanti*

Alfredo, mama, brother Alberto, sister Dania, and stepfather, Jerry.
Havana, Cuba.

champagne, Quik powdered chocolate mix, Kern's juices, peanut butter, a variety of ice-cream, pasta, sauces, Sony TV's, VCR's, radios, Microsoft programs and so much more. The place was packed with Cubans waiting to purchase the American delicacies with their hard-earned (?) dollars. I was back in the States as if I'd never left.

It was almost 6:30pm and still no show. "Alfredo, how long will it take to make the arrangements?"

"A couple of days."

"Then do it and let's get out of here."

We shook hands and as he was ready to cycle home, he joked with a smile, "If they come, you call me."

"Oh, sure," I replied in raised eyebrows. "I'll be waiting."

As I sat out on the patio enjoying the warm tropical breeze with a cold can of Coke, Patricia stopped by, having just returned from an outing around Havana with some of her fellow students. Taking a seat at my table, she asked, "How are the plans going for the Tour?"

"Not that well, but Alfredo and I are making progress."

"Well, what do you expect?" she smiled. "You're down here by yourself when you should've come with a group like *Global Exchange* and done your Tour that way."

I sat straight up in my chair and leaned back in a forced relaxed mode, returning her smile, tooth for tooth. "I don't do tour groups. Not my style."

"Of course you don't, because you're doing this for your own fame and glory. You have no idea what the situation is like here in Cuba. These people are poor;

they have no money. You're not top priority to them," she spewed, leaning closer toward me. "They have so many problems that they're dealing with that you're on the bottom of the list. What you really need to do is immerse yourself in their culture. At least we're trying to do something-- "

"Yes, of course you are," I said, my tone cold. "I can see the immense help and contribution you're giving by taking a Spanish language class here instead of some stateside school."

Her lips pressed tight, she began to breathe heavy, ready for the second attack.

"You're just here for your own fame and glory. Yeah, we're here under the pretense of learning to speak Spanish, but we also came down with supplies trying to help them, trying to make a difference."

Mangy, flea infested bitches were howling just outside the courtyard from where we sat, as my eyes began to wander down Patty's thin, sleeveless T-shirt. With each new level of tirade, her breathing became more rhythmic. I smiled to myself as her breasts became full, her nipples erect as I stated that, "I really don't care about my personal fame and glory, since I've had it for years. So really, what more do I need? All I wanted was for my host to be honest and up front with me. If this were going to cost, fine. How much? Let's get down to business, but don't stick me with these surprises upon arrival."

"Well that's just what they did," she sneered with a smile. "All they want is your dollars; all they want is for you to spend, and that's exactly what you're doing," she laughed. "They stuck you here, and you have no choice but to spend your money in order to survive."

I momentarily left the enjoyment of the show her breasts were performing and replied, "Not for long." I wouldn't give her the satisfaction of seeing me boil, as I took a drink. "Since I have to spend my money, I'll do it my way. This Tour will happen now that I have Alfredo."

Something about the self-assured way I carry myself, coupled with my confident tone and attitude, makes people want to kill me. It's been said I have a talent for bringing out a person's true character, whether it be good or evil. Patricia sat across from me seething with rage, trying oh-so-hard to smile through it all.

"Well, then, it seems you have it all figured out. But then, what do the Cubans get out of this? At least you're getting paid for this by your sponsors. They don't need the publicity. They need help, they're starving..."

"Patty, get off your high-horse, idealistic bullshit. Whatever deals I have when I return home is no one's business. And as far as the poverty and starvation these people seem to be having, it's mostly their own fault. Granted, the embargo does hurt them to some degree, and has to go, but it's not the root cause of their problems. Forty years ago when Cubans were Capitalists they had it good. But then they got greedy and wanted more. They thought a Communist-Socialist way of life would be better. Castro came in to fill the void, and the gamble didn't pay off. They lost and now must suffer the consequences. That's what happens when you turn your back on God. He lets you have your way."

A San Francisco Bay Area liberal like Patty evidently does not want to hear such cursing. "You think you have it all figured out, don't you? You just expect to come down here and do your tour and expect them to help you out. Well, who do you think you are? You're not important-- "

"Never said I was," I answered. "But I have a job to do, and it's going to get done before I return home."

Her breasts were really up and erect at this point, as I leaned into her, placing a comforting hand on her arm.

"Listen," I said soothingly. "Let's cut out the politics and personal vendettas, and enjoy each other's company over dinner. Afterwards, we can return to my room for dessert..."

She shot straight out of her chair so fast that some of the people around us glanced over to see what the commotion was all about. "What you're doing is a complete waste, and we'll see how far it gets you."

"I'm trying to make advances," I consoled, looking up to a pair of twin peaks. "Would you like it if we went back to your room after dinner? Either bed is fine."

She spun on her heel, joining her group while I took my leave, retiring to my room.

What makes people so full of hatred toward a stranger? Whether someone comes to Cuba bearing medical supplies under the guise of being a student, or does a one-of-a-kind cycling tour that generates enough press coverage to get out the message that the embargo has to go, he's doing what he can in his own way. No one should blast another in what they're trying to do; everyone should have their personal motives in check.

By Patty's rantings and ravings, it seemed to my Spirit, she wanted some personal fame and glory for herself; that she must look in the mirror and feel utterly, hopelessly worthless. You can do more with a bicycle in love, then with a lot of so-called *good intentions* in hate.

About 7pm, there was a knock at my door. There stood Humberto, wide-eyed and quite excited, trying to rattle off something in his limited English.

"*Kebin*...come...down...now."

Not even realizing what was going on, I followed him, and saw Alberto-- and then standing next to him was one whom I presumed to be the infamous Jose Palaez.

The introductions were made, the handshakes given. I excused myself a moment to return to my room to grab my briefcase and make a fast phone call to Alfredo.

His sister Dania answered, and because she couldn't speak English, the message had to be very slow, and very limited. "Kevin...Jose Palaez...*El Morro*."

She repeated the message. "Okay."

That was all I could do, so I raced back to my guests, who were waiting outside on the patio.

A stocky-built man in his 50s, with a head of curly gray hair, Jose Palaez carried more than his weight in the cycling community. His over-sized paunch attested to the fact that he was obviously leading a well-satisfied life; it was a gut that would take years to work off on a bicycle-- if he were to ever get on one. In general, this continues to amaze me about those corporate executives I deal with in the industry. The majority of them haven't been on a bike in years, judging by their waistlines, and if they were to try to get back into some kind of reasonable shape, they'd probably keel over from a heart attack. It's embarrassing to watch them try convincingly to sell a healthy lifestyle via the bicycle to the public. Somehow their talk just doesn't measure up.

Palaez's arrival and entourage had the staff buzzing about like busy little bees as they hovered over us, acting as servants, but really wanting to be close enough to listen in on our conversation. The American "students" were close by as well, looking over from time to time, talking in low whispers. I caught Patty's narrow gaze and tight lips, and wondered how her nipples were doing.

Alberto, Palaez and I huddled in a corner, going over the itinerary, as cold Cokes and snacks were served slowly around the table. Did the staff have to be that obvious in wanting to listen in? Never has someone of such importance and high position within the government come to the *Morro*.

"Mr Palaez apologizes for being uninformed of your arrival," stated Alberto, speaking for Jose.

I diplomatically accepted the apology and asked if Rafael Noriega mentioned or passed along the new itinerary.

Alberto looked over at Palaez, then turned to me hesitantly. "No, only when you would be arriving."

Originally, when the Tour was an official go in May, I sent off three different choices for my host to choose from. In addition to beginning immediately, I suggested a couple of months later, in July; or sometime between February through April of the following year. Without much word, I had to call Noriega for some kind of decision, to which he answered that my host would leave the choice up to me. When a sponsor of mine suggested after the hurricane season, in November, I went back to check out some facts and found it to be a good choice.

Taking the map in his sausage-like fingers, Jose scanned the route and made comments concerning the various terrain that Alberto interpreted.

Jose had some misgivings about the proposed route from *Maisi* to *Cabo San Antonio*, the two extreme ends of the island. Beyond *Baracoa*, Cuba's oldest town, and largest easternmost community, he stated, "the roads are generally unkept. More dirt and gravel than pavement, and very steep. One section rises some two thousand, four hundred feet."

"No problem," I answered. "The bike was designed to handle any road condition and terrain."

Jose wasn't really listening, as his eyes continued to scan the route that laid unfolded across his belly. "I suggest you fly to *Guantanamo* and begin the Tour there. It is close to the US naval Base where we could gather some good press coverage."

"Yes, that is a good idea," I agreed. "But going from one end to the other would also get us a lot of press coverage. This will be the longest cycling tour in the history of Cuba," I smiled enthusiastically.

Jose sat there like a frowning Buddha, staring at me blankly, long after Alberto finished with the interpretation. Again, he perused the map. Scanning the route, he shook his head, and said half-heartily, "The first part of the Tour from *Maisi* to *Manzanillo* is mountainous, but after that the terrain would change to flatlands."

He took a few deep, strained breaths, mopping his sweaty forehead with a handkerchief as Alberto caught up to his interpretation. Continuing, I wondered if he would have a heart-attack before negotiations were finalized.

"The last part, beyond *Trinidad*, would be hilly once more." In effect, I was looking at a week of boredom sandwiched between two rollercoasters.

"Would special permission be needed to cycle and climb your country's highest natural point, *Pico Turquino?*"

When plotting the Tour in the last year, I made sure we would pass right by the mountain that was located along the Southern coast outside *Santiago* in the *Sierra Maestra* range. At 6542 feet, the mountain was doable as a day excursion, and since most governments have a certain amount of paranoia when it comes to their treasured wonders, I needed to know what loopholes to jump through.

"No," said Palaez. "You will be able to climb it."

He stated it so matter-of-fact, off-the-cuff, that it seemed too easy to be believed, but having no way of knowing what to believe at the time, I tossed off the remark. Afterwards, Alfredo would confirm Jose's remarks about *Pico Turquino* to be true.

We continued our discussions concerning transportation and accommodations. On these subjects, Jose sat back with a huge grin on his face, his hands joined together resting on his stomach, while Alberto spoke for his boss.

"Mr Palaez has the power to make all the necessary phone calls for security and to the various sporting facilities located in every province which could house you during the three-week Tour."

On the transportation, Jose felt we could either have a driver per province, or, say, a group of three, changing every week.

"One could come out of *Guantanamo*, another from either *Camaguey* or *Ciego de Avila*, and the last one from Havana."

"I like the three drivers idea," I stated as I sat on the edge of my seat, excited that we were finally getting under way. "One driver per province would be a total of thirteen, and that would be too much to handle."

Alberto and Palaez nodded in agreement. Everything was going along smoothly, until the question of finances arose.

Alberto asked, "How much did you bring with you to pay for this Tour?"

Here's where we were going to place our cards on the table, where the rubber was about to meet the road. In my mind, I could hear Patty's evil "you deserve it" laugh. I sat back in my seat, took a drink of soda, and let the question formulate in my mind. We were now at the make-it or break it stage. My mind began to wander to my sponsors, the world-- *if I lost this Tour, they would see me as a failure. They wouldn't know all the dirty little details. All they would see was the end result, and their harsh and strict judgment would be a verdict of guilty by reason of insufficient planning.* There would be no plea for mercy and understanding from my countrymen. This was one reason why Cuba would be my retirement Tour: the hassles acquiring the sponsorship dollars was just too much.

"Why do you want to go to that *in-Fidel's* country for anyway?" sneered my own mother.

I had tried to explain my point of view that "they're people like us. We should try to reach out to the great dictator in love, peace and friendship." But the philosophy wasn't getting through to my Christian mother, who had become a product, like many other Americans, of a mass market campaign to hate whom you're told to hate. It was placed upon my generation, who knew only of a lifetime of embargo, to make the necessary changes in whatever way we could.

When Alberto's question came up, I simply asked "Why wasn't this mentioned in the two years we'd been planning this Tour, during our correspondence?" He asked Palaez, who had shook his head in return.

Instead, they came up with a serious figure of $5000US, thinking the Tour could only be done for that. I tried to suppress my contemptible laughter, knowing that Alfredo's earlier price of $100US was more realistic, and calmly stated that all I had on me was $1000US. That was the truth, and I held my ground.

It was strongly suggested that I postpone the Tour until March or April-- "When we would all be more ready," stated Alberto.

"That's not going to happen," I smiled. "Since I'm already in Cuba and we have the time, we should move forward."

Alberto gave the interpretation with trepidation.

The truth was, there was no way I was going to leave empty-handed-- especially as I had already done press coverage back in the States and was about to do with CNN in Havana. To return home now meant someone else could steal the Tour out from under me.

Jose's cold, forceful stare would probably make almost anyone cower, but then he was dealing with me and against my hard looks and intimidating presence that just wasn't going to happen.

I said what I had in terms of cost, I knew what we could do this Tour for, and I had a back-up plan that they didn't know about. The next move would be theirs, and I would counter accordingly in this Cuban game of chess.

Palaez blinked and lowered his defenses. Alberto found a new source of hope in his voice as he interpreted, "Mr Palaez would like twenty-four hours to make the necessary arrangements, and then another meeting will be held."

Jose gave me a cat-bird, knowing smile as he sat across from me, and I wondered just how much English he could really understand that he wasn't letting on. According to the itinerary, we were suppose to begin the Tour over a thousand miles away in *Maisi* within two days, and no way was that going to happen. My only choice was to grant the request and hope that not too much time would be lost.

Diplomacy is a give and take, tug of war, in which both sides must achieve results and save face at the same time.

As the meeting was about to end, Alfredo arrived, a bit red in the cheeks and somewhat winded. He had gotten my message and successfully decoded it. His presence now confirmed what I had already suspected-- he was as hungry for this Tour as I had once been for cycling atop China's Great Wall. I just hoped he would never be like me where the fun of cycling has been lost to becoming a job. That's why I needed this Tour-- to see if I could find the fun again.

Alfredo receiving a 2 *peso* (8 cents) ticket for cycling against traffic.
I was spared for being a foreigner.

Introductions were made all around, as we drifted into the lobby of the hotel, the staff still buzzing about. I threw in a new curve. "Alberto, tell Jose I want Alfredo along to act as guide and interpreter."

Palaez shifted his gaze from me to his nervous assistant, the sweat forming along Alberto's brow.

"I do not know if that would be wise. Arrangements can only be made for you."

"Don't know if you don't ask," I smiled.

Jose was waiting, and when he heard the new "suggestion," he turned to Alfredo, asking him questions in their native tongue, to which Alfredo would answer, "*Si, si*... of course, *si*..."

Much to Alberto's relief, his boss was comfortable with Alfredo's background and experience in tour cycling, nodding, "It will be fine. I see no problem and will include him in the overall agenda."

As we exchanged farewells, handshakes and phoney laughter, Alfredo and I watched the group of men drive away. The ol' uneasy feeling returned to my gut, gnawing at me like a bad habit.

Apparently, Alfredo felt the same. "What do you wish to do?"

"Go ahead with our plan. Start the paperwork, and let's get out of here."

He nodded in agreement, got back on his bike, and disappeared into the night. I stayed outside a moment, standing in the courtyard that I now regarded as an oasis, a safe haven from the filth and poverty that was spread out before me. I listened to the sounds of waves crash against the concrete wall that lined the *Malecon*. The scent of salt filled the warm air. The moon was nearly full. *Salsa* music streamed through the open windows of dilapidated buildings, and bare-chested men and short-skirted women walked the streets in search of relief from their boredom.

Although I felt uneasy with *senor* Jose Palaez, it was just the opposite with Alfredo. He was a man I was comfortable with-- a man very much like myself. I knew the success or failure of this Tour rested almost entirely upon his shoulders, for all I had to do was the cycling. And I was confident that the Lord would be with us and see us to the end.

My only remaining thought now was to get out of Havana as quickly as possible and experience the freedom of the open road and the sweeping countryside...

It was time to go to work.

CINCO

5

HAVANA, CUBA
NOVEMBER 14, 1997

"Kevin?"

"Yes?"

"It's Jean."

"Yes."

"Thank God you're alive!" she burst out crying. "When I didn't receive any word from you through your Canadian contact, I became worried. I thought maybe you had been kidnapped or something, and I'd never hear from you again."

"Now I know I love you for your mind and not your body," I cooed.

"Oh, stop making fun of me," she barked into the receiver. "I was really worried about you."

"Is that the same as saying you love me and miss me and care a great deal about me?" I laughed with a tease.

"You know it is," she stated flatly. "I called, didn't I? My actions speak louder than words."

"Yes they do," I replied, rising out of bed. "And how were you able to get through to me directly?"

"Without telling the people, our government seems to have relaxed sanctions on dialing direct to each other's country. But at three dollars a minute, we pay the price."

With that said, we didn't waste time and precious dollars on the small talk. I quickly brought her up to date on all that had happened thus far. That, although I felt uncomfortable with the outcome of last night's meeting, the Lord provided me with a helpmate named Alfredo, and we were going ahead with an alternative plan, leaving Havana as quickly as possible.

"So you'll have no security? No entourage?"

"None," I replied, pacing the room.

"But what if something happens to you along the way?" Her voice rose an octave at the mentioned thought.

"Then what of it? So be it. Thy will be done," I snapped. "What could you do to help? Contact the State Department? You know I already face being arrested upon my return. Best thing to do now is go ahead as planned."

She was quiet for a moment. "Yes," she agreed. "You're probably right. You need to get to work."

"If I can hold out." I coughed hoarsely, pounding my chest to loosen up the concrete bile within me.

"It doesn't sound as though you're getting any better since you left for Cuba."

"Sounds worse, I know, but I'm trying to take it easy. I rest as often as I can, and am taking my vitamins. But there's still plenty to keep me busy."

"It's probably the traveling from cold to warm, and not knowing from day to day what's happening with this Tour that's bringing you down in untold stress."

"Perhaps," agreeing with her diagnosis. "But as soon as we can begin and get on the trail, I believe my spirit will improve. We just need to get started."

"Everyone at the church is praying for you," she stated, changing the subject to a brighter one. "We haven't seen any reports on TV or in the papers yet."

"I know," I relaxed, as I viewed the photos of Jean and my *Lhasa Apos, Hanzhu* and *Jia Tu* beside my bed. "I'll be doing an interview with CNN today. Expect to see something within the next couple of weeks once the Tour is underway."

All the other major networks and the Associated Press didn't have offices anywhere in Cuba. Cable News Network did, because the boss, Ted Turner, came to the island himself to set up shop a couple of years back. Once the CNN piece hit the airwaves, other stations around the united States would pick it up, then the newspapers from the wire service. That would be the only way anyone could follow what I was doing or how I was getting along.

It was good to hear a familiar voice again-- Jean's voice most especially. But it was difficult when saying good-bye.

"And you love me and miss me and can't wait to hold me in your arms again, right?" I teased.

"Well," she laughed, "I do miss you...but only sometimes. When I stop a moment from my work to think about you."

"*Mon ami!* You actually think about me sometimes? I'm honored! Touched! It must mean you love me."

"You know I do," she laughed, easing the tension of having to say our good-byes.

"Ay! What's that ye say? Speak up! I can't hear ye."

She giggled. "Stop it! You know I care for you."

"Ay? Ay! Speak up woman! Ye blasted she-devil!"

"I love you okay," she screamed into the phone. "You're such a pain. Now do

Some of the neighborhood boys hitching a ride.

what you have to do and come home."

"I look forward to making your wish come true."

The sound of the dial tone was followed by the most dreadful feeling in the world: loneliness. This is when it hits you hardest most of all.

The only solace I could think of was to continue my work, to assemble the bike for its Cuban debut. Once completed, it was time to don my stars-'n'-stripes uniform. Captain America was about to make his first public appearance in the Communist country just 90 miles off the coast of Florida. Today's reactions would determine the tone for the rest of the Tour. I descended the stairs with the bike to cheers of ooh's and aah's.

"*Kebin*, my man, how are you today?"

"Fine, Humberto, fine."

"Es beautiful bike," he motioned with a kiss. "How much?"

Like the daily gathering of the crowds with each new Tour, questions concerning the bike follow me throughout. So let's get this over with here and now on all the intimate details and creation of *La Bicicleta...*

To begin with, it took some 18 months to hand-build the Klein prototype at a rough cost of $20,000. For those who don't ride a bike often enough to become familiar with some of the industry's terms, think of the main frame of a bicycle as an upsidedown triangle. The top bar is called a top tube. The bar to the right where your handlebars protrude from is the bottom tube. And the bar that your saddle is attached to is called the seat tube.

The 19.5 inch aluminum frame is unique, in that it boasts the fattest top tube

(11 inches) in the industry, thus eliminating the need for a bottom tube, making it one of the best climbing bikes in the world. Full suspension, the rear frame is of a triangular design that pivots upon hitting a bump on impact. The front shock takes blows all day instead of my shoulders.

Much of the componentry is made of a combination aluminum and titanium. The Beast has 24-gears (a standard automobile has four to five speeds you shift through); bar ends that attach to a one-piece stem-handlebar, allowing my upper body to stretch in three different positions during the course of a regular 12-hour cycling day, which is most important to relieve stress, strain and tension; 22-32-42 chainrings and 11-12-14-16-18-21-24-28 rear cogs (for all you techno buffs). The size and thickness of each tire are: a 26x2.35 front and 26x2.10 rear make for better maneuvering in the dirt, especially if you hit a patch of sand. It gives you a moment to quickly adjust, thus avoiding that all too unnecessary face plant.

The red-white-blue, stars-'n'-stripes paint job was relatively the same as the **American Summits** bike. Also: five-spoke Aerospoke carbon fiber wheels (in the same colors as the bike itself), IBC hydraulic brakes, Avocet altimeter cycling computer, Pinnacle cut-away seat which relieved pressure of the groin (which becomes a blessing when cycling some 10-12 hours a day), and probably the most popular feature of the bike, the Powerpost seat adjuster I controlled from the handlebar. This is the lazy man's way to ride, especially on those rollercoaster days.

Typically, the seatpost would stay in one position until I headed for a steep downhill. Then I had to dismount, lower the seatpost in order to get the weight back (unless you enjoy going over the handlebars), and continue the mad descent. With the Powerpost, however, you simply click a button for the seat to adjust-- depending on the type of condition you're faced with-- and continue on your way. Never need to dismount, never break cadence. It takes maybe an hour to get used to, and a lifetime to appreciate. Like many of the features of the bike, it would be difficult to go back to the old way of cycling I once knew. The two new items I really had to get used to were the Shimano clipless pedals (I always felt uncomfortable in that locked-in feeling), and the motorcycle-like Grip-Shift gear shifters which, over the course of 1200 miles, made me a seasoned pro.

With nearly a dozen companies contributing to the overall design, the created work of art weighed in at about 10 kilos or 22 pounds, and there isn't another bike like it in the world. We were here to put on a show, and a red-white-blue, stars-'n'-stripes one at that.

There were always daily problems on the Tour, but a couple of them were never foreseen. For instance, my name being on the bike. Normally this wouldn't present a problem, except I kept getting comments like, "Kebin Foster the famous movie actor?" This has plagued me since 1990 upon my return from China. Kevin Costner, *the famous movie actor* made his mark by winning a pair of Academy Awards for *Dances With Wolves,* and ever since then I have had secretaries go quiet, or catch their breath, or ask me to repeat my name just to make certain they didn't misunderstand whenever I called on sponsorship. It does become irritating now and then, and on the **Tour de Cuba**, it got to the point toward the end where I finally had had enough of the question and screamed, "Yes!... Yes! I am! Do you want my autograph?!" and promptly scribbled my name on a piece of paper.

The other incident had to do with my bike sponsor's name. Along with being the fattest top tube in the industry came the largest signature planted on it. When being seen in the photos, no matter how small I may look in some of them, you can't help but spot the logo, and whenever people heard my name and saw the large appellation, they would often combined the two, exclaiming, "Kebin Klein, the famous fashion designer?" to which I would finally have enough and scream, "Yes!... Yes! I am! Do you want my autograph?!" and promptly scribble my name on a piece of paper.

Starting out from the hotel, I headed west toward Alfredo's workplace, the 15th Municipal District sports complex, where there happened to be a group of school-children, the bike's inaugural crowd. As soon as I stopped, the magnetism of the bike drew them closer with squeals and wide-eyed expressions of delight. I was surrounded as they admired the sophisticated piece of machinery.

They all rattled off at once in very fast Spanish that I couldn't understand, peppered with minor English phrases of, "Is beautiful!" and "How much?" This was followed by many little hands touching every part of the bike, their eyes mesmerized by the colors and the overall design.

I spoke what little I could with them, finally asking for Alfredo, to which they earnestly pointed to his office.

Alfredo wasn't in, but since I was already out, I decided to go exploring parts of Havana. I made my way toward the *Plaza de la Revolution* and down a few pot-holed side-streets, among many looks and whistles from people as I passed by in a red, white, and blue blur. In all my peacock finery, I stood out in a dull world.

According to my itinerary, today would've been the start of the Tour some 1000 eastward miles away, but energy-wise I knew I wouldn't have been up to it, as I continued to fight the battle of the sore throat and concrete chest.

To be done that day was the afternoon interview with CNN at the historical *Hotel National*-- a beautiful monument to the old style 30s architecture that Havana is known for, where the rich and famous, kings, queens and heads of state reside at $150US per night (cheap by their standards). It is a palace-like fortress that juts out toward the Caribbean, ending at the *Malecon* with a magnificent waterfall-fountain.

Dressed the way I was in uniform, I felt somewhat uncomfortable as I strode into the terraced parking lot. I was being bodily blocked to enter the building by the valet who raised his hand in a halt position, pointing to an area where an attendant looked after the two wheelers. In places like this everyone pays in dollars, so instead of a *peso* to watch the bike, it became one dollar-- or rather two. Alfredo came riding by just at the right moment. Uncanny.

Returning to the front door, I was again stopped by the valet, shaking his head and holding up his halt hand.

"Now what's the problem?"

He pointed to my bandana and uniform and said something in Spanish.

Alfredo answered, "He say you canno' enter the hotel dressed the way you

The historic *Hotel National* along the *Malecon.*

are. It is American flag, and in places like this, they no like American flag."

Smiling, I informed Alfredo, "Tell him to go play with himself, I'm going in."

"You cause trouble if you do," warned my interpreter.

"Because I'm an American who happens to be wearing his country's colors?"

"*Si.* If I wore these colors, I would be arrested and thrown in jail. The government no like your country's colors."

"Which are the same as yours," I shot back.

"*Si,* but you have more stars," laughed Alfredo.

"I'll show you some stars," I countered. "Tell him we're here for an interview with CNN."

Alfredo did-- plus he must have mentioned some other things, the conversation taking more than a moment.

The valet spoke with the front doorman, who spoke to someone at the registration desk, who allowed us to enter the imposing sepulchre. Wouldn't *Open Sesame* have done just as well?

The lobby was like a palace, done in shades of brown tile flooring, with brown marble columns supporting the weight of brown cathedral ceilings. Before arriving at the island, I had read that renovations to the *National* cost the Cubans some $15 million dollars, and now I could see why. Some people were milling about in a busy-like atmosphere, dressed in country club attire in shades of watercolors that made the boldness of my attire stand out even more, as they looked me over with contempt. Others were sitting in overstuffed chairs reading the daily paper.

At the front desk, we asked to be paged to CNN's room. We were brushed off by a wave of the hand and told to use one of the phones that were sitting on a table behind us.

Not being able to get through to anyone, we were just about to leave when someone called out to me. Turning to the voice, we were greeted by a large, stocky man named Tony Valdez, CNN's soundman. He shook our hands warmly.

"Guess you didn't have a problem spotting me," I joked.

"Well, you certainly stand out in that uniform."

"Yeah, I also had some trouble getting in." I explained to Tony the hassles, including the fact that I wasn't allowed to bring the bike inside.

Tony quickly found someone in charge, rattled something off in Spanish, and returned to us.

"You can bring it in, but you must carry it across the lobby. They're afraid you might scratch the tile floor."

I laughed, but agreed.

As the three of us entered through the glass doors to the back courtyard, I stopped in mid-stride, my lower jaw hanging loose.

"Did I just die and enter Heaven?"

"No," said Tony. "You're still in Hell, and this is the best it has to offer."

The best was a spacious green lawn that extended straight to a blue sea Caribbean. Natural stone tiles were inlaid in the manicured grass carpet that cut across the lush lawn in walkways where the spit-shine shoes of immaculately-styled guests clacked against the sparkling marble. Victorian-styled white iron benches were placed at intervals for the pedigrees to take in the three-sided view of the waters. This was a different world than the one I had recently been a part of. The comfort of all creature comforts, as I took a deep breath and smiled like a donkey.

"And on this day ye shall be with me in Paradise."

Tony introduced us to Rudy, the cameraman, and as we began to set up the shot and discuss what we would do, along came a busy-looking petite beauty dressed in white. Princess Charming? Between phone calls from her cellular, she introduced herself as Lucia Newman, head bureau chief in Cuba, and the one who would be doing the interviewing.

I had seen Lucia on TV in the past and was familiar with her work in covering events in Havana during the *Brotherhood to the Rescue* plane shoot-down incident of February, 1996. I found her reports to be smart, intelligent, sophisticated and her beauty far more revealing than what her official company photo makes her out to be. Yeah, ol' Ted Turner sure knows how to pick his women.

"How's the search for the McDonald's going?" asked Lucia with a smile, as she extended her hand.

"Closest I could find so far is the *Habana Club*" I volleyed, taking her hand in mine.

"A great place to unwind."

"I'll remember that once the Tour is over."

As the interview got under way, we discussed the merits of the bike and why I was in Havana, casually chatting away even though I knew whatever was said could be edited out in the final piece. I just had to go with my views.

Lucia stood off to the side, out of camera range, while Tony checked the sound quality, with Rudy inching ever so close with his camera for those tight, close-up shots.

"As our countries' representatives, Alfredo and I are about to do the longest cycling tour in the history of Cuba," I stated to the camera, as Alfredo stood near Lucia, beaming with a proud smile.

"It's not just the achievement of doing such a Tour, but that we symbolically represent our nations. And we hope to show, that, through us, we can work together in peace and friendship, thereby putting an end to this decades long nonsense called the embargo."

"And you feel that by doing this *Tour of Cuba*, you'll be able to achieve that goal?" asked Lucia.

"I would be naive to think that," I parried. "But I, like many other Americans, do feel that enough is enough on persecuting Cuba. If we can lighten up and do business with China and Vietnam, then we can open our arms to this jewel of the Caribbean."

"And how have your experiences been?" smiled the princess reporter.

"The poverty was to be expected," I sighed. "But the people have been warm and gracious despite their hardships caused, in part, by this embargo. This is what makes the united States look bad in the eyes of the world. We have politicians back home that profess to be Christians, yet their actions say otherwise. Well, maybe it's time we do something different and show some love, especially during this particular upcoming holiday season. Because really, that's what the Christian faith is all about and why our Saviour came to teach: To love thy neighbor as thyself."

Lucia kept quiet, smiling off-camera, allowing me to say my piece.

When I get off on something, I've been known to hang myself, but I had days to prepare what I wanted to say, so I continued. "I've been in Cuba several days now, but the number of American products I've seen already is ridiculous. Are you sure there's an embargo? The majority of American corporations are working through their Latin and European affiliates, bringing their products in. It's great that they know a ridiculous law when they see one."

I was really on a (head) roll now. All revved up, which Lucia was only too happy to sit back and report on Captain America putting the noose around his own neck, knowing that what I was saying was going to be shown back in the States to a lot of pissed off politicians. If you gotta go, go out big.

"I love my God and my country more than life itself, but we've been hating Castro since before we really got involved in the Vietnam War, and now we're doing business with them. So what's wrong with Cuba? Castro's not going to leave horizontally or vertically until the Lord wants him to, no matter what some Senators say or do," I commented, jabbing a finger toward the camera.

"He's a Socialist-Communist, and he's going to die that way, which is sad, because the moment his Spirit leaves his body, he's going to wake up in Hades, to a smiling Satan, saying, 'Welcome home.' And Fidel's going to think he's dreaming, because all his life he's been saying that Heaven and Hell don't exist. But guess what...," I paused for effect, opening my arms in a shrug. "Of course, he's going to have plenty of company, many old friends and comrades."

If I seem brave with the liberal media, it's because I understand the politics well enough to know that they will never air my views. And if they ever do, so be it. I stand by what I say, because I am fueled by my passions and convictions. I will go to the grave with them.

Concluding our interview, I had one last shot to get in. "Clinton can't be re-elected to a third term, therefore he has the perfect opportunity to break with this tradition of hatred by lifting the embargo once and for all."

"That's good," said Lucia. "We got enough material to work with. Now we need some shots of you cycling."

"Where?" I asked, looking around the manicured courtyard. "Here?"

"Sure," she answered nonchalantly. "Go around a couple of times, but do it fast before we're caught and get thrown out."

I smiled with mischievous delight, rubbing my hands together, and mounting the bike. I bet this was going to be a first for the *National*, as I sped past the well-groomed guests sitting on the richly painted iron benches as they tried to spiritually connect with the blue waters of the Caribbean. Some of them reeled in horror at the thought of being run over by a pair of knobby bicycle tires, while a few of the younger men smiled and gave me the thumbs-up sign.

Even Lucia got into the act when she saw the fun I was having, and decided to take the bike for a spin, screaming, "I can't find the brakes! Where are they?"

I was close enough where I could run to her rescue before she fell and ruined her perfect, chiffon white pantsuit. Grabbing her by the waist, she let go of the bike, clinging to me as I held her in my arms.

"Uh, pardon me for getting so familiar," I blushed.

"Not at all," she replied oh-so properly. "You couldn't help yourself." There was an awkward silence between us as we stared at each other. "You can let me down now."

"Oh... yeah... right," I stammered, releasing my hold on her. "Sorry."

"It happens," she quipped, straightening herself.

Rudy, through his viewfinder, was laughing. "Great footage. Good stuff."

"Yes, and let's all be thankful for the fine art of editing," I shot back. "Could I get a personal, unedited copy though?" We all had a good laugh.

Lucia wanted to go to a nearby park for footage of me interacting with other Cubans and their reactions when seeing the bike.

"I have to warn you, Lucia, I've been known to get mobbed."

"That would go well with the piece," she mused.

When filming a news piece, reporters want to get as much footage to work with as possible. Once, when I was generating publicity for the China tour, I worked with CBS for three hours, with the end result being a five minute piece on the six o'clock news the next evening. As an actor, I understand this, and would want to do the same if I were in the reporter's position.

While Princess Lucia rode in her chariot with her attendants, Alfredo and I cycled to the park. This was good, because then Rudy could film us in motion through the streets of Havana. Gotta get all you can.

When we arrived, we found a group of men of all ages sitting on park benches under shaded trees, trying to conserve their energy from the blazing sun.

That didn't last for long.

Decaying Old Havana along the *Malecon.*

"Hey, *amigo*, es beautiful bike. How much?" asked the tall, good-looking fellow that was more or less the unspoken leader of the group that followed him to where Alfredo and I were, as Lucia and company filmed from a respectable distance.

When I told my new-found friend the $20,000 price tag, he momentarily staggered back into the arms of his friends, his hand over his heart in mock fashion.

He rattled off something in Spanish to Alfredo, who replied, "*Si*, is true."

"Would you like to ride the bike, *amigo?*" I smiled, offering him my Beast.

He glanced toward the edge of the park, and saw Lucia and company filming. He didn't need a second invitation as he jumped on the steed and rode for the camera.

"Careful with the hydraulic brakes," I yelled out to the wild-eyed, frenzied fan. "She may try to buck you."

He rode around the small, triangular, concrete park, laughing and yelling with delightful glee; waving to his friends with each pass. Rudy seemed to be enjoying himself, too, capturing it all on film.

When the young *gaucho* returned, his group of friends swarmed around him, vying for the next turn, as I sat back and watched the festivities.

"Doesn't it make you nervous to see them handle your bike in that way?" asked Lucia, as she came to the bench where I was relaxing.

"Not at all," I nonchalantly replied.

"But what if one of them should ride off with it, never to be seen again?"

"And where would they go?" I laughed. "Where could they possibly hide a one-of-a-kind bike?"

"Perhaps you're right," she relaxed, taking a seat beside me. "I think this will make a good human-interest story for the people back home as well as for Cubans."

"Great. That's what we want."

"The other news agencies will probably pick up on it throughout the country. It could be a hit."

"One can only hope and pray."

Just then Lucia's cell phone buzzed and it was back to business. There was another story to go to in another part of Havana. Rudy got enough footage to his satisfaction.

Before going our separate ways, Lucia called out from the car, "I'd like to get a copy of your tour itinerary, so that we can keep in touch. Maybe we can do some filming of you along the way as you return closer to Havana."

"Sure. Be glad to. You're my only link to the States."

"We have other offices at the *Hotel Libre*. Meet us there. We won't be far behind."

Heading up *La Rampa* Street, Alfredo and I arrived at the ultra modern Hotel, a neighbor of the older, more sophisticated *National*, and just down the avenue. I headed for the lobby while Alfredo stood guard over the bikes across the street.

The front guard saw my red, white and blue, star studded physique coming toward him and obligingly blocked the opened entrance.

"Hey, *amigo*," I smiled, pointing past him to the lobby. "Me... go in."

Folding his arms in front of his brick walled chest, he shook his head. "No."

I continued to smile, inching closer. "Me... CNN. Es okay."

He stepped aside for another, plainly dressed couple to enter, and when I tried to follow, he physically pushed me back to my surprised look. No more smiles.

"I've put people in the hospital for that," I sneered in his face, matching my fleshy chest to his granite. "Me... CNN... now!"

Forget what you read in the guide books about the staff being able to speak in your native tongue. Reality indicates otherwise.

When the next "no" came, I shoved him off balance enough to get part of my body through the door, yelling out to the people in the lobby, "Anyone speak English?" The crowd just looked at me with blank stares for a moment, then went back to their own business.

Finally, the dreary doorman said, "*Uno momento*," and proceeded to call someone else over on his walkie-talkie. A security guard arrived, and the two bruisers conversed in Spanish.

The guard looked at me and said, "No come in." He walked away.

Do you really think I was going to stand for that?

I was now red in the face, and when the door dunce relaxed his guard and turned his back on me, I shoved him out of the way, racing toward the guard.

"Hey, pal, CNN... me...upstairs." That was all I could get out before the front door gorilla got a wrestler's hold on me, ready to bodily throw me out of the Hotel. By now, some of the guests in the lobby had forgotten what business they needed to urgently attend.

The guard told the door mouse to release me as he walkie-talkied the head of security. I guess I overstepped my bounds and figured I was now about to be placed under arrest. Perfect! With CNN right in the same building. Just like having a major accident while visiting a hospital.

Thankfully, the head of security could speak enough English to be understood, as I stated briefly, "I'm here to do an interview with CNN upstairs, and I'm dressed this way because it's my uniform."

He motioned his guard to leave us as he took me to the receptionist, who then asked for my passport. Looking it over, she filled out a security pass, handing the documents back to me.

"When you return to the lobby, hand the pass back to the receptionist," smiled the security chief.

I thanked him for his help. Another obstacle overcome, but I knew this was just practice for the Tour. There would be more of the same. I could count on that.

The 20th floor presented a magnificent view of Havana and its harbor, and I could imagine how it must have looked at night, the shanties anonymously cloaked behind glittering lights-- the same lights of the yachts and the clubs that lined the beach.

I walked to the end of the hallway where CNN had a row of rooms they used as offices and an equipment center. Lucia was not far behind.

As she made a copy of my itinerary and schedule, she asked, "Be in touch from time to time on your progress. We'd like to follow your story along the way."

"Sure. And perhaps you could relay messages for me back home," I inferred. Lucia and I could be of help to each other, which really wasn't a bad arrangement.

Because our government can't violate the media's first amendment rights, they have direct dialing access. This I remembered from my China days. Guess the politicians are more afraid of the spotlight than their constituents.

Returning to the dismal, cockroach motel *Morro*, Alfredo said there was to be a gymnastics meet and private party tomorrow at the stadium where he worked. He thought I should attend, so that I could meet his boss and discuss getting the paperwork in order for the Tour. I love this guy, always thinking; the mind always planning ahead.

When we parted company, I headed to the corner PanAmerican store to buy my daily liter of juice that I'd been taking with my vitamins. I selected the drink quickly, but no sooner did I get to the back shelf where the juices were than the manager grabbed my arm, shaking his head concerning my attire.

Because they were near closing, I didn't have time to change out of my uniform. I instinctively pulled away, and showed him my money. "Hey, pal, green is the only color you should be thinking about."

I went to the register to pay and left. Yeah, Cubans may love Americans, but they hate when we show off our colors.

SEIS

6

HAVANA, CUBA
NOVEMBER 15-16, 1997

The day began with an early morning call from Alfredo. He was waiting for me in the hotel's lobby. I had been awake for hours, going through my gear, constantly packing and repacking, trying my best to get it down to one bag that would have to last me the entire three-week Tour. What to take; what not to? Do I really need this or can I do without? How important is this item to me? Can I survive without it? Questions like these went through my mind with each item-- each piece of clothing, each bit of gear. Even then I could only manage a minimum of two small knapsacks. I knew from experience that I could still cut it down by 50%, but then, which half? Unfortunately, the answer would only be known after the Tour was completed.

Upon reaching the lobby, I was met outside in the courtyard by Alfredo and his 2-year-old daughter, Illessa. Cute as a chipmunk and somewhat shy, Alfredo has her on weekends.

"Her mother and I divorced soon after she was born, because I was never home. Always off on bicycle tours," Alfredo tried to explain, while his daughter played monkey on his back.

"I was not even home when she was born," he mentioned matter-of-factly as Illessa swung on her father's arm with squeals of delight.

"My wife, she no like me absent so much. Even now, my daughter's birthday is in January and I will be on another bicycle tour with a group of Americans," he said with a touch of melancholy in his voice.

"Is it worth it?" I asked.

"It is what I love to do and can make much money to buy things for my daughter," he responded, as he looked upon his smiling girl.

"But then you risk losing her by being a part-time, weekend father."

"*Si.* But then after this tour, I will be famous among my friends," his voice rose, his eyes grew wide. "American and other tour groups will hear about what we have done and will pay me well for my knowledge of the island."

The three of us arrived at the gymnastics competition in a matter of minutes, and upon entering the facility we, or rather the bike, created a mild disturbance. The small crowd gathered in front of the gym floor parted like the Red Sea in awe and wonder, allowing the majestic bicycle to pass undisturbed, as those closest to us in the stands cocked their heads in unison from the performers to us. When I leaned the Beast against the wall, a group of young men encircled it like buzzards around a carcass. Regardless of the flashy paint job, even if it were uniformly black, it would still draw attention due to its unusual shape and style. No Cuban has ever-- nor will probably ever-- see another one like it in his lifetime.

As we watched the young female performers do their routines, I noticed the condition of the interior, with its peeling paint and bare concrete walls; rows of benches that should be replaced before an accident happened, and the floor with so many tiny boards missing looked like Swiss cheese. It reminded me of this game I used to play as a child called *Break the Ice*, where you and an opponent would take a little plastic hammer and break tiny blocks of ice from a raised platform until one would give way, creating a downfall of the entire structure. This day, I wondered how many more blocks needed to fall out before the floor gave way under the weight of the performers. Not even the ghetto gyms I was accustomed to in my youth were as bad as these that future Olympic athletes trained on. If our corporations were allowed to legally do business with Cuba, I reflected, instead of skirting around on the fringes, there would be better facilities for these children; the companies would be supporting the programs in the neighborhoods they happened to be in. I am ashamed of those big conglomerates that could well afford to help. If they could find the loopholes to bring their product into the country, then they could find a way to bring their charity in as well. If I were Castro, I'd be doing my own embargo with these bigwigs: *Fund some of these individual programs, set-up scholarship opportunities, improve the neighborhoods, or get your product out of my country.* You'd see some changes real fast. It's all one big poker game... Just don't be the one to blink, that's all.

After the competition, Alfredo took Illessa and I to another part of the complex, a locked and gated area where an individual stood at attention, allowing only a certain clientele within its borders.

Inside was an Olympic-sized pool which many young men and women enjoyed. Older ladies sat off to the side in discussion groups; the men hung around a beer keg that was about the size of a propane tank, complete with its own trailer and engine. The Cuban men love their beer as well as their rum, women, music, and laughter.

During the next few hours, Alfredo managed to round up several important men in charge of the complex. The most notable was Profirio Gonzalez, the

An afternoon crowd gathers around one of the smaller beer kegs for a glass or gallon and some good conversation.

man in charge of this particular municipality. A tall, bearded, rather handsome man of rugged, chiseled, pirate looks. Although he spoke no English, we could communicate through Alfredo, who did most of the talking, explaining the Tour and my immediate need for a guide. I kept quiet, trying to get a sense of what Profirio was thinking, but he remained stone cold, walking over to the bike to inspect it as we all drank beer and rum.

"Think of what the publicity will mean to our district," mentioned the flea in the sow's ear.

Profirio smiled, running his hand smoothly over the top tube of the bike, as if it were the bare back of a woman.

Alfredo turned to me. "Without valid permission, I will not be able to go with you. And, more importantly, Cubans and foreigners are not allowed to stay together in the same hotel, or even travel to certain tourist places."

"Then by all means, speak to your heart's content."

Profirio asked the usual questions about the bike, which Alfredo duly answered.

"How much?"

"Twenty-thousand."

Profirio's eyes went wide. "In dollars?"

"*Si.*"

"What is the weight?" picking up the Beast.

"Ten kilos."

"What is it made of?"

"Aluminum, titanium, carbon fiber."

Silence. Profirio never even took his eyes off my baby, lustfully smiling at her.

"Stop by the office Monday morning to discuss the Tour further."

Alfredo turned to me with a thumbs up sign, giving me the interpretation once we were out the gate. For now, we all raised our cups of beer together in friendship.

"It would be best to have a letter of introduction from Palaez, but the bureaucracy takes too long," said Alfredo, during a lunch of pizzas at a mom and pop place.

"With Profirio we be okay," he assured me, taking a bite of the six-inch circular pie, which was nothing more than fried bread dough with some sauce and cheese at a cost of five *pesos* per pie.

His daughter, Illessa, laughed and giggled when trying to bite into her pizza, which was the size of her head. She rocked back and forth in her own world of amusement, singing a native song to herself.

"On Monday we meet to discuss the Tour, then it take another day to get the letter. Then we go."

"You make it sound so simple," I shook my head in disbelief. "Governments never move that fast."

"*Si,* but we go through the local level," he answered between mouthfuls of bread dough. "It be okay."

"You're the man with the experience," I shrugged, finishing off my first Cuban pizza, while starting in on my second. "If all we need is a letter of permission and introduction to get us through your country's 13 provinces, then let's do it. Whatever's necessary."

Since our intense encounter a few days ago, I had not seen much of Patricia, but that particular blessing wouldn't last long, as I heard her voice upon approach.

"So, how's the world famous tour coming along?" she asked with a devious smile.

I was relaxing out on the patio, waiting for Carmen, the cook at the *Hotel Morro*, to bring me my dinner when the inevitable happened.

"Fine," I answered nonchalantly. "No problems."

"That's nice." She left, laughing in a contemptible tone.

People who try to make other people feel like shit, are nothing more than shit themselves, and I refused to let a piece of shit like Patty belittle me.

Then there was the opposite with Carmen. A beautiful and statuesque woman with short, black hair and an infectious smile.

I usually took my meals late and alone, just before the kitchen closed. By then, everyone else had wined and dined and were enjoying a good *cohiba*. Tonight was no different, giving Carmen a chance to relax and practice her English with me.

"You like my cooking," she asked of the fish and rice, and fish stew.

"You are a master chef, Carmen. *Bravissima!*" I answered, blowing her a kiss in a grand gesture.

She laughed with delight. "I cook with love, much love, for you," she said with a pearly-white, toothy smile. "You are a beautiful man."

Music by the Bee Gee's was playing across the street as I returned her smile, thinking, *Yeah, and I'm also an American. Want to come home with me? Hey everyone, look what kind of souvenir I brought back from Cuba...*

Boys, a little advice: If you're looking for a wife, look no further than to the jewel of the Caribbean. The women are absolutely georgeous. They can cook, clean, and make wonderful mothers, and they'll love you with an intense passion, expecting only the same from you in return. Have you ever noticed how Florida resembles the shape of a penis, and Cuba's just hanging from the end of it? I know there's a metaphor in there somewhere.

Carmen wouldn't be the only *femme fatale* chasing me during my time in Paradise. It was just another problem I had to deal with, one I couldn't take seriously. Realistically, the only reason I was swooned over was not for my looks, but rather for the enticing view of my passport.

Sundays are usually set aside for rest and meditation upon the Lord for His many blessings He bestows upon His children. You can do this in a church or, if you're Alfredo, you do it by conducting cycling tours of Havana with the many tourists that infiltrate the city-- this day being one with six American women. He asked if I'd like to accompany him. Me? Pass up the opportunity to be with a company of women? Besides, it would be fun to really get out and see the city from an expert's point of view.

The women, from across the united States, were in Havana on a conference. That's how they were able to stay legally.

"Doesn't any American come to Cuba just for vacation and to have a good time without any excuses or legal loopholes?" I asked one of them before our outing.

"Not if you want to return without problems," smiled the short redhead without missing a beat.

"Yeah, but if we stop skirting the issue and be more honest then perhaps others will join in."

"But who really cares," laughed a towering, dark-haired beauty. "The Helms-Burton law is a joke. Like Jesse, it has no teeth. No one pays attention to it, except, perhaps, the corporations who are chomping at the bit, because, they can't pump more of their product into this country than they'd like to."

During our tour, we visited the old part of Havana, the University, the *Plaza de la Revolution*, and places along the *Malecon*. Neighborhoods so run-down that it made my ghetto a heaven.

"We have our own version of Chinatown," mentioned Alfredo, the tour guide.

Nearby, was a block of buildings completely covered by brightly colored murals that made it look as though it came from another dimension, or at best, a bad acid trip. It was certainly the most colorful part of Havana I'd seen since arriving in the country. I couldn't help contemplate if the Cuban people who painted such divine, stunning colors, didn't do so to wash away the drab exsistance they really lived in. Whatever the reasons, Alfredo didn't stop long enough to explain, as we rode off to another site.

A block of murals in the old part of Havana.

At the Farmer's Market, I ran into CNN's Tony Valdez doing some shopping.

"Hey, Kevin! I'd thought you'd be gone by now."

"So did I. Just a couple more days."

"Great! Have some fried *yucca*," he said, shoving a piece into my hand. "The story's being held off for another week or so," he mentioned between *yucca* bites. "Lucia's putting together some scenes from your **Great Wall** and **American Summits** tours we have on file in our Atlanta office. We're going to incorporate a little bit of everything into the overall piece. It'll be an eye-opener."

"Sounds good," I replied, munching on the breaded *yucca* that resembled something like our fish sticks. "Hope I get a chance to see what it looks like at some point."

"Oh, sure. We'll have a copy of it at the office when you return to Havana."

While at the market, I went to buy some fresh garlic-- a head cost a *peso* (about 4 cents)-- but my smallest bill was a 10, and the guy couldn't break it. As I was ready to leave, a Cuban purchased the garlic for me, which, given their monthly income is a great cost. I thanked the man kindly, remembering another verse that would be a part of the Tour: *Love Thy Neighbor as Thyself.*

Another guided stop we made was to a craft market, next to the old Capitol building, which looked like a bomb hit it. Of course, I try to compare Havana to Washington, DC, and there's just no way that can be done. No gleaming, shiny buildings. They cost too much to repair and keep clean, so Cuba makes due with what they have.

"Say, Mister," said a voice from behind. "Can you spare some change? Any little bit will help."

Turning around, I was greeted by a thin, scrappy-looking, elderly gentleman of average height, with salt and pepper hair. His hand was trembling as it reached out.

"Excuse me?" I answered.

"Change. Can you spare any?"

"You speak really good English."

"I used to live and work in Miami during the 50s as a world-class photographer."

"And you came back to this?" I asked in wide-eyed disbelief.

"It was my country. I wanted to return." He shifted his weight, avoiding eye contact with me. "Say, that's a really nice bike. How much does something like that cost?"

I was silent for a moment. I really didn't want to tell him, because he already felt bad enough panhandling, yet I didn't want to lie to him either, so I quickly and nonchalantly answered, "Twenty-thousand."

His lower lip dropped, and his eyes grew wide. "My God! Are you some kind of racer or something?"

"Yeah, something like that."

"I wish I had my camera, but then my Social Security only pays me 98 *pesos* a month, so I can't afford any film."

"You live on four dollars a month?"

"Yeah, but I pick up extra dollars as an interpreter. Write letters in English for my people who have relatives in America. And ask the tourists for any spare change..."

His voice trailed off as his hand went back up. I took a couple of bucks out of my backpack and handed them to him.

"Thanks," he replied, shoving the money quickly into his pocket, his eyes shifting from side-to-side.

"Before Castro legalized the dollar in '93, we'd be thrown in jail if we were caught with any. But the cops who caught us with them could keep what they found."

"And you, the people, stood for this?"

"Not much we could do. There's still a lot of loyalty towards Castro, but being honest, there ain't gonna be too many tears when he dies. Hopefully, things will improve once he's gone. We'd like the country to become more Capitalistic, like it used to be in the fourties and fifties."

He was getting fidgety, always looking around.

"Is there a problem?"

"Naw... it's just that if Cubans are seen talking to tourists, especially Americans for too long a time, we can get arrested if a cop shows up. And you, my friend, stand out in that uniform. Say, that's a really nice bandana."

"It's my only one," I answered in a cold tone.

"So you wouldn't want to part with it, huh? It would get me a couple extra month's spending money for food and medical supplies."

"I can see you really miss the united States," I smiled.

"Yeah... yeah, I do." He looked down toward his worn-out shoes and frayed pants.

"So, 98 *pesos* takes care of your needs for the next month? You run out, you run out?"

"Pretty much the way it is. Oh, I have a small, three room apartment, and I get medical assistance, but it's of poor quality. If you want any proper treatment, the best medicine, you have to pay the doctors in dollars. And everyone gets a monthly ration book."

He pulled a floppy, dog-eared one out of his handbag that I could peruse. In it were colored coupons for bread, rice, vegetables, and other staple items.

"It's only good if the items are available for that day. If the ration center don't have, or they run out before you get there, you're out of luck. And if you don't use all your rations for the month, they can't be transferred to the next. You just have to make due without."

"But there are many of your countrymen wheeling and dealing on the side to bring in the extra dollars and buying what they want. With your talent for reading, writing, and speaking English, you should be able to do well, instead of lowering yourself to handouts."

"Yeah, well, we all have to get by somehow."

"So, Communism works, huh?" I smiled, with a wink.

He returned the gesture in like kind, freeing himself to speak his mind. "Communism is full of shit and don't let anyone tell you different. My people had it good before Castro, but then they bought into the lie that the government would take care of all their needs. Hell! You have it real good in your country, my friend. Don't let them bastards in Washington tell you otherwise."

"There are still some of us that believe, *We the People* still rule, and that the hard work philosophy is still the backbone of America."

"Good," he smiled, patting me on the shoulder. "Screw this Communistic bullshit! There's no incentive when everything's given to you. Communism doesn't allow you to progress."

"Unfortunately, my friend, the united States is becoming more democratic, more Communistic everyday. My people feed off the government's breast and call it father. They turn their backs on God our true Provider, thereby making us a bastard nation in His eyes."

His mouth hung open when listening to my words, and when he found his speech, all he could say was, "Man, you really know your shit, don't you?"

"I read...and observe."

The blue sky was beginning to turn black. Ominous clouds began to form, as thunder was heard in the distance.

"*Kebin!*" shouted Alfredo from a distance, his arms waving to me. "Come on. We are leaving."

"Thanks for helping me out, my friend," said the elderly gentleman, offering me a warm handshake.

"The conversation was worth it," I replied, as he turned and blended in with the crowd.

The tour of Havana ended along the *Malecon* when a fantastic thunderstorm hit, spewing forth buckets of rain upon us. We ran for cover trying to wait it out, shivering under doorways. Soon, a tour bus stopped by to bring the women back to their hotel, thus leaving Alfredo and his companions with the half-dozen steel bicycles.

Getting the bikes back to the *Morro* would be a slight inconvenience, but Alfredo always has his ways of working things out. He took some old tire tubes and bungee cords and strapped the bikes together in tandem-form, allowing us to ride and carry them back to the *Hotel Morro* more easily between downpours.

We were soaked to the skin when Alfredo and I parted company. He went back to his house, while I returned to my room. The only comfort was in taking a cold shower. I never realized until now that hot water was a luxury.

About 5pm, when the rains ended and the day began to cool down, Alfredo stopped by for a visit and to go over some details concerning the next day's meeting, as well as to clue me in on Cuban philosophy.

"The government is always thinking business, always thinking tourism. I think they want you down here because they think you would be good for tourism, good for business. But maybe now they decide you no good for business or tourism, so they forget about you. That is the way things are here. If they can use you for business, that is okay. If they canno', they let you go and forget about you."

"You really think that?" I asked between rounds of cold Cokes, as we sat in the front courtyard. Noise from the baseball game on the bar TV filtered outside. "Palaez will just let me sit here at the *Morro* until I get tired and decide to go home?"

"*Si,* that is the way it is here; that is how they do. It would be nice if they help, because they have a lot of power, but we can do it with my superiors. It will be okay," he assured me, flashing me a conspiratorial look that reminded me of some of my old Mafia relatives-- or at least a bad Marlon Brando *Godfather* imitation.

"Tomorrow, you should think about changing some dollars into *pesos*," advised my partner. "We will need them to pay the drivers when we hitch a ride to *Maisi*, and to buy supplies."

"How much do you think we should start with?"

"Mmm, not more than one hundred dollars. We can pick up more along the way if we need to."

"Then what?"

With the map of the route before us, Alfredo sat up in his chair, excited to show me his plan. "We will find a driver who is going to *Santiago* or *Guantanamo*, and we pay him two hundred *pesos*." He guided me along with his fingers, pointing to the different cities. "That is a lot of money for a driver if you pay him in *pesos*. But if you give him, say a single American ten dollar bill, then it no' seem like much, even though it be one dollar more."

He sat back and laughed, taking another swig of his Coke. "We fight now for our independence. We say, forget the government, and go on our own and do it. That is the Cuban way. To fight."

Later that night, I returned to the process of weeding out my equipment to the bare bone minimum. Alfredo's family had volunteered to store the rest. I went from the most to the least important-- and that meant deciding on exactly how much film and audio tapes for journal entries to carry. The rule of thumb is that no matter how much you pack, you can always shelve it by half, and throughout my life I have found this to be true. Except no one tells you which half to bring, and what to leave behind-- so aside from the journalistic supplies, there were some toiletries, vitamins, my music (for psychological purposes I don't go anywhere without my Bach and Christmas carols), a pair of dress pants, two T-shirts, an extra uniform, two pairs of socks, two sets of underwear, a poncho and light jacket. Even this was cramming it.

Although we would have no entourage and no security along the way, the good part was that we were on our own to veer off the route or change it if we wanted to. We could put in as many or as few miles as we wanted.

I may not have shown it, but I admit that I was scared as I viewed the photos by my bedside of Jean and my little *Lhasa Apso* girls, *Hanzhu* and *Jia Tu.*

Love? Is there such a feeling? I thought I knew at one lustful point in my life, but that was just a case of mistaken identity. When Jean came into my life just before the **American Summits** Tour, I fell head over heels hardcore for her, but over the years it's been a rollercoaster relationship at best. She's told me so many times she'll never marry me, that it's begun to penetrate my thick Italian skull.

Why do I stay? I don't know.

Do I love her? Yes...and...

And my girls?

They give me what Jean cannot. Love. Affection. They wag their tails, and shake with delight after not seeing me for hours, days, weeks at a time. They beg me to hold them in my arms as they ferociously lick my face and neck, fighting to see who wins sitting in my lap.

They are my loves, and Jean has become my best friend whom I trust most in the world with my life, my very soul. I exist because of her.

If I fail in completing this Tour, my sponsors will be upset, but to hell with them, I can always pick up another gig.

But if I fail in redeeming myself, then I fail in Jean's eyes, and become a true failure. She, more than anyone else, believes in me; builds me up into believing in myself. Not even my blood family has the capacity to do that, and that is why, over time, she has replaced them.

And why, no matter what, we will remain the best of friends-- for richer or poorer, in sickness and in health, in good times and bad times, 'till death us do part.

SIETE

7

HAVANA, CUBA
NOVEMBER 17, 1997

It had been a week since my arrival in the capital of Cuba, and I was still stranded at the same hotel I had been conveniently dropped off at. And not a word from my hosts since Wednesday's meeting, I reflected, as I sat outside at a table in the courtyard, basking in the warm, tropical sunshine.

At 9am Alfredo arrived, joining me for breakfast to go over any last details before our meeting.

"It is very important to convince my boss that this is an historic tour we are doing for peace and friendship," mentioned Alfredo, sitting on the edge of his seat. "If we do not convince Profirio, then all is lost."

"Relax, Alfredo. I've been through this before. We've come this far. The Lord will not let us down."

With a cocked head and crinkled brow, he took a drink of orange juice. He said nothing about my *so called* faith, but trusted in his ability to do whatever it would take to get the permission papers.

We arrived at the Sports Complex on time, soon discovering that the meeting was delayed a couple of hours.

Alfredo took this *opportunity* to attend his daily English class at the school next door where he worked.

Walking toward the building, we came to a life-size bronze figure which stood at the entrance of the school it was named after. It momentarily threw me off guard, as I stood frozen, my mouth agape. "This is the name of your school?" I asked in disbelief.

"Yes," answered Alfredo, blinking in bewilderment.

"Your school's name is Abraham Lincoln?"

"*Si*. He was a great Socialist and one of your great presidents, who freed the slaves."

I stifled my laugh. "Yes, and then introduced other forms of slavery called commerce, and Communism."

"*Si*," agreed Alfredo. "Lincoln was a good Communist. We learn about him in school, like you."

"No way, my friend," I laughed, shaking my head. "We don't learn about *that* Lincoln where I come from. My information comes from books written in 1865, shortly after he was assassinated. The Civil War came about, not because Lincoln cared about the slaves, but because he wanted to wrestle the abundant trade from the Southern States."

"*Si*," agreed Alfredo once again. "The Civil War began, because Lincoln wanted to make everyone equal, and the South did not want that, so he take from them and give to the poor. He was a good Communist and Socialist."

"That's bullshit!" I eyed Alfredo. "I work hard for a better life, while someone else sits around and does nothing? Or maybe they just aren't blessed like me? So they feel they have to be equal, and decide to take what I have? Even go to war with me? That's bull! God says, 'Thou shalt not covet anything of thy neighbor's.' Lincoln took what he wasn't allowed to take. That's why we had a war between the North and the South."

"But then everyone come out equal."

"No way! The South lost big time. Everything was taken from them. The slaves became the masters, the masters became the slaves."

I stopped momentarily to catch my breath. Alfredo took it all in, listening to my point of view of what the real 1860s history books talked about, written by the men and women who wrote during the time all this chaos was happening to them at the moment. As I continued, I mentioned to my friend, "Just before the war ended, when Lincoln saw the death and carnage at Gettysburg, he gave his life to Jesus Christ. But by then the damage had been done, and shortly thereafter he was assassinated."

"And became a hero."

"Yeah," I grieved. "Dead heros are popular in America, too."

While Alfredo went to his English class, I headed back to my room at the *Morro* to get in some much needed catching up on my journal entries. By 11am, I was back at the school when Alfredo emerged with a crudely handwritten letter.

"I write this while in class," he said, showing me the piece. "It say, we are on a mission of peace and friendship between our two countries. That we are doing this bicycle ride across Cuba to end the embargo."

"Sounds good to me. Whatever it takes."

"Do you belong to a cycling club?" asked Alfredo.

"No."

"Then to some kind of group or organization?"

Again, the reply was no. "I'm not trying to be difficult, Alfredo, but in doing these particular events, it's natural to be alone."

"It would be better if you represented a group. That would mean more to my bosses."

We thought about this, and then I said, "You can tell your bosses that I represent my country, and my people are tired of this unwarranted embargo, so I have come here in the name of peace and friendship to put an end to this hatred once and for all."

His eyes lit up with a Cheshire Cat grin. His chest swelled like a peacock as he furiously wrote, incorporating my words into the overall letter. "Ah, *si,* very good. This could work."

Profirio's office was a few hundred yards from the school. A two-story concrete block of a building, it had absolutely no shape, style or color to it. It was as though a child had designed it, merely cutting out holes in the square for doors and windows, which, at best, were in dire need of replacement. Alfredo and I walked up the concrete steps to the foyer.

Across the street, I noticed the guarded Swiss Embassy. The United States had an interest office there, and many Cubans stood in line waiting to get in, wanting to leave the country.

"Did you know to get a passport costs two thousand dollars?" asked Alfredo.

"You mean 2000 *pesos,*" I corrected him.

"No. Two thousand American dollars." My mouth dropped. "That is the cost for all the paperwork and the physical. It very difficult to leave the country. These people in line, their families in America send them money that they save. Then, the passport good for only two years, but many of them no come back."

He asked how much a united States passport costs, which I stated as being $65US. And it was good for 10 years.

This time his mouth dropped, as he rolled his eyes, and cocked his head.

"In my country," I said, "they don't care if you leave, because the government knows you'll return to the land of many freedoms."

As we entered the building, I asked Alfredo, "don't you think there's something wrong with a government that keeps you in the country by force, or at least tries to make it very difficult for you to leave?"

We locked our bikes against the rack inside the foyer, and began climbing the stairs to the second floor, where Profirio's office was located.

"*Si,* but that is the way it is for now. Maybe someday it will change when Castro is gone."

He told me that once a person had a passport, he could renew it every two years at a cost of $50US. He himself has the valuable document in hand, keeping it handy for that dream of someday coming to America and doing a cross country bicycle tour. I told him that trip would be about three times the length of what we're about to do.

"Then this Tour will be good training for me," he laughed.

I sat just outside the office on an unpadded iron chair, while Alfredo went in to discuss the matter of the Tour with his bosses.

Looking around, I noticed the painted walls were peeling, their flakes lying about the floor. Across from me was another office, where a woman sat at a chipped and damaged wooden desk, some of its drawers missing. She was dressed in a soiled uniform, typing a letter-- triple copy with carbon paper in between the sheets on a 30-year-old typewriter, the top of which was missing. The ribbon looked like a transparent filter, ready to be replaced.

There was nothing of beauty about the place. No plants to bring in the outdoors, no photos of family or anything else to line the walls with. It reminded me of many offices I had seen in China, and I wondered if all Communist countries were dismal-- or just their governments.

Aside from a couple of other desks and chairs, there stood, like sentinels, metal filing cabinets that had seen better days. When I was eventually called into the office, Profirio was sitting on a torn cushioned seat across from a battered couch. Alfredo and a couple of other gentlemen were gathered around in the cramped office. One of the men I recognized from Saturday's rum and beer pool party. One other man was a stranger to me.

I pulled out the section map of their country, showing the route of the Tour. Their eyes lit up like little boys who were about to partake in an escapade as they huddled over the map, following the route with their fingers, talking in rapid, excited tones in their native tongue. The bait was cast; the hook, taken.

The man I was unfamiliar with spoke in English. "Perhaps you could postpone the Tour until next Spring when we would all have a chance of being better prepared."

I nodded in agreement, my fingers to my lips in a praying formation. "That does sound better, I admit, but since I am already in your country, and we are ready to go, why not do it now?"

They all looked at one another for a moment, spoke some words, shrugged their shoulders about the Spring return idea, and continued onward with the idea of preparing the necessary paperwork for Alfredo and I to leave the next day.

Alfredo let out a silent sigh of relief and proceeded to go about his business.

"Gentlemen, this a wonderful opportunity to bring our sports complex some good publicity. To show that Cubans and Americans can work together in peace and friendship."

He stood around us in the middle of the room, waving his arms like a grand *maestro*, conducting the course of the conversation to suit his purposes. His voice rose in pitch and vibration, along with his facial expressions.

"We did a CNN interview that will be shown in both countries. We will be famous and show that we love Americans even if their government hates us. I believe this bicycle tour across our country will help to end the embargo, and bring more Americans here to visit us."

Alfredo was on a holy roll, with the spirit of seduction leading him ever onward. The enthusiasm was catching as I sat back and watched his bosses. Their eyes grew wide. They sat up straight in their seats. Their breathing stopped! Yes! Yes! Hallelujah! Let us bond together in unity for this magnificent endeavor!!!...

Actually, they sat about looking at one another, said a few words between them, and asked me, "When you return to your country, would you write some letters and make some phone calls to the corporations in our behalf for some donated sporting equipment for our children?"

I nodded. "Yes, I can do this."

The people's organic garden where the product is grown and harvested for the benefit of the community.

"Then it is settled. We will draw up the papers."

One of the men brought out a box stuffed with deflated soccer balls with the McDonald's (from Spain) logo on them. This was the closest I would get to the golden arches until I returned to Los Angeles.

These people, I thought, while viewing the hand me downs, knew how to be grateful for the little generosities that were bestowed upon them.

When Alfredo and I returned to Profirio's office later that afternoon to check on the progress of the letter, we brought along a seven-year-old bottle of rum as a diplomatic *thank you* gift. This turned out to be an excellent suggestion on Alfredo's part, for Profirio broke out in a wide smile and offered me a hearty handshake. It was I who was grateful.

The papers would not be ready until the next day, so Alfredo and I headed back to the *Morro*, where he escaped to the bar to watch the basketball game with some of the guests and staff, while I went for my daily liter of juice, as my concrete chest was now down to miserable slush.

Lord, I have seen filth and poverty here as I've seen nowhere else in my life's travels. The corner PanAmerican store is guarded like a fortress with a huge chain-link fence surrounding it, topped by razor-sharp barbed wire. Drunks and vagabonds of both sexes and all ages loiter about on the sidewalk begging people that come in and go out of the store to help them. You try to do what you can, but it just isn't enough, and you must, at times, turn a deaf ear and a blind eye to the surroundings. Yet even that doesn't seem to help, as one young man followed me out of the store and to the *Morro*, first asking for money, then for whatever I just happened to buy. Finally he pointed to his worn-out, torn, toe-exposed shoes, then to my own comfortably-worn sneakers and asked, "Me have them?" This was just getting to be too much, and everyday I wondered when I'd be able to leave.

Hanging outside the courtyard with some of the staff that had now become my groupies, I was greeted by another young man named Ramon. He was a jolly little Leprechaun of a fellow whom I met several days before. He always had a big smile when greeting me, and seemed to take his life's situation in stride. Like many others, he fell in love with the bike, and asked if he could ride it around the block. Cubans would never allow this with their own two-wheelers, but I was much more free-- bold, really-- thinking, *Where could they possibly hide such a creation?* But when Ramon didn't show up after about 15 minutes, I did become somewhat concerned.

"Oh, *senor,*" he smiled, "I have ridden many bikes, but never in my life such a one as this. She is beautiful."

He was married with two children and said he made $2US a month from his job. His shoes, like many other of the Cubans' I would meet along the way, were well-worn, and his clothes had holes in them. He said he was going to be 24 years old the next day, and he wanted me to attend a party at his house, just around the corner. As a birthday gift, I casually flipped off a $5 bill-- not thinking anything significant of the gesture. To Ramon it was a gift from Heaven, not to mention two and a half months' salary.

"Oh, *senor,* my friend! *Gracias, gracias*."

Alfredo and I never did make the party, but we presumed Ramon had a good time. Drinking and sex were to be the main courses. For many people in poverty conditions, they are a way of escaping the harsh realities of everyday survival.

Toward the end of the day, Alfredo wanted me to take everything we would not be carrying back to his place, so I hauled my stuffed bicycle bag into a waiting taxi. A half-hour later, I found myself at his apartment.

I was down to the bare bone survival minimum. The room seemed bigger and lonelier. I wondered if everything would go according to Alfredo's grand plan. Of course, I couldn't do anything more than simply step out in faith, as I have done so many times in the past and will continue to do until my dying day. How else could I possibly please Him that has given me so much in life to live for, so much to be thankful for?

Yes, I tell myself, looking in the mirror near the bed. *Yes, we are really, truly, finally going.*

It's what I continued to tell myself until sometime during the night, when sleep finally took over from an exhausted, stressful week.

OCHO

8

HAVANA, CUBA
NOVEMBER 18-20, 1997

And on the eighth day, God said, "Ye shall leave the *Morro*... but not until one last diversion is placed in your path."

It was during the morning hours with a visit from Carmen, the hot-blooded, statuesque, Amazon beauty who appeared in my doorway with a smile and a sway of her hour glass hips. It was a dicey situation that I didn't want to confront. She entered my room with a cat's eye stare, making herself comfortable. Her tight, painted on shorts left nothing to the imagination, as she sat there on the edge of the bed, her creamy smooth thighs parted slightly, along with her lush, full lips.

I needed to start the Tour. I mean, I *really* needed to get out of Havana and on the road. Carmen nuzzled up beside me as I sat next to her, whispering in my ear, "I...uh...no practice sex for long time."

As if I really needed to know this? "Ummm, that's good, Carmen. Sex is a hassle. No good. No like."

Because of her limited English, I tried to talk slowly and use simple words, but even then I was misunderstood. Her eyes widened. "No! Me like sex...I...uh... like...with you."

She leaned toward me and gently bit my earlobe to a rousing sensation that made me blush and get instantly aroused. Again, she whispered, "Me, love you... make much love with you."

I shook my head, and crossed my legs, laughing at the thought of the sinful pleasure of going a few rounds with this Wonder Woman, but reality intervened. To Carmen, I was only an American, and that meant a ticket out of Cuba. I had to accept the amorous affection for what it was. I decided to take a chance and turn the tables, because some people like the chase until the chasse stops and becomes the chaser. I was hoping my perception of people was on target. God help me if I were wrong.

I turned and kissed her, falling down with her on the bed. "We make love here, Carmen?" I asked, rolling on top of her, as we joined at the groin. "We make love now?"

"No...no good," she answered, shaking her head. Her eyes grew wide with fright.

"Here...now," I pleaded, working my way down to the inside of her thighs.

She sat bolt upright, trying to pull me away from my intended goal. "No! *Kebin!* No' here...my job."

"But, Carmen, I love you. I want you." I pressed into her. We both fell back onto the bed.

"No...no' good here." She struggled to free herself from beneath me, finally pushing me away and jumping off the bed. She went to the vanity table to fix her hair and straighten her clothes. "You a *cwazy* man," she smiled at me through the mirror. "No make love now. After...you return... *Habana.*"

"Well," I sighed. "If you insist, then I must endure."

I called the bluff about whether she was ready to play romper room or not. I mean, what if management were to find out one of their employees were giving extra special attention to one of the guests? *Madre de Dios!*

When Alfredo arrived about the noon hour, he found Carmen and I sitting out in the shade on the terrace. All smiles, he produced the much sought-after letter of introduction that contained not one, but four different signatures and stamps from the various municipal departments. Now we were important. In a nutshell, the document, in Spanish, basically gave our names and identification numbers, and stated that the Tour was for peace and friendship between our two countries, in protest of the current embargo, and any assistance that could be given would be appreciated.

With the letter in hand, it was finally time to check out of the *Morro*. I took photos of many of the staff riding the bike and of Carmen and I together.

"You call me when return *Habana?*"

"*Si, si,*" I nodded.

And so, with my backpack, Alfredo and I cycled back to his place, stopping on the way to change $100US into 2300 *pesos*; my pockets bulging from the overflow of paper.

We were now on our own, moving forward from here on out. Since the previous week's meeting with Jose Palaez and Alberto, there hadn't been any word from them, not even a phone call. This was inconceivable to me, so irresponsible. I thought about how Noriega called from Washington, DC, just before I left the States, announcing that there was a meeting being planned with Castro after the Tour. Palaez would be the one setting it up, but now...?

By going forward with this Tour, I was the reluctant rebel once again. But the objective was going to be met. Yes, I would love to meet Castro; I even prepared for it by bringing along some gifts to present to him once the Tour was completed and we were back in Havana, but the job came first-- no matter what the final consequences would be.

With the ever delightful, Carmen.

With pockets full and a single backpack stuffed to capacity, we arrived at Alfredo's dwelling unit, where he packed a pair of rear side panniers with his belongings, spare parts and tools, topping it off with my denim knapsack that held some audio tapes and other miscellaneous items. Alfredo, who would bear more weight than I, shrugged it off, saying, "I am used to it from the many cycling tours I do with other people throughout the year." But with his packs and steel frame bike, the total weight was more than I could lift. I wondered what we would be leaving along the roadside just to get through this adventure.

Shortly after 4pm, we waved good-bye to his family and headed toward the truck stop depot at the edge of town, by the harbor and railroad station.

"This will be the best place to hitch a ride, because all the trucks from around the country must come to this spot to refuel before returning home," advised Alfredo.

Hitch-hiking is an art form in Cuba. Although the nation has an airport in every major city, a railway system that goes as far as *Santiago*, and a main highway that divides the country in half, the problem that all three have in common is the cost or the hurdles a Cuban must jump through in order to get a ticket to a particular destination.

Examples: Alfredo and I could fly to *Santiago*, which would cost him 90 *pesos* ($4US)-- as opposed to me who would pay the equivalent in dollars. Or you can take the train as far as it'll go, which would cost someone like me with a bike about $35US, and for Alfredo a mere 20 *pesos*. But the problem, other than the cost (most Cubans save their money for food or rum), is time.

I could get a plane or train ticket anytime I wanted, by simply walking up to the counter and paying for it. But someone like Alfredo, a native, would have to fill out forms, submit them with the proper amount of *pesos*, then wait about a week for his ticket to arrive. Even the government, it seems, don't like their own currency, so they make their people jump through a few hoops. That way, they'll have time to fill up the seats with foreigners paying in American dollars.

"And you go for this discrimination?"

"That is the way it is," he answered, shrugging his shoulders. "It has been this way all my life."

"That still doesn't make it right," I snapped. "My country is more Communist-Socialist than yours. At least we're fair by only having one form of money system that everyone uses. Foreign or domestic, rich or poor. We don't care who you are. Green is green."

Also, when hitch-hiking, you never know when you're going to leave. You could be waiting on a ride for a few minutes, a few hours, or a few days. Generally, when Alfredo and I were hitching rides before and after the Tour, we waited anywhere from 15 minutes to 15 hours, depending on the circumstances-- such as the one we were in at the moment.

The truck station could be better called the carbon-monoxide pit stop, because of all the pollution and thick, black smoke that poured out of not only the trucks, but the passing cars, and the factory's chimneys across the street. We were at one of the most congested areas of Havana, and after a couple of hours of catching up on my journal entries and choking on poisonous fumes, I began to feel nauseated. I finally had to don my sponsor's charcoal face mask in order to breathe.

Alfredo mingled with the crowd. They were either roaming or lying about with their luggage close by, as he asked where they were going and how long before the trucks would be heading out.

Returning to the curb, he squatted down beside me and laid out the facts. "Most of these people have been waiting here since early this morning; the drivers since last night. All wait for the fuel truck."

"And how long before it arrives?"

"Who know?," he shrugged. "Could be hours or days. All we can do is wait."

"Balls!"

"*Si.*"

I began to think how easy we have it in the States, where we can just pull in at any gas station in the country, fuel up in a matter of minutes, and be on our way. In Cuba, it was a waiting game in which no one knew when the wait would be over. How these people could sit and laugh and carry on, was beyond me. They just relaxed and resigned themselves to the situation, taking it in stride. Waiting-- like going without-- was a part of life.

The truck stop area was completely surrounded by a chain-link fence, topped with barbed wire. Everyone who was looking for a ride waited outside the gate near the guard-house, or on the sidewalk. They were always careful to clear the area of trash or spit, or in some cases animal dung. If one was to wait all day, one needed a place to lie down.

For the majority of our waiting time, a police car was stationed just across

Waiting for a ride out of Havana at the truck depot.
After awhile, the smog got to be too much.

the street, opposite the main gate. Watching us and occasionally giving tickets to those who walked on the grass of the nearby park or didn't cross the street in the proper manner.

Some of the drivers would sometimes come out to talk with the people or get something to eat, and this was when we could find out who was going where, and plot our course. If we knew which drivers were going to the farthest end of the island, we could position ourselves to be one of the first to jump on before their trucks filled up. Also, by talking with the drivers, we could make our own private deals, thereby cutting out all other competition on space.

Since we had the time, and Alfredo knew I wanted hands-on involvement with the people and his country, he taught me how to read the license plates.

In the united States, all you have to do is look at a plate to know what State the vehicle is from. In Cuba, all plates have the country's name stamped on the bottom, so you must learn the code. All plates begin with at least two letters, and by learning how to read them, you know which truck goes to which province.

A license plate that began with the letter H stood for Havana, which was a province unto itself; B stood for the county of Havana. Other letters we saw were P for *Pinar del Rio*, V for *Villa Clara*, S for *Santi Spiritus*. If two or more provinces began with the same letter-- such as the triple provinces of *Cienfuegos, Ciego de Avila*, and *Camaguey*-- only one would get the initial letter C (in this case *Camaguey*), while the other two provinces were regulated to an F (*Cienfuegos*) and A (*Ciego de Avila*).

Nearly every truck from every province was represented, except the two we were looking for, U for *Santiago de Cuba*, or the magic N for *Guantanamo* (because G stood for *Granma*).

We could have taken the first truck out the gate, onto which people were able to climb onboard, but the license plate began with an M for *Matanzas*, which was the next province over. We declined the ride for one that would get us as close to our destination as possible, figuring the shorter the ride, the longer the wait in between. We knew our best chance was to hold out now, however nerve-wracking it was becoming.

Alfredo hooked up with a young man who was moving a household of furniture to the province of *Holguin* (O). Alfredo's voice rose in pitch as he slapped me on the back. "He say we can hitch a ride with him when his friend's truck is fueled."

"And when will that be?"

"Hmmm," thought Alfredo, scratching his head. "Who know? Maybe tomorrow, I think."

"And is that going to be alright with his friend?"

"But of course," Alfredo answered with a strange look as if I should know Cuban procedure. "By taking us, the driver make two hundred extra *peso*."

"But of course," I replied, mocking my friend. "The more cattle he take, the more money he make."

Viewing the map, *Holguin* was next to *Santiago*, so if we couldn't find an N or U truck, that would be our best bet, as it would carry us three-quarters to our destination over the course of some 20 hours.

The last truck we saw leaving the compound was a T (for *Las Tunas*, about the middle of the country). We called it quits after a six-hour wait, heading back to Alfredo's place.

The next day, it was more of the same. Alfredo and I were up early. His mother fixing us a big breakfast before we headed out the door by 8am, ready for round two of waiting for a truck at the carbon monoxide center.

Cycling to the truck stop, Alfredo kept turning to see how far I was behind him. "Come on! Faster!" He'd call out, waving his arm for me to catch up to him. "If we are late, we will miss the truck."

"Don't worry about it," I yelled out to him. "We're early. The Lord knows our needs."

"But does He know the driver's?"

When we arrived at the fueling center, none of the people or drivers were found to be anywhere.

"You see! You see," shouted Alfredo. "We lose our ride, because we no' here early enough!"

"No way. Look at all those trucks in there," I pointed beyond the gate. "The people just went home to bed. They'll return."

And they did shortly after. Many of them we recognized from the previous night-- including the man who was moving to *Holguin*, telling us his driver friend was still there. The fuel truck hadn't arrived yet.

Alfredo broke out into a smile. "We early."

"The Lord knows."

We waited a few more hours for the fuel truck, and by early afternoon decided to check out some other areas nearby. There was always time to return to the center, if all else failed.

About a mile to the east of the fueling center, we actually found a semi going to *Holguin* that was carrying a pair of trucks on a flatbed, and thought this would be a great way to go. Since we knew we would be traveling all night, we could sleep on the front seat, as Alfredo and I would each have a truck to stay in. This was definitely better than the other *Holguin* offer where we would have to sit up, all crammed together in a cab for nearly a full day. But alas, it was not meant to be. The driver explaining he didn't know how long he would be in Havana. It could be an hour, a day or a week. We couldn't take the chance, and moved on.

Although we didn't know it at the time, Providence intervened on our behalf: The next day, just outside the capital of *Holguin*, we came across that very same truck, only it was laying on its side, off the road. The cargo was smashed to pieces.

Alfredo said what I was thinking, "That could be us in there."

"Yes. God has been good to us."

"Ah, I don't believe such nonsense. We were lucky."

"Luck is a Luciferin term. It was Providence."

Although Alfredo, the atheist, brushed off this incident as coincidental, he kept quiet for several hours.

And so we continued searching for a truck to take us to *Santiago* or *Guantanamo*. Finding neither, we headed back to the depot, where the man we had met earlier who set up the ride to *Holguin* with his driver friend approached us with slumped shoulders. Not a good sign.

Alfredo and he conversed for several minutes off to the side until finally returning to me.

"He say his driver friend canno' take him, because he is carrying a cargo of oversized tractor tires, and there is no room for him and his furniture."

I placed a hand on the young man's shoulder. My heart went out to him, for I knew the difficulty he faced. There are no professional moving companies in Cuba, because no Cuban could afford such an expense.

"I am sorry to hear that, my friend. We will find another ride."

"No," he replied, patting my shoulder. "I arrange with my friend. You take my place."

"But that is not right," I said.

"Es okay, my friend," he replied, giving me a hug. "You go. I find someone else." We shook hands, and then he turned and left.

Thus, we hooked up with Mario and Dennis. The price was set at 100 *pesos* each, and we would be riding all night, arriving in the capital of *Holguin* some 17 hours later, early the next morning. So, for about $9US, we would cover nearly two-thirds of the country in a single move.

Before climbing aboard our transportation, I wanted to take some photos, but Alfredo covered the lens with his hand. "No photos here. I know...you want to take picture so you can tell everyone back home how we waited two days for ride."

"So? It happens. No big deal." I proceeded to take a picture, but this time, Alfredo stood in front of the lens.

"No show nothing bad about Cuba."

"What's the matter? Communism afraid of a little light?" Alfredo decided to be diplomatic and not answer, as I put my camera away, but warned, "Let's not make a habit of this. I want the freedom to take photos when I want."

Mario and Dennis were the yin and yang of truck drivers. Mario's jet-black skin was the darkest I had seen yet on the island, and I wondered if perhaps, some of it was more grime and grease than pigmentation. His mannerisms were large like his frame, and he resembled an Australian aborigine, but better dressed in gritty overalls. He didn't talk, but shouted. To describe something, he'd use grand hand gestures where his audience would have to stand several feet back, or else get hit by a flying arm. When he laughed, several teeth were missing. He was a well-cut gem.

His partner, Dennis, was just the opposite. About a head shorter than Mario, his coloring could be called white, but doubtful as he wore just as much grease as his companion although it didn't show as much on Mario. Dennis was more laid back in his conversation and mannerisms, but would share a good laugh with Mario when it was called for.

A middle-aged woman was joining us part of the way, and because there was only room for her in the front cab, Alfredo and I climbed aboard with the tires which smelled of fresh rubber. We became black upon their touch. Alfredo's bike was strapped on the outside, atop the tires, while Mario had stuffed mine inside the tubes.

"Hey, Mario, put mine on top, too," I called out to him. He shouted something to me in return, waving his arms, and going about his business. Alfredo laughed.

"He say, he no' want problems with someone trying to steal your bike when we stop to rest."

As we began to drive out of the city, Alfredo and I took a seat on the back of the rig, just behind the sleeping compartment. The day was beginning to cool down. We were finally on our way and the excitement grew within.

About two hours out of Havana, we made a stop off the main highway to a ramshackle house sitting in the midst of a sugar cane field that doubled as a restaurant. Trash, toys, broken down trucks and parts littered the surrounding building, not to mention different shapes and piles of dung from the various animals in attendance. It would, we knew, be our only opportunity to eat until the morning, and we were starved.

The family consisted of a set of parents and a young girl of perhaps five years of age. The front parlor had a couple of chairs and a television for visiting guests. Obviously, this was Mario and Dennis' regular hangout before their long journey back to *Holguin*, for no sooner had we reached the front door, than did the man of the house greet the truck drivers with a warm smile, open arms and a pair of newly

Alfredo's bike strapped to the top of a truck full of tractor tires. We slept inside the rubber tubes during the 17-hour journey to the capital of *Holguin*.

opened bottles of beer. When the little girl saw me, she quickly hid behind her father, watching me in wide-eyed fascination. Apparently, I was her first foreigner in this part of the countryside, and never once did she take her eyes off me the entire time we were there, even when I tried to play with her by making faces or winking.

This would be the first real meal of chicken, rice, *yucca* and beer that I would be paying in *pesos*. A bountiful feast-- the chickens were fresh off the block (their siblings were walking around the yard), and all for a mere 50 *pesos*, about $2US. Maybe Alfredo was right and we wouldn't need more than $100US to do this Tour. But I knew I wanted to have days of rest, do some sightseeing, and generally have some fun. And that would-- as it does everywhere-- take dollars.

With our bellies full, we were on our way. Everything seemed to be going great, until...an all-night rainfall. We were forced to dive into the tires for protection, which, packed close together, prevented the water from leaking in. But have you ever tried sleeping in a giant-sized tire before? It gives new meaning to the phrase, *curvature of the spine.*

Needless to say, we tossed and turned, and tried to prevent ourselves from cramping up, but it was to be a restless night, and I wondered if it'd be like this all the way to *Maisi.* Would we need a day just to revive our battered bodies, I asked myself, as we continued on into the unknown void of the night.

By 4am, when we stopped to stretch, Dennis, the driver, invited me to sit in the cab. There was an extra seat available, now that we had dropped off our female passenger somewhere along the way. Alfredo was still asleep, curled up within one of the tires. I would come to learn during the Tour that he could sleep anywhere under any conditions.

For the remainder of the journey, there was very little rest. Mario, Dennis, and I shared coffee and rum for the next several hours, until we reached our destination. As morning broke, I had the chance to see a beautiful Caribbean sunrise, with its yellows, reds and oranges against a cobalt blue sky. I watched the rural countryside coming to life, all the people and animals readying themselves for a new work day among miles upon miles of sugar cane.

We arrived just outside the capital of *Holguin* early. I momentarily dozed off, but was awakened by Mario's shouts. Bleary-eyed and disoriented, he removed our bikes from the truck. I fished in my backpack for the money, handing him ten-20 *peso* bills. He thanked me with a hearty handshake and a slap on the back that produced the arousing effect of instantly waking me up. A moment later, he was back in the truck. And off they went, disappearing, the dust from the road camouflaging their departure.

When the dusty conditions cleared, I felt as though I were coming out of a dream. Surrounding us were some of the townspeople. Some looked us up and down with contempt, others out of mild curiosity. After several moments, they walked off, going about their business.

Was it me, the alien invader, the American flag bike, or the fact that Alfredo and I were covered in dirt and grime; black rubber marks were smeared across our hands, faces, and throughout our clothes. We stretched and yawned, doing mild calisthenics in the middle of the road.

"Man, I could use a *masseuse* and a *Jacuzzi*," I commented between stretches.

"*Si*," agreed Alfredo about the *masseuse*, but added, "What is *Jacuzzi?*"

"Heaven," I replied. "Especially if you can get the *masseuse* in with you."

He cocked his head to the side wondering what to make of my comment, then decided to leave it alone, as we got on our bikes, looking for a street-corner vendor for something to eat.

At *Holguin*, the best place to hitch another ride was near a police check-point. We were inching our way closer to our goal of *Maisi*.

The second letter on some of the license plates was Z, which distinguishes a truck from an automobile, so, in effect, *Holguin's* trucks began with O-Z. I termed it that we were in the land of OZ, looking to get to UZ (*Santiago*) or NZ (*Guantanamo*).

Stopping at a truck depot or border check helped, because many drivers usually don't want to stop for every hiker, regardless of the money. We ended up waiting under some shaded trees along with a few other people. It was about 10am, and already the temperature had climbed to 90 degrees.

After an hour's wait, a government truck stopped to pick us up. It was heading to the next town-- *Urbano Noris*.

"I no' like this," expressed Alfredo, as other people were climbing aboard.

"Why not?"

"Government truck cost more."

"You want to wait all day for a cheaper one? We're already a week behind schedule on this Tour."

"But they charge us twenty *peso* each. It too much."

"I don't care. I want out of here. Let's go."

Urbano Noris was another dusty town where goats and pigs roamed the streets as freely as the mangy dogs. Construction was underway; rebuilding was taking place, as it was with other towns we passed along the way.

We waited another three hours for a truck heading toward our destination. Part of the time Alfredo and I slept, or I'd play constant catch-up with my journal. An elementary school was nearby where the uniformed children were involved in a fierce game of football (soccer to us).

When the next truck arrived, the fun began. The lethargic crowd that had been waiting in the heat of the day found renewed energy. This far out into the country, transportation is few and far between. There was a good-sized group of us, so we were on a first-come, first-served basis, and that meant crowding, jamming, pushing and shoving to get a place. After awhile these trucks began to resemble cattle cars, and we, the pieces of meat, going off to the slaughter house.

"Hand me the bikes," shouted Alfredo, who was one of the first to board the truck.

We were actually in a worse position than the other passengers because of the bulk of our gear. Since Alfredo was the expert with traveling in this mode, I did what he said and followed his lead.

Once aboard, we were off to the next town, *San Luis*, some two hours away. Standing the entire time wedged between other people with luggage and bicycles, we traveled at speeds of up to 60-70mph. If we were to ever flip over, there'd be plenty of carnage scattered by the roadside, but hey, it was only costing us a mere five *pesos* each.

"You see," said Alfredo, pointing a finger in my face. "A private truck is cheaper than government."

Sometimes the trucks have a canopy on them, which is wonderful when it happens to rain, or you are left out in the open, exposed to the elements. Ours was open, therefore...

We were dropped off at a junction just outside *San Luis*. There we waited another hour or so with a hundred other tired and travel-worn people. From the heat, we were all in a lethargic state of being, moving in a quagmire of discontent. Some of them would casually glance over at me and Alfredo. Others, mostly the young men, would brave toward the bike to inspect it with lustful eyes. While waiting for a truck to take us to *Guantanamo*, a magnificent, brightly-colored, detailed rainbow welcomed us. Like Noah after the flood, I took this as a sign that God was continuing to be with us. We were in good hands now that we were far away from the smog of the city. My breathing was better and there was less of a concrete feeling in my chest.

As I sat under a shade tree with the bikes, preparing my daily notes, Alfredo made the usual rounds, talking with the various people about where they were going: "Have the trucks been coming along at regular intervals?; Anything heading eastward?"

Returning to me, he reported, "I think the best plan is to ride our bikes into *Santiago*.

The cattle being transported to their next destination.

There, we will spend the night with a friend and get up early tomorrow morning."

"Can't we get a truck into *Guantanamo* instead?"

He shook his head. "No good. We have a better chance of finding an empty truck in *Santiago*. This better idea, I think. We be okay."

It was about 4pm, with only a couple hours of daylight left. The way traffic was, it didn't look good for us, and after spending the previous night in a tractor tire, we were both thinking of a shower. We mounted our bikes and rode the 20 miles into the capital of the province. The first half was flat, but the second part was a spectacularly refreshing downhill run.

Just before our plunge toward the capital, we came across a young man emerging from a sugar cane field. He had a machete in one hand and a bunch of stalks in the other. He was dressed in nothing more than a pair of shorts and sandals, and he was tying his dinner onto the back rack of his bicycle.

"I've never tried raw sugar cane before. It must be a delicacy," I commented to Alfredo who interpreted this to the young man.

He laughed at the statement, then lopped off a two-foot section with his blade. When I tried to pay him a few *pesos*, he refused, saying to me through Alfredo, "This is your first experience, so it is an honor. There is an entire field to choose from," he motioned with a wave of his arm.

"How do you eat this?" I asked Alfredo.

"You just chew on the stalk and suck the juice out," he answered nonchalantly.

Chewing on the sugar cane stalk was like biting into a piece of balsa wood, and I was afraid if I were not careful, I'd end up with splinters between my teeth.

The juice seemed to pour out of the fibers. It was very sweet and gave me a burst of energy; we hadn't eaten most of the day.

While I was indulging my tastebud, Alfredo mentioned, "This field is for the people who are poor and starving. They are allowed to go into certain fields and take what they want."

"And no one says anything?"

"Never," laughed my partner. "There are fields like this all over the country. Oranges, guavas, pineapples, coconuts, papayas, bananas. All for the taking to feed the people."

Evening fell when we reached the bottom of the mountain. Gliding into the city of *Santiago de Cuba*, we were met by bright lights, *salsa* music and vendors selling their wares. There were pedicabs, and people on horseback or walking along the streets. An enormous statue of a noble officer on horseback greeted us; he seemed to be waving to us to move onward toward our destination.

Alfredo led the way, and, within a few minutes, we darted off the main path to a run-down part of the neighborhood, meandering our way through fallen concrete slabs and a polluted water system until we came to an apartment unit Alfredo obviously knew well.

On the first floor, we were greeted by a beautiful *senorita* named Ida. Her skin was the color of chocolate cream and her laughing eyes complimented her perfect smile.

She invited us in, smiling and bowing slightly as we entered her humble abode with our bicycles; making us feel at home by asking us to sit and relax while she brought out drinks and snacks. In short time, she and Alfredo were chatting comfortably away, catching up on the latest news of family and mutual friends.

Alfredo pulled out a manila envelope from one of his panniers and handed it to our hostess, who smiled and blushed with delight as she opened the package. Inside was a letter in English, along with a few dollar bills, and a small atlas of the fifty united States.

"I was here almost a year ago with another American group," mentioned Alfredo as Ida leafed through the items. "We cycle from *Santiago* back to Havana."

Ida turned to her friend, asking him for something. Alfredo nodded in reply, "*Si, si*," then turned to me. "She no' can read English, so I will read the letter to her."

After a few moments, Ida placed the items back into the envelope, then showed us where we could bathe and shave while she went to the market to gather some items to prepare us a meal. Again, it would be a cold shower, but even still, there was something refreshing about washing away the grime of the road.

Ida spoke little English-- barely any really-- but she made us feel comfortable with her warm smile and laughing eyes. Her tiny two-bedroom apartment was decorated simply, with a couch, a desk, a couple of chairs, a black-and-white TV set, a shelf with some books and mementos on them, and some colorful posters hanging on the walls. The spare bedroom had two beds and a dresser with an attached mirror; her own bedroom contained a single bed covered in mosquito netting. The entire area was well-infested with the pesky creatures and Ida's apartment was no exception. I was thankful I had remembered to bring the repellant.

Ida cooked us a fine meal of rice and beans (*congris*), fish, tomatoes, and onions, topped off with rich, black coffee. It was a feast, but to Ida, she shrugged it off with a pleasant pearl-white smile. It was simply something she threw together.

Before retiring, Alfredo and I viewed the map.

"We will awake at five and be at the center of town no later than one hour after," informed my guide. "This will give us the best chance of finding an empty truck to *Guantanamo*."

"When do you think we'll arrive in *Maisi?*"

He thought a moment, then answered with confidence, "Tomorrow evening. We will have all day."

"But *Guantanamo* is the last major city in the East."

"*Si*," nodded Alfredo. "The further we pull away from *Guantanamo*, the less chance we find transportation."

I nodded silently at this piece of reality, not even realizing my hands were in a praying position.

Alfredo laughed nervously. "I have never been past *Guantanamo*," he confided in me. "This will be a first. A real adventure." Was his worried look equal to my own?

We also decided to leave as much of our equipment as was not needed for the next few days. We figured to begin the Tour in *Maisi* on Saturday and be back to Ida's place the next day. That was roughly 200 miles, according to the map, and would be a long stretch for me who hadn't been on a bike in over two years. Fact is, I hadn't done over 50 miles in a day since China and I wondered if I was up to the challenge.

"We can do it," he nodded. "It will be okay."

I could only hope and pray, but with each step-- each mile we were closer to our goal-- I was getting more and more excited. Would we really reach the end of the island sometime tomorrow? The eastern edge of Cuba? It was just too good to be true, but I was obsessed in reaching this town out in the middle of nowhere.

We were now a week behind schedule, and just to be able to arrive in *Maisi* was a milestone in itself. Starting the Tour would present new and different challenges of their own.

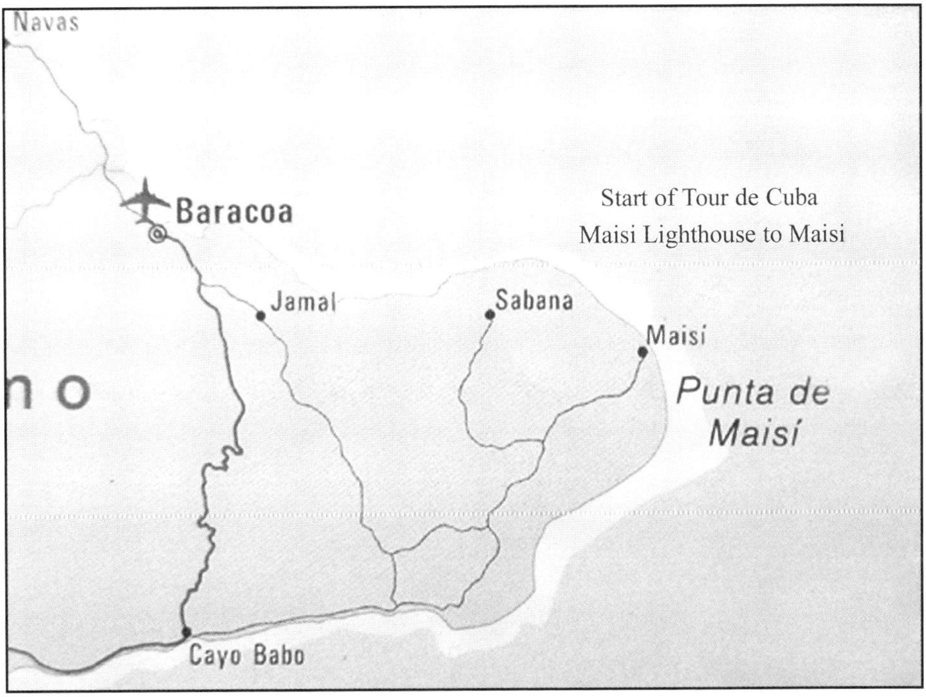

NUEVE

9

SANTIAGO DE CUBA
NOVEMBER 21, 1997

1st DAY OF TOUR :	**LIGHTHOUSE at PUNTA DE MAISI to MAISI**
DAILY DISTANCE :	**8 miles or 13.3 kilometers**
TOTAL DISTANCE :	**8 miles or 13.3 kilometers**

It was still dark when we awoke at 5am, and already the temperature had reached 75 degrees. We quickly got dressed while Ida, still in her bathrobe and slippers, more sleep-walking than fully awake, prepared rich, black coffee served in thimble-sized cups with sweet rolls on the side. The coffee was potent, and although I don't touch the stuff at home, when I'm away and on a tour, the survival mode kicks in and I find I will eat, drink, and do whatever's necessary to get the job done. This coffee, I found, could wake the dead, which was just what we needed.

We headed out the door within the half-hour, Alfredo promising to return by

Sunday evening. Ida gave a sleepy smile, waving us good-bye with a yawn. By the time she really wakes up, I thought, she'll probably think it was all a dream-- except for the fact that Alfredo and I left a good deal of our belongings at her place.

Although the temperature was climbing, a wind was coming in from the coast. And in the cool breeze, we arrived at the center of town, where trucks and private vehicles were lined up to take the daily cattle of people East, West or North.

"You see," said Alfredo, "the best idea is to start here when the truck no' full. Along the way many people will come, and then we no have room for us and our bikes."

Perhaps he was correct in his thinking. After all, we had a good night's sleep-- the mosquitos having very little to nibble on with our bodies covered in repellant. We were able to shed some of our weight, at least for a couple of days, and that would help me get back into the groove of the road.

The hum of activity was happening around us. People were milling about, talking with the drivers about where they were heading and when they would be leaving; street vendors were setting up their carts of freshly-prepared food and drink; even the sky hurried from blackness to a twilight blue.

Alfredo quickly found a driver who was going to *Guantanamo,* and for 40 *pesos* we were on our way by 6am. Half the dumpster-sized truck was full with people dressed for work; others carried packages they were taking to whatever town they were going to be dropped off at between the twin cities of *Santiago de Cuba* and *Guantanamo*. Their reactions to me and the bike were nothing more than a casual glance, since they see many foreigners passing through. Only in the country where the little towns stood off the beaten path, were the people more curious about who I was and why I was in their country.

Inside, the open-aired truck had benches lining the sides for whoever were the first aboard. Alfredo and I had the choice of sitting, as did many of the other men, but gave up our seats to the ladies. At first, we had room enough to move, but by the time we reached the truck's final destination three hours later, we were packed like sardines, standing all the way.

As usual, Alfredo stayed on one side of the truck, striking up a conversation with a fellow passenger, while I was opposite, taking photos along the way. If you keep yourself balanced, and do the right camera adjustments (I like to use a manual camera as it allows me more control than an automatic), you can get a lot of great "car shots." Jean, having more than a half-century of photographing experience (not to mention a house full of awards), taught me this neat little trick (and how to operate a 35mm in general) as a way to utilize my time more effectively.

The Cuban countryside came into full view, reminding me of California's San Joaquin Valley, which I had left behind exactly two weeks before. Lush green vegetation piled high on both sides of us like a cursed Northern snowdrift. It stretched far to the horizon to meet with the blue of the sky, as the sun rose majestically like the *crescendo* of a great symphony. Nature's show, and we had front row seats.

Hopping off at *Guantanamo*, Alfredo had already made the next arrangements with the young man he befriended on the truck. "We need to ride three miles to the next stop."

I looked over at the young man, who nodded his head in agreement, already on his bike, waiting to go. We stopped for a quick breakfast of fresh papaya juice along the way. When we reached our destination, our young friend bid us farewell with a smile and a handshake. With the heat increasing to near triple digits, it was time to break out the sun screen lotion and find shade whenever possible.

By 11am, Alfredo and I found a truck going toward *Baracoa*, the oldest town in Cuba. The driver said he would stop at the junction of the seaside town of *Cayobabo*. For another 40 *pesos* and two hours of further travel in upright positions, we found ourselves heading ever eastward.

My companion during this stretch of the journey was a chicken. His head peered out from a burlap bag, giving me a startle upon first encounter.

"Well, hello there little fella. You someone's dinner tonight?" I asked, as he craned and turned, looking about, squawking his displeasure at being held against his will, and disappearing every so often within the confines of his captivity.

Roughly an hour out of *Guantanamo*, the road conditions began to change from smooth pavement to pot-holes to gravel to dirt, to a combination of any of the above. But the discomfort was mitigated by the sight before us. As soon as we entered the district of *San Antonio del Sur*, there, at last, were the crystal clear, ice blue, blue-green waters of the Caribbean. We had reached the coast, and it welcomed us with short waves topped by small whitecaps. The air was thick with the smell of salt. It was exactly 25 years ago when last I was in this part of the world with my parents on the nearby island of *Saint Croix*. My senses were back in their youth. I felt comfortably at home.

As we stopped for something to eat and drink in the town of *Imias* (or is it just *Maisi* spelled differently?), we came across a weekend carnival.

When the drivers are hungry and stop on the side of the road, their cargo do not climb out, the vendors rush to you with trays of freshly-prepared items, such as fried *yucca* or banana, bite-sized pizzas, cookies, bottles of *refresca* (juice like our Kool-Aid), and coffee.

Alfredo yelled down in Spanish to the vendors for bottles of cool liquid and some food.

"What are you ordering?" I asked.

"It does not matter," he yelled across the truck to me. "Just give me *pesos*."

So many people were pushing and shoving; so many arms flying and hands grabbing that it became one gigantic struggle for survival. We were subjugated to no more than mere animals, like the desperate, starving dogs below us, who hoped we would drop some morsel of food before them. Unknowingly, this meal-on-wheels would be it for the day.

Whenever you're in unfamiliar territory and in the survival mode, you must eat as the opportunity arises, else pay the price afterwards.

The main street of *Imias* was tree-lined and paved, looking almost Americana. Tents were placed on both sides, where children enjoyed rides of merry-go-round horses and flying chairs. There, vendors displayed their goods, and people strolled up and down the avenue licking ice-cream cones and trying not to make a mess of their

Vendors attempting to feed the cattle en route.

cotton candy. It was just like my days of youth when the biggest thrill was having the traveling Fair set up at the local plaza parking lot.

"We will be cycling through here this time tomorrow," mentioned Alfredo, through mouthfuls of food and drink.

"Then it'd be a good time to stop for lunch."

"*Si. Guantanamo* is the poorest province of Cuba. The sooner we are out, the better chance we have to find food."

As the driver started up his massive truck, we continued on the winding road toward the seaside hamlet of *Cayobabo,* where we were dropped off with other passengers. The truck continued on to the coastal resort town of *Baracoa.* From here to the last major town of *Maisi,* the road would be one of dirt, gravel, and pot-holes big enough to keep you awake. We would be doing a steady climb all the way to the easternmost point of the island.

We waited at the truck stop with another group of people who were hitching rides along the way. We were definitely in no man's land. Alfredo got settled into a comfortable position on a bench inside a three-walled concrete shelter, while I took a seat along the outside shaded edge to work on my notes and take in our new surroundings.

The town was nothing more than a group of concrete buildings with scattered houses on both sides of the main road-- the only road in town. There were no side streets. A single female vendor stood a few yards away from us, selling homemade ice cream in cardboard cones to a group of young men who buzzed about her. Naturally, bees are attracted to sweet things, but the ice cream in Cuba is not like what we are used to in America. It's soft, almost to the point of mush, but it is cold and sugary and, in the heat, it's delightfully refreshing.

A young man, presumably the town stud, strode up to the ice-cream stand on his motor scooter, laughing and waving to his *amigos* in grand gesture. He was the proud peacock, strutting his stuff to impress the *senorita*, while buying a round of cones for the *caballeros*. He stayed a long time in conversation with the ice-cream *chiquita*. From observation, he was from a well-to-do family (the fact that he had the only motor scooter in town showed that)-- as one could be in this deserted part of the island. He was king in this area of perhaps a few dozen or so, and he relished in it with gaiety, laughter, and not a care in his little world.

As I was amusing myself with his flirtations, a voice broke the silence of my imaginary world with a boom that announced, "Jesus Christ is my Lord and Saviour."

Turning toward the sound of the bold announcement, a pleasant-looking young man was beaming a smile at me from the other side of my bike. He was dressed in a pair of clean, white pants with a striped white and blue shirt. Introducing himself as Abel, he was going to a town about midway toward *Maisi* to teach Christianity to the people, as he showed me his Bible.

There was a certain glow about him usually associated with newborn Christians. He smiled at me and his countenance was angelic. His eyes radiated a light and love that showed his soul was calm and at peace with his faith. Because of his cleansing by the blood of the Lamb, he was completely reborn, like an infant; fresh, pure. Unlike the hard-core, world traveler I had become (with 30 years of service to the Lord), who's outer skin had turned to thick scales by years of gossipy, back-stabbing, envious, black-hearted, hypocritical Christians who do what they do to their fellow man *in the name of the Lord*, yet are no different than their non-counterparts.

At times, I have been ashamed to even call or associate myself as one. I don't fit in with the religious right, because like Jesus, I don't care for religions that, "Break my Father up into denominations." I'm not *perfect* enough for most Christians who live in a cocoon all their lives, and "praise the Lord," for their blissful state of being. I want to learn. To experience new and different cultures. To seek truth. To travel and be one with the people. Not to be *of* the world, but in it and a contributor to advance the cause of Christ. To occupy while I'm alive on this earth. To be a thorn in Satan's side and a jewel in the eyes of Jesus. And to remind myself that being a Christian means to suffer.

Yes, I backslide. Miserably at times. But I know Jesus is there to pick me up, brush me off, and send me on another mission. Because of Him, I am able to change, grow and learn.

Looking at this boy, I try to recall those innocent days when I was a *babe in Christ*. Although my faith continues to be strong, somewhere along the way, my heart has grown cold, bitter and cynical toward an evil and corrupt world. I wanted so much to believe in the good cause again. That in the end, the guys in white do win. Perhaps, with Abel's kindly presence, the Lord was giving me a gift of hope that I could cherish and hang on to.

"You have a beautiful bike," pointed Abel, awakening me from my thoughts.

"We have time before the next truck arrives. Why don't you take it for a ride."

"Do you mean it, *senor?*" His eyes lit up.

"Of course. It would please me."

"You are most kind. Bless you."

As soon as he hopped on the Beast, some of the people, who were taking shelter from the heat, sat up like dead dogs to take notice. Even the loyal, ice-cream *caballeros* and succulent *senorita* shifted their attention from the *macho*, motor scooter man, to Abel, which didn't sit well with the *man about town*.

"What a blessing it was to ride such a superb bicycle," beamed Abel upon his joyous return. "Bless you."

"I'm glad you enjoyed it," I smiled in return.

"Would you like to see my collection of coins?" he asked, already retrieving a cigar box from his few, precious belongings. Before I could answer, he was sitting beside me with open box in hand, full of coins from various countries.

"These are from the many tourists I have met that have come to Cuba," he announced, as we went through various-size coins from Germany, France, Canada, the united States, Russia, and Africa. Aside from his Bible, this was probably his most prized and cherished possession.

"Financially, it is impossible to leave my country. But if I look at my coins, I can dream and feel that I have been around the world, and that makes me happy."

It was a simple, honest statement like this that jarred my soul into realizing how blessed the Lord has been to me all these years. Sometimes we need to be shaken into remembering the little things we take for granted, like health, peace of mind, a warm, comfortable bed, a hot shower, abundant food, and still a nation under Jesus Christ and not Communism, regardless of who wants to deny this solid fact our forefathers fought and died to give us.

"Thank you for showing me your treasures," I said to Abel. "May I contribute some coins of my own?"

"*Senor*, you have done much for me already."

"Not as much as you have done for me, my friend."

I dropped several new coins into his already vast collection, then turned to Alfredo, "I'm going to take a ride down the road, see the rest of this town."

"What if the truck come and you no' here?"

"There are no side streets. Where could I get lost?"

At the town limit of *Cayobabo*, there's a colorful billboard depicting an event that occurred over a hundred years ago at the other side of town, on the beach where a national monument had been erected.

On April 11, 1895, Josi Marti and Maximo Gomez, along with a group of exiled Cubans, landed on the shores of *Cayobabo*, just outside of town. It was during the War for Independence, and their aim was to free their people from the Spanish, who ruled with an iron fist at the time. The ensuing battle marked the beginning of Cuba's freedom from Spain.

Looking at the billboard, I wondered, if alive today, what Josi and Maximo would think of their efforts. Did they pay off? Was Castro, the heir, keeping the faith?

Arriving in the sea coastal town of *Cajobabo* 102 years after Josi Marti's famous return during the (1895) War of Independence from Spain.

As I proceeded further along, taking in the simple structured homes that lined the main road, I stopped and walked to the white sandy beach where I could look for miles in both directions and not see another soul. I listened to the sounds of the waves crashing against the rocks and lap near my shoes. I observed the many different forms of seashells dotting the coastline, picking up a few gems that caught my attention. I felt at peace here in the solitude; and I have often felt that way, whether it be in a winter wonderland in Alaska, or the burning desert of the Gobi and Inner Mongolia. To go where few people have been intrigues me, for it is where I can feel close to God and seek His face.

I returned to Alfredo and the group after a couple of hours. After all, how much is there to see in a one-street town? A truck arrived heading to *Maisi*. The last one for the day, according to the driver, as we all piled in to endure another two-hour, bumpy ride. This time there were so few of us that we actually had the chance to sit. The condition of the dirt road, though, was so bad on the tail bone that it was better to stand.

As I studied the terrain of what we would be cycling on in the morning, I was thankful to God we were not doing the Tour from the other direction. Even though I had heard this section was steep and gravelly from Palaez, at a 45-degree angle, I would not want to cycle it during the heat of the day-- heat in which you would have to be well-prepared. Being caught out here under less than desirable conditions (that is, being low on food and water and not being in fine physical shape) would be suicidal.

Abel got off at the small hamlet about midway to *Maisi*, where we shook hands.

"God bless you, my friend," he smiled cherubically, grabbing his suitcase.

"And may peace, strength, health and our Lord be with you in your work ahead," I responded.

He stood by the roadside, waving enthusiastically upon our departure.

Pulling away, I watched the young man walk across the street to a group of buildings that were no more than cold-water shacks. I reflected that he was about to do something more worthy, more valuable than anything I had ever done in my entire life... saving souls by bringing his people to know Jesus Christ in a more intimate way; and that was a different kind of fight for a different kind of Cuban.

Patria O Muerte, Venceremos! -- Fatherland or Death, We Shall Conquer -- Cuba's national saying was everywhere, including being stamped on their coins, like our own *In God We Trust* (which, incidentally, was given to us by Abraham Lincoln shortly after converting to Christianity and just before his assassination in 1864). Cuba's verse can be taken another way in Abel's case; and in my heart, I prayed for him and his lifetime mission ahead.

Again, Alfredo struck up a conversation along the way with a couple of dirty, ragged teenage girls who happened to live in *Maisi*. The dirt road seemed to narrow, as the giant jungle leaves from the trees tried to engulf us. Standing up in the truck was not an option unless you enjoyed getting slapped in the face by a palm leaf. Sitting down was out as well. Every five seconds we'd hit a pothole, sending us bouncing along on our tail bones. The best we could do was squat, or bounce along with the terrain. The situation was tolerable if you could laugh at the circumstances, and think of the back of the truck as a large trampoline.

"Hey, *Kebin*," shouted Alfredo over the noise of the truck's engine. "These girls are sisters and say we can leave our stuff at their *hacienda* while we go to the lighthouse to take some photos."

"That's very kind of them."

"*Si,*" said Alfredo, "Mia say we can spend the night with them."

"*Gracias,*" I answered, nodding to them.

The girls giggled at my Spanish. Mia, the 18-year-old, smiled and batted her eyes at me. I began to imagine what kind of a night we would be spending with our newly-acquired hosts. Alfredo gladly accepted for both of us.

About 5pm, our driver pulled into the dusty-clay center of *Maisi.* He accepted no charge from any of us, waving us off with a smile. I shook his hand and thanked him. Retrieving my bike and knapsack, Alfredo and I walked off with the girls to their house just a few yards away. Our final tally in what it cost us to get to this place in three days of bodily abuse was some 305 *pesos* for both of us and our bikes, or just a smidgen over $13US.

The Tour began now, eight days behind schedule. I wondered if we could make up the difference as I scanned the old Western style, literally end-of-the-road, town. Was this a dream? Were we actually here?...

And then Alfredo broke through the fantasy, by announcing, "Come, let us go to the lighthouse."

From our vantage point, we could see the towering beacon of strength several miles away near the coastline.

Although *Maisi* is the first town in Cuba to see the rising sun, it's also the first place to get dark, and after 5pm it was time to relax, not begin cycling. Our proposed route to the other end of the island, would be in following the sun, so that over the course of the next few weeks, we would actually gain daylight.

"I don't know Alfredo," I cautioned. "It looks too far away for us to be able to make it in time to get any photos. We should just wait until early morning."

"It be okay," assured Alfredo. "It only a few *kilometers*. Not far. Our stuff be okay with the girls."

They were sitting outside on the front porch with their father, watching and smiling at me the entire time.

"I don't know," I repeated. "Once we get down there, I still need to change into my uniform and set up the shots."

"We have time," said Alfredo, mounting his bike. "Come, let us begin the Tour now. It all downhill from here."

"Which means we'll be traveling back uphill in the dark, and that's not a good thing."

"We be okay. Come." And with that, he didn't even wait for me to answer, as he sped off for the lighthouse.

It was a fast downhill all the way, and I was surprised that neither one of us took a serious fall as we negotiated the hard clay surface, trying to beat the clock, as it were.

The *few kilometers* Alfredo so *wisely* judged, actually turned out to being some 13.3 or eight miles, according to my cycle computer.

Although we made it to the bottom in still-light conditions, it was, nevertheless, too dark for the camera to pick up a strong, clear-edged photo.

"Damn!" I cursed myself, searching through my knapsack.

"What is it?" asked Alfredo.

"I left the flash at Ida's place. No way am I going to get any decent photos now, and the beginning and end of each Tour is the most important. We may have to return tomorrow."

"Naw," said my partner in confidence. "We be okay. I take photographing class. I know what to do. You change into your uniform, while I set up a good shot."

With darkness falling upon us, I didn't have time to argue, as I changed out of my dusty, well-traveled clothes, and back into the red, white and blue; the stars and stripes of my country's colors. Whenever I don my uniform, I am transformed, alive and tingling all over. I am, once again, Captain America on another adventure. And with that feeling comes a certain sense of power and purpose.

As I was straightening out my headdress, Alfredo commented, "I wonder how many times you will be arrested looking like that?"

"If you're going to be the first, you may as well do it in your country's colors."

The start of the **Tour de Cuba** at *Maisi,* the easternmost point on the island.

While Alfredo was popping off a few shots, some of the people that lived within the shadow of the lighthouse came with blankets and bottles of beer and rum, to rest and relax on the beach nearby. I thought how if we had our gear, I would've spent the night out with them. But instead we had ourselves a long climb back to the main town in blackout conditions, neither one of us having any form of light to guide our path along the way...

Since we were now officially on Tour, I reset the bike's computer mileage to zero. From here on in-- lighthouse to lighthouse, point to point, *Maisi* to *Caleta Larga*-- we were going to know the exact distance of the longest cycling tour in the history of Cuba. **The Tour de Cuba** was underway! And what a beginning we were about to have...

About a half-mile from the lighthouse, we passed a small, single-strip airport, where government and private planes fly in.

"Drug smugglers use this place, coming in from the nearby islands of Haiti and Jamaica," mentioned Alfredo. "Even parts of South America."

Any sunlight was now gone. We were completely in the dark. An eerie feeling. My handlebars were off center by a fraction, and because the bike was made to precision, the front tire felt wobbly. I stopped at the edge of one well-lit house to make an adjustment to my handlebar stem when the family came out to the front porch and invited us in.

Since it was already dark, what could we lose? Alfredo and I took them up on the offer, thereby giving me a chance to work on my bike in full, lighted conditions.

The family consisted of grandparents, parents and a couple of children. All were friendly and hospitable, but especially the grandfather, who went out of his way to see that Alfredo and I were comfortable, wanting very much to talk with me, as visitors are a rare sight in this part of the country. With Alfredo as interpreter, we could.

"Where are you from?" Was the usual question. When I answered America, his eyes grew big, and the family surrounded us. "*Americano!* I have not seen one in over fifty years. What part of America?"

Their drinks consisted of rich, black coffee and water. Alfredo announced, "The region we are in is famous the world over for its coffee beans."

The family shook their heads in agreement, and while we were enjoying the kick-ass brew, grandfather shuffled off to the back room to produce a small bottle of rum, insisting we mix some with our drink, giving us that extra special jolt.

Grandfather being the most talkative, asked us, "Why are you here, and where are you going?"

We explained what the *Tour de Cuba* was, as I pulled out the section map, laying it out for them on their dining-room table. The rest of the family crowded around, and looked on in wide-eyed amazement, as they followed my finger of the highlighted route through every province, from where they were to the opposite end of their country.

"You are at the very beginning of our Tour," I said. "The first family we have come to."

Grandfather laughed with joy, clapping his hands. "Oh, my friend, in all my years I have never been through my country the way you will see it. Bless you."

We drank a toast of rum without the interference of the coffee. Clicking our glasses and patting each other on the back, we fellowshipped with one another in laughter and drink. I wished I had my camera flash, silently cursing myself once again for not being prepared.

If there is any possibility, I, for one, do not cycle in the dark without the proper lighting. A friend of mine living in Washington, DC, once related the story about a buddy of his who was cycling home one night after work-- sleep-cycling, really-- when he took a nasty fall, skinning his arms and face, receiving swollen lips and a black eye. When later asked how he got this way, the cyclist simply said that he ran over a bum sleeping in his path. The man was inebriated, so when he awoke the next day, he more than likely never knew how he got that single tire track across his forehead or why he felt such discomfort in his chest.

But most Cubans don't have the luxury of bicycle lamplights, or often the opportunity to wait until sunrise, so they have become much better equipped to handle the situation. Among other things, poverty makes you strong and determined, and Alfredo was just as good at covering ground at night as he was in the day. He was a cycling machine who never knew when to stop.

"Alfredo, this is bullshit! It's Russian Roulette out here. We're going to get hurt before the Tour starts," I'd yell out from time to time.

"Do not worry," he'd reply. "Just cycle in the middle of the road, and you no' fall. We almost finished."

"Oh, yeah," I countered, "Let me tell you the story about this bum..."

This went on for about six miles, until a truck came by our way, and I made the bold move of stopping it. Four men got out to see what the problem was, and Alfredo returned to act as interpreter in front of their headlights.

"They canno' give us a ride into town. This is a government truck, and are forbidden."

"Yeah? Then why did we ride in a government truck in *Holguin?*"

He gave a slight smile and responded, "That government truck could. This one can't."

"You are so full of shit! I can't believe you expect me to believe that."

"Is true."

"Balls! Money is money. Make a deal."

The leader of the group looked over our papers, then talked a while with Alfredo.

"He say you can be arrested for bribery."

My jaw slightly dropped. "You're kidding? In a Communist country? What is this world coming to when you can't trust greed anymore?"

The men got back into the truck and took off as I cursed under my breath.

"You see," said Alfredo, "They no' can take us."

"You going to tell me bribery doesn't work in your country?"

"*Si,* but only if they know they no' get caught."

We continued onward and upward for another mile or so, until a second truck happened to be going our way and actually stopped to offer us a ride. Though we were almost to the top, we took it.

That was probably a mistake.

"*Halta!*" announced the overweight, under-achieved military officer when Alfredo and I were getting out of the truck, shortly afterward.

He motioned us to him with a crooked finger. Speaking in Spanish, he asked for our papers and passports. Alfredo quickly handed his over, while I took my sweet, slow time, much to Alfredo's worried look. Other subordinate officers and personnel surrounded us, checking out the most famous-- and probably the most colorful-- bike they had ever seen.

"So, what's the problem, *El Capitan?*" I inquired, as he studied my passport most carefully.

He turned to Alfredo, evidentially asking him why we were in his district. My partner reached in a side pocket to retrieve the document that explained what our mission was all about. It didn't seem to do any good, though-- he walked toward the fenced compound that housed the headquarters-- with us in tow. We were *guests* there for the next couple of hours.

"Oh, I fear we are in big trouble now," said Alfredo, while we waited in the foyer with an ever-present guard nearby.

During the waiting period, Alfredo was given permission to bring our bikes within the compound area and return to the house nearby to gather our gear.

"What are you worried about?" I asked. "We haven't done anything wrong."

"We in an area we no' suppose to be in."

"Isn't that why we have that piece of paper? Four stamps on it. We're very important."

"No joke, *Kebin*, please. We are in trouble."

"Balls! I'm hungry. Let's go find something to eat," I said, getting out of my seat.

Alfredo remained in his. "We canno'."

"Why not?"

"You under arrest."

"We are?"

"No. Just you. I free to go."

"Yeah? And what makes you so special?"

"They think you a drug smuggler."

If man were allowed to judge an individual by their looks, I would end up spending a lifetime in jail, and then be sent to Hell for all eternity-- which is another reason that I thank the Lord that He's in control of us all and all situations. Nothing ever gets by Him, and on that last great day, He will be the ultimate Judge. He will weigh our hearts, and take into account whether or not we realize He is Lord, Master, and Saviour. I know beyond any doubt that He will do justice when it comes to me. Good or bad, up or down-- His decision will be fair and right.

Of course, at the moment, I was being judged by my hard, intense looks, and the fact that within our gear was a large, plastic, zip-lock bag containing a white powdery substance. That did not go well in my favor, but who knew we would end up in a situation like this?

Before leaving the States, when I was organizing my gear, the powdered energy drink came in an awkward, round, plastic container that took up space, so it was natural for me to transfer it to a bag that could lie flat and pack well. So it wouldn't bust open and spread all over the rest of the equipment, I taped it up. Now, in this Cuban jail station at the eastern edge of the island, when brought to my attention, yes, it did look familiarly like a couple of kilos of cocaine. Still, this fact didn't bother me, because all they had to do was test it or taste it or both.

When the *Commandante* returned to us in the waiting room, he was holding the powdered drink in one hand, my passport in the other, and giving me a narrow-eyed, beady look somewhere in between.

Through Alfredo, I asked, "If I were a drug smuggler, would I be dressed so flamboyantly?..."

"Please, *Kebin,* no use so big words," moaned my interpreter.

"Would I be dressed like this with a bike to match?"

"*Si,*" mumbled the head officer. "It possible to throw us off track. You cause us confusion and pass right by."

"Boys, you've been left out here too long. Time to get back into the real world," I commented.

My partner was allowed to go across the street, from where a half-hour or so later, he returned with juice and some guava sandwiches-- all he could find. It's an interesting combo that Cubans seem to like, where the guava fruit is made into a paste and shaped into a rectangle bar about an inch or so thick. It's then cut into slices and placed between a bread roll. Quite good, actually, if you prefer gummi bears between bread, or jello *ala* roll. It fills you up fast. That's important, to keep the belly full.

Another hour or so went by. I was so tired of sitting that I got up and walked out the front door, much to Alfredo's fear and the wrath of the front desk officer.

"You should not be so bold," cautioned Alfredo.

"This entire scene is ridiculous. We've done nothing wrong, and I'm just outside the doorway."

I watched some people hanging out in the town square enjoying themselves at the local *cantina* across the street.

A poster of Havana's top officials hung on the east wall, looking more like mug shots of some most wanted list than politicians. From time to time, I could hear the head man on the phone in his office in the back calling out my name and passport number. I figured he was on the line with someone at the capital. Didn't know I was that important...

Emerging, he was stone-faced as he spoke with Alfredo.

"The *Commandante* want to know when and where you arrive in the country." I supplied the answer, to which was given to the officer with another reply. This one had to be good, I imagined. Alfredo looked like he had lost a little color in the cheeks, as he announced, "You name no' on passenger lists on any of the flights."

Isn't it amazing how incredible the mind can assimilate vast amounts of information in order to come to a quick and reasonable conclusion, working out the best method for all parties?

The process of my mind went something like this when confronted with the latest news...Summary: hard looks, powdered drink that looks like cocaine, drug smuggler, airport by the lighthouse, no record coming into Havana. Situation: dead man. Solution: *Mucho big cojonas!*

"This is bullshit," I screamed, getting into the *Commandante's* face, a finger pointed at him for good measure. "I'm an American! I've done nothing wrong! I flew into Havana. Now get back on that phone to the airport and have them check it out further."

Alfredo interpreted about as fast as I was screaming, and we added that he could also check out the institution where Alfredo works and my past host, the Ministry of Sport. And he could have his superior in Havana make a phone call to Rafael Noriega in Washington, DC, to verify who I was.

The officer was quite calm as he exchanged words with Alfredo who repeated them back to me. "He say we need permission from Ms Rosa Elena Simeon, the Minister of Environment, to be here."

"Tell him we were not aware of this when we left Havana, and I would just love to sit down and have a talk with her about some serious pollution going on in this country."

Alfredo was evidentially tactful in his interpretation, the calm response being, "He say it will probably be until tomorrow for your story to check out."

"Tell him we're tired. We want a place to sleep."

More words were exchanged and Alfredo's identification book was given back to him. My passport, however, was confiscated.

"He say no' can afford to keep us here, but to go to the *Hotel Ascencion* up the road. He will call them to say we will be there."

I stood my ground a moment, looking the *Commandante* in the eye. "Cheaper to keep my passport, huh, pal?"

We retrieved our gear and headed out the door to a waiting crowd, curious about our plight. It seems we had caused much excitement in *Maisi* that Friday night. I imagined they were thinking how not only had an American not been in their part of the country for as long as anyone could remember, but he ends up getting arrested, causing much speculation and vain imaginations-- to which I probably added to them by refusing to speak with anyone.

Alfredo and I got on our bikes and rode the two dark miles to the hotel-- another dive that needed to be badly condemned. No one ever said my life was boring.

The only hotel in town, the *Ascencion* was of old architecture. It had become dilapidated over the years and mainly used by locals by the hour or the day. The tiled foyer was large, and a grand staircase went to the top floor of the two-story building. A long reception desk stood near the entrance, over which a pair of women-- one younger, the other older-- posted watch. Business didn't look to be that good, I noted, as we checked in.

The women tried to be pleasant by striking up a conversation with us, but I wasn't in the mood for anything except sulking.

Alfredo was more talkative, as he was relieved of the ordeal we had just gone through, and suggested we each have a shot of rum or two before retiring to our room in order to relax and help us sleep better. The younger woman poured, while I paid the 20 *pesos* for the two large rooms to the older one.

The bikes were supposed to stay in the lobby, but I refused, so for me they made a special waiver, because they didn't really want to be responsible for a piece of machinery that was worth more than the entire town.

"The young *senorita* say she will show us to our rooms," smiled Alfredo, as he downed his first shot of rum quickly.

"Wonderful," I deadpanned. "I am looking forward to being shown my room by such a beautiful escort."

Alfredo interpreted my response, and laughed at the young lady's reply to me. "She say she have a boyfriend."

"If I want to get laid, I'll ask her directly. Why don't you interpret that for me?" I incited.

The girl asked Alfredo what I said, to which he diplomatically shook his head. We finished our drinks, and then followed our escort upstairs.

Each room had a large, double, sagging bed-- the springs nearly popped through-- which sat on a cold, concrete floor. The sheets were stained with whatever your imagination allowed; I spread my own cloth on top. There was a large refrigerator ready for drinks and food as well as a chest of drawers with a vanity mirror. The bathroom had a shower and toilet that didn't run, but the hotel staff did provide two five gallon buckets for bathing and flushing. There was no sink. To access the 60-watt lightbulb in the middle of the room, we would have to connect the wires. Being electrocuted once in my life, I avoided this, but Alfredo was brave enough to do the honors.

His room was basically the same as mine, the exceptions being that he had a sink in the bathroom (which really didn't matter since nothing ran anyway), and he had no light at all. Both rooms had open windows. I had noticed that most Cuban homes did not have glass in the windows, but slabs of wood about half an inch thick by about four inches wide, fitted into the framework and connected by a pole that the people simply lowered or raised to close or open, much like you would do with blinds. On our windows, some of the wooden pieces were missing or smashed, so the mosquitos came and went whenever they felt like it. But we did have our trusty repellant with us for a good night's sleep.

When we were settled in, Alfredo said, "I go back into town to buy some food for tomorrow, since we will be leaving early, and nothing will be opened."

"Very optimistic, aren't you?" I asked, handing him some money. "I would get lonely without my passport."

As I took a cold sponge bath, I felt completely drained of life as I reflected upon the day's events and the course this Tour had taken thus far.

In three days and six trucks we reached the end of the Cuban world-- an adventure in itself, really-- only to be arrested upon arrival. I have been arrested at least once per tour, so I figured it would happen while in Cuba, but not on the first day. This was a bad sign. At least in China, I was arrested on the last day, and on **American Summits,** it was more or less in the middle. Evidently, I was off to a great start. And surely word had reached certain people back in Havana, most notably Alberto and Palaez. If I thought I had a chance of meeting Castro upon our return to the capital, it was all but blown now. I felt bad about the situation, but when you don't know the rules, what are you supposed to do? The main concern was getting the job done; to finish the Tour. That's the ultimate goal; the main reason I came. We hit a snag, but it had been dealt with and by the next day it would be behind us.

That was a comforting thought to me as I lay atop my sheet. The temperature on my watch read a comfortable 75-degrees.

Many hotels I've stayed at made you feel welcomed by placing baskets of fruit and cookies, homemade jams and jellies or flowers in your room. At the *Ascencion* all rooms were supplied with a packet of three condoms, which I would've gladly traded for hot running water. But, hey! what a great deal for 45 cents, and such a comforting thought to sleep on.

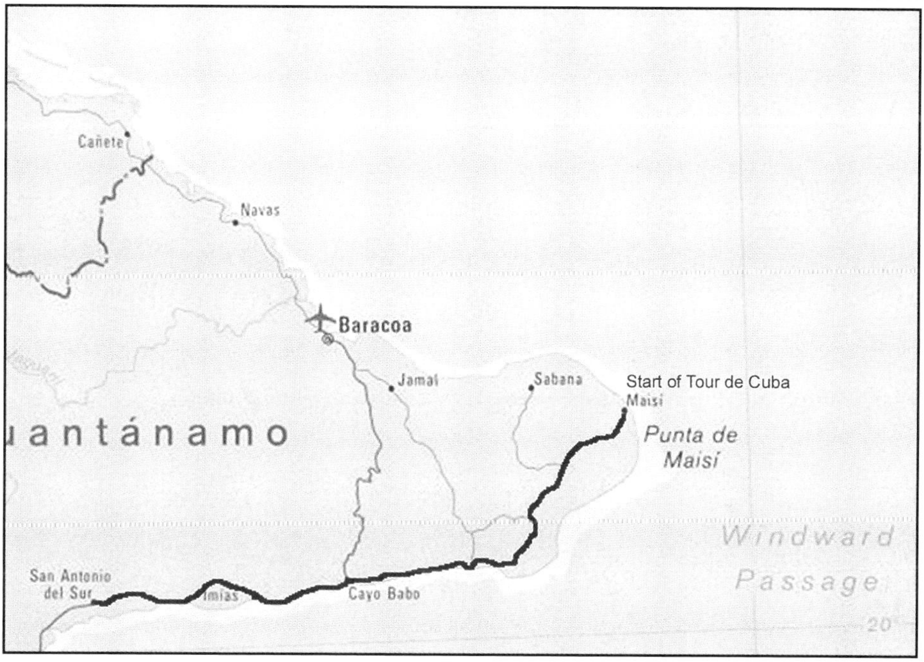

DIEZ

10

MAISI to SAN ANTONIO DEL SUR
DAY 2
NOVEMBER 22, 1997

DAILY DISTANCE : 55 miles or 91.7 kilometers
TOTAL DISTANCE : 63 miles or 105 kilometers

Originally, when Alfredo and I were planning out the Tour's schedule, we initially said we would rise at 4am and begin an hour later, so that we could get in the most miles before the heat of the day overwhelmed us. But being placed under arrest and having my passport confiscated on the first day was not part of the plan, which meant a delay-- in this case, one of more than three-hours.

As we made our way back to the police station, I began to think how today was the 34th anniversary of president John F. Kennedy's assassination. For some people back home, it's considered a national day of mourning, while in many parts of Cuba, the loyal Fidelists celebrate with cheers for the death of the man who had tried at one point to kill their beloved leader. I suppose it's just how you look at a given situation, and what part of the world you happen to be in at the time.

By 8am, the *Commandante* returned my passport with an apology that everything must be checked out. "*Maisi* is the last point on the island and is very susceptible to drug trafficking." He gave a nervous laugh. "You don't find many Americans in these parts."

"*Si, si*," I nodded in controlled understanding and patience as I pocketed my passport for a quick retreat.

He asked Alfredo a question, to which my partner replied in nervous laughter, shaking his head.

Alone, I asked, "What was that all about?"

Alfredo blushed. "He want to know if you were the famous movie actor."

Outside the police station, many of the town's children had gathered around my bicycle, a common occurrence on tours such as these. As I approached them, an authoritative voice called out, barking an order that made them scatter to several dump trucks. They packed themselves in like cheerful cattle about to be shipped off to the slaughterhouse, and began to sing songs, laugh, and call out for me to take their pictures as the trucks drove them off in the direction of the lighthouse.

"What's going on, Alfredo?"

"During the weekdays, while adults go to work, the children attend school, but today, Saturday, everyone, including the children, work for the country."

The area was well-known for its coffee crop, so the children helped in the fields with their parents, turning over their day's labor to the government. They didn't grumble or complain, but merely accepted this as a fact of life, that all must work for the benefit of the good. Cuba doesn't have a welfare system as we know it in the States.

"And on Sunday, it day of rest for everyone," smiled Alfredo.

"Except us."

"*Si*. But then we no' work for the government."

"*Si*. Spoken like a true Capitalist."

I couldn't imagine Americans doing that sort of thing on Saturdays. Yet these people accepted it as a part of life. They're content with what they have-- and that showed when they would give generously of their meager material possessions or manual labor.

Taking some final photos of the town, a woman called out to us from her front door, offering us rich, hot, black coffee produced from the area's crop. It was the best I had ever tasted in my life. And it was breakfast. Not only for us, but most of the townspeople as well.

"*Imias* is about sixty kilometers away, and there are no restaurants until then, so we must leave quickly."

After taking the last of the "start" photos, we packed our gear, thanked our hostess for her generosity, and began the rollercoaster ride to *Cayobabo*.

Along the dirt road, jungle route, we passed a small group of people carrying multi-layered, white-frosted cakes in hand, preparing for a wedding that day. There

Everyone, including the children, work for the government on Saturdays.

was such joy in their faces, I couldn't help but wonder if these people had to save all year in order to arrange such a feast.

Within the hour, we were working our way out of the dense, emerald brush into what I can only describe as an open-aired cathedral. The Caribbean Sea stretched out far below us like a blue mirror, sparkling in the warm sunshine. Virgin, white sandy beaches invited us to inhabit them, and from our lofty vantage point, we could see for miles the Paradise that will someday be overcrowded with resorts and tourists.

With an elevation of over 3000 feet we were at one of the highest levels we would reach on the tour.

I love a good downhill. I love speed, and so we were starting off this tour the right way. At first, Alfredo and I were hesitant, egging each other on with, "You first" gestures, because neither one of us were wearing helmets or any other body protection, except thin shorts and shirts.

When you're staring down the barrel of a 3000-foot drop, it's normal to become queasy. And as for me not wearing a helmet, I never liked them in the first place. My longtime sponsor Bell, didn't want to be a part of this Tour (nor any other helmet company to be fair), and when you begin to attain such speeds as we were doing, a helmet doesn't matter. Now I've done it. I've broken my image as a role model and have made people mad. Keep reading though, I'm sure you'll find other things to criticize as well.

We began slowly, testing out our brakes on the loose gravel. Alfredo would follow a slight distance behind, then ride up beside me, meeting my cautious eyes with his. He'd pass me, then I to him, then he to me, until our fear of splattering the

Freshly baked cakes for a festive wedding celebration.

road with our flesh and blood was replaced by our competitiveness.

The weight was with him, so he eventually pulled past me, as I found a comfortable, tucked-in, aerodynamic position which allowed me to keep up. I watched the computer's figure soar upward to a final reading of 45.5mph -- the second highest speed I've ever recorded in my career as a bicyclist-adventurer-explorer (the highest, 52mph, was in 1994 on the slopes of Hawaii's highest natural point, Mauna Kea during the **American Summits** tour).

Alfredo and I would barely reach the 45mph mark a few more times during the tour, but never past what we did this first full day. We were on a rollercoaster rush all the way to *Cayobabo*.

Just outside that seaside town, we came across an inlet of fresh water where a group of women were washing their clothes. They laughed and sang while some of their children played off to the side. They were in shorts and T-shirts, their dirty clothes in wet piles beside them. For freshness and cleaning, aloe vera plants were in constant use as they scrubbed the cloth, soaked the material, and beat the dirt out onto the rocks.

"This a good place to stop and do our wash," announced Alfredo, dismounting. He began to rummage through his side packs for all the dirty clothes he could find. We both had a pile after the last couple of days.

As we approached, the women became subdued and quiet, looking over toward me and then glancing to where their children were. I stayed at a reasonable distance so as not to scare them away. I realized at this end of the island, rarely is

Some of the women outside the town of *Cayobabo* helping me wash my clothes in the nearby river.

there any type of foreigner. Alfredo, on the other hand, was bold, literally jumping right into the river near the female crowd and got busy doing his wash, whistling while he worked.

Curious by my appearance a few of them began a conversation with Alfredo, to which I would hear the word *Americano* being said several times. I figured he was telling them about our tour and where I was from, as I tried to figure out the proper method of river washing my soiled clothes.

One of the ladies, a big-busted, husky native took pity on my cleaning methods. She boldly broke away from her female companions and wadded to me, offering her assistance by snatching the wet shirt from my hands and cleaning it herself.

"*Gracias*," I gratefully accepted.

Soon, a few other *senoritas* joined their friend, and, I had a happy little harem doing the work for me. Needless to say, I felt like Tom Sawyer-- watching others whitewash the fence while I sat back and admired the work.

A pack of goats came by to check out the activities and take a drink of the cool, fresh water, while Alfredo finished his load and was arranging the clothes on his bike, draping them where he could to dry. Shortly thereafter, the women were through with what few articles I had.

"*Gracias, gracias*," I said, bowing to their giggles and laughter.

I reached into my jersey's back pocket to produce some *pesos,* but the women just shook their heads and hands in protest.

"Alfredo, ask them to please take the money for their help. It would please me."

He did, and they still refused. "They say, it was their pleasure to help you. That is payment enough."

"*Gracias,*" I repeated, bowing to them once more. They did, however, agree to take some photos with me.

We arrived in *Cayobabo* near the noon hour. The temperature was nearing the triple-digit mark, and there was still no food to be found.

Alfredo was used to the heat and lack of fuel for the engine. I wasn't. He was a workhorse going on sheer will power. I couldn't. He pushed himself because he never expected anything from anyone in return, whereas someone from the *Land of Opportunity* was taught that if you worked hard, you'll get ahead in life. To look at Alfredo, one wouldn't think he could drive himself ever further. From my own poverty-ghetto experiences growing up, I understood that drive, and if Alfredo could've been given the chance when he was younger, he would've made a great professional cyclist.

Fortunately, the Lord blessed us in *Cayobabo*. We came upon a man in town that happened to have an abundance of homemade banana ice-cream he had just finished making. Our resting place was under a shaded tree just across the street from his house, so when he viewed our heated, exhausted condition, he emerged with the welcome treat. For a *peso* a serving, we would take all that he could supply. It was cool. It was refreshing. It was a life-saver until we could reach *Imias* a couple of hours later.

And then the party began-- or was that festival?

What we saw coming through that part of the area the previous day was still going strong. The main street was blocked off to traffic. People were laughing and dancing in the streets, milling about to and fro, checking out the vendors' merchandise that lined both sides of the sidewalk. Others waited for the homemade ice-cream and cotton candy that was being churned out, and children were running about, waiting to join their friends on the mechanical rides. In all my red, white, and blue glory, I seemed to fit right in.

My attention was more directed toward food, and where we might be able to acquire some, when Alfredo called out. Off to the side, at one of the many beer booths where he was quenching his thirst, he motioned me to join him and the owner.

"This man, Aturro, I met last night at the police station. He say he know a good place to eat."

Although he could neither speak nor understand English, Aturro nodded in agreement as though he knew what we were talking about. Even engaged in conversation, he still scanned the crowd passing by his booth, calling out to a younger man to keep the beer flowing while he personally escorted us to the establishment.

Aturro was my height, but stocky in build, and reminded me somewhat of the singer Aaron Neville. A jolly, happy sort of individual. As we headed toward one of the (supposedly) better restaurants of *Imias* he seemed to know everyone in town, greeting them with hearty laughter and handshaking; slaps on the backs. Aturro had many ins and outs with the other local business owners, as shown when we entered the restaurant and our local guide was able to get us the best table in the place (that is, the one which was somewhat cleaner than the rest of the cheap, dirty linen-covered tables). The setting was casual. The flies seemed to outnumber the customers 10 to 1.

We took a table in the corner, where I positioned myself so I could keep an eye on my bike, locked outside. A small crowd-- as usual-- had gathered around it; and although there have never been any problems, I just couldn't help falling back on my East Coast street upbringing: You don't turn your back on anyone.

The main food for the people of Cuba is pork (the government keeps the beef), but my heart was set on fish. Cuba has plenty of that, too, but the people generally can't afford it.

"If you want something that is not on the menu, Aturro say he can get it for you," said Alfredo, with Aturro hunched low in his seat, nodding in agreement.

"Would the restaurant have fish?"

"*Si,*" nodded Alfredo. "It can be arranged."

He turned to Aturro, said a few words, then the big guy got up and headed toward the cashier, who went to the cook in the back.

When Aturro was gone, Alfredo turned to me and suggested, "Since we can pay in *pesos*, we should invite Aturro to eat with us."

I had already thought of the idea. Being from an Italian background, there would be no way I could eat in front of someone without sharing in like kind. So when Aturro returned to our table and said fish was being prepared for me, I gave the invitation, to which he bowed slightly, saying, "*Gracias*."

And with that he ordered another pitcher of beer.

For a couple of starving cyclists, the meal was manna from Heaven, though the only one we would have that day. A local white fish, breaded, with *congris*, fresh tomatoes and cooked banana.

Needless to say, we devoured the feast, downing it with pitchers of beer until we completely satisfied our cravings. The price came to 16 *pesos*-- roughly 64 cents. There were times, I remember, during the Tour when I could have bought everyone's meal in the place and never felt the pinch in my pocket.

Outside, we gathered to take keepsake photos. Aturro was trying to talk Alfredo into having us spend the rest of the day in town, where the evening would be even livelier, and much as I would have loved to take him up on the offer, we had a certain schedule to maintain. So many miles to log.

And the women in this town, as they were throughout the country, were getting to be a distraction. One young *senorita* strolled past us in shorts so tight and so revealing that it produced the desired effect. Aturro noticed this (the craned neck probably gave me away), and quickly decided to help his new *amigo* by offering to speak to the young lady on my behalf. Would I not wish to spend the rest of the day and perhaps the evening with such a lovely creature?

Just as he was within a shoulder's tap of her, I intercepted. "No, Aturro," I shook my head. "*Nada.*"

He looked at me wide-eyed, and then toward that lovely, pear-shaped backside that was walking away from us, and then back to me. "*Nada?*"

I looked at what was leaving, and sighed. "*Nada.*"

Aturro and Alfredo enjoying a beer during the carnival weekend in *Imias.*

He didn't believe me for a moment, as he took me by the arm, dragging me toward her. I dug in my heels.

"No, Aturro. No! Alfredo, help me out here."

My interpreter was laughing. "You no' need my help."

I stood in front of Aturro, blocking his path. "Wait, *por favor.*" He stopped and looked at me without emotion, waiting for me to say something.

"Alfredo, tell Aturro, I appreciate his hospitality with the lovely *senorita*, but we don't have time."

"We can make time for that," pointed Alfredo to the wet dream wonder, who was now just several feet away, talking with a group of other lovely ladies.

"Look, Alfredo, it's like this: you can't have sex anytime you feel like it."

"Why no'?"

Aturro was bobbing his head back and forth as though he were watching a tennis match, wondering what was going on between us.

"It's not like that in America."

"But we no' in America."

"And don't I know it," I moaned, rubbing my forehead. "In America, the men have been so castrated by the women, that we've become inept. We're no longer used to such forwardness."

He tried to convey what I was saying to Aturro, who looked at me in shock.

"Aturro ask how women in America castrate men."

"By their words, their actions. Women in America don't like to think of themselves as sex objects."

"But the women in Cuba enjoy men looking at them. They are vessels of pleasure for us."

"You're right. I should never return to America, but spend the rest of my life here, enjoying the many vessels with all the pleasure I could produce."

This entire scene was topsy turvy to my ingrained way of thinking. If I understood it correctly, the men of Cuba enjoyed sex as a national pastime, an inherent right. The women of Cuba viewed themselves as vessels of pleasure, and are thrilled that a man would crave them in such a way. So I could have any woman with just the snap of a finger. What was I missing here, and why would I ever want to return to the united States?

"What do you want to do?" asked Alfredo.

"You want to spend the night here?"

"If we do, we cycle over one hundred miles tomorrow."

"Exactly. Let's go."

We gave our thanks and bid our good-byes to our generous host, Aturro, and headed east toward the day's destination, *San Antonio del Sur*.

Of course, after spending two and a half hours in *Imias*, the leg muscles had cooled down considerably, and were not ready to go the final 20 kilometers (12 miles). The engine had become cold and was difficult to warm up again. This is why a cyclist cannot be stationary for long. On a Tour like this, lunch should be no more than 20 minutes. To rest longer than that, you may as well end it for the day This I would have done, but the thought of doing over a hundred miles tomorrow didn't sit well with me.

My legs protested this indignation until we reached our goal, but we took it slowly so as not to tear any muscles in our calves, thus ending up in bed for several days.

At *San Antonio del Sur* we were slapped with another calamity: There was no room for us at the inn. In fact, there was no inn at all for that matter. We either had to make a deal with one of the locals or cycle another ten miles to the nearest campsite.

The legs chose the former. I rested at an outdoor *cantina,* while Alfredo made the rounds to wheel and deal, returning a half-hour later. "We can have an entire house for sixty *pesos.*"

"Done deal. Let's go." I tried to rise from the chair.

"It too much," he protested. "They rob us."

I sunk back down in my seat. "Does it have beds?"

"*Si.*"

"Is it comfortable and private?"

"*Si.*"

Coasting along the gravel road. In the background is the *Point de Maisi.*

"Does it have a bathroom and a place to bathe?"

"*Si.*"

"For less than three dollars?"

"But it too much..."

"Let's go."

The best part about the bargain was that it was only a mere 50 yards from where we were, for which my body was thankful.

I skipped the shower because I was too burned from the day's sun, and was satisfied enough from the late afternoon meal that I was ready to pass out.

A simple house on the main street of town. The living room area consisted of a table and some chairs. The two bedrooms were spacious-- the beds comfortable enough for anyone who was near comatose-- and the bathroom was just outside the door, past the family's future meal, the pig.

I performed the nightly ritual of placing photos of the girls, Jean and my *Lhasa Apsos, Hanzhu* and *Jia Tu,* near the bed, while listening to music from one of the half-dozen tapes I brought along. I felt like dead clay on the edge of the bed, my hacking cough still with me.

It was a 55-mile day, I reflected. That was something I hadn't done in years, I was sorry to admit, but for the moment, I felt good, the muscles strong. I wondered if I could keep that pace for the duration of the Tour, especially since Alfredo wanted to make *Santiago* sometime the next night. Judging by the map, we were in for a long, hard day. I knew from the outset, at least the last year, that although I didn't put in much training for this adventure, my body was strong-- in good enough condition that I estimated the first week of the ride would be bothersome at most. My body would fight me at first, but by the second week we should be in sync, and by the third and final week I would be back in as good of shape as I was during the Great Wall of China event.

I passed out to the sounds of *Silent Night.*

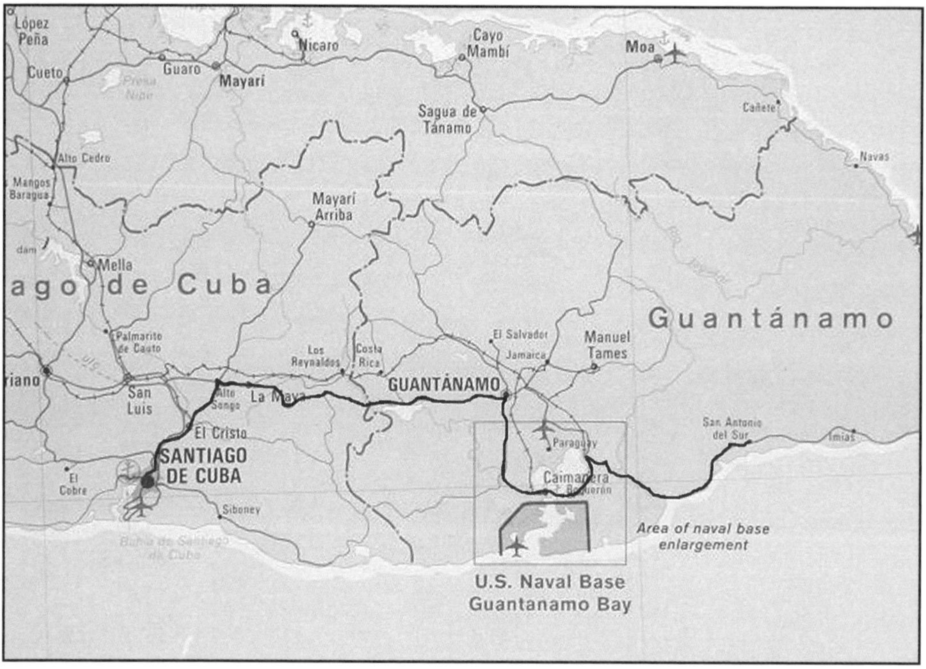

ONCE

11

SAN ANTONIO DEL SUR - SANTIAGO DE CUBA
DAY 3
NOVEMBER 23, 1997

DAILY DISTANCE :	**98 miles or 163.3 kilometers**
TOTAL DISTANCE :	**161 miles or 268.3 kilometers**

"The second full day of a tour always the most difficult, but in time you will get better," predicted my companion.

When I began to seriously lay out this Tour a couple of years before, I always had in mind an average of 40 miles per day. A good figure. Comfortable. Plenty of time to see the sights, relax, shoot photos and take notes.

But from the moment we awoke at 5am, Alfredo had a particular goal in mind and he was bound and determined to see it through.

I've seen that look in myself many times. Wide eyes. Frenzied, determined, methodical, going about my business. Hands shaking, voice quivering at the expected, reachable goal. It borders on sheer madness, and all anyone can do is stay out of my way. I knew then that I'd just have to get through it alive: This particular Sunday was not going to be a day of rest, but a kick-ass event.

"Just one more hill," would be Alfredo's encouraging theme throughout the day.

"You lie," I'd pessimistically shout back.

We left *San Antonio del Sur* at first light 6am, in the cool morning of the day. The sun was just beginning to rise behind our backs, and we were among the first people in the nation to see it shine.

My empty stomach was growling more than it had the day before-- we had at least had a small cup of coffee to feed upon. *Guantanamo* was 40 miles away, and we had nothing more than our water bottles and some vitamin E tablets to chew whenever the urge of hunger arose.

"Ah, we just go and find food when we can and drink water. Too much in the stomach is no good," said Alfredo, practicing what he preached.

"Why don't you try some of this energy drink I was almost arrested for?"

"Water is good."

"But this has carbohydrates that will take the place of hunger," I advised.

"But if you no' think of food, you no' feel hungry," countered Alfredo.

"You would've made a great professional cyclist if you were only given the chance."

"*Si*."

"But listen, Alfredo, when you sweat, you lose electrolytes; energy, it needs to be replaced."

"But if you no' think about..."

"Will you shut up and try it!"

He did. And that was a mistake. From the moment he took his first drink of the clear, cool, sweet liquid, he couldn't get enough of it. From then on, the next problem was in trying to ration it, so that we'd have enough to last until the end.

Going along the coast was always pleasant. I could never tire of the scenery and the sound of the waves crashing along the shore. It kept the mind in a stable, steady cadence, like my music did for me at the end of a long day. Time and miles disappeared. The trick in a long tour is to never look at the whole, but the individual day instead. Make a game of it, marking your continual moving line forward on the map, recording the mileage. This was the most fun at the end of the day; I always felt as though I had accomplished something worthwhile.

Whether in life or in my job-- such as these seemingly impossible Tours-- whenever I need to get through some task, the constant thought; my mantra is: *This won't last forever, this won't last forever, this won't last forever...it'll eventually end one way or the other.*

Those four simple words, *This Won't Last Forever*, keeps me focused at the task at hand, because really, nothing lasts forever, not even one's own life. Bad things that happen to you can't last forever-- though neither can those at the other end of the spectrum.

I do these Tours, sometimes risk my life, to seek God's face. When the routine of life begins to bore me, it is then that I need to seek Him out, to renew my faith. I have my faults just like everyone else, but I realize it's all a part of growing and that this life...won't last forever.

So I take it all in, and I encourage others to do the same. Once around the merry-go-round, boys and girls. Grab those brass rings while you can, and know that your Creator is nearby to pick you up when you fall, to brush you off, give you a hug, and send you on your way.

What can I do to better this world while I'm here? I constantly ask myself. From the outside, riding a bicycle in various countries around the world doesn't look like much, I agree, but on a deeper level, countries that I do choose-- places that do not attract the tourists out of fear induced by the media or threats posed by their governments-- cause me to explore them. Can I advance the cause of Christ and peace? If a bicycle, a mode of transportation that's in every country on this planet, can act as a symbol, then so be it.

Somewhere along the 40-mile way to our first major city, we came across tough-looking buzzards sitting on a fence, steadily watching government cows from a safe distance, while some military boys were going about their maneuvers. We watched them doing their drills for a while.

"It is best that we move on," cautioned Alfredo, nervously eyeing the boys and their bayonets. "If we stay much longer, we may be arrested."

At another section, goats occupied a three-walled, concrete-covered bus stop, seemingly waiting for the next ride. Throughout the countryside of Cuba, we'd see goats roaming about everywhere-- just as mischievous, cocky, and arrogant as their American cousins. They went where they pleased, doing what they pleased, until they were chased away.

About 10 miles outside *Guantanamo's* city limits, we came across a building marked, *Restaurante/Cafe.* These establishments dotted the entire length of our route, and nearly every time we stopped in the hope that something edible would be served-- not just the staple rum and cigarettes.

In this case, we were partially blessed with juice and one-pound bars of chocolate.

For a *peso* a cup, we could drink our fill. No matter how thirsty we were at any given time, Alfredo and I could never drink a dollar's worth-- 23 cups.

We also bought the one pound, half-inch thick chocolate bar for 20 *pesos*, or as Alfredo put it in more economic terms, "Two rooms at the *Hotel Ascencion* in *Maisi.*"

Upon knowing I was from the united States, the owner's eyes lit up, his arms raised in a hallelujah praise, as he shouted, "Ah! *Americano!*" Bringing his arms down about me in a grand-fashioned hug.

"Please," he smiled. "Allow me to practice my English on you. It is rare for an American to visit my humble cafe."

"But, *senor,* are you not close to the military base?"

His eyes lit up again, and his moustache curled with his smile. "Ah, *si,* let

Arrogant goats waiting for a ride.

me show you something."

He took me by the arm, and lead me out the door, all the while asking me the usual questions of where I was from, how long I would be in Cuba, the length of tour I was undertaking...

Outside, he viewed the Beast propped against a side of his building's wall. He marvelled at the machinery, clasping his hands in worshipful prayer. "She is beautiful, my friend. Never before have I seen a bike like this!"

Then, taking me around the corner, I came across a plantmill on the water's edge. It took the Caribbean Sea and turned it into salt, but this was a usual sight for him-- the point of interest was beyond that.

"You cannot see from here, but just out there on the water's edge is the US military base." He smiled broadly as though he had just leaked a National security secret.

I knew we were about as close as we were ever going to get, but it was too far away to get a decent photo. Still, I liked the sea-salt making facility, so I readied the camera for some shots when a hand covered the lense. Every photographer hates that, but it turned out I was about to lay a fist on a policeman.

"No." He pointed a finger at me, shaking his head.

"Hey, pal, back off." I pointed a finger right back, proceeding to go about my business.

The brave soul stood in front of my view, continuing to shake his head. "No."

"You're asking to be hit, aren't you?"

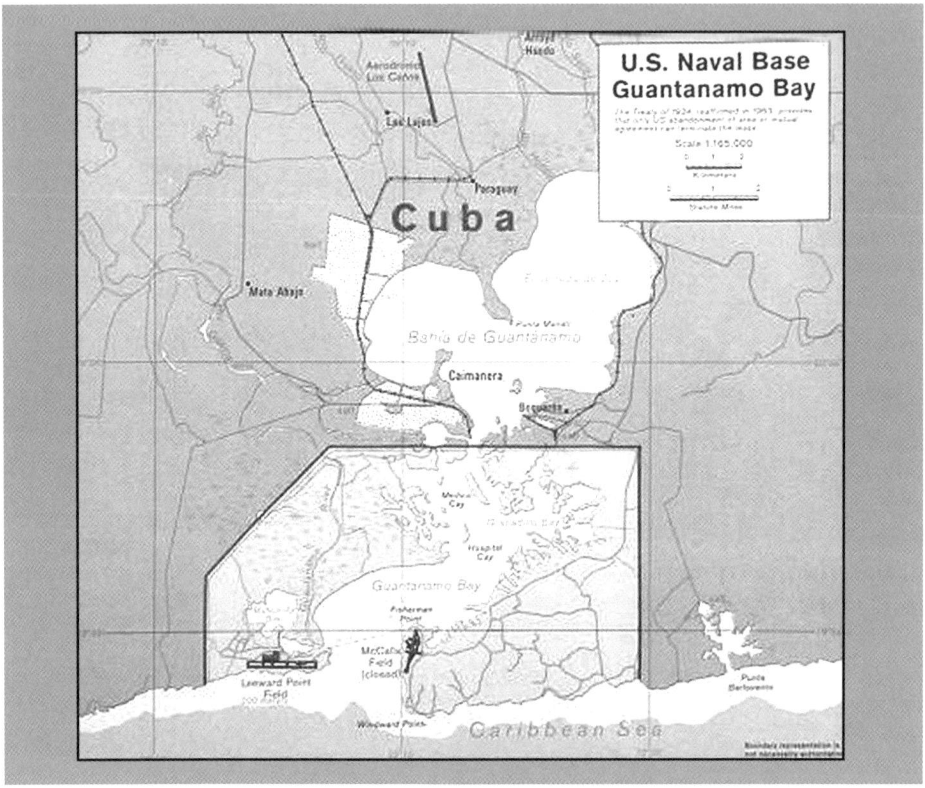

The proprietor began talking very fast in his native tongue, explaining who we were, that we were only taking pictures of the factory.

The patrolman wouldn't listen. Turning to Alfredo as interpreter, he shouted to me, "Identification! Now!"

"Get lost."

"*Kebin,* please, no make trouble," pleaded Alfredo, as he nervously handed him his little ID booklet that every Cuban must carry with them at all times, which contain their photo, ID government number, and vital statistics.

The officer glared at me, holding out his hand for my passport. I threw it at him, which hit his chest and fell to the ground. We stared at one another in a Mexican stand-off until Alfredo diplomatically picked-up my passport and handed it to the man in black.

As I began to pack away my camera and supplies, the officer explained to Alfredo, "Our government has a military compound nearby that keeps an eye on the American base. This is a very sensitive area to be in. It would be wise for you and this *Americano* to leave."

I thanked the owner for his hospitality. Shaking my hand, he bowed slightly, "I am terribly sorry for what happened here, my friend. Please, do not let it spoil your image of Cuba. We are a friendly people. We love Americans."

"I understand, my friend. It's alright."

As we got on our bikes to leave, the last image of the area we had was of the police officer shouting angry words at the owner.

"Don't you think it strange how that policeman just happened to show up out of nowhere?" I commented.

"Not so strange," replied Alfredo. "We are being watched throughout this Tour. Someone saw us coming here and reported us, that is all."

"Communists are so paranoid."

"You know," smiled Alfredo, changing the subject. "The American government pay Castro fifty thousand dollars a year to lease the land for the base, but because he no' like America, he never cash the check. When the lease expire, he going to throw them out."

Regardless of the constant reports of Castro's ill health, I can see why he intends to hold out long enough to redeem some satisfaction for all those times the American government tried to kill him. Revenge, in some cases, could be the miraculous remedy one needs to sustain his life.

By 10:30am, we arrived in the heart of *Guantanamo*. I was refreshed by the boost of energy from the chocolate and ready to find a place to relax and have a bite to eat.

That wouldn't be difficult. The center of town consisted of a Green, as we call them back in New England. A plot of grass in a large square shape with business establishments surrounding it.

A large, spartan, concrete monument adorned one side of town. It was devoted to the heroes Marti, Maceo, and Gomez of the Independence War of 1898. Much of the battle took place between *Cayobabo* and *Santiago de Cuba*, so there were many monuments and much history along the way. We were immersed in it, the many scenes depicted in murals and sculptures, monuments and sepulchres.

We found a large cafe that served juice, beer, pork, *congris*, bread, and other items-- all paid for in *pesos*. We filled our empty tanks before finding a place under some trees on the Green to nap.

"We rest awhile before we go to *Santiago*."

"How far do you think it is?" I asked.

Alfredo looked at the map. "Hmm, not more than one hundred kilometers."

"Sixty miles! That's another full day."

"*Si*. But we make up time we lose in Havana."

What was in our favor was the weather. With the cloud cover, the sun never had a chance to turn up the full heat. This was another reason to take advantage of the day and put in as many miles as possible.

As we were lying under the shaded tree, Alfredo commented, "If we could cycle one hundred kilometers a day, we would make up the lost time by the end of the Tour and never notice it."

"One hundred kilometers a day is doable. One hundred miles is not. I'd still be able to get in my photo shots and work on my notes."

This was just one of the mind games we played on ourselves to pass the time, but it could become a reality, we thought, and that excited us.

Leaving the first of 13 provinces behind!

The two hours we spent in *Guantanamo* were quickly gone before we found ourselves back on the road toward our next major city of the day. The rest proved beneficial. In the first hour we did 13 miles and averaged 10mph thereafter, as opposed to doing half that amount without rest.

"Look!" shouted Alfredo, pointing to the giant, concrete letters that spelled out the region's name. "We have reached the border of *Guantanamo*."

It was a mini-victory, as we took photos atop the hillside sign. We had just cycled through our first province-- only a dozen more to go.

We arrived at the outskirts of *Santiago* just as night fell, the last ten miles being all downhill. At any other time, that would be the reward after a long workday, but when you have to do it at night with no headlights, other cyclists and automobiles whizzing by you, and people walking along the side of the road, well... splashes and crashes danced in my head. I prayed for no pot-holes or bums to be in my direct path.

"You see! You see!" exclaimed Alfredo. "We have made it! We almost there!"

I could hear the little night-owl, but I couldn't see him. I was as blind as a bat without radar. Ordinarily, a ten-mile downhill would be a rush to a cyclist who's had to work nothing but uphill climbs all day. Since *Life* magazine printed the quote shortly upon my return from China, my motto has always been, "Work the uphills and pray for a good downhill." I ached to release the brakes and go fast so bad, but caution and landing in a Cuban hospital prevented me from doing it. No, rush of the wind for me this time. A complete waste of a good downhill and brake pads.

By 7pm we had reached Ida's first floor apartment. It was a welcome sight, mosquitoes and all. We had done 98 miles of mountainous terrain in 13 hours and survived.

"We only spent three dollars," I said to Alfredo.

"*Si*," he acknowledged. "We can do this Tour for less than one hundred dollars."

"Only if I stay away from those resorts."

"*Si*. It too expensive."

Whenever we didn't stay at resorts where we had to pay in dollars, our daily expenses would amount to roughly $3US; $5US at the most, and it would take an incredible amount of time and effort to spend $7US.

Alfredo was pleased to have reached his goal. "It good day today. We can do this everyday."

"No way, *amigo*," I said, shaking my head. "One hundred kilometer days, fine. But no more one hundred miles. Once is enough for me on this Tour."

Ida, a lovely sight to behold, dressed in modest apparel, shyly spoke with Alfredo, pointing toward our bedroom, before returning to the kitchen.

"She say, she wash our clothes while we were gone and clean the bedroom for us."

Turning toward Ida, I said, "*Gracias*." She smiled with laughing eyes and a crinkled nose, bowing slightly.

While Ida prepared us a meal of fish, *congris*, cucumber, and avocado, Alfredo and I, still hot from the ride, took cold showers and relaxed in the living room, watching a black and white documentary on the Beatles, the hottest musical group in Cuba at the moment.

Dressed in loose shorts and T-shirt, Alfredo asked, "What happened to your legs?"

He had noticed my scarred legs when we were cycling around Havana, but never felt comfortable asking about them. Now that we're together on a 24-hour, 7-day basis, he felt he could talk to me about whatever was on his mind.

"About thirty years ago, I got caught on a live, high tension wire thirty feet up, and was electrocuted."

"Shit," said Alfredo, in a dropped jaw.

"With sixty-five thousand volts and thirty amps running through my body, the electricity had to emerge somewhere. The holes throughout my body is where it came out."

"And you no' die?"

"Well...that's a matter of opinion. No one walks away from an accident like that without being changed. I had lost all memory since birth, and had to relearn how to walk again."

"You no' remember your mama and papa?"

"Not until the doctor told me who they were. The electrocution opened the door between this world and the ones beyond. I've been to Paradise and Hades. I've met Jesus and Satan. There's another life beyond this one, Alfredo. Believe it."

He sat across from me in stunned silence, mouth unable to close, taking in-- or trying to-- everything I was telling him. Ida noticed her friend's inanimate form from where she was a few feet away at the kitchen stove. She called out to him, asking what we were talking about. That seemed to jar him awake, as he repeated what I said.

She got so involved in the story, that she nearly burnt the food she was preparing for us. "*Madre de Dios*," she exclaimed, making the sign of the cross.

Shaking his head as though he were trying to wake from whatever dream he was having, he replied, "I no' believe. You make this all up."

"The charred holes that pierced through my body are real. I know what I saw was real. Don't ever let the Devil trick you into thinking that the hereafter is an illusion. We all must die, and where we end up for eternity will be real indeed."

"Then how come you curse and drink and like to have a good time? Christians no' do this kind of thing."

"I am not perfect. I am far from it. Most Christians want to be Jesus Christ. I have no desire to be."

"But you say you are a Christian."

"Yes. But like Jesus, the man. Not Jesus, the God. No one can be Jesus, the God. Jesus, the man knew how to laugh and cry and feel pain and compassion. His first recorded miracle was turning water into the best wine in town. He knew how to have fun. He knew how to live in the world, but not be a part of it. He understands the war we have between the flesh and the Spirit."

"I do not know," said my partner, shaking his head. "It is all too much for me."

"Sometimes it is for me as well. All I know is, Jesus died for you just like He died for me, because He loves us, and wants us to live with Him. We choose to ignore that, then we go where we belong...to Hell."

As Ida prepared the meal, Alfredo kept a running translation on what we were saying. She'd cross herself several times, and would nod in agreement.

We washed the meal down with soda, rum, and coffee. Alfredo told Ida and her neighbor, Marcella, who had joined us later on for drinks, stories of our last two days on the road, including my arrest in *Maisi.*

"...he a crazy man. He no' scared about being arrested. He tell the *Commandante* to go play with himself." Alfredo announced, making an obnoxious gesture with his groin.

The girls howled with laughter. I laughed along at Alfredo's antics as I sat semi-paralyzed on the couch, too tired to do much of anything else. My body was sore and stiff, my mind ready to shut down.

Marcella smiled at me, then spoke to Alfredo, who in turn translated. "She ask if you want a massage."

It was a tempting offer, and I dropped my guard momentarily when I answered, "*Si.*"

Being an American, and judging how aroused the Cuban women are by us, combining this with a massage would be entering dangerous territory. I should've called it off.

But it was already too late. Marcella left us, returning a few minutes later with some lotions and other supplies. We retreated to the spare bedroom, where I stripped to my shorts and let Marcella work her magic.

Late 30s and several inches shorter with reddish-brown hair to the neckline, Marcella had the strength to work out the tight spots and cramps where it needed it the most, the back and legs. I could feel her enormous energy revive and rejuvenate me. Somewhere along the way I wandered off to dreamland, neither understanding, nor caring a word Marcella was saying until I felt her breasts upon my shoulder blades.

Turning over, I saw her hovering over me with nothing more than a smile, trying to work off my shorts.

"Marcella, no, *por favor*," I begged, trying to whisper; Alfredo and Ida were just outside the door. I pointed in that direction, so she would understand.

She giggled, placing her finger to her lips, and laid down beside me. Snuggling close, she took my hand and placed it on a breast. I didn't have to understand what she was saying, because the body language was talking loud enough, and I knew if I had stayed in the current situation I was in much longer, I would've lost all control, audience or not. I hurriedly reached down for her clothes that laid beside the bed on the floor, and handed them to her.

She looked at me wide-eyed with a slight smile. "No?" she asked, shaking her head.

"*Si*," I answered.

She rolled on top of me, kissing passionately. *What a tongue*, I thought. *Yeah, I could get into this. Now, if Jean were here, I'd be totally safe. She's always been good at keeping other women away from me.*

"No?" she asked again, smiling.

I sighed. Sometimes it's great to be *of* the world.

While she got dressed, I left the room to avoid suspicion, covering my condition as best I could. I really needed a drink to relax me down to a normal level.

In fact, I needed a lot of drinks, practically keeping the bottle of rum to myself. Moments later, Marcella emerged looking as refreshed as I was tense, and the four of us (actually three, as I kept to myself) continued with stories until Marcella left for her own place-- but not before again trying to coax me with a look, a cock of the head (did I just say that?), and a smile into going with her.

When Marcella left, I went into the bedroom to gather my daily notes to work in the living room, while Alfredo got ready for bed. Ida walked in and began to smile bashfully. We couldn't figure out what it was until she pointed to a shelf above Alfredo's bed. There hung Marcella's bra.

Alfredo laughed, full and loud. "What did she do? Massage you with her breasts?"

"I have nothing to say on the matter," I stammered, leaving the room with blushed cheeks.

Alfredo was asleep well past midnight, when I finished my notes. As I was setting the papers aside, Ida emerged from her bedroom. Her white nightgown looked radiant against her creamy, brown skin; her shoulder-length hair was up in a 'do.

She seemed to half sleep walk toward me, placing an arm around my shoulder, looking to see what I had written-- though I knew she couldn't really speak English, let alone read the language.

She bent down to kiss me, and I felt my arms wrap around her slender figure. My fingers caressed her soft, velvety hair. Her fragrance uplifted my senses, making me drop my guard, as I held her closer, our lips pressed tighter. The combination of her perfume, the rum and my run-in with Marcella were all taking their toll. I felt myself wanting Ida in the most passionate of ways.

She straightened, walked toward her bedroom door, and turned to smile before disappearing into the darkness.

One-night stands are nothing more than a tease, I knew, and I detested them. Better to play with yourself than to love someone passionately for a brief moment, knowing that you'll never see her again in this life.

It's such a bullshit tug-of-war between the cursed flesh and the purity of the Spirit. Oh, how I wanted to make love and be loved. How I wanted to feel like a man again. Flesh upon flesh. Intertwined. Esoteric erotica. *You can have it, Kevin. It's all yours for the taking. Just follow what's behind door number one.* Screw you, you cursed imp!

With the bottle of rum before me, it was then I decided to play suicide and drink myself into oblivion.

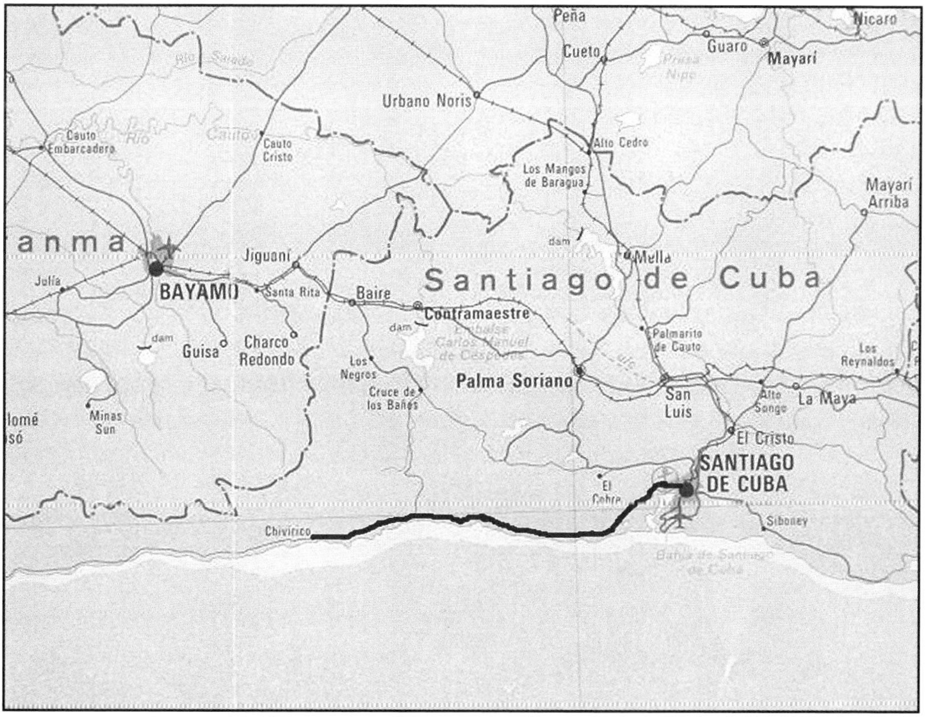

DOCE

12

SANTIAGO DE CUBA to CHIVIRICO
DAY 4
NOVEMBER 24, 1997

DAILY DISTANCE : 45 miles or 75 kilometers
TOTAL DISTANCE : 206 miles or 343.3 kilometers

Alfredo was up and ready to go by what had become the usual 6am departure time. I, on the other hand, was slightly inebriated, having lost to a bottle (or was that two bottles?) of rum, coupled with very little sleep. Getting me revved for the day's journey ahead was taking a Herculean effort on my companion's part.

"Come. We have much territory to cover today," begged Alfredo, grabbing

With Ida outside her place in *Santiago de Cuba.*

my arm and pulling me up like a winch.

"Alright, alright," I moaned. "Just give me a few minutes." And then crashed back into the soft mattress.

"This no' good. You need to go to bed early."

"We need to do less miles."

Ida was somewhat drowsy herself. Stumbling toward the kitchen, banging into walls along the way, as she made a full pot of Cuba's strong, kickass coffee.

By 8am, I was coherent enough to be placed on my bike and pointed in the right direction. I looked like I felt.

Ida, on the other hand, looked stunning in her workday uniform. She took care of the administrative duties of the apartment complex; her office was just next door. Staying to romance her would be a pleasant distraction, as we said our good-byes. I thanked her for her hospitality and was on my way. At some point during the day, when Alfredo and I were long gone, she would find the ten dollar bill I left for her on the bedroom dresser. In my mind, it really wasn't enough for all that she had done for us, but then to Cuban thinking, it was a month's pay.

Santiago de Cuba's monstrous grave site monument to Josi Marti, Cuba's National Hero. Marti lies in a flag-draped coffin, above ground, just under the pillars.

Santiago is significant in Cuban history. Within a mile after leaving Ida's place, we came across the town's cemetery; and my eye caught a four-story tombstone honouring the person buried beneath it, Josi Marti, one of the gods of the island.

It was hexagon-shaped in gray stone masonry, with statues carved into the corners of the building as though standing guard from coming invaders. Six arches decorated the bottom portion, with four sets of stairs at the corners. A base divided the tower and the ground floor; the ground floor was reserved for Marti's shrouded coffin. The entrance was lined with stone pillars on each side of the walkway, standing as somber silent guards. There were palm trees just outside the structure. In Cuba, as in parts of New Orleans, burials are placed above ground, the coffins sealed in decorative stone. By far, Marti's memorial was the largest I had seen throughout the Tour, and I wondered what Che Guevara's would be like now that his bones were returned from Bolivia after 30 years. I cannot imagine what Castro's will eventually become when he departs this world. Those three men could be considered the Father, Son and Holy Ghost of their country, so much are their personalities intertwined with the people.

Alfredo pointed west from Marti's grave, saying, "A few miles from here is the Moncada Army Barracks, where Fidel began his assault on Fulgencio Batista's government."

"Ah, the infamous July 26th (1953) Movement."

"*Si*. Fidel and his men were captured and sent to prison for two years. When he was released, he go to Mexico to form another revolutionary group."

"Which landed a year later in the *Sierra Maestra* mountains just outside of town."

"*Si*. We will be passing their headquarters sometime today or tomorrow."

"So, one dictator was replaced by another."

"*Si*. That is the way it is."

We continued on the rollercoaster terrain from the previous day's route, maintaining a parallel to the southern coast. Because of this, the highest point of our climb was 190 feet; the average for the day being a mere 30 feet. In my hangover condition, it was a blessed relief.

"If we can make the base of *Pico Turquino* today, you will be able to climb Cuba's highest point tomorrow."

"Good-luck," I moaned, my legs straining to keep up with Alfredo's maddening pace.

"We can do it!" He raised his fist in victory.

"You lead, I'll try to follow," I belched.

Ever since the **American Summits** tour, I'd been fascinated with nations' highpoints. At 6542 feet in elevation, *Pico* was doable, another first to bring a bicycle to its summit.

"How far do you think we have to go to get there?" I asked the expert, as we kept a fair cadence along the shore.

"Hmm, I say no more than one hundred kilometers."

"Sixty miles? Are you crazy? Where did you pull that figure out of?"

"It true. More or less."

In reality it was 135 miles from *Santiago de Cuba*.

"No way. Even if you're right, I can't go that far. Not in my condition. I don't have it in me."

With each crash of the waves against the shore, my head pounded like an off-key church bell. Just the motion of the water if viewed long enough made me queasy. By the time we reached *Santiago's* city limits, it was 9am, the temperature at 90 degrees. This had disaster written all over it, with all the proper combinations in order for me to take a serious fall.

Trying to shake off my desire to vomit, I escaped into my mind, as Alfredo pulled farther away.

According to the map, *Chivirico* was the next major town at 45 miles away. *Pico* another 15 (or so we thought) after that. My butt, hands, and feet were beyond numb, and I wondered if I could get permanent nerve damage. I cursed myself for not training: My mind was more confident than my physique. My years as an adventurer were catching up to me. I had become over-confident, thinking of Cuba as a mere joy ride. I had begun to believe in my own publicity. And now I was paying for it. Only my fear of failure was keeping me from cashing in my chips and checking out.

Alfredo obviously felt none of what I was going through. To my envy, he cycled carefree-- laughing and singing-- enjoying the current surroundings. At times, he would outpace me by more than a mile and beyond. All I could do was watch him grow smaller and smaller. He was a racehorse that had to be let loose to fly. I wasn't particularly worried about losing him since there was only one road along the coast. When he wanted to, he'd stop and wait until I caught up.

Small cemeteries dotted the road along the coast. Some gated, others in the open space; some buried underground, others above. All were marked with crosses of various materials, from wood to concrete, and adorned with colorful pieces of material, beads, and flowers from their families.

As we stood between the quaint little burial grounds and the sea, my historian and tour guide explained, "About a hundred years ago, only a single ship per week would sail along the coast, picking up the sick to take to the closest hospital."

"In *Santiago?*"

"*Si.* Usually, or *Guantanamo.* Sometimes the people couldn't wait and traveled along the coast. If they die along the way, then they were buried where they fall. All these crosses and monuments you see along the shore are a reminder of the people's hardships they face."

"Not all that different now, is it?"

"No. We still fight. Fight all the time," Alfredo's voice raised in pitch along with a clenched fist. "Fight slavery, inbreeding, prison, dictators..."

"Embargo."

"*Si.* Embargo. Each revolution make new laws, new government. We poor, but we fight."

"Someday you will become a Capitalist and be fat and lazy as many Americans. You will exchange your fighting Spirit for material comforts."

"When Fidel die, many changes will take place for my people. Our children may have a better life."

"And that could be good."

"*Si.* Or no'."

As we stood along the shore paying silent homage to the people who lived in these mini necropolises, we realized how close we were to a transition phase. The areas we were cycling through today, tourism doesn't exist, along with its aftermath...sewage, crowds, and corporate garbage spewing the pristine beaches. We were on roads where you won't see another soul in any mode of transportation for hours on end.

One reminder of the present did hit us in the form of graffiti. On a section of cliff, painted in huge yellow letters, were the words *Helms-Burton Act, No Good. Jesse Go Home.* The embargo's reality, it appears, reached all areas.

For days after leaving Havana, my diet consisted of a combination of various foods, fruit juices, ice cream, and rum. Coupled with the rising temperatures, hilly terrain, and the motion of the waves, it finally caught up with me. I had to pull off to the side and vomit, heaving out liquids. My stomach twisted and turned in knots.

There was a golf course-green park along a section of well-manicured beach where I could stop. Many couples were at the *playa* (beach) with their children; teenagers off to a secluded swimming hole. Alfredo and I found some shaded trees and set our blankets on the ground.

As I lay down to rest on the soft, cushiony grass, staring out onto the reflecting sea, I saw my ever-busy companion eye me over. Seeing that I was alive and relatively responsive, he pulled out a notebook and began compiling his daily notes.

"In the first two hours we only do 15 miles," complained Alfredo.

"I know. I'm sorry. The heat is stifling."

"*Si*. But it worse in summer. Many people who come to Cuba canno' take our heat."

"We're not going to make it to *Pico*. I can't."

"*Si,*" reflected Alfredo, looking out toward the horizon, the waves crashing against the rocks. "We do many miles yesterday. We no' do so much today."

"It won't be like this, Alfredo, I promise. It's just this first week is rough. I'll get better."

"It okay. You rest. I work on my notes."

Filled with disappointment and anger over myself, I turned to my side and promptly passed out. Alfredo woke me a couple of hours later. It was early afternoon, and the temperature had climbed to the triple-digit, ear wax melting mark, sapping the last of anyone's energy. If we were ever going to get in our daily quota of miles, we'd either have to begin cycling at first light, or I'd have to get used to this chocking heat that could knock you out like a furnace.

We continued at a fairly good pace, but the 100-plus degrees was still bearing down on me and I had to stop every half-hour to catch my breath. Alfredo would be only a short distance away, looking back from time to time, stopping when I did. If he wanted to make me feel better, the least he could have done was vomit whenever I had to.

Poor Alfredo, I thought, as he'd wait patiently every time for me to resume. I felt like an anchor slowing down a racehorse. Because of my condition, he was forced to be an inchworm.

"I'm sorry, I'm sorry," I kept saying each time we stopped. "The heat, the heat..."

He'd nod in understanding. "It okay. In summer, even I canno' ride. It so hot, it impossible."

Thoughts of cycling through the 130 degree Gobi Desert during the **Great Wall Tour** flashed in my mind. At least I was prepared for that, dammit! I knew what I was up against and trained for it. I took this Tour too light, and only the strength of my mind, and my fear of failure would see me to the end.

"I ride ahead," said Alfredo. "I know of a hotel nearby and will make arrangements. We take it easy today, and do better tomorrow."

"Okay. I'll follow along."

It took another three hours for me to reach our day's distance. I came across Alfredo waiting for me at the entrance to the *Hotel Guama*. It was a resort for Cubans, which meant, if accepted, we could pay in their currency.

With our four-stamped, official-looking government document in hand and a pair of brass *cojonas,* Alfredo marched into the office to work his magic. I imagined he was always figuring the more money he could save me, the more he'd get paid.

Even though Alfredo never mentioned price when we talked about his services, I had already determined in my mind that if he got me through his country, I was going to pay him handsomely, so I left more than enough at his mother's place to cover any unforeseeable expenses.

This hotel was strictly for Cubans that paid in their own currency. According to government rules and regulations, foreigners were not allowed access to fellowship with the natives in resort areas, and vice-versa.

As Alfredo explained, "Cuba has an incentive program for all the workers. If you do your job well, or more than your share, your boss promote you with some luxury."

"No extra money to let them buy what they want?"

"No. They receive coupons for maybe, a new bicycle, extra food rations, or a weekend at a resort like this. If a foreigner come along, then sometimes they can stay if the owner feel like it, but then they have to pay the same in dollars, not *pesos*."

Case in point with the *Hotel Guama*: The fortunate, hard working Cubans paid 15 *pesos* per person, per night, per room. Because I was a rich American (we're all rich, you can't fight the myth), I was expected to pay the same in dollars.

However, we had a special, government sealed document, which meant that if the owner were sympathetic to our cause in why we were doing this Tour, then he could permit us to stay a night at the *peso* price.

The *Hotel Guama* was out in the middle of nowhere, on a desolate part of the coast. The sun was beginning to get low on the horizon. If Alfredo couldn't talk his way through this one, I'd have to cough-up $30 for us, else ride through the night until we found some area to rest.

"The owner say okay," informed Alfredo, when he emerged from the front office. "We can pay for the room in *pesos*, but he will have to charge us dollars for dinner."

And the only restaurant in the area was the one owned by the *Hotel Guama*. Since I wasn't in the mood to eat, I accepted this arrangement, and we signed in.

Still, Alfredo couldn't resist a challenge to spend as little money as possible during this Tour. The old adage: *If it's for free, it's for me,* would definitely apply to my wheeler-dealer partner.

"Alfredo, I'm fine with the arrangements. Let's go."

"But I can do this."

He explained to the owner that for security reasons, he was accompanying me, and we didn't carry much *dinero*.

"I understand," said the round-faced, over-weight host. "But I need to see some dollars."

Alfredo was forced to adhere to the conditions.

The resort consisted of about a dozen well-placed brick cabins scattered along the lagoon. Each cabin had a well-kept bathroom (but no hot running water); large bedroom with two queen-size beds; and livingroom, complete with TV, telephone, tables and chairs. There was still so much room left over that it seemed palatial; was palatial by the standards I was used to thus far in Cuba.

I would have thought Alfredo would be happy to lap in luxury after all we had been through thus far, but he kept strangely quiet, until a smile crossed his face. The loud clap of his hands startled me from the prostrate position I was now in on the bed.

"Maybe if we go to the bar and buy the owner a drink and pay for it in dollars, then maybe he will let us pay for everything else in *pesos*."

"You are a devious man. Let it go, Alfredo."

"No, I can do this!"

So we left the comforts of our room and headed to the *cantina.* We found the owner at the bar with a nearly empty beer. Only a couple of the employees and bartender occupied the place. Could the timing have been more perfect?

Ordering a couple of the local brew, Alfredo mentioned to the owner to join us. He humbly accepted. I extended the invitation to the other men, including the bartender. For the next hour we drank. Alfredo and I shared stories of our Tour thus far. The total bill came out to six dollars.

As an added gesture, I asked if they'd like to take a photo with me and the bike. I could play just as well as Alfredo. If we were going to suck up, we may as well go big.

"*Si,*" said the owner with wide eyes and open arms.

He had been eyeing my bike since we first arrived. Before I could ask again, all the men were out the door, walking fast, then running toward the Beast. Boys will be boys, but the owner's large beer-gut bounced the others out of the way. As soon as he sat on the bike, it flexed to the full extent. Up to that point, I don't remember ever giving the bike a strained weight test.

The owner rode around the parking lot, bouncing along and laughing. He waved an arm and shouted words of joy (at least that's what I imagined) in Spanish to his employees.

He weaved and bobbed around me as I took photos, while the other bar flies shouted and gestured for him to stop and let them have a try at it.

After working up a good sweat, he generously allowed anyone else to take a spin on, "The most beautiful bike I have ever had the pleasure of riding!"

After much hand shaking and some hearty slaps on the back that made the bile in my chest rise up, he announced in great fanfare. "*Amigo,* I like you. You may pay for your meal in *pesos*."

"*Gracias,* my friend."

When everyone who wanted to try the bicycle was exhausted, Alfredo and I returned to our cabin to change into our swimming trunks and head for the lagoon.

"You see," smiled Alfredo. "I knew it could be done."

Having rented our own private piece of Paradise, we swam in the warm water, watching the sun set. Fish darted to and fro between us in the semi-clear sea.

For dinner, we consumed three plates of ground beef, *congris*, and banana, with two beers and tea. So much for not being hungry. The total price was 23 *pesos*-- one American dollar-- instead of the $23US that was originally mentioned.

The six-dollar beer investment had been well worth it.

The biggest expense of the day was calling my Canadian contact. I had tried to call Jean directly, but for some reason, the operator couldn't get through, saying that only major cities and resorts could contact the United States directly.

I brought him up to date, telling him the Tour was now well-underway, and that Jean needn't worry.

"I can't believe you pulled it off," he laughed.

"We still have a long way to go," I reminded him.

Since CNN had covered the departure, it would be airing sometime that week. My bud said he'd be on the lookout, and once again assured me that he would give Jean the news.

I wouldn't know when I could call again-- probably not until returning to Havana, within a month.

The night was cool, the stars shining bright. I stood in the middle of tranquility and listened to the sound of the waves lapping against the shore.

Today was a good learning lesson. I needed to take this Tour seriously. No more all night playing around. Work was work. There would be times for fun, but that came second to the task at hand.

And then it occurred to me...

That 15-minute call to Canada cost me $35US. The *Hotel Guama* did all right for themselves after all.

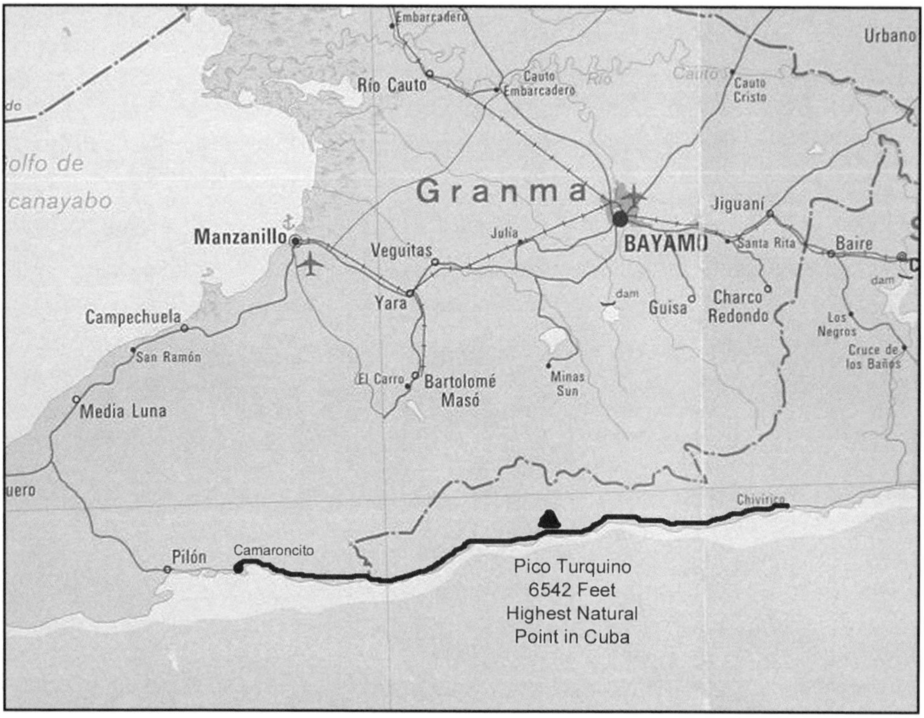

TECE

13

CHIVIRICO to CAMARONCITO
DAY 5
NOVEMBER 25, 1997

DAILY DISTANCE : 57 miles or 95 kilometers
TOTAL DISTANCE : 263 miles or 438.3 kilometers

Being able to stay at the *Hotel Guama* was a blessing I would be thankful for. I had seriously underestimated the distance between our lodgings and *Pico Turquino*-- not 15 miles, but 36.

In the previous day's condition, I wouldn't have made it. But a short workday and a good night's rest rejuvenated my *Alma* (Spirit). When Alfredo was up and ready to go in the early morning hours, I was ready.

Continuing to follow the coast, between the *Sierra Maestra* range and the Caribbean, Alfredo and I cycled through small, dusty, poverty-stricken towns with obscure names attached to them.

Again, we met with history. Small cemetery parks dotted the coast, honouring the dead heroes of Cuba. They're maintained by local volunteers who live nearby, and consider it an honour to be of such service for those who fought and died to free Cuba from oppression.

Coming upon yet another one of these parks, this one had a single-story monument of white granite standing erect like a sentinel. A bronze plaque was fastened to the stone with inscriptions of the soldier's names who died on the site, having battled former dictator Baptista's men in 1958. It was in this area that Castro and his guerrilla band hid out upon returning from Mexico at the end of 1956.

Here, Alfredo decided to take a short detour to show me Castro's old headquarters, a perfectly preserved unit nearly a generation old. It consisted of the main building, where strategies were planned, along with a couple of palm-roofed huts where the men slept. The entire manicured grounds were fenced off; the Cuban flag flew within the camp.

"This whole area protected by Fidel," motioned Alfredo with a wave of an arm.

"In the last few days, we have seen many monuments erected and dedicated by Fidel."

"*Si*. He is well-preserved."

"Do you admired your leader for what he's done?"

Alfredo shrugged his shoulders. "He give us the dollar. He try to help his people. He no' like Capitalism, but that is what the people want, and when he die, we will have it."

Alfredo never really had much to say about the leader he's known all his life. He just accepted Castro as a fact, a statement, a part of his world.

About 12 miles from *Pico Turquino*, in one of the desolate, dusty towns, we came across a middle-aged Canadian couple who had just finished climbing the country's highpoint. They were hitching a ride back to *Santiago*.

"We hiked in from the east," replied the distinguished-looking gentleman. "It took us three days to reach the summit."

"How was the trail?"

"Well-worn as expected," answered the Canadian's well-worn wife.

"You'll have very little problems," countered the husband, "But the last mile is a bit steep."

"*Si*," nodded Alfredo to me. "That is true, for I have climbed the mountain twice."

Knowing how close we were, my heart began to beat very fast at the wonderful news I was hearing. My breathing was rapid. My smile infectious. But still, one thought kept gnawing at me like a bad habit.

"Any problems with the authorities?"

"None," they both replied.

"Where are you entering the trail from?" asked the man.

"From the west."

"Then you'll have to be careful with the guards."

Fidel Castro's old 1958 headquarters in the *Sierra Maestra* mountains during the Revolution with Baptista. It is now an historic preservation site.

"Guards?" I hated the sound of that.

"Yes. From the way you're going, there are three guard stations. One at the summit, another in the middle, and still another at the entrance. They could give you some hassles, though we never had any."

I nodded my understanding, taking in all they had to say, along with Alfredo's confirmations. When a truck stopped to take the Canadian couple and others to *Santiago*, we parted company with handshakes and good cheers.

"What do you think?" I asked my partner.

"Difficult to say. We will know when we arrive."

About an hour later, as we rounded a corner, there in the distance, we could see the top part of the mountain itself. It was the highest point in the country all right. The giveaway sign was the cloud formation in a cloudless sky. An afternoon storm was brewing.

I had come to learn this mark of observation from the **American Summits** Tour. Especially in the West, where the highest of highpoints occurred, storm clouds singled them out. One reason why we would climb some of these beasts in the middle of the night was so we would be back in the safety of our camp well before mid-afternoon, when the unpredictable happened.

The next town was a short distance from us, and as we got closer, the skies darkened; the winds beginning to pick up in strength. We were about to be hit with an afternoon shower.

When we reached the town of *Ocujal* five miles later, one of the locals came walking into town with a sack of rocks on his back. About 10 years older than myself, he was in superb shape. Every muscle was outlined and carved by the Master's chisel. It made any indoor body builder with all the creature comforts pale in comparison. He had holes in all parts of his clothes including his shoes; his toes were exposed. I made him an offer of 100 *pesos* if he would join us on the expedition and help carry the bike and supplies. Placing a bicycle atop another country's highpoint would be a first, especially if the mountain's height was so accommodating, as Cuba's was.

"*Si,*" smiled the man.

Speaking through Alfredo, he added, "The price is more than enough for a day's work. *Gracias.* But you should check with the local guides. You may need special permission from the military."

He pointed to his house, where he could be reached.

"If everything is all right, I will join you."

Special permission? I didn't like the sound of that, and why would we need such consent anyway? I had already checked with Noriega in DC and Palacz in Havana, and both said it would be fine to do the climb. Was there now a toll master only the locals knew about?

It was near the noon hour, and the entire town seemed to be deserted. We found a small five-room motel where we could spend the night, but no one was at the desk. A group of young men hung around the building, and we inquired about guiding services to *Pico.*

"One of the locals is a guide," announced the men. "He will be returning in an hour or so, and can help you."

Across the street was a chiseled-stone restaurant that was out-of-place in this area. It was a fine-looking building in a nearly non-existent town. Better than its looks was the fact that it was open. They actually served a dish called *spaghetti* although their *meat sauce* left much to be desired. I didn't realize chunks of tomato counted as meat, but I suppose if one were to stretch their imagination to the limit... Alfredo and I consumed a couple of plates each, along with juice.

One of the local guides returned shortly. He was bare-foot and nearly bare-skinned. He spoke with Alfredo, who informed me of the bad news.

"He say all foreigners need special permission from the government, from Rosa Elena Simeon, the Minister of the Environment, to climb the mountain."

Rosa Elena Simeon. The same one mentioned at the police station in *Maisi,* who's permission we needed to do the eight miles from the *Point of Maisi* to the town. Was I in a surreal dream, or just being cursed by this phantom woman from Havana? And would her name crop up again on the last day of the Tour with the desolate section to *Caleta Larga?*

Okay, I figured, we had a problem and it needed to be dealt with. Problems I can handle. Stonewalling I can't.

Alfredo, the guide and I cycled to the base of *Pico* to speak with the guard stationed on duty.

Merely a boy with a rifle, his dirty, tattered, unkempt uniform and toe-exposed shoes made him look more like a beggar than a soldier in Fidel's army.

Along the southern coast, following the *Sierra Maestra* mountain range.
In the background is Cuba's highest natural point, 6542-foot, *Pico Turquino.*

As we began the talks, the guard informed us that, "Before February, any foreigner could climb the mountain, but now you need special permission."

"Why?" I asked.

"Because the government fear a foreigner will come with a virus and introduced it into the forest, killing all plant and animal life. Not to mention the people."

"That's bogus! This is why we can't climb *Pico*?"

"Not we. You," Alfredo corrected. "I can climb the mountain because I no' a foreigner." He seemed to smile more at the ridiculousness of the situation than of my predicament-- though to him, I imagine, they were one and the same.

"Ask him what the procedure is."

"He say...we have to call the officer in charge in *Santiago*...who call the officer in charge in Havana...who, if they say yes, will draw up the papers...send them to us here...and then you can climb the mountain."

"Great! How long?"

"A week."

"Balls! Do I look like a guy that's carrying a deadly virus on me?"

Alfredo smiled, blushed, then reached into his pannier side pocket to produce our official-documented paper. He began to work his magic on the young guard, who nodded in agreement with everything Alfredo was saying, but orders were orders.

"This is pointless." I threw up my hands. "Where's his superior?"

Alfredo asked, and the guard pointed behind us. Turning around, we could see a man on a donkey, meandering slowly toward us. His olive green uniform was as dirty, tattered, and unkempt as the boy's. When the Captain approached us, there was no formal salute between the men; being casual was evidentially the order for this unit.

Again, we went through the process of showing him our papers and reciting our story. He never said a word while looking at our documents and map of the Tour's route. Stone cold stiff in both speech and mannerisms. He just sat on his ass looking down on us with contempt. It was going to be a hard sell to get through this barricade.

"Doesn't anyone make a decision on their own around here?"

"Not if they want to keep their jobs," answered Alfredo.

"Let's make the call to Havana, see if we can get something going."

Alfredo asked, the Captain casually answered.

"He say the nearest phone is 36 miles away in *Chivirico*."

The Captain sat like a statue. I went ballistic. "I don't believe this crap!" I cried. "No communication whatsoever? No wire service? No telegraph?"

The Captain shook his head after the interpretation.

"Well, I'm glad to see they're prepared for that deadly oncoming virus." Silence all around, eyes on me as I paced back and forth. After a couple of deep breaths, I turned to Alfredo. "Perhaps we could pay the processing fee to the Captain."

"Ah, you want to make a bribe," smiled my partner.

"I'm talking about speeding up the paperwork. Cut through some of this Communist crap red tape, that's all."

"I know you."

"Just do it."

He did. The Captain smiled.

"The Captain say you could be arrested for that."

I returned the smile. "You're a butthead, *amigo*."

Alfredo diplomatically refused to interpret, but did on my next question, "How were the Canadians able to climb without permission?"

It seems they had a reason for approaching the summit from the other side during the night-- actually three very good ones. Confirming what the Canadian couple told us earlier in the day, the Captain explained that if they had taken the route we wanted to undergo, they would not only have met the guard at that station, but another one in the middle, and a third one a mile from the summit. Perhaps you might bypass the first or second, but you would be caught by the third and sent back down. Going the other way in the dark enabled the couple to casually walk to the summit, undetected, until the descent. Then, the top station discovered what they had done and sent them on their way. But by then it was already too late.

"But the Captain say do not worry, they will be arrested in *Santiago*."

The ass on the ass showed no emotion.

To say I was pissed was an understatement. Six years! Six stinking years of planning this tour; the itinerary. I knew what I wanted. So did Noriega and Palaez, and each time the highpoint was discussed, I was assured there would be no problem--

even as recent as two weeks ago when meeting with the Minister of Sport. Lousy, worthless bureaucrats!

While viewing our map of the route across the country, *El Capitan* informed us that we would need special permission to do the last 30-some miles to *Caleta Larga* or face the same obstacles. Just like how we unknowingly needed special clearance to do *Maisi*, but we somehow got past the guards-- which was why I was placed under arrest.

Personally, giving a lame excuse about spreading a deadly virus at the highpoint of Cuba in order to keep foreigners away shows the government's folly. The issue is one of control. The majority of nations know that there are people in the world who would like to climb a country's highest natural point, so they either shut them down by taking over, or producing enough hoops for the individual to jump through to make it nearly impossible to reach the objective. I am amazed at how easy it is for anyone, foreign or native, to be able to enter the united States and travel where they want. In fact, out of the 50 States, only California and Alaska come to mind as needing any type of approval that would require sufficient notice.

The Captain nudged his donkey away from us and rode off from whence he came. There was no further discussion. All I could do was stare off at the trail a few yards in front of me, beyond the guard's gate.

"This will give you an excuse to return," sympathized Alfredo, as he got on his bike and waited for me to do the same.

Our almost guide bid us farewell and cycled back to his town. The horse was dead. No use flogging it. I shook my head in disgust and slowly, agonizingly, got on my bike. I was so pissed the rest of the day, I never felt the next twenty miles, nor even noticed passing into the next province of *Granma* as we made our way toward *Camaroncito*. It was just as well: The coast was barren and desolate; there was not a soul in sight.

"I recognize this formation," announced my guide. He pointed to a group of rocks that towered out of the water, attached by a spit of sand.

"In the beginning of the year, I lead a group from *Santiago* to Havana and we pass by this place."

He took a deep breath and smiled at his resourcefulness for remembering this area after such a long period of time had elapsed.

"The people I guide take photos of families we stay with, and then send them to me. If I come back the same way, I have something to give to the family, and they, in turn, let me stay with my new people another night."

I love this guy's mind!

We would be spending the night with a man named Diego and his family. Already through the mid-point of his life, and standing at a rough six-feet, Diego was in excellent physical shape. He achieved this physique by farming the 200-acre mountainside retreat he called home and by swimming and fishing in his own private part of the Caribbean-- there was no one else in the vicinity for as far as you could see.

The split log house which he built himself was an average-size home for most people consisting of one large living room area with bedrooms off each side. A

With Diego (at right) and his family on their 200 acre ranch along the priceless coast.

very simple structure that suited the family's needs. Several feet away was another building about half the size, that was used for cooking and eating. At the opposite end was the outhouse.

There were penned areas for cows, goats, pigs, chickens and a Cuban delicacy, rats-- rodents bigger than any I'd ever seen back home.

"These are just the babies," mentioned Alfredo, as Diego pulled back a trapdoor to reveal the parents, which were the size of my *Lhasa Apsos*.

Diego and his wife had four children, two sons and two daughters. One of the girls had recently married and lived with her husband not more than a few hundred yards away on the family property. Of course, the Cuban government owns all the land, which the people farm, turning over a portion.

"It is a small price to pay for the view," mentioned Diego, through Alfredo, in casual passing.

Alfredo, Diego and I headed across the road to the private beach, where the water was lukewarm. The sun was beginning to set below the horizon.

"If I knew you were coming, I would have caught some lobster," said Diego.

As it was, while we relaxed at the shore, his wife and daughter prepared one of the many fatted hens they had in stock-- unless, said Diego with a smile, "You would enjoy rat instead?"

To the outside world, these people would seem to have nothing; their only creature comfort being an old radio hooked up to a car battery that gave them the news and some music. That's it. No TV or lights-- no electricity, for that matter, save the battery. They had literally only pennies to their name, but then they didn't pay taxes.

While the mother and the daughter prepared the meal in the kitchen unit adjacent to the main house, the men sat out on the front porch, smoking and laughing on whatever they amused themselves with. I watched the sun set below the horizon, illuminating the sky in glorious pastel colors.

Because their eating facilities were quite small for everyone to fit comfortably, Diego motioned Alfredo and I to sup first, being the honored guests. The meal was a small feast of rice and vegetables, the fresh chicken fell off the bone and melted in the mouth. Since dessert is a rarity for the family, I pulled out the half-pound of chocolate I still had with me from *Guantanamo*, that made the meal complete.

For the nightly entertainment we all sat out on the front porch. The son and daughter's boyfriend in conversation; Diego and Alfredo in quiet thought, having a smoke; the mother and daughter laughing at a private joke.

Through Alfredo, we spoke about our Tour. Where we had started from and where we hope to end. The daughter wanted to know if I had any Beatles music, which was the popular craze at the moment. I didn't, but I did play other rock and roll I had with me on my battery-operated cassette player.

I began to dance to the music on the porch, and tried to invite her to join me. Would she not want to learn some of the dance steps? She pulled away from me, shaking her head and squealing with delight. The rest of the family laughed and clapped along.

Her boyfriend, through Alfredo, asked, "What is the going rate for black pearls in your country?"

"I don't know." I had to honestly admit. "I'm sure they'd fetch a good price. They're considered a rarity."

"There is a buyer from Europe that is interested in obtaining whatever supply I can retrieve from the waters."

"Are there that many black pearls in the area?"

"*Si,* if you know where to look and can dive deep enough."

As the last rays of the sun finally faded away, we could see the lights from Jamaica on the horizon. Being such a warm night, we wanted to sleep out on the porch, so Diego retrieved some mattresses from the house.

With no illumination interfering with our view, the evening sky exploded with a multitude of stars as the crashing waves put us to sleep.

What more was there to life than this? I wondered.

I was content.

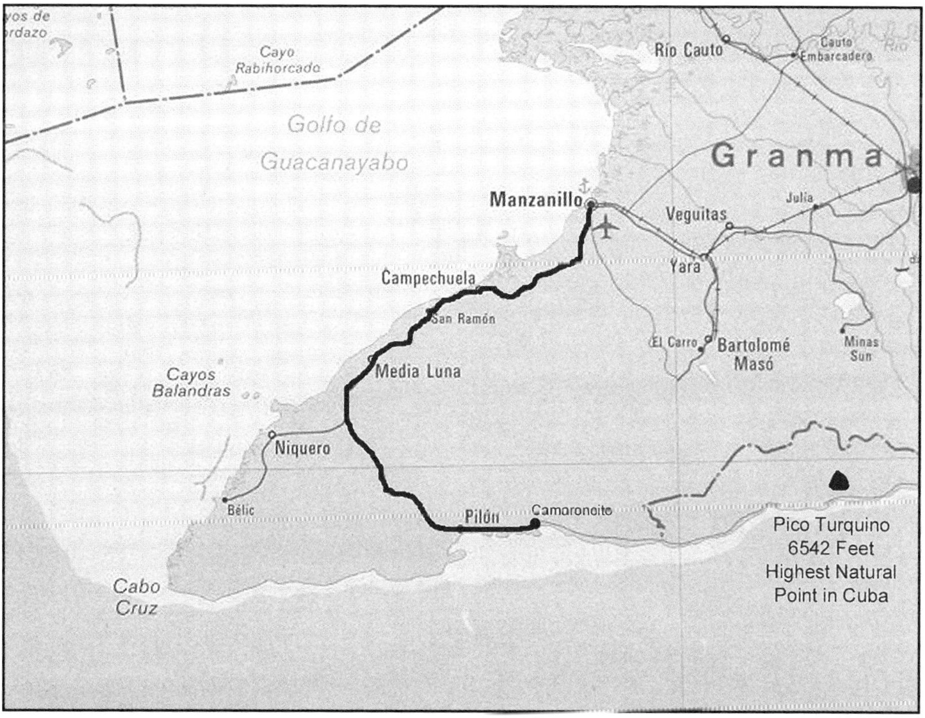

CATORCE

14

CAMARONCITO to MANZANILLO
DAY 6
NOVEMBER 26, 1997

DAILY DISTANCE : 74 miles or 123.3 kilometers
TOTAL DISTANCE : 337 miles or 561.6 kilometers

About 4am I thought I heard the sounds of an animal crying and people milling about us, but it was hazy in my sleep, and I thought it was a dream. A few hours later, the supposed dream took shape in the form of a brown-wooled baby lamb. Its umbilical cord was still hanging from his belly as he took his first few unsteady steps, following his mother along in the penned-up area of the front yard.

We watched the lamb play and frolic, discovering its world and surroundings, among the other animals, before preparing to leave our Eden. We shared some rich coffee with Diego and because of his extended hospitality toward us, I left him some dollars.

He bowed slightly, saying, "I wish you well on the rest of your journey. The next time you are in this area, you must stay longer."

"That's a promise." I smiled as we shook hands.

Alfredo and I accompanied Diego's son and daughter to their place of work, down the road at the nearby banana plantation. We four cycled side by side, sometimes racing one another, sometimes sauntering along, until we parted ways with a wave and smile.

If one has a choice during a cycling tour, the best way to begin the day is on a flat surface. This is always a gift, as it gives the leg muscles a chance to warm up. Today we were given a 16-mile present to *Pilon*.

The scenery was much the same as the previous day: quiet and desolate. Alfredo and I would be off in our own worlds, running through the course of the day.

In the early morning hours, with the sun rising and the temperatures still cool, it was rather tranquil. But by day's end, I would be sick of whatever the scenery had to offer. There's just so much Paradise by the handlebars one can take in at any given time.

We stopped once at a one-room schoolhouse to view a dozen or so uniformed children standing in front of a white-marbled bust of Josi Marti and the national flag, reciting their pledge of allegiance.

As I took photos, Alfredo entered into animated life.

"I have an idea," he pointed a finger heavenward. "If we buy pens or pencils for the school children of *Caleta Larga*, we may be able to gain permission and complete the last section of the Tour."

"What kind of an idea is that?"

"The local authorities may not let us cycle the last section to complete the Tour. But," he smiled, "if we buy some things for the children or the people of the last town in Cuba, then the authorities will allow us permission, because now we have gifts."

"And you think that'll work."

"Of course," Alfredo said with open arms. "We bring gifts. They no' refuse us. Then we get the job done."

Was it any wonder why no one, foreign or native, ever cycled the entire length of the island, I asked myself, *When the government had control of the beginning and end sections? Not to mention the highpoint?*

We arrived at the outer edge of *Pilon* just in time as vendors were setting up their stands for roadside breakfasts of pizzas and *bandito,* a thick juice of ice and fresh fruit, made in a blender. People were milling about, waiting to catch a ride into the town itself, or for other unknown destinations.

Within a half-hour we were veering away from the coast into more jungle-like terrain, going slightly north toward the next town of *Media Luna*, Alfredo's birthplace. For the next 25 miles, we would be traveling through lush green countryside, abundant with sugar cane, coconut, and banana plantations.

Along the way, we encountered our worst hill of the day, with an elevation of some 1000 feet. With the sun at our backs, the heat bore down on us with its full force. I began to feel the energy slowly ebb away from me.

A tractor going slightly faster than we were happened to be bringing a group of field workers to the top. One of them called out, a cigarette dangling from his mouth. He offered his hand, which I gladly accepted, while Alfredo latched onto a passing truck. By this method we were able to do a fast 400 feet before the downhill came upon us.

However, this method is dangerous and not for the faint of heart and weak wrist. You feel the strain in your tendons, as the hands play a tug-of-war with one another. Since one hand is being held that only leaves you with one hand free to hold onto the handlebars, and try to maneuver the potholes and bumps in your path. If you fall, or the bike gets sucked under the truck's wheels, would you remember to let go of the person or truck you're hanging onto before your wrist tears from your arm?

During our trek through the countryside, there were more places and more monuments devoted to Fidel's early conflicts in battle, but one such memorial-- a single, simple, white-stoned, house-shaped tombstone, shaded by palm trees-- was devoted to Carlos Manual de Cespedes, a wealthy planter who was widely regarded as the Father of Cuba. The dark bronze plaque noted that on October 9, 1868, de Cespedes freed his slaves-- one day before the popular uprising went into effect, freeing the rest of Spanish Cuba.

When de Cespedes took action on October 9th, followed by the entire country the next day, it began the Ten Years' War. De Cespedes headed the revolution that demanded independence and the abolition of slavery. Spain retaliated and won by a protracted show of force. The war ended with the signing of the *Pact of Zanjon* in 1878, which provided reforms and the gradual eradication of slavery, but not total freedom from Spain's iron grasp.

As we approached *Media Luna*, the surrounding greenery opened up to reveal a picture postcard environment, with cotton candy clouds over a blue Caribbean Sea.

Alfredo's birth town was like any other dusty road community-- only the population was larger; roughly 10,000 souls inhabited the area.

Riding through the center of *Media Luna*, we were followed, out of curiosity, by fellow cyclists, and chased by stray dogs hungry for some fresh meat. Alfredo's face brightened upon returning to his hometown. A hero's welcome for the well traveled cyclist. The first thing we did was search out the old *hacienda* where he was raised the first few years of his life.

On a corner of a side street stood a sky-blue adobe structure no bigger than most resort bungalows. What was once a house filled with the laughter of children was now a government office.

"I stand in front, and you take a picture," said Alfredo, as I did what he asked.

While we were setting up, he mentioned, "This is where my mother met my father."

"In *Media Luna?*"

"*Si*. When Fidel took over the country, he wanted everyone to learn to read and write, so he mount a campaign. Thousands of people from Havana go

Alfredo in front of his birth house at *Media Luna*. The place has now been turned into a government office.

all over Cuba to teach."

"And your mother was sent here?" I snapped a few photos of Alfredo with his bicycle near the front door.

"*Si*. She live and teach here for two years. My father was one of her students. Then they get married."

When the shots were taken, Alfredo came across the street to where I stood, looking at the house he once lived in, while I reloaded new film into the camera.

"I born here in 1963, and after a short while, we move to Havana. About ten years ago, my papa died. Sometimes I miss him."

I nodded. "That's nice that you still miss him."

"Is your father still alive?"

"Yes, but he doesn't like what I do for a living. Thinks I should get a real job." I laughed. "At this point in my career, I couldn't afford a nine-to-five job. Anyway, just before I came to Cuba, we talked on the phone. He said I was dead to him. That he never wanted to see or hear from me ever again, and then hung-up."

"Shit!"

"Yeah, he is. That's the way life goes sometimes."

Once we finished the business of reminiscing, Alfredo and I rode off toward a small, outdoor cafe that bordered the town's park. There, we had an extended lunch of drinks and *congris*. I asked the waitress if they had fish, but she shook her head.

The rest break gave us a chance to catch up on our individual notes. I thought about my own family and how they would be spending the next day, Thanksgiving.

As per usual, whenever I stop long enough to rest, a crowd gathers around the bike. For the purposes of whatever privacy I could attain, I place my bike off a ways-- in this case, across the street near the park. It's always close enough to keep an eye on it, but far enough away to give me some breathing room.

"You know," said Alfredo. "*Media Luna* is also the birth town of Celia Sanchez, Fidel's lover and confidant."

"Really?" Amazed that history was still following us along on this Tour. "I've heard Sanchez was Castro's only true love."

"*Si.* When she die, Fidel never the same."

The school children in the area were on their way home when they came across the Beast. Still dressed in their red and white uniforms, they marveled over the bike before looking around for the owner. Who would be crazy enough to leave such a beautiful bike unattended? When they saw my red, white and blue figure beneath an umbrellaed cafe table, they drew forth. This gives new meaning to the phrase, *magnetic personality*.

Insisting I take photos of them, they got so close to our table the waitress had to shoo them away and place a portable fence between us and them.

Taking the scene in with a smile, Alfredo continued with what he had been saying. "Fidel's first wife, a daughter and granddaughter live in Miami."

"Yes, I've heard of that. And they speak out against him every chance they get."

"I don't think he care. He has ten children from other wives and lovers, but he only care about Sanchez."

"How did she die?"

"She find out she had cancer, so she kill herself on her sixtieth birthday. Fidel make the house she born into a museum. In the park over there, is a statute of her sitting next to a waterfall fountain."

He pointed several hundred yards away. Since we had time, I walked the area, taking photos of the various surroundings. Along the street, all along the park, the buildings had a Southern 1930s flavor about them. The front *verandas* were wide, supported by large, round columns. The double doors swung open to cathedral ceilings. Painted in pastel colors, the majority of them were businesses.

One of the houses, a couple of buildings away from us, had been converted into a clinic for expectant mothers. During the mid-afternoon they sat outside in the shade of the palm trees, calling out to me to take their picture.

While I surveyed the area, a Havana University classmate of Alfredo's cycled by and spotted his old friend. For the next hour, they reminisced about those college days and caught up on the latest news from one another. He, too, was a recreational director.

Alfredo turned to me, saying, "I, too, was offered the job in my hometown, but I decided to stay in *Habana.* There is more opportunity."

"I agree. There's more chance for advancement in the city. But then there are many benefits to living in the country."

"Not for me. I no' live in *Habana*, we no' meet, and I no' do Tour and become famous."

A fountain-statue of Celia Sanchez in the park of her hometown, *Media Luna*. A lover-confidant of Castro's, she committed suicide on her 60th birthday after learning she had inoperable cancer. Her house is now a museum.

"Living in a small town in the country allows you to really get to know the people and have peace of mind."

"But no advancement," countered Alfredo.

"I give up."

Throughout the morning, I had been lamenting to my partner that tomorrow, Thanksgiving, was a special day in my country, and that this was the first time in my life I would not be home to enjoy the festivities.

"What is this Thanksgiving?"

"Big holiday. Lots of food. No *congris*, I can tell you that," I answered, unable to take another bite of the stuff.

"But why do you celebrate?"

"About four hundred years ago, a group of men and women left their homes and families in England, and came to America, because they couldn't worship the Lord the way they wanted to. Because of their faith, God blessed them and the country. That's why we have Thanksgiving. We are thankful to Jesus for the many blessings He has bestowed upon us."

"Ah! They fight for their freedom. This is good. I understand."

"Yeah," I sighed. "No pumpkin pie this year. No turkey that melts in your mouth. No stuffing and candied yams..."

As I was torturing myself with fond food memories, Alfredo would turn to his friend, translating what we were talking about, and tomorrow's particular holiday.

"We've been following the coast for days now, and I'm supposed to believe there's no fish in any of the restaurants we've come across? That's a crock."

"*Uno momento*," said the young man, as he went inside the restaurant we had been patronizing the last couple of hours to talk with the owner.

Speaking mainly to myself with Alfredo close by, I reflected, "It really is selfish for me to think this way, when the Lord has blessed me abundantly. I still have my health, and people back home who love me. And if nothing else, I've been given the gift to live an extra thirty years since the electrocution. There'll be plenty more Thanksgivings in the future."

After a bit, the young man returned. He and Alfredo exchanged a rapid volley of words.

"Do you wish to buy a kilo of fresh shrimp for forty *pesos?*"

My eyes lit up. Two point two pounds of shrimp for roughly $1.75US?

"*Si!*" I said, my hands almost trembling with anticipation, my mouth watering.

A few minutes later we had the delicacy in a plastic pouch. As an added blessing, it was entirely prepared.

I was ready to devour it then and there, but Alfredo grabbed it and quickly strapped it to the back of his bike. A prized carrot as an incentive to the day's goal, *Manzanillo*, some 34 additional miles away...

"Can you no' taste the shrimp," yelled the taskmaster, picking up speed along the route with me in hot pursuit.

The blinders were on. I saw nothing but the bounty.

About halfway to our goal, just outside the town of *Campechuela*, Alfredo wanted to make another stop to show me another monument devoted to another important figure. Juan Manual Marquez had fought and died in Castro's revolution.

"This one special," he'd say, but then he always said that.

We stopped.

Surrounding a sugar cane field in the middle of nowhere, the gated area was carpeted with a well-manicured, lush green lawn. Part of it sloped upward to form a small hill that met the backside of the eight-foot high, curved, cream-colored stone.

Cut rocks formed into a puzzle and laid in concrete made up the walkway, which led to the monument. There, an image of Marquez was cut out of a single piece of wood. Palm trees formed a semi-circle about the structure.

The bronze plate attached to the stone wall mentioned that Juan Manual was born July 3, 1915, and died in 1956. The real background would come from my guide.

"When Fidel was fighting Baptista's troops, Marquez was wounded and left for dead. A guard reported this to his superior, who want to see the body. So the guard return, but find Juan alive, so in order to cover his error, he kill him and dump his body here, in this spot."

Listening as I was taking photos, I replied, "You mean to tell me, because the guard didn't want to look like a fool to his superior officer, he kills Juan, and dumps his body in this sugar cane field, in the middle of nowhere?"

"*Si.*"

"Just another sign of the times."

An old Cuban planter working the sugar cane fields.

By 5pm, we had arrived at the coastal city of *Manzanillo*. Before we left Havana, I remembered, Alfredo's neighbor had given him the address of her sister, extracting a promise that we would not only see her, but spend the night at her place as well. In America, it's hotel chains. In Cuba, it's an introduction that gets you in the door of a person's home.

As if on cue, Alfredo mentioned the arrangements. What would sweeten the deal in this case would be the letters and photos Alfredo had in his possession from his neighbor to give to the sister.

At the town's center, street vendors sold juice and other food items on every corner, and near-empty shops were filled with people eager to buy whatever the shelves contained.

As we turned down some side streets, the crowds began to thin. After a bit, we arrived at our destination-- possibly the worse section of town to live in. Paint was peeling from the buildings, roofs were rotten and flaking off, broken concrete formed the basis for the exterior walls, sidewalks were strewn with filth and sewage, and there was the heavy, humid stench of human and animal waste. Not a single person was in sight.

Alfredo knocked at the address given him by his Havana contact. The old wooden door creaked open slightly. Words were exchanged before the woman was confident enough to show her full self. A slim, dark featured, attractive beauty roughly our age; her eyes, stunning jewels of black onyx. Her name was Melba, and just behind her dress peered her 10 year old daughter, Elaina.

The four-room, train-style house was of a simple structure. We entered the living room area with our bikes-- in the part of town we were in, Alfredo and I had silently deemed it unwise to leave our most valuable possessions unguarded. Of course, having the bicycles inside with us got to be a bit cramped, as each of the rooms was roughly 10x10 feet.

The next two rooms we passed through were Elaina's and Melba's bedroom, and then the kitchen with a tiny bathroom in the corner. Outside the kitchen was a small rectangle-shaped patch that was considered the backyard. In it hung the laundry and was kept a future meal, a small, pot-bellied pig.

We arrived near the dinner hour, and Melba, obviously not expecting anyone, didn't have enough food to feed us-- let alone for her and Elaina. When we produced the kilo of shrimp, her eyes lit up along with a wide, toothy smile.

"I will be pleased to prepare this for you and your friend," said Melba, through Alfredo.

He waved his hand, as though he were the Pope about to give a blessing. "There is enough for all of us."

Her smile got brighter. She illuminated the room.

"*Gracias,*" she bowed slightly to both of us. "*Por favor.* I fix, you shower and rest."

After washing off the day's grime and changing into more comfortable clothing, Alfredo said he needed to make a call to a friend back in Havana to take over some of his recreational activities. He asked where the nearest operator would be. Since the meal would not be ready for a while, Melba mentioned that Elaina could take us to the public phones.

At the communal pay phone building near the center of town, a small group of people waited in line to place a call with one of the two switchboard operators. Upon entering, there was a lounge area with cushioned seats and a couch. Off to the right were ten glass booths in rows of two with an aisle down the middle. After giving one of the phone operators the number you wish to call, you took a seat. When your name is called, you're directed to one of the private stalls. We were there at least a half-hour. Elaina was always close to my side with watching eyes and smiles.

The equipment the operators were using seemed to date back to the 1920s.

When Alfredo was through with his call, I mentioned, "You know, I've seen operating equipment like this in old photos and in museums."

He laughed. The telephone operators asked what was so funny, and he repeated what I said. They giggled and laughed, and responded through Alfredo, "If we were as modern as America, we would be out of a job."

In a strange way, they had a point.

On the way back to the house, we came upon a store that sold nothing but bottled water and Coca-Cola-- which was obviously so valuable that the doors had to remain locked.

When Alfredo announced, "*Americano,*" the middle-aged woman smiled, stepping around the refrigerated counter to let us in.

Two luxuries I required every four or five days while on the Tour were a resort (or the equivalent) and a cold coke, regardless of the fact I had to pay in dollars.

I justified my reasoning by convincing myself that it was needed for sanity purposes. You get tired of warm water and living like an animal. I could still remember the bitter cold of Alaska's mountains; this time I wanted to focus on fun-- and the people of Cuba have no problem with that. This, too, I rationalized, would be a remembered gift for Elaina, as we had the locked store all to ourselves.

While in the well-lit store, a young, trashy, mis-shapen black woman began knocking on the window. The proprietor tried to shoo her away, but the tramp was unmovable. When we left, she followed us down the street, calling out to me with kisses and tapping me on the shoulder.

Ignoring this, she boldly came alongside us, showing me a *peso* and holding out her hand; her gap-toothed smile trying to seduce me. In any language I can understand begging.

She showed me her middle finger and said something. Alfredo laughed. "She say she screw you for a *peso*."

"Thank you for that interpretation," I sighed. "I think I could've figured it out for myself."

Elaina looked up at me wondering if I was going to take this woman up on her offer. She held my hand tight, and tugged me away, as my new-found pest continued to antagonize me with her words and gestures.

I had had enough of the games, and stopped to face her with my own words and gestures. "I wouldn't screw you if you paid me a *peso*."

She belched, and the smell of alcohol mixed with the stench of her body odor nearly made me vomit.

Continuing on our way, she tagged along, speaking once more. Elaina said something in an angry voice, trying to shoo her away. You were not going to mess with Elaina's man.

"She say she kiss you for free," Alfredo smiled.

After more walking and bribing, she turned and left. Grabbing my butt for good measure, she sashayed down the street. I probably should have given her the lousy *peso,* but at the time, I just wasn't in the mood for beggars.

When the three of us arrived back at the house, Melba had prepared a fine meal of rice mixed with the shrimp, fresh vegetables, and a pitcher of juice. Since the four of us couldn't all fit around the living room table-- the bikes took up most of the room in already cramped space-- Melba insisted Alfredo and I eat first, followed by herself and Elaina, who at least wanted to sit beside me until her mother had to scold her out of the room with a smack of the apron on her bottom.

At night, Melba gave up her queen-size bed and shared the twin with her daughter, who wanted none of mom, but all of me.

As I was undressing, Alfredo stayed off to the side, looking away from me awkwardly.

"What's the matter with you?"

"I...have never slept with a man before," he squirmed; his *macho* manhood at stake.

"When you pass out, it won't matter," I nonchalantly replied. "Unless you want to sleep on the floor with the roaches." Then I crawled into bed.

True to form, we were out cold when we hit the pillows. But then, what would anyone expect when you put in 18-hour days?

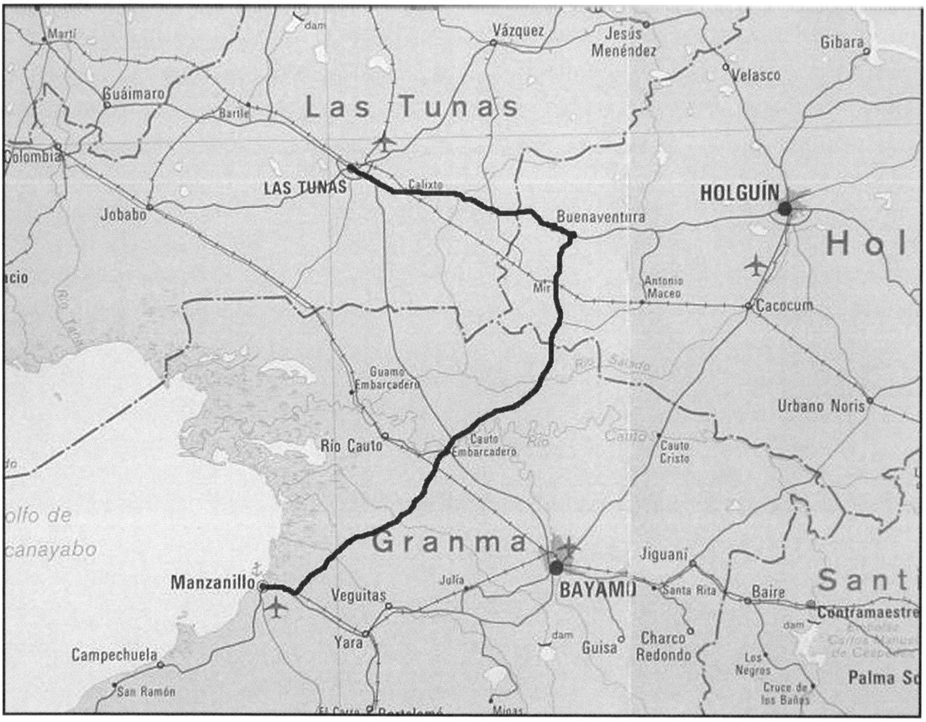

QUINCE

15

MANZANILLO to LAS TUNAS
DAY 7
NOVEMBER 27, 1997

DAILY DISTANCE : 61 miles or 101.7 kilometers
TOTAL DISTANCE : 398 miles or 663.3 kilometers

The first week of the Tour had been along mountainous, coastal terrain, but according to Alfredo, the next several days would be flat. Judging by our map, we wouldn't be near water again for at least a week, until we reached the *Bay of Pigs*. That day's route took us north before heading west again through the middle of the country. Our day's goal: the capital of *Las Tunas*.

Of the 13 provinces (actually 14, because Havana is considered a province unto itself), 11 of them share the same name as the capitals of their respective territory. Only the province of *Granma*, where we were, had a capital named *Bayamo*, while *Villa Clara's* center name was *Santa Clara*. On Tour, only the capitals of *Granma, Holguin* (which we arrived by truck), *Villa Clara, Matanzas* and Havana would not be cycled through.

If we were to complete the distance Alfredo had in mind, we would actually pass right through *Holguin*, since we were just nicking the western corner of the province.

Both before and after the Tour, people have often asked why I simply didn't cut straight across the island.

There were two reasons: one, it would have been boring; and, two, I wanted to cycle through each province. No matter how small or trivial it might seem, I wanted to project a sense of unity. The route was the thread joining the country together, with the bicycle as the needle.

That would have to be another two-in-one day, for if we could make it to *Las Tunas*, we would make up time. Also, according to the original itinerary, there were to be four rest days, but if we trimmed those as well, we could make much larger gains. Much like shaving weight off a bike or gear from a backpack, every little thing we could think of-- doing a double day, cutting our rest days by half, putting in more miles than the schedule called for-- would ultimately gain us time that we lost in the beginning. Maybe not eight days' worth, but certainly enough to where we could finish it off in a respectable manner.

We began at first light, thanking Melba for her hospitality by leaving over a pound of shrimp and some dollars as an appreciation for taking us in unannounced and being a gracious hostess as well. Alfredo was already out of bed and packed before I had a chance to know what was happening. He didn't seem to have any problems sleeping with another man-- at least none that he mentioned.

Before heading out to the open road, we stopped at the local marketplace for a breakfast of pizzas and *bandito*, which were among the food items the people had for sale at the various booths. Evidently, pork sandwiches were always a welcome sight to the natives, but one I could pass on no matter how starved I was.

The pizzas in Cuba are not at all like what we would expect in America. They were mainly fried bread dough, sometimes served from a round five-inch pan, or folded in half. Usually they had goat cheese sprinkled on top, perhaps sauce if it were available. Once in Havana, we found a place that made large, 12-inch diameter creations, topped with sauce, cheese, onions, mushrooms, and peppers-- all for the price of $2US, paid in advance.

The *bandito* was always made in a blender with ice, but what you received depended on whatever fresh fruit was available in the area. It could be banana, papaya, mango, pineapple or any other variety, but, regardless, it was cool, chunky-liquid fruit that slid easily down the throat. A wonderful way to begin the day.

Alfredo wasn't joking when he said this next stretch would be flat. In the 60-odd miles to *Las Tunas*, we only gained 500 feet in elevation. So gradual was the climb that we never felt it.

My palms and wrists began to bother me; my fingers would be numb and tingly until the end of the day when they could rest. Being on such flat terrain had at least one advantage: we could cycle sitting straight up, without having to place our hands on the bars for miles, and still keep our balance.

Our view consisted of a lush green world of banana, coconut and sugarcane fields. Workers would be along the edge of the field, near the road, cutting the tall grass with their machetes (I never once saw a lawnmower), while Cuban cowboys herded their cattle to market.

We were in wide-open spaces. The blacktop road became the dividing line that cut through the plantations. The quiet, the rhythm of it all, was so tranquil; so solitaire and beautiful, that my mind wandered as my body slipped easily into a comfortable cadence without effort or thought.

It was Thanksgiving back home, but I was in a joyful mood in Cuba. Thoughts of our shrimp feast the previous night and the near completion of the first third of the Tour-- a task that had taken six years to organize, brought a smile to my face and a faster stride in my pedal.

"Hey! Why you in a hurry?" shouted Alfredo, as I passed him by in an American-colored blur.

"It's a beautiful day, and there are no more hills to climb," I shouted back, continuing my pace.

It was another warm day; our tans were getting darker. I thought about my biological family in the East and mid-West. They would be shivering, no doubt, perhaps spending the day feasting next to a cozy, comfortable fireplace. It was the beginning of the Christmas season.

My thoughts shifted to Jean and my spiritual family in California. I knew the members of my church continued to pray for me. They would be receiving reports from various news services on the progress of the Tour. Exciting to some and giving others gray hairs, no doubt.

And my beloved Jean...my best friend in the world. She would be with her own family this day. Children and grandchildren traveling from north and south. The house would be full of laughter and conversation, the warmth of the wood stove burning, music playing in the background. Every year since 1993, she had taken me in as part of the family. This would be the first year without her, and I wondered if this were not some dreaded omen of what the future held for us, if this were not the first physical sign of the gap beginning to expand between us.

Since the end of the **American Summits** tour, she's been progressively determined to widen the distance without a valid reason, while I've been trying to keep the relationship fresh and exciting. The generational difference in our years has never been an issue, since both of us consider age as nothing more than a number. Although it'd be an asexual union, I'd marry her just because of our deep, devoted friendship with one another.

"But I don't want to marry you, because I don't love you enough." She has said enough times over the years.

"If I left you, you'd miss me after awhile."

"Yes...yes, I would," she'd admit. "But your lifestyle is too dangerous for me to handle. I can't take the constant worrying I do when you're away."

"Ah! See! That means you love me!"

"But not enough to make a lifetime habit of it."

We'd go on like this for hours until we exhausted ourselves. Thank God it was only once a year. Whether we wanted to admit it to ourselves or each other, we were bonded to one another until death separated us.

At the city limits of *Manzanillo* rested a stone arrangement several feet in height. There was a gap in the middle where an iron bell hung with the words, *Bienvenicos a Manzanillo*, – *Welcome to Manzanillo*. Just in front of the structure was a huge cast-iron train wheel with a mature tree growing through one of the six slots. Each of the provinces was known for some type of product represented by an appropriate symbol-- in this case, the industrial fortitude of *Manzanillo* and the province of *Granma.*

Wide open spaces had a disadvantage, in that the towns would be few and far between, which meant a rationing of food and water for the next few days.

When we came upon *Cauto Embarcadero*, a tiny roadside industrial town, we were able to find a shack of a stand that sold nothing but *refresco*, a light juice similar to our Kool-Aid, that came in many flavors, such as peach, cherry, orange, grape, pineapple, lemon, pear, and a host of others. The product was made in China, and came in small packets that you simply tore open and added the proper fluid to make a couple of quarts. At a *peso* per packet, this became a God-send as a replacement to plain water. Provided, of course, you could ever find the stuff for sale, it was that elusive.

The young businessman would not sell us the packets, only drinks for a *peso* per cup. He was beginning his capitalistic climb, and we honored it.

The continual crowd of children gathered around the bike. Their eyes grew wide at the unusual design, as their tiny hands glided over the colors. Even the young, heavyset owner of the juice stand examined the piece of machinery like an art lover would a masterpiece painting. I took the hint and asked if he'd like to ride it.

I didn't have to ask a second time. The children parted for him like a swath, and, in a single moment, he hopped on the bike, cycling up and down the main street. He maneuvered around a bulldozer that was tearing up the old asphalt, riding through the debris with confidence, as though he were an expert. He had some trouble with the tiny, clipless pedals. One foot would slip off, then another, as his face registered animated shock at trying to hang on and not topple. The children laughed and screamed with joy. He managed quite well in a short period of time. When he was through, he needed a good supply of his product to cool down.

Doing another two-day-in-one marathon could be a killer, I knew, reflecting on the trip between *San Antonio del Sur* and *Santiago de Cuba*. But the area was so flat, we made great time to *Las Tunas*, arriving by 2pm.

Alfredo never seemed to tire of offering pretty young women a lift into town.

"You see," smiled Alfredo as we approached the city's skyline and abundant congestion. "We have made up another day on the schedule."

"I know," I yelled over the noise of the traffic, as we dodged in and out of the stalled vehicles. "If this is the way it's going to be for the next week, we can easily make up for the time we lost in Havana."

Alfredo seemed to know exactly where he was going, making a beeline for the capital's sports complex. No stopping, the blinders were on for him, and I followed closely behind. Within the hour, we had reached our destination. At the front desk, Alfredo gave the names of friends who coached at the complex to the woman, who placed the call.

Soon, a couple of *amigos* came running down the stairs, shouting, "Alfredo!" There was much hand shaking, hugging and slaps on the backs. I did the diplomatic thing by sitting off to the side and keeping quiet.

Because of our letter of introduction from Alfredo's workplace in the nation's capital, we were able to spend the night free of charge at the swimmer's dormitory where past, present, and future Olympians coached, lived and trained.

While waiting in the main foyer to be escorted to our room, Pedro, one of the directors, came bounding out of his ground level office.

"Hey! Alfredo," he shouted with open arms.

"Hey! Pedro," returned Alfredo's shouts.

They hugged, laughed, and generally carried on in much the same manner as Alfredo did with his earlier friends. Why do friends like to punch each other in the arm when they haven't seen one another in so long? I could never understand this ritual. They spoke to one another so rapidly, that even if I understood the language, I wouldn't have been able to follow along.

About medium height with a wide mustache, Pedro reminded me of a Cuban Groucho Marx. He seemed always animated in his facial expressions, being unable to hide his emotions. *He'd be a lousy poker player*, I thought.

When Alfredo said we would be staying the night, he felt compelled to show us our quarters himself.

The complex takes the best athletes-- children of all ages-- from the eastern part of the country, and trains them, educates them for whatever sport they happen to excel in. The rest of the country, or west of *Las Tunas,* attend the facilities in Havana.

Riding our bikes to the swimmer's area, we came to a section of blue pastel-colored buildings. Set up much like one would see apartment buildings in a housing complex, each section had a green yard and shaded trees. A walkway formed the divider for the men, women, children (who lived with an adult supervisor) and coaches. This last area was where we would be spending the night.

Our dorm slept twelve. There were six bunks with metal closets and shelves, a TV arranged where everyone could see it, shower and toilet facilities around the corner. Very Spartan in manner, the concrete walls were undecorated, and it smelled like an athlete's habitat.

No sooner had we picked an empty bunk and dropped our gear than a young, clean-cut coach came through the doors.

He scanned the room of men, and then made a beeline toward me, extending his hand. "I am Ibrahim," he announced in a deep, strong voice that went with his powerful grip.

"Come. I show you gym where we train current and future Olympians." He wrapped an arm around my shoulders and guided me out the door. Alfredo and Pedro followed.

"Say, Alfredo, how is it that all these people know I'm here, since it's only been a half-hour?"

"Word has spread throughout the complex that an internationally famous cyclist has arrived."

"So much for the chance to rest."

What I saw upon entering the makeshift gymnasium was archaic, to put it mildly. Instead of the state-of-the-art, latest gizmo, pumping iron equipment we capitalists have come to expect, the Cubans use whatever happens to be lying around. Literally. Whatever means they have at their disposal is going to be it for them. And to think that, although the country is roughly the size of California, it's fifth in the world with total Olympic medals, is amazing.

To train the children in the proper swimming position, old bicycle inner tubes are sliced, fastened at one end to the child and by the other to a wall outside the pool. For flotation devices, pieces of plexiglass are formed from the children's hands, cut, and then strapped to them.

For muscle buildup, weight-training consisted of dumbbells made from a pair of concrete blocks with a rod rammed through them. The curling bar was made from a car axle, with wheel drums welded to each end. The leg curling table had truck springs to work the thighs and calves.

"Come," smiled Ibrahim. "You try. Do."

Other athletes stopped what they were doing in their workouts and gathered around us.

"Ibrahim, I can't. My leg muscles have cooled down."

"You try," he insisted. "I time you."

"Alfredo, help me out here."

"No push. Just go easy. It is only a friendly game of competition."

"Not exactly the answer I was looking for."

As Ibrahim readied his stopwatch, I took a seat, wrapping my legs around the truck springs.

"I count thirty seconds," informed Ibrahim. "Go!"

With so many pairs of eyes on me, I was forced to go on display. Tearing a leg muscle to prove some *macho*, athletic ability, and ending the Tour here and now, was not what it was all about. With Ibrahim's muscular, brick wall build, there was no way I could beat him in this contest, so I did the best I could with a count of fifteen.

"Okay," smiled Ibrahim. "I do now."

We changed positions, as he gave the stopwatch to Pedro. When the signal was given, Ibrahim held on tight and began pumping the legs furiously, smiling the entire time under the creaks and groans of the truck springs. All eyes were on me, and all I could do was laugh and applaud. That off balance reaction seemed to take the crowd by surprise, and soon were joining me to Ibrahim's delight.

The place looked more like a welder-masonry shop than a gym, but these young men and women were hungry. It didn't matter how fancy their equipment was so long as it did the job, gave them the final results they were looking for.

In many nations, sports is a means of getting out of poverty. I was all too well aware of that, for I always thought becoming an actor would give me the world traveled, internationally famous life I craved. Yet, in the end, it was sports that did it-- all through the simple mode of the bicycle.

After the tour was over, Ibrahim, Pedro, Alfredo and I sat outside in the warm sunlight.

"We do not have much," began Ibrahim, "But we use what we have to train our children."

"And most impressive," I replied. "Many other countries could not have achieved as much as you have."

"But we could do more if we had better equipment."

Alfredo and Pedro kept quiet, listening, while Ibrahim sat on the edge of his seat. The set-up was just too obvious to ignore, but what was I in for?

"And how can I be of help?" I asked.

It was the question to break the ice, as Ibrahim sat back in his seat, relaxing with a smile.

He pulled out a piece of paper from his back pocket with a list of things written on it. Well, it was the Christmas season after all.

"When you return home, we like you to call some of your corporations to help with new gym equipment, if possible."

Ibrahim handed me the paper and I scanned the list.

"Swimming equipment would also be helpful," continued my new friend. "Books on new swimming techniques, video..."

"English or Spanish?"

"Does not matter. Important thing is to know latest swimming ideas to be more competitive."

I folded the paper, placing it in my back pocket. "I'll see what I can do when I return."

Back in our dorm room, I mentioned to Alfredo, "It's amazing what can be done with old concrete and car parts."

"When you are poor, you must improvise."

"I know that all too well," I replied, as I climbed to the top bunk. "In my country, we would never allow our athletes to use such primitive equipment, much less make them build it themselves."

"America have everything." Alfredo flopped onto his own bed to nap. "We would take what America throw away."

Staring up at the ceiling, I commented, "Wouldn't it be wonderful, Alfredo, if governments would step aside and allow ordinary people like us to embrace and fellowship with one another in true friendship? What miracles we could achieve."

"*Si*," laughed my friend. "In Heaven."

"I hope and pray in our lifetime, I can one day return to a prosperous Cuba."

"*Si*. And I will be rich and famous."

When night descended a few hours later, Pedro came by our dormitory to take us to a restaurant.

"One that has good food and could be paid for in *pesos*," said my frugal friend.

"I know just the place," he said through Alfredo. "Just a short walk from here where most of the coaches go. The food is the best in town."

"And will you join us?" I asked.

He waived the offer. "No, *amigo,* I do not wish to impose."

"What impose?" replied Alfredo in a quizzical look. "We have enough for our friends."

I looked at my partner a bit wide-eyed. "And I'm suppose to be watching the *pesos?*"

"It will not be much, and we may be able to stay another day and rest," smiled Alfredo.

"I insist, Pedro. *Por favor*, join us."

"*Gracias*," he nodded humbly, and led us to the trough.

Alfredo read all the items to me from the Spanish menu until I chose the fish, *congris* and salad. Alfredo and Pedro choose the same, but substituted fish for chicken.

There were about a dozen or so round tables that were occupied by the locals. A line was waiting to be seated.

Adrian, Ibrahim, Alfredo and Pedro at the *Academia de Natacion.*

The flies were kept to a minimum, and the establishment even contained a fully-stocked bar of domestic and foreign liquors. The names of the drinks sounded exotic. I wanted to try them all, but mixing alcohol has never been my forte, so I stayed with the one called *Dragon*, a sweet greenish-colored concoction.

True to Alfredo's perception, during the course of the meal, Pedro asked if we'd like to stay an extra day.

"And you will not have to stay at the dorm. I would be honored if you came to my place instead."

"A most generous offer," I replied, "But we do not wish to put you out of your way."

By now, Alfredo knew my mannerisms. "*Si,* Pedro. *Kebin* is right. We do not wish to be a problem."

"Na, na, na, na..." Pedro rattled with a wave of his hand. "There is plenty of room. You will be my guests tomorrow. After dinner, I will show you the town."

There were no further arguments. After a week on the road, we were ready to let our bodies rest.

The meal was absolutely superb with all the main and side dishes laid out before us. A bountiful feast on this Thanksgiving night. I simply had to have another round of everything, including the *Dragon.* Alfredo and Pedro relaxed in their seats, opting for another round of beers. When the bill finally arrived, the total amount came to a whopping 23 *pesos*-- exactly one American dollar. I considered how I might've paid for everyone's meal in the place and never feel the pinch in my pocket. What a delicious fantasy. Trying to tip the friendly waitress was no good either; she kept returning the money, even following us out the door.

Back at the complex, the three of us gathered our bicycles and headed for the center of town where the core of activity took place. It was a warm evening. Men were selling cold beers from ice buckets on a corner, while party music played in the near distance. Across the street, the movie theater was showing the latest film, *Batman Parasiempre*, with Val Kilmer as the new Dark Knight. It was at least two years old, but for the price of a *peso*, I'd have been interested in seeing it in Spanish.

The *bicicleta* scored another hit with the crowd that gathered around it for a look, a touch, a chance to sit and pose with it. Once again the stunningly beautiful women of the island made friendly moves. Their hard bodies, in tight skirts, showing legs that went on forever, were oh, so seductive. Could I ever get tired of such beauty? Could I ever stop talking about such beauty? At times I was thankful to have my constant escort beside me, and sometimes I wanted to cut him loose and dive into sinful pleasure. Let's face it, at moments like these, sinning is fun, but oh, the possible, infinite, consequences you could end up paying for the rest of your life.

"Come," said Alfredo, tapping me on the shoulder and waking me from my fantasy. "Pedro want to take us to a private party the complex is having."

I bowed gracefully to the young *senoritas* who surrounded me and the bike. Alas, parting really is sweet sorrow. We cycled back to the complex, to a fenced-off area where the private party was being held for the young student-athletes. The drink was *refresco*; the dance, disco. Everyone was in the dancing mood, twirling and spinning. Laughter could be heard throughout the parking lot and across the street.

Pedro knew the man at the bar, who retrieved a bottle of rum from under the counter. The three of us indulged ourselves until I was ready to let loose.

I started off just dancing to the DJ-supplied tunes. Some disco, some rock, and even a bit of *calypso* that came back to me after a few routines. The younger crowd seemed to enjoy my moves, or perhaps just seeing an *Americano* up close and personal. A couple of the teenage *senoritas* were brave enough to join me, and the others quickly followed suit until we were just a mass of bodies bumping and grinding, caught up in a dancing circle. The young crowd's facial expressions grew to wide proportions, as the sweat poured forth. What time zone was I in? What decade? What world? In a magical instant, I had lost twenty years and was back in high school with *Saturday Night Fever*. It was wild! It was fun! It was decadent! And I loved it! No reason why one can't party and then leave alone in contentment. It doesn't always have to be sex, drugs, and rock 'n' roll.

Afterwards, I thought about how thankful and blessed I was to be in such a position. To be born and raised in a free country, to choose your own life, to follow your own path, or wherever the Lord has set your heart.

Yeah...there was much to be thankful for, on this, of all days...

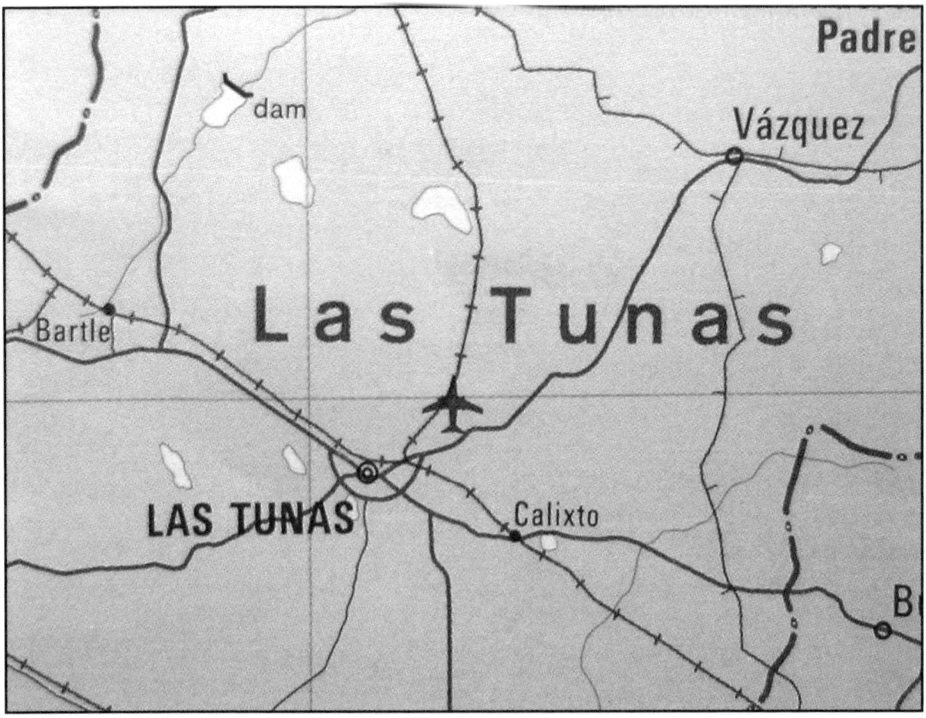

DIECISEIS

16

REST DAY in LAS TUNAS
DAY 8
NOVEMBER 28, 1997

A day of rest? You must be joking. There's no such thing when you're on a Tour of this magnitude. The mind must be constantly going over every minute detail. You may not be physically active, but you're still on the go. In a sense, that day could be called a resting workday. An oxymoron if ever there was one.

We were in the midst of a party town, had been on the go since leaving Havana ten days earlier, looking at an early wake-up call, facing 90 miles of cycling to *Camaguey*...Tell me, what would be your answer?

It had been a toss and turn, restless night of sleep. My muscles felt tight and cramped; my body desperately wanted to shut down both mentally and physically, but my mind, my Spirit would not do so until I was back home in familiar surroundings. Only then would I let my guard down.

I overslept a couple of hours, waking up by 6:30am, Alfredo rose a half-hour later, and Pedro joining us a half-hour after that.

Packing up our gear, and saying our farewells to Ibrahim and the rest of our dorm mates, we took a short bike ride to Pedro's place, a spacious two-story dwelling on a side street about a mile or so from the complex. Pedro, his wife, son and daughter lived on the top floor, while our host's parents lived beneath them. Once we were shown the spare bedroom toward the back of the house and had settled our gear, we parted ways.

"I must return to my office," said Pedro, "But make yourselves at home. Whatever I have is yours."

"*Gracias,*" replied both Alfredo and I. When Pedro left, Alfredo wanted to head to the marketplace.

How you find such a place is easy: you cycle through a particular area where a large crowd gathers in the early morning, and that's the marketplace. The one in *Las Tunas* was set up like a flea market, individual booths running down opposite sides of a main aisle, offering different types of services.

Alfredo craved his pork like I savored fine resorts, so naturally the first booth we stopped at had prepared pork sandwiches; pieces of meat in a plain, dry bun.

"How can you eat this crap?" I said with disgust.

"Is good," mumbled Alfredo.

"It has no cheese, no mayo, no lettuce, no nothing."

"*Si,*" he gulped down hard. "Just the way Cubans like. No fancy. Just plain."

The head of the swine sat next to the rest of his body on a silver-colored cookiesheet. Why I got an image of John the Baptist then was beyond me.

Aside from the swine sandwiches, there were booths with the regular pizzas, *bandito, refresco*, fried bananas and *yucca*, and other eatable items. Some were recognizable, some were not.

The centerpiece of the bazaar was filled with fruits and vegetables. People would arrive daily to buy their needs, using baskets, pillow cases, or some other form of container to transport their foodstuffs home.

Then there were the services that catered to one's vanity: the barber, the shaver, the *masseur,* the shoeshiner. Household items were also for sale-- but you had to arrive before the supply ran out, or else you'd be forced to go to one of the PanAmerican stores. And there you had to spend the much sought-after, elusive dollar.

"What do you wish to do today?" asked Alfredo.

"Go back to Pedro's place and catch up on my notes."

"That no' fun," brushed off my partner. "We go to a park I know. Very private. No one bother you or the bike."

"Oh? Does such a place exist?"

"*Si.* I know. I show you."

"I know a place, too. Pedro's. Indoors. Quiet. No one can see me. Complete privacy."

"Park is private, too," insisted Alfredo. "Only a few kilometers from here. I need to cycle everyday. It make me feel better in the legs."

So we went to this park that was "only a few kilometers."

It ended up being about ten miles away.

The park had a flowing brook running through it, and several bungalows in a shaded, wooded section. There was a main stone building that housed the bar and restaurant from which music and festive laughter echoed.

We parked our bikes in a clearing just outside the stone building. Alfredo stayed with them and worked on his journal, while I walked off to a more excluded spot.

For the next couple of hours, I was able to get caught up on my daily notes. I had long since abandoned the tape recorder. With Alfredo constantly by my side, how was it possible to talk about him?

About a hundred yards off, where I had left Alfredo, the party seemed to be getting louder. Walking back in that direction, I noticed a skinned swine with a long metal pole skewered through it, leaning against a concrete partition, ready to be placed on the spit.

Turning around to a tap on my shoulder, a male partier dressed in female clothing, gave me a wink and blew me a kiss from his cherry-red lips. If it wasn't a male, then I didn't know my drag queens, or else this was the ugliest woman with a bad case of facial hair, I had ever seen.

"My name Rodolfo. Come, we dance."

He grabbed me by the arm, and led me to the dance-floor where several other couples were bumping and grinding. The party was in full swing, and Alfredo was right at the core, dancing and drinking with a couple of foxy-looking, long legged, skin-tight, *senoritas.*

"A nice, quiet place to work, huh, Alfredo?"

"*Si,*" he laughed. "We have a good rest day, no?"

Aside from the stuffed pig, there was *congris, yucca* (a vegetable much like squash), wine, beer, and rum. The group numbered around two dozen from throughout the *Las Tunas* countryside.

This was a party group and there was no way we were going to get away with keeping to ourselves in work, especially when they found out I was an American. Now who could've told them that? Alfredo was as slick as I was in getting his way.

"Hey Klein! Klein," called out one young man with a few lusty ladies by his side.

"You talking to me, *amigo?*"

"*Si,*" he smiled. "We see your name on the beautiful bike. My friends and I want to know if you are *Kebin* Klein, the famous fashion designer?"

Alfredo had only told them my first name. The second part they took from my sponsor off the frame, thus putting the two together, arriving at their own conclusions. I didn't feel like getting into a long explanation.

"*Nada, amigo; senoritas.* No relation."

"Is okay," he smiled. "You are still welcomed."

"*Gracias.*"

I was doomed throughout the Tour to be referred to as either, *Kebin* Foster, the

Pig on a stick? Skewered swine? Anyway you look at it, it all adds up to party time!

famous movie actor, or *Kebin* Klein, the famous fashion designer. Whatever happened to Kevin Foster, the famous adventure-cyclist? Somehow, he got lost in the shuffle.

"*Americano, Cubano, amigos*," they all shouted, bringing me into the dance circle. The women, with their short dresses and long legs, were a stunning, erotic display to watch. What man among us could compete with their seductive dance? Some fancy, groin-grabbing disco moves on my part thrilled them to shouts of ecstasy. It made Rodolfo so hot, he took off his top, sliding his form next to mine. Everyone laughed and clapped at his sweaty, hairy, bra-laden chest, his skirt flowing about him like a *prima ballerina*. We drank the afternoon away, many of us losing our inhibitions.

"You know, Alfredo," I shouted over the music. "No matter how long I live, I can't get used to the sexual forwardness from your women."

"*Si*," shouted my friend. "In Cuba, sex is a pleasure. An enjoyment. Our women enjoy pleasing the men."

"I think the only way to subdue these women, is to gag them, tie them up and give them a lobotomy."

"But then it is just sex without the passion."

You know? He's right.

I had once heard about native American Indian customs and superstitions. Apparently, many natives believed in the power of the sperm as having life and energy. Squaws felt the more sperm in their wombs, the more power they were able to produce; and if they could gather a white man's semen it would make them more

Daisy and Rafaela.

powerful than anyone else in their tribe.

That went for the men as well. Many Indian cultures were happy and willing to give their wives or daughters to the white man, so that as soon as the foreigners filled their squaw's bellies with the "white magic," the men could shortly thereafter enter into their women and partake of the abundant power and energy that flowed from them.

I thought about these legends as the men at the party would point out their women and show me where their bungalow was located. They would ask me if I thought their women were beautiful by placing their fingers to their lips, asking, "*Bene?*"

And what's more frustrating was that the women didn't mind this attention at all. They seemed only curious, wondering which one of them I would choose--or would I rather take them all? Funny, but the question never came up regarding whether or not it was to be one at a time or all at once. With my limited Spanish, it was difficult to convey my feelings that I was having enough fun without the extracurricular activities. Alfredo was no help.

"They want you to choose, so choose," was his reply.

I felt like the prized stud surrounded by so many beautiful, willing participants. How much white power did they think I could produce in the next few hours?

One dark-haired lass named Rafaela kept closer to me than the other ladies for some reason. Her smile, the way her dark hair flowed, the flirtation of her eyes--my Italian grandmother would call this the evil-eye-- were intoxicating. Rodolfo and some of the other local boys insisted on pushing me closer to her, but I just couldn't

The party coming to an end. Rafaela and Jacquelina behind number 44; Rudolfo giving the horned salute with Luis by his side.

handle that type of forwardness. I backed away.

Finally, one of the women named Daisy took the reins and got down to business with me, language barrier or not. Using a combination of simple words and charades, she wanted to know why I didn't want to make love to one of the women, since they and their bungalow were available... I found it awkward to say I would love to get laid right about now, but just wasn't interested in one night (or one day) stands.

"*Senora?*" She asked if I had a wife back home.

"No."

"*Senorita?*" She was wondering if I had a girlfriend.

"*Nada.*" I replied, half-lying. Yeah I had a girlfriend, but the relationship was asexual, platonic, friendship... hell, even I didn't know what my relationship was with Jean, so how could I explain that to them? Maybe I should've said yes, but the effects of the wine and rum made me answer before I could think.

Daisy's brow furrowed. "*Senors?*"

"No!" I made that point quite clear. My interest was not in *senors.* Alfredo laughed so hard, he nearly toppled over a bench, dousing himself with his drink.

Finally, I remembered a word. "*Dios,*" I said, pointing up to the sky. That seemed to settle the curiosity.

Maybe it would've been easier to have gotten laid after all.

During the party they all wanted me to take their pictures-- by themselves, with my bike, with me, in groups of different combinations. At one point I ran out of film. One young man named Luis offered to take me back to Pedro's to retrieve more film on his motor-scooter if I would put a liter of fuel in his tank. I agreed.

About a half-mile down the road, we ran out of gas. Cubans are so poor they can't even afford the luxury of a full tank; they have to pay for the petrol in US dollars, and their labor is paid in *pesos*. More proof that two different money systems don't work.

We walked and pushed the scooter for another half-mile or so, until we managed to find someone that siphoned off a small amount of fuel to make it to the next gas station.

When the attendant came out to serve us, he wanted the 75 cents for the liter up front, but I motioned for him to fill the tank. I didn't want to deal with problems of being stuck again. He looked at Luis for a moment, wondering what to do, and Luis seemed to be as confused as the attendant was, obviously wondering if I could afford such an extravaganza.

I motioned again more insistently, and the attendant filled the tank.

The amount came to $3.70US. When it was paid, Luis' overjoyed facial expression grew so out of proportion, I feared it'd leave a permanent mark. He shook my hand, slapped me on the back, and from that point on, referred to me as, "My brother."

When we returned to the park, the pork was just being removed from the skewer, ready to be distributed to a hungry, exhausted, drunken crowd. I began to take pictures furiously, while Luis related the story of my benevolence to the group that was now crowded around him like a football squad.

The others looked over at me in awe, shaking their heads in confused wonder that I would do such a thing so nonchalantly. I think I somehow added to the rich myth.

The white meat of the fresh pork was mouth-watering, and as the party wound down with the setting sun, we all exchanged addresses so I would know where to send photos.

We hugged, we kissed, we laughed. We didn't want the day to end, but they had rides to catch in many different directions. It was one of the best *rest* days I had.

Alfredo and I were back to Pedro's house within the hour. While the wife made a meal of rice, meat, cucumbers, and papaya juice, we decided to stay in.

We listened to music from the Beatles (Pedro's) and Barry Manilow (mine). I became an audience to the children's English lesson of simple phrases, like: "How do you do?," "Where do you come from?," "What is your name?"

I critiqued their assignment, on which they did very well, and added some new phrases to their vocabulary, such as: "May I go out and play?," "May I help you mama... papa?"

They'd really have something to tell their friends and teacher Monday morning: a real, live *Americano* spent time at their humble home.

Day by day, mile by mile, we were bridging the gap between our two countries. The politicians could scream and shout at one another all they wanted to, but it would be us -- the common people-- that would produce the change.

Americano-Cubano, amigos!

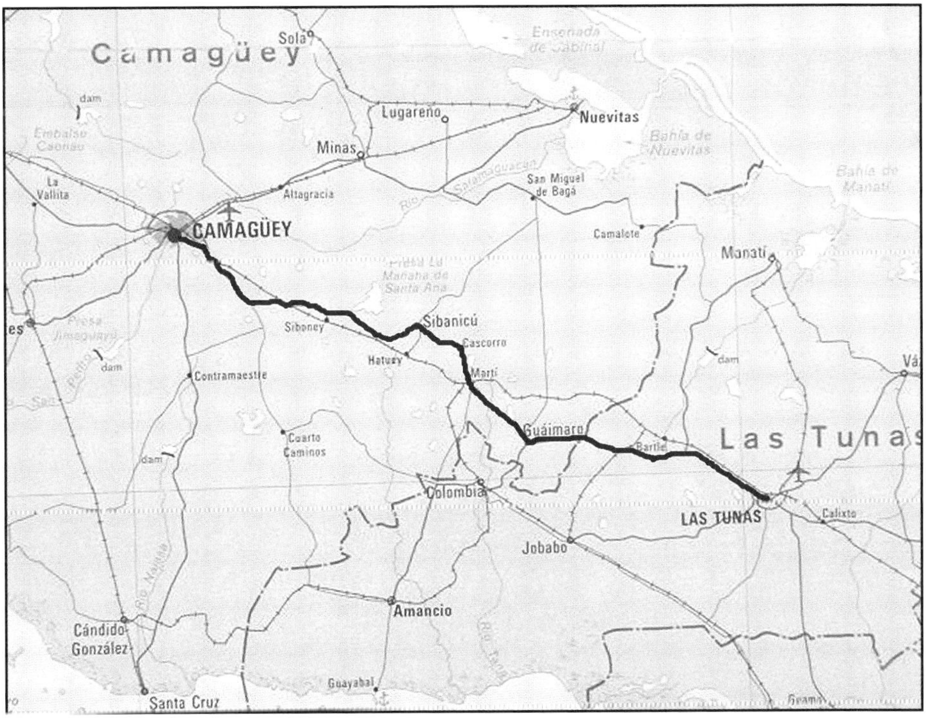

DIECISIETE

17

LAS TUNAS to CAMAGUEY
DAY 9
NOVEMBER 29, 1997

DAILY DISTANCE : 82 miles or 136.7 kilometers
TOTAL DISTANCE : 480 miles or 800 kilometers

It was a day of mental and physical milestones.

Physically, we were at least a third of the way through in Tour miles, and about half on days left. At three weeks, I was also half-way through my time in Cuba. Though my visa had an expiration date of December 3rd, I could get an extension if the Tour could not be completed in the length according to the itinerary. This I wanted to avoid at all costs. I was uncomfortable with the thought of experiencing a Communist Christmas.

Another physical problem that arose left me literally drained. In the nine hours it took us to reach our next destination, I was on and off the bike so many times trying to find a place to relieve myself that it was a small miracle we made it to *Camaguey* at all.

When we began our day at 5am from Pedro's house, it seemed like any other morning along the Tour. We had something to eat and a shot of rich, black, Cuban coffee; thanked our host; and waved good-bye, cycling off into the dawn.

A couple of hours later, we reached the border. We took photos near the new province sign, next to the large, red clay water jars that were symbolic of *Camaguey's* renowned liquid product.

During this stretch, Luis passed by, with a friend in tow, puttering along on his motor scooter. He waved frantically, shouting with joy, "Hello! my brother! Hello!"

I returned the gesture and the greeting before he disappeared from sight.

That's when the diarrhea developed. The first time, I paid it scant notice. Just another normal bodily function. Pull off to the side of the road (in this case behind the *Camaguey* border sign) and do your thing.

But then, about every 10 or 12 miles, or nearly every hour, I found myself having to take a detour. The indication of approaching sickness was that my lower intestines would begin to rumble, moaning and groaning until they were ready to explode. I was then forced to abandoned the route, giving myself over to a lower authority.

This was not exactly an easy thing to do, having been faced with untold miles of flat terrain. And all day it was endlessly level: No trees, not even a field of any kind; this made a private matter even more difficult.

Thankfully, there were bridges along the way, and that would be, in a phrase, a pit stop. I wasn't the only one that had the idea, I found. Others before me had the same problem. The flies were in dung heaven, as I made my way around the minefield, finding a spot to add to their treasure trough.

To say I felt like crap was putting it mildly. But it was totally my own fault. PentaPure, my water filter sponsor, had supplied me with enough product to get me through the Tour without incident, but then I got cocky, (sorry) working up a sweat with the *senoritas* during the previous day's festivities at the park. I had thus forsaken practicality for partying, and now I was paying the price.

Being sick on a major Tour is never on the itinerary, even though I always need to calculate for it. Being minutely sick can be disastrous, even fatal in failure. This couldn't be happening to me. Not now, not at any time-- but the problem was mine, and I had to deal with it. Fortunately, I still had half a roll of toilet paper that would just see me to the capital city.

The only *non-deposit* stop we made was when we reached the town of *Guaimaro*, where the first Cuban Constitution was drawn up and signed during the Spanish-American war.

At the town border, there were several stone steps leading up to a three-story concrete pillar. Off to the right was a building that housed the country's early documents and other historical artifacts. Throughout our travels thus far, I found more money and devotion placed upon the upkeep of the historical monuments, than I did on the people. At least it showed where the government placed its value in the chart of society.

Along the way, we also passed by a cattle ranch owned by the government, where two bored bulls were getting it on.

Alfredo pointed and laughed. "Look at the homosexual bulls. Quick, get a picture."

One bull broke free of its pen, and several of the Cuban cowboys came storming out of a corral ready to rope the beast. He bucked and kicked, being fought into submission by the *gauchos*, until he was led back to the rest of the herd. It was probably the most excitement the wranglers had all day, and was a detour for this *gringo* from his immediate problems.

When we reached the capital of *Camaguey* I was red in the face, yet Alfredo looked like he just went around the block instead of the 80-plus miles we completed. Perspiration was draining from my pores. All I wanted to do was find a place to rest. Our first stop through town was the *Hotel Camaguey*, a large, expensive-looking building, possibly the largest hotel in the city.

At the rental car facility, Alfredo spoke with the head man, a distinguished-looking gentlemen with a serene spirit. Of average height with salt-and-pepper hair and a moustache to match, his name was Jerry. He came out to greet me with a broad smile. His eyes twinkled and he spoke excellent English.

"As I was telling your friend here, this hotel is very expensive if you are just planning to rest. However, I have a friend at the *Hotel Caonao* that could give you a room at a good price."

He handed me his card with the information printed on the back. I thanked him for his help and complemented him on his English. He bowed slightly and smiled, obviously pleased that someone who must have looked as terrible as I, would take the effort to banter pleasantly.

"As we get closer to Havana," warned Alfredo, "finding places to stay and pay in *pesos* will be difficult."

"But only through the middle section," I noted. "Once we get beyond a certain point toward the western end of the island, we'll be able to go back to *pesos*."

The *Hotel Caonao* (pronounced Cownow) was a lovely, off-the-road retreat with palm trees on the sculptured front lawn and valet bicycle parking in the back. About what one would expect from a mid-priced hotel in America, the room rate for being "friends of Jerry" came to an enormous $10US.

In Cuba that's the only price you pay. It doesn't matter how many people are in your room. There's no bed tax, tourist tax, State tax, county tax, and any other tax anyone could think of. The rooms were clean; the beds were comfortable. There were lukewarm showers if one desired, and the place had a restaurant.

Once the details were taken care of, it was just a matter of time before I dropped my backpack off in a corner, stripped out of my uniform, popped a couple of penicillin (thought maybe it'd help), crawled under the covers, and quickly fell asleep.

Although the temperature was in the 90s, I couldn't stop shaking and needed two blankets. I got hot after a while and threw them off, only to cover myself back shortly thereafter. I tossed and turned in moaning restlessness.

When Alfredo came to wake me for dinner some four hours later it was as though only a moment had passed. I declined.

"But you need to eat something, for strength."

Just the thought of food made me want to vomit. Alfredo's knitted brow was of deep concern, and I suspected he had seen this before on many other tours. If I went back to sleep and never woke up, that would've been all right with me, but my cycling partner pulled and tugged, propping me up, helping me to dress and ignoring my protests.

"You will feel better when you have something in you."

"I'm just not hungry. I need to rest."

"Come," insisted Alfredo, pulling me up out of the bed.

"I'm going to vomit on you. I mean it."

"I jump out of the way," he countered, continuing with the task of getting me out the door.

"You are such a pain in the ass."

"But not as painful as it is for you."

He eventually got me out the door and into the restaurant. Somehow I managed, but my legs felt like soft rubber. I was dehydrated. Walking the brief route to the place, I wobbled and nearly fainted.

There were not that many people present, so we were seated immediately. Alfredo's usual enormous appetite made me feel green. The waitress came by, placing her hand upon my heated forehead, shaking her head in a motherly, concerned manner. All I could handle were several glasses of water-- why bother with the purifier now, I wondered-- juice and some sliced oranges. By then I had to excuse myself, and I hurriedly made it back to the room and the throne, emptying out a liquid stream of what little meal I had. The book, *A River Runs Through It*, had new meaning for me.

I was now in serious jeopardy of not being able to finish this Tour. Would I return home with another failure under my belt? Since Alaska, I had to redeem myself.

"Oh, Kevin's slipping," the sponsors would say. "He's getting old. Can't handle it anymore."

Would I be forced to retire looking like a loser? That's not how I wanted it to end. Not that way; not on those terms. There was still time left in the schedule, still a chance to completing this thing. But I needed to let the parasite run its course; to rest.

The heat, the food, the killer 60-to-80-mile-a-day pace, the lack of sleep because of all the paperwork to get through were combining to take its toll. My body was beginning to shut down, and there was nothing I could do to fight it.

Three weeks were left before I returned home. Could I possibly cycle another 800 miles and finish?

Home...what a beautiful, sacred word. Home. The ranch. The country. The Christmas Season. How I missed Jean and the girls. How I wanted to hold them and hug them all.

And Alfredo. He was a good man. He wanted to see this Tour to its end as much as I did, for this would be a personal achievement to him as well. The longest cycling tour in his country's history... It would be a first, and he, the only Cuban to ever do it.

He was a good choice for this undertaking. The best companion anyone could ever have. I knew I wouldn't have had a chance without him. Loyal. Trustworthy. No better friend could one have, and the success of this Tour would lie with him.

Yeah, I thought, as I laid in bed, he pushes me to go the extra mile or 30, but he's patient and understanding, and realizes the difficulties I have in adjusting to his country.

I may have gone to Cuba to do a Tour, but God brought Alfredo to me; had him waiting there for me. It was fate. It was destiny, and no matter what, we were going to finish this Tour. We would see it to the end, no matter how long it took. There would be no turning back.

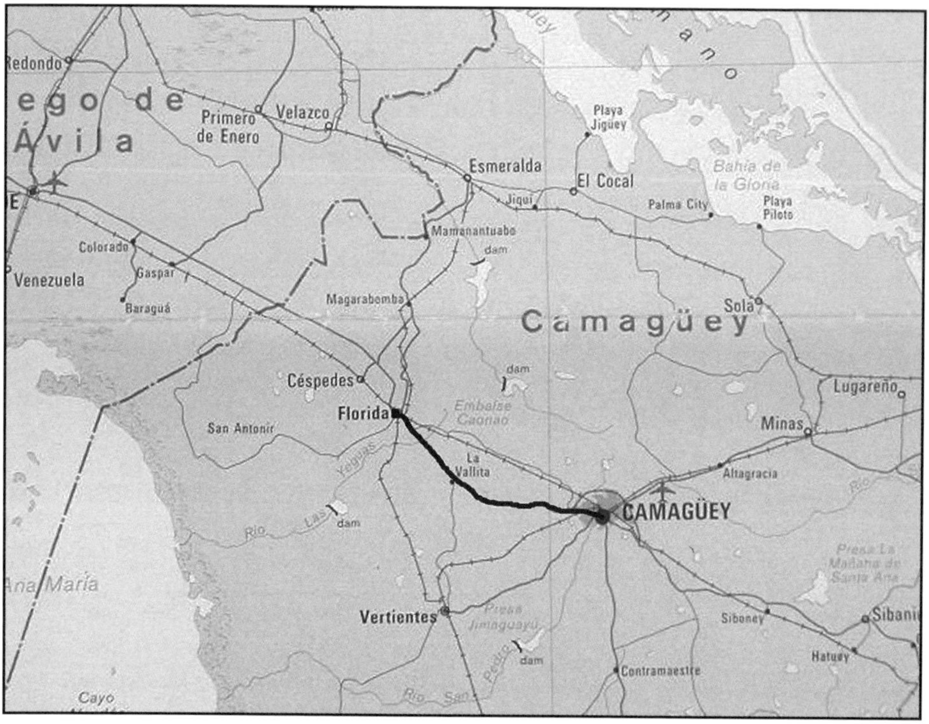

DIECIOCHO

18

CAMAGUEY to FLORIDA
DAY 10
NOVEMBER 30, 1997

DAILY DISTANCE :	**28**	**miles**	**or**	**46.7**	**kilometers**
TOTAL DISTANCE :	**508**	**miles**	**or**	**846.7**	**kilometers**

"*Kebin, Kebin*, come. It is time to go."

I thought I was dreaming, the shaking just a reaction from the virus or whatever I had. But the voice brought me back to a state of conscienceness.

"Come, we go."

Alfredo was suited-up, fit and ready for another beautiful day of cycling. It made me sick. "To hell with that," was my reply as I rolled over to continue what little sleep I was able to get.

It was a restless night going from bed to bathroom. If I could, I should've just slept sitting up on the toilet. I mean, really, how much crap could a person have in them?

My head hurt, my body ached. I could feel every muscle and bone with every movement I made, and, of course, the more you go, the more you dry out. My lips were parched, my skin rough and dead. I needed to stay an extra day-- I wanted it, I begged for it. *I demanded it!*

"We can't, because all the rooms are reserved." His eyes shifted, unable to meet mine.

"And I'm supposed to be full of shit?"

"It will pass," sympathized my partner.

"Yeah, flaming asshole has a new meaning for me," I snapped. "Look, I just need to rest. Tomorrow I'll be better." I didn't want to hear anymore. I wanted to sleep.

Alfredo persisted. He viewed our map of the country, pointing to the route. "Can you no' make it here?"

"Here" was a mid-sized town called Florida, about 25 or so miles away. At that distance, I figured it may as well have been the State it was named after.

"I don't know," I moaned. "Maybe. Just give me another hour or so." It was almost 7am, and Alfredo was obviously anxious to be on the way. But if I could make it to Florida, I knew, he would be happy to settle for that.

"You must eat something and keep cycling. It will make you feel better." The thought of food made me nauseated, and imagining placing my tender butt on that hard saddle seat made me curl into a fetal position.

Another hour passed. In that time, I was at least sitting up and half dressed.

"You are doing very good," Alfredo encouraged. "Just a little more and we be on our way."

I crashed back into bed. Alfredo looked up toward the ceiling. "Why me, God? Why me?"

"I'm exhausted. Can I go naked?"

"Not unless you want to go to jail."

"One with a toilet?"

"The jails in Cuba are the toilets."

By 9am, he was practically pushing me out the door.

"Oh, you look much better. We go far today."

"You're such a junkie for miles."

"*Si.* I love to ride. We do good today."

The next four hours were painfully slow-- painful to my tired buttocks, painful to my mind. About every six miles I had to stop and rest-- just catch my breath, I was that weak.

Thankfully, and with much gratefulness, I never had to make a pit stop. And that was a blessing in the continued flat, open terrain. There were still those times when I wanted to pack it in, as I watched Alfredo pull farther and farther away from me until he became a black speck on the horizon. No question about it. It was a work day.

When we reached Florida, there were two places to stay, located respectively on either side of town. The first one we approached was the *Motel Florida*.

Cycling up to the driveway, I saw that the hut-like buildings needed to be condemned. Some of the roofs were caved in, windows and doors were missing. What clinched our decision not to stay was when the guard at the gate told us there would be no extras like water, electricity-- or a working bathroom. *Oh, is that all*, I thought.

He did, however, mention that about three miles on the other side of town (or the other end of the main road) there was another place called the *Hotel Florida*. Could it be worse?

It was the exact opposite. The palace-- excuse me, place-- was monstrous. Alfredo and I made our way to the front entrance, my mind reeled at what the price would be for such extravagance.

Alfredo evidently picked up on my thoughts-- not that it would have been difficult: my mouth must have been wide with awe, my eyes glazed over with the sight of it all.

"The next hotel from here is about fifty miles away."

I was doomed.

The grounds were immaculate, a lush green carpet with palm trees. At a discrete distance from any disturbances, there was a gazebo-bar where a waiter was serving drinks to satisfied customers. Off to the side, we could hear the laughter from many people, splashing away in the Olympic-sized, clear water pool.

We must have looked like a couple of road rats just off the street. I knew I felt like it, too.

We entered the establishment where perfectly-dressed Cubans seemed to part for us. Oh dear, I marveled, and I forgot to put on my deodorant today.

The marble floor was polished to the point that your reflection shot back up at you. There was a tourist gift store off to our right and the bar-restaurant-game room to our left.

The surroundings were a dead give-away to what we were in for. And since I was going to be hit with a financial jolt I had no way of avoiding, I just had to deal with the situation as best I knew how: Pray. Pray real hard.

"That will be twenty-one dollars," smiled the beautiful young receptionist.

Was my hearing going as well? "For both of us?"

"*Si*--I mean, yes sir," she answered with another smile.

Hallelujah! Praise the Lord! But then I realized that the Cubans who were staying were allowed to pay the same price in *pesos*.

Yes, you have to brush these things off with the understanding that the Cuban people are poor, while we filthy, capitalistic Americans are rich.

Bikes were not allowed in the room at any excuse. They had to be taken to the back, where they were given an identification number and locked in a guarded area. The price: two dollars for me, 2 *pesos* for Alfredo. It was rather a big difference when one amounts to 8 cents, while the other is...well...two dollars.

"I keep telling you, Alfredo, my country is more Socialist, more Communist than yours," I reminded him, as we headed with our gear to our top floor room.

"America is no' Communist," he laughed.

"Sure it is. We don't care if you're rich or poor. Everyone pays the same price, regardless."

"It is the same with Cubans."

"Balls! You come to my country and see if you can get a discount, because you're a Cuban. They'll tell you to step aside. Green is the only color Americans care about."

Getting into the elevator, we continued.

"A place like this, your people can stay for *pesos,* while all foreigners must pay in dollars. Big difference."

"Because all foreigners are rich."

"They teach you that in *Social* Studies?"

Our room was located at the end of a long, narrow hallway. If anyone wanted to get by you, it would be a feat of accomplishment.

"It could be worse," commented Alfredo.

"Yeah? Like how?"

"Because I with you, I, too, could be paying in dollars."

"And why aren't you?"

"Because I show them the special, stamped document."

In our room, we found such features as a balcony, color TV, refrigerator, a toilet that flushed, a sink that worked, and a shower with lukewarm running water. Never in Cuba was I able to find a really hot shower; they just don't believe in it, I guess.

Once settled, Alfredo changed into his swimming trunks and was out the door. I settled for the shower massage therapy, and the relief of the toilet. When you're feeling that sick, it's the creature comfort surroundings that help; the little blessings that count.

After a short rest, I joined Alfredo out by the pool. He was enjoying a beer and watching the young ladies splashing near him. I was feeling somewhat better, but my stomach was still doing flip-flops.

While Alfredo ordered snacks for himself, I helped myself to some soda crackers and a Coke at the bar.

When the staff tried to collect some dollars from Alfredo, he naturally put up a fight.

"I ordered the *hors d'oeuvres* for myself, not for him," he pointed to me a few feet away. "Besides, I am Cuban."

"That doesn't matter," said the young lady. "You are with him, so everything has to be paid in dollars."

"I refuse to pay in dollars," Alfredo answered, without looking up at her.

Sure, he could've gotten the money from me, but he wasn't asking, and I wasn't volunteering, because I really wanted to see how he'd get himself out of this jam.

The young lady persisted. Alfredo resisted. She went off to get one of the managers; a walking wall of a bouncer.

I stayed with my soda crackers, munching furiously with excitement. This guy could eat Alfredo, the pint-sized sausage, for a breakfast appetizer, but that wasn't bothering the brave *bendaho*. He stuck to his rights. I stuck with my dollar Coke. The two men spoke very rapid Spanish until the argument was settled.

Alfredo could pay in *pesos.*

But we both got hit that night for dollars at the restaurant. I ate very little and was too tired to fight. Returning to my room I watched *Major League II* on HBO.

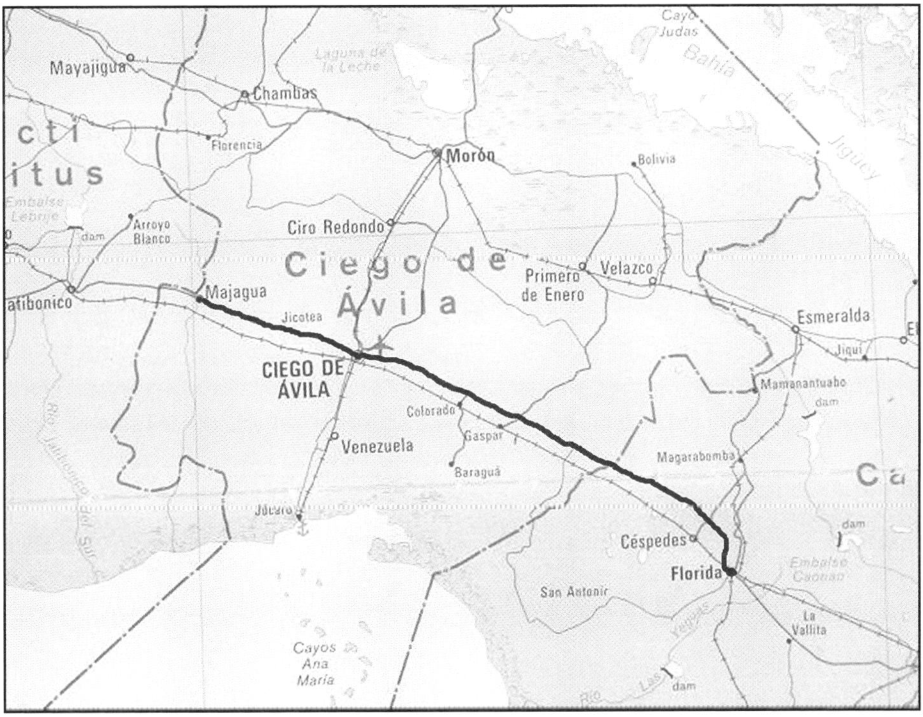

DIECINUEVE

19

FLORIDA to MAJAGUA
DAY 11
DECEMBER 01, 1997

DAILY DISTANCE :	**61 miles or 101.7 kilometers**
TOTAL DISTANCE :	**569 miles or 948.4 kilometers**

5am arrives fast, especially when you're up late watching American films with Spanish subtitles on Home Box Office. And it doesn't get any easier when your partner has a specific goal he wishes to attain.

"Are you out of your stinkin' mind?"

The question seemed perfectly legitimate, considering what he was attempting to drag me into.

"*Si,* we can do it!" he said with a cyclist's confidence.

"*Trinidad!* In two days?"

"*Si.* It no' a problem."

According to our former itinerary, we were to arrive at the 500-year-old town in three days, not the two Alfredo was pushing for.

"We only have about two more days of flatness. This is the best part to make up for the lost time."

"But don't you think trying to get to *Trinidad* in a two day stretch is pushing it? I still have a case of the runs."

"Look," said Alfredo, pulling out the map. "After *Trinidad*, you want to go north. That is very bad."

"Why?"

"We have to cross the *Topes de Collantes*."

"So?"

"It is a devil mountain. So steep. Not even crazy people try to cross it with bicycles. Sometime trucks no' can make it to the top. Staying to the coast would be best."

"But then we miss the entire province of *Villa Clara*, and I want the bicycle through every part of Cuba."

"But it will take us all day. Very little miles."

"Have you ever crossed the mountain by bike?"

"Are you mad?!" Alfredo stepped back in mock fear. "You do not know this mountain. You wait and see."

As I continued to view the route, Alfredo went about the business of packing his gear.

"I think two days to *Trinidad* is too much to handle, and still try to take photos and keep up with my notes."

"We gain time now, we lose it on the devil mountain."

"Once we reach the summit, it's downhill, right?"

"*Si.* But we will never reach the capital that day."

"What if we change course?"

"Along the coast?" Alfredo's eyes lit-up with a smile.

"No. After the mountain, we should be able to make it to *Manicaragua*," I said, pointing to the spot for Alfredo to take a look. "From there, we can change course, shooting straight across to the capital of *Cienfuegos*."

"*Si*," said Alfredo, scratching his head. "That will work."

"And give me part of the province, thus maintaining my goal."

"*Si.* If we go two days to *Trinidad*, we take rest before going up the mountain."

Little by little we were advancing upon the time lost in Havana. If we did what he wanted, we would gain another day. But in my condition, I knew, it would be a killer pace once again.

"Alright, let's give it a try."

For the most part, the worst seemed to be over. I only had to make half a dozen detours instead of the two dozen of the day before, but what little toilet paper I could scrape together was quickly running out, and I was forced, at times, to resort to tearing sheets out of my journal. Lord, I needed another miracle in a country that was short on supplies of everything, whether you had money or not to pay for them.

We reached the border as the sun rose. It danced upon the horizon, tickling the sugarcane fields. As *Camaguey* is known for it's water, the province of *Ciego de Avila* is famous for it's pineapple-- *la pina*, as the locals refer to their cash crop.

It was also at the border between the two provinces that we came across the famous monument to a cyclist. An Emmy award-winning, documentary filmmaker bud of mine once told me that he heard there was some statue devoted to cyclists, but couldn't get all the details; he didn't even know if it were a myth or not. Either way, I said I'd check it out.

Unbeknownst to me, several years before, when I was planning the route for this Tour, I inevitably marked the spot we were passing through.

As was with most Cuban memorials, this eight-foot high marble and granite obelisk was erected by the side of the road, in the middle of a desolate nowhere. About two-thirds of the way down the shaft was a bronze plaque depicting a symbolic cyclist. At the base of the structure was another metal plate with the Mexican cyclist's name, *Agustin Alcantara*, and the date of his death, February 25, 1979. No other information was given. That would have to be supplied by my knowledgeable guide.

Unlike other roadside historical stops we've been making along the route, this one I was interested in.

"All the Latin nations came for a cycling competition. It was right here at this border that the accident occurred. *Alcantara* was badly injured, so they put him in a truck and take him to the hospital in *Ciego de Avila*, but he die on the way. No one know exactly when he die on the route, so the monument was placed here, where the accident was."

As I took photos, I asked, "Who put up the monument? The government?"

"No. The people of both provinces, five years after the accident, since it happened on the border."

Right out in the middle of nowhere, miles from the nearest town in both directions. Only hikers, cyclists, and those on horseback would notice; motorists flying by at 100 kph would probably ignore it. Somehow it seemed fitting.

About 9am, Alfredo and I stopped at a small town named *Colorado* for a light breakfast. Alfredo ate voraciously as usual, while I picked at my pizza. People were milling about from booth to booth, drinking and eating on their way to work, or catching up on the local gossip.

A couple of hours later, against a brewing storm and constant headwinds, we reached the capital. Making our way to the immigration office to see about an extension on my visa, we arrived at our destination just as the rains came crashing down. Perfect timing. Thank You, Lord.

This was a necessary stop, because the date on my visa said November 3rd, which meant there were only 30 days to renew, which meant now. However...

"The thirty days of the visa begins when you arrive in Cuba, not when it was issued to you in Washington, DC," said the immigration officer through Alfredo.

If that were true, then I had until the 10th of December, which to the best that we could figure out from the map and the miles we were putting in, would place us

At the monument to a fallen cyclist on the *Camaguey-Ciego de Avila* border.

somewhere near the capital of *Pinar del Rio*.

"Nine days to *Pinar*," I said. "Think we can make it?"

"*Si*," nodded Alfredo. "We can do it."

"What happens if time runs out?"

"Trouble."

"That's inspiring."

"A visa can only be extended at a province capital," informed Alfredo. "The next one is *Sancti Spiritus* tomorrow. After that it is *Pinar.* If we do not arrive at the appropriate time, we will have to return to Havana."

"To hell with that idea. We return to Havana when the Tour is over and not before then."

By the time we settled the situation, the downpour had stopped. As we were looking for a place to have lunch, I peered around the corner and chanced upon a sign that translated as *National Academy of Cycling.*

Just a group of buildings around a courtyard, the Academy was the place where the coaches and Cuba's future cycling stars lived, ate, slept, and generally did nothing but become cycling machines.

Upon entering the facilities, we saw a group of male teenagers huddled over a bicycle. They were in the process of repairing it, as a staff of doctors and nurses would be operating on a patient. They were so engrossed in what they were doing, they never saw us standing nearby.

That wasn't the problem with the staff of coaches seated in the office just off to our right. From their glass front view, they jumped from their seats, trying to squeeze out the door all at once.

"Welcome, *amigos,* welcome!" shouted one of the men.

By then a couple of the boys repairing the bike looked over to see what the commotion was. When they spotted the bike, their eyes lit up. Tapping their friends to attention, they, too, in short order, joined us.

"Never in our lives have we seen such a beautiful piece of machinery!" said one of the coaches, as he knelt down with some of his athletes to inspect every bolt and cog.

One of them pointed to a button on my handlebars.

"What does this do?" he asked?

"Why don't you press it and find out," I answered.

He did, which popped the seat up from the downhill position to the straightaway level. Some of the boys near the saddle jumped back in astonishment when it sprang to life, laughing nervously along with their coaches.

"May I try it?" asked another coach, wishfully.

"Of course. You may all ride it if you like."

The invitation excited the entire compound, as the boys tried to fight for position, only to be scolded by their adult supervisors into forming an orderly line. When Humberto finished his test run, he had abundant questions and comments.

"What are the wheels made of?" he asked, all the while keeping his eyes on the bike and the different riders.

"Carbon fiber," I answered.

"And the brakes. Are they hydraulic?"

"*Si.*"

"I have never known such stopping power."

"If you're not careful, you could be thrown from the bike. They have also been known to crush ordinary rims."

"I believe."

The other coaches who took the Beast for a spin asked about the weight, the cost, the particular materials that were used, the angles at which the tubes were cut and positioned.

"This is incredible technology," said Humberto, shaking his head. "No matter how well we prepare, we could never compete with such a disadvantage."

"But remember," I pointed out. "It's not the machine, but the engine that sees the race to the end."

"*Si,*" agreed my new friend. "But if both engines are well-conditioned, the machines could give a slight edge, and that is all that is needed to win the race."

They were about to have lunch, and invited Alfredo and I to fellowship with them. We accepted their kind offer.

During our lunch of bean soup, rice, mashed beans, salad, bread and water, served cafeteria-style, many of the coaches who, in their prime, had cycled in such races as the *Tour of Mexico, Tour of Italy*, and *Tour de France.* They asked if I knew such American cycling celebrities as Greg LeMond, husband and wife team Davis Phinney and Connie Carpenter, as well as several others.

"Yes, most of them I know personally," I answered.

They beamed with pride, announcing, "We once raced against them."

Given a small tour of the facilities, I found the conditions in which the teenage athletes and coaches lived in were far below that of most poverty standards. In some cases, it was just downright filth. Their bathrooms were devised of a long trench to urinate in, while another area consisted of holes to squat over. Showers were nothing more than rusty metal pipes poking out of a concrete wall that cold water poured out of. Their sleeping quarters were no better. Cots and bunks thrown in a colorless, concrete gray room with wood-chipped dressers to store what little clothes and possessions they had brought along with them. My own dogs lived better than they did.

This was the reality for these young boys. The dream for them was to work, study and train hard, so that, *Deo Volente*, God Willing, some of them might break through the barrier to succeed in glory. Poverty makes one strong, and hope is all that some people have to live for. This, I have understood from birth. Take an individual's dreams away, and what's left? It is not a sin to want a better way of life.

After a couple of hours of conversation, exchanging addresses, taking photos, and handing out tubes of liquid Teflon called TriFlow for their bikes, Alfredo and I headed out of the city.

Off to a small border town some 15 miles away-- in order to set ourselves up for the next day's *Trinidad* run. And, of course, we didn't like to stay in the bigger cities.

The winds continued kicking up in our faces throughout the afternoon, so it took much longer to make the next town than what we had anticipated.

Once again, the Lord was obviously good to us when we came upon a resort facility in a jungle-like setting. It was complete with an abundance of trees and a calm river where we could swim and wash our clothes. The best part of the deal was that we could pay in *pesos.*

"The manager say he no' want to rent us a room, because it is the day to wash the sheets," said Alfredo, upon returning from the front desk.

"Alright, here's what we do," I said, looking over at the manager who was cleaning off the counter. "I'll sit here in front of her view looking exhausted. You tell her we've come a long way and can't possibly go any farther."

"She no' believe that story."

"Tell her Americans aren't as strong as Cubans."

"Hmm," nodded Alfredo. "This, she may believe."

Back went my partner, while I found a corner seat to place myself, looking utterly devastated from the road miles we put in. I was a pathetic sight, but it was the best routine we could come up with on such short notice, and by Alfredo's body language, he was pouring it on thick.

"*Si,*" said the plump woman with the sympathetic, motherly look. "There is a room for twenty *pesos*, if you are not too particular about the conditions."

Who? Us?

The room was adequate for our needs, and, once settled, we headed for the river with our dirty laundry. Finding the water to be warmer than the cold shower, we decided to bathe ourselves as well.

Across from us were a group of boys climbing a giant tree, 30 to 50 feet high, and jumping off one of the limbs into the river below. They called out to me to take their picture as they dove time and again. We were not in the best part of the day, and there was too much shade for a decent photo, but I humored them nonetheless, taking several shots.

The river separated the hotel and restaurant, and between the gap spanned a rope-and-wood foot-bridge that shook with every step. The restaurant itself was of huge proportions-- large enough to accommodate wedding parties. I felt out of place without the proper attire; Alfredo was just hungry. He ordered the horse.

"It give you strength," he held up his fists. "You try."

I wasn't as hungry as a horse-- and certainly not hungry enough to eat one for that matter. I was still in the flip-flop stage, so I played it safe with the crab and rice, drinking plenty of bottled mineral water. Even then I couldn't finish what I ordered. Fortunately, I had a human garbage disposal by my side. I wondered if staying drunk would help my condition?

The situation remained the same. At times I felt hot, then cold with the shakes, needing an extra blanket at night. I crawled into bed exhausted, wanting to sleep forever and a day. I didn't even care that I had to share my quarters with the lice, fleas, ants, mosquitoes, or any other creatures that roamed about us.

The heat and humidity was ever constant. I was sweating day and night, sometimes wondering why I bothered to bathe at all. I felt dry and parched continually; drinking to no end, as I remembered those China days and the kidney stones that followed shortly upon my return to the States. I would drown myself in fluids before suffering that condition once more.

Ah, the good ol' Summer days of one's life, I thought. The glory fades with age, but the memories linger on. Is that how it happens once I hang up my cleats as I plan to when this Tour is over? It's been a good run, a fun run, but now it's time to move on to the next level, the next phase of life. In a way, these Tours, these adventures have brought me closer to God. A yearning to seek His face. The cycling doesn't mean much to me anymore. When it's over, it's over. I won't miss it, because I'll have moved on to something else, another set of dreams to fulfill.

After the next day we would be past the half-way point of our journey. If we could make *Trinidad* we would have earned another rest day, and that made me as giddy as possible, under the circumstances.

God bless the little blessings.

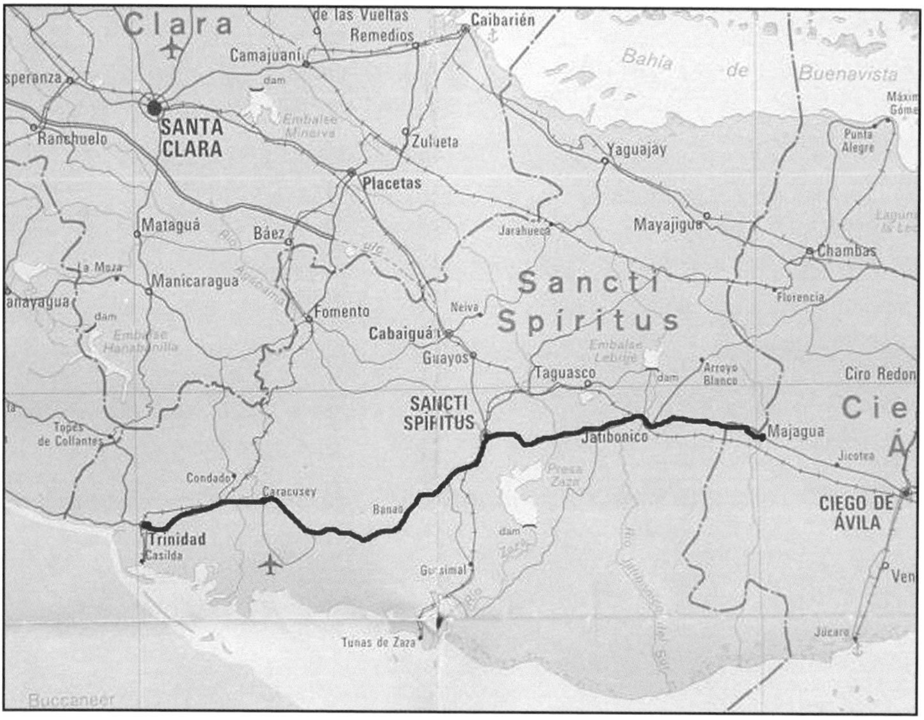

VEINTE

20

MAJAGUA to TRINIDAD
DAY 12
DECEMBER 02, 1997

DAILY DISTANCE : 80 miles or 133.3 kilometers
TOTAL DISTANCE : 649 miles or 1081.7 kilometers

I awoke in a wet bed, and momentarily thought I had lost all control of my bladder. Upon further inspection, I realized that the fever had broken during the night. Hopefully, the illness I'd been experiencing since leaving *Las Tunas* had finally passed, although I still felt weak and shaky.

Aside from the sweat of the fever, the hot, humid nights made everything damp. When dressing into a new uniform, it was like putting on wet clothes. We couldn't wipe the perspiration off with our towels, because they couldn't absorb any more liquid than they already had. Trying to write on our map, or scribing some early morning notes, was also impossible, because of the dampness.

"How do you feel, Alfredo?"

"Not so good," he replied, placing his own damp clothes on his sweaty body. "Too much humidity. Everything damp."

One other problem began to return: the loss of feeling in my hands. It was an odd and irritating sensation as though someone had whacked my funny bone and I couldn't shake the feeling. Perhaps less time on the bike after the Tour was over would help, but then again, I was alarmed at the notion that I may have permanently damaged something, that I'd have to live with this condition the rest of my life. The Lord is the Great Physician, and I trusted in Him.

Within a half-hour upon awakening, Alfredo and I were dressed and out the door. We were getting better at being up and out, but it was particularly easy that morning, since we had an incentive. A day of rest tomorrow if we could make *Trinidad* by nightfall.

"It is only sixty miles away. That is nothing," stated the expert.

"You're full of it. More like eighty," I countered.

This was another routine for us: arguing about the miles we had to put in for the day. My bicycle computer was the final authority in speed, distance, mileage, time and altitude, and Alfredo and I tried to out-guess it often. It was just something for us to do, another mind game to get us through another day of work.

So what goes through one's mind when doing some long, torturous, soul-searching journey? Don't know. Can't speak for anyone else, but from my point of view, thoughts fluctuate between the here and now and the hereafter.

Lots of thoughts about the Lord, and how hypocritical I feel putting myself in His place when judging me. If I were God, I'd send me to Hell. When I try to focus my mind on the good and benevolent-- certain times of my youth, when I can still recall some innocence within, images of women and breasts, passionate weekends spent in bed with some of the most beautiful women I have ever been privileged to make love with enter my psyche, and I can't seem to dismiss them -- that's when the guilt enters.

I try to shake the ecstasy for the ecclesiastical, only to end up in agony.

Work is work and play is play. I love both. Pleasing a woman sexually is as much of an accomplishment to me as meeting a day's goal. When you live on the edge of life and face death as often as I have, being in the tender arms of a soul mate is a very comforting experience. Jean's my best friend in the world, and I'll love her till death us do part. But sexually there's nothing between us. She just never wanted to devote and commit time to sharing her life with someone else other than her hobbies. Some people are just meant to be asexual, because the very thought and act of love-making, of exchanging bodily fluids, is a turn off. For years I've tried to be patient and understanding. We've spent hours together in conversational therapy, but to no avail. Somewhere along the way, I just gave up, returning to the pursuit of my goals. I've left a crack in the emotional door, because I can't completely close it and throw away the key. Friendship allows the door to our souls to stay open. There's nothing else I can do about it, but continue to hope...

On our way out of town, the only thing open and available to us at this time of the day was a local *Rapido.* It stood by itself on a desolate section of road. A beacon in the still darkness of the new day. The only other customers besides Alfredo and I were the truck drivers heading to Havana with their goods. A chain of *Rapidos* link the island, and they serve a variety of items. Always on hand were coffee, cigarettes, and the national liquid, rum.

By then, Alfredo and I had become so lax in our discipline that it was nothing for us to begin the day with a shot or two of rum. It served to see us through the next few hours, until daylight came and the food vendors were in service.

I remember doing an interview once for a health magazine. The reporter wanted to know what my nutritional regimen was when in training; how many miles would I usually put in per week, and how it all went during one of my grueling, seemingly impossible tours. I lied, giving the pat answer of doing a breakfast of steak and eggs or tacos and burritos. I've never been big on the first meal of the day. My training miles consisted of zilch, and when on a tour, I advised being as disciplined on nutrition as possible. After all, I rationalized, I had my sponsors to think of.

After our dance with the rum, Alfredo and I headed west. The sun rose on our backs, spreading its beautiful orange-yellow-rust hues before us.

"You ever notice how the mornings are darker since we left *Maisi*," I asked Alfredo.

"*Si.* We are following the sun."

"Yeah," I laughed. "We were the first ones to see the sun rise, and by the time we finish this Tour, we'll be the last ones to see it set."

By 6am we were following the black-fume-spewing trucks to *Jatibonico*, choking all the way. This continued for the next hour. We'd get behind them until they slowed to a crawl, then pass until the trucks received a second life and ran past us, flying dirt and gravel in our faces. Sometimes the roads were so narrow, it was either the oncoming truck or us to move out of the path, and no way does a cyclist win over a trucker.

Alfredo would come to a stop, and get as far off to the side as possible. Me, on the other hand, would confront the diesel demons head-on as close as I could before veering off.

"You crazy." Alfredo would shout. "Do you want to die before you finish the Tour?"

"Just a little Russian Roulette to get the blood flowing in the morning."

"*Si!* The blood will flow out of your body when you are hit. Someday you will come too close."

At the turn-off outside *Jatibonico*, we and the truckers parted company. They headed north toward Havana, while we continued on our course toward the coast.

Already I had enough cuts, scratches and bruises over my body to serve as memories for months. I figured I'd spend weeks explaining, "Oh, yeah, you see this

A Cuban farmer in the *Jatibonico* region.

one? Yeah, I got it playing dodge with a Dodge. This one? Oh, I got that when I tried to swerve a swine."

The countryside was a mixture of browns and greens. Palm trees dotted our way. Fishermen congregated in the rivers and inlets, readying their catches for the day. I came upon an elderly farmer who seemed to have stepped off the pages of Hemingway's classic, *The Old Man and the Sea.*

Passing through the small, roadside town of *Jatibonico*, we saw that food vendors were already setting up their mini carts and propping up their multi-colored umbrellas. It was hustle and bustle time. The crowds were already in attendance to buy their breakfast and be on their way to work or destinations known only to them. The mood became festive, as though the circus were coming to town. Alfredo was able to acquire his plain, dry pork sandwich. I stuck with the local juice.

It was literally eat and run. We made our way toward the capital, *Sancti Spiritus*, arriving a couple of hours later. Another mind game we played with ourselves, especially during those last several flat days, was to connect the dots. In the morning, we would view the map, scope out our route for the day, then mentally connect the dots with the upcoming towns, wondering how long it would take us to reach each one.

"How long do you think it'll take us to *Jatibonico?*"

"Hmm," studied Alfredo, "An hour."

"I figure at least another two to *Sancti Spiritus*."

"Maybe less. Perhaps we can make *Trinidad* by the afternoon."

"No way," I shook my head, looking at the distance on the map. "Maybe by dinner. Before it gets dark."

"But by lunch would be better."

"You're dreaming, pal."

We put ourselves through this mental mind torture daily until there was no more Tour to be done. Eventually, I suppose, you either run out of tour or sanity.

"We should just get up in the morning and go all day until we reach the end for the day," complained Alfredo.

"And when do I get in my photos?" I complained back.

"Who care about picture?" brushed off my partner with a wave of his backhand. "There is nothing to see out here."

"The problem with you, is that you're not human."

"*Si.* I a horse. I go all the time." He pounded his fists into the air.

"Just because you ate one last night doesn't mean you have to be like one."

"We put in one hundred miles a day, we be finished with Tour by now."

"Do you think you'll ever do a Tour like this again?"

"No. Never again like this. A first and a last."

"Then shut-up and enjoy it."

In *Sancti Spiritus*, a sign read: *Trinidad 42 km.* Could that be right? *Trinidad* by lunch?

"You see," smiled Alfredo, riding up alongside me. "*Trinidad* by lunch."

"You're full of it," I countered. "My calculations couldn't be that far off."

"You no' read the sign back there?"

"If I'm wrong, I'll be the happiest one to admit it."

A bit further along, though, another sign proclaimed: *Trinidad 66 km.*

"Excuse me," I said, coming alongside my partner. "I believe the Lord has given us a sign of redemption."

"I do not want to hear it," growled Alfredo.

The center of *Sancti Spiritus* was a hubbub of activity. Men with private cars converted into taxis were ready and willing to take any and all rich, dollar-paying foreigners to *Trinidad* or whatever other destination they had in mind. More vendors and hawkers of all ages were out in full force with food and drink. Shouldn't these children be in school? Mangy dogs, chickens, pigs, goats and sheep, along with their appropriate droppings, were freely roaming about.

I was ready for breakfast, so I consumed the usual pizza and juice. To be sure, there was never much choice for food on the road, but when you're hungry, you'll eat the same thing day-in, day-out if you have to. It's not enjoyable, but it is necessary.

"Hey, mista', where you go? Have ride for you," someone called out to me.

"No thanks," I turned away.

"Good car. *Trinidad*, for you, twenty dolla'," cried another, right in my face.

"No!"

More called out to us. Every time I turned away, another section of the mob faced me. From within came the same shouts.

"*Trinidad.* Yeah, sure. Sounds good to me, but then it doesn't matter what I'm saying to you, does it, because you can't understand a word of it, can you?"

They looked at me with the dumbest, blankest smiles I'd ever seen. After awhile, they'd awake from their hypnotic state and begin rattling off the same English verses they'd been taught to repeat.

Some walked away upon the first brush off, others kept trying. But then they, too, would walk away. One middle-aged man was being quite persistent in giving us a ride to *Trinidad*, bikes and all.

"*Amigo,*" he smiled. "You bike. *Mucho grande!* Twenty dolla' *Trinidad*, okay?"

"Wow! Twenty dollars. That is such a generous offer, I just don't know what to say. I'm just going to have to sit here and think this over while I eat my breakfast."

He gave me the same, dumb smile as the others. Just stood there with his best, yellow-stained, crooked smile he could bring out in himself, not understanding a word I was saying. He finally got smart and went to Alfredo, who turned his back on him and walked away.

He returned to me. "Come," he grabbed my bike. "You *Trinidad*. Now! Twenty dolla'."

I slapped his hand. "Whoa! *amigo.* I'm still thinking about this. Tell you what. We take your car and our bikes and leave you here."

He just stood there and smiled. "To *Trinidad?*"

"*Si,*" I smiled. "Or until we run out of gas, and then we'll leave your piece of junk by the side of the road."

He shook his head in trying to understand what I was saying to him, finally going back to Alfredo for an interpretation, who was trying to lose himself in the crowd. Unable to get a response from my partner, he returned to me, taking a seat, as I turned sideways, doing my patient best in body language to ignore him.

"Hey, *amigo.*" He tapped me on the shoulder.

I continued to ignore him.

He came around to the other side of me, blowing cigarette smoke in my face, smiling. "Twenty dolla'. Now."

I returned his smiled. "I'm going to kill you right here in front of all these people and enjoy it."

He just sat there and smiled. Alfredo was ready to go.

For some strange reason, I actually felt better when I rode the bike than just sitting around doing nothing. Maybe Alfredo made sense: I'd probably still be in *Camaguey* if the choice were left to me.

We did the next 20km in about 40 minutes, thanks in part to a tractor blocking the winds for us. You get to your goal any way you can (with the exception of $20 rides)-- and drafting counts.

A short juice break in *Banao* and then onto *Caracusey* for a half-hour rest period...

During these times of rest and photography, people generally approached us to admire the bike and strike up a conversation. This allowed them to practice their English.

"Did you cycle from Havana, *amigo?*" They smiled.

"*Maisi,*" Alfredo and I would answer.

"*Maisi?*" Their brow would knit together, as they'd look at one another in confusion. "Where is *Maisi?*"

And then we'd pull out the map, because it was much easier to show than to explain.

"*Madre de Dios,*" they'd exclaim, their hands to their faces, trying to hold their jaws from dropping too far to the ground. "You are cycling from one end to the other?"

"*Si,*" returned the reply from Alfredo and I.

"But no one has ever done such a thing."

"That is why we are the first," Alfredo would smile.

Just outside the seacoast town of *Trinidad*, Alfredo wanted to make one of his rare detours to show me an old-family winery. The area was rich in vineyards.

"This entire area was given by the Spanish to a single family over a hundred years ago," said Alfredo, opening up his arms wide to take in the view. "There was no grapes here. Nothing. The family work the land."

"It's beautiful," I remarked, taking photos of the surrounding buildings and countryside. "The ancestors of the original family must be thankful."

"They would if they owned it," replied Alfredo.

"Don't they?"

"No. When Fidel take over, he stop land grants, and return all this area to the people."

"You mean the government has their greedy paws into what it took the family so hard to work for?"

"*Si.*"

The magnificent Spanish-styled, seven-arch *hacienda* had become a fancy jacket-and-tie restaurant-- with, of course, a superb wine list. Nearby stood a seven-story tower that to me, was more like an old Saturn V rocketship than a lookout.

For one dollar, I was allowed to venture up the winding staircase to the top. There, I was afforded a picture-perfect view of the surrounding landscape, all the way to the coast and the town we were about to enter. Alfredo declined to join me, staying instead with the bicycles.

Climbing each story, I got some wonderful shots of the buildings below and the mountains off on the horizon. There was a couple building an addition onto their home, a mother hanging her clothes out to dry. Tourists flocked below me, shopping for items to bring back home. Tour buses were picking up and dropping off. And the countryside...lush, fertile, green, with tree-covered humps for mountains, gently sloping off in the distance. This was future golf course country. The reality would be in my lifetime.

"Can you see de mountains?" yelled Alfredo from below.

"*Si,*" I answered as I was taking some shots.

Alfredo and I at the tower.

"We will be climbing that big one after tomorrow."

And it was a monstrous-looking devil. About as tall as the nation's highest, *Pico Turquino*, it was, in fact, the second highest at just over 6000 feet. Called *Topes de Collantes* by the locals, it was the beast Alfredo had been trying to get me to change my mind on for the last several days; he opted instead to go by way of the coast to *Cienfuegos*. I would love to oblige, but that would mean bypassing the entire province of *Villa Clara* altogether, and that would forever grate on my nerves as breaking the chain of unity. Looking at it from the tower made me glad we were going to rest the next day.

Just before beginning the long downhill into *Trinidad*, we met several more cyclists along the way, including a couple from Switzerland that Alfredo had met the previous year. They gave us a name of a place to stay, so, along with Alfredo's other contacts, we were well-prepared.

The vineyard countryside of Trinidad with the dreaded *Topes de Collantes* in the background. We would be cycling up this beast of a mountain in two days.

A peek into Paradise.

"Is good we meet them, but I have my own contacts," said Alfredo, as we began the long descent into *Trinidad.*

"Are we in for a surprise?"

"You will see," smiled my friend. "When we come to the edge of town, we will be surrounded by young hooligans."

"And what will the little imps want from us?"

"Money," he laughed as we picked up speed.

"Want to tell me something else I don't know?"

"We will be hustled. They will want to show us a place to stay for fifteen dollars. They get five from the owner."

"Nice set-up."

"*Si.* Very capitalistic."

As Alfredo had already pointed out he had his contacts, we didn't need to be hustled. But it didn't stop the young *banditos* from trying, as we swooped into the city, while they swarmed upon us like buzzing vultures.

"Hey, mista' where you from?" asked one young entrepreneur off to my left.

"America."

"Hey, *Americano!*" he shouted as his buddies chimed in.

The cobblestone streets were narrow enough without cyclists trying to ride four abreast. Weaving in and out of traffic and people while trying to avoid crashing into the hawking hustlers was a mental game in logistics and master control of your machine. I wonder if Hemingway ever felt like this when running with the bulls?

"Have a good room for you. Real cheap."

"Go away," I snapped at the young flea.

"What do you want to do?" asked my partner.

"Bask in glorious, heathenistic, capitalistic luxury."

"What does that mean?" he countered.

"It means we go to a hotel with lots of luxuries. Relax and spend money enjoying ourselves."

"It cost too much," replied the tightwad who had other ideas.

Was he serious? The *Hotel Alcon*, the fanciest, beach-front, pamper galore place in town was only $60US per night for the both of us. "Let's go for it!"

"Mista'. Hotel cost *mucho dinero.* Have better place."

"Are you still following us? Go away."

"I have a better idea," smiled Alfredo.

I knew exactly what he had in mind as we cycled down a street lined on both sides with connecting, 2-story houses. After a couple of weeks riding, sleeping, eating, bathing and going to the bathroom together, you know each other's habits and thought patterns.

"No. I'm not interested."

"What!" he laughed, avoiding eye contact with me. "You no' even know what I propose."

"Mista', nice room down here." By now all the young buzzards gave up on us for some new meat, but we still had one left that we couldn't shake. "You pass the street. Come, we go back. Good room. Clean."

Alfredo bolted past us and I quickly followed suit. Our young scab was cut loose, returning to his pack.

"You are so full of it," I said, catching up to Alfredo. "I know exactly what you have in mind."

"We go to a friend's house. I have photos for them."

"No!" I protested, cycling through the streets. "I do not want to rent a room in someone's house, because then you have to be entertaining and I don't want to be entertaining!"

He wasn't even paying attention.

By then it was past 4pm; the sun about to set. Time was running out. Forget the kicking and screaming, I told myself. It doesn't work with Alfredo. He leads, I follow, and that's the way of it. No choice. Simple as that.

The occupants of the house consisted of the parents (dad was at work), two married daughters, and three granddaughters. They rushed to offer us cold drinks and warm conversation; and were obviously excited at seeing Alfredo once again. Giggling and gleeful, they were just as excited on receiving photos of themselves from whomever took them the last time.

Alfredo and the women spoke in their native tongue; none in the family was able to speak English. I flopped in a comfortable chair to relax with a cool glass of *refresca.*

When the ladies heard I was from America, one of the daughters, speaking through Alfredo, said, "My husband escaped from Cuba on a raft three years ago and is a truck driver in Miami."

"That's the last you'll see of him, *senora.*"

"No, he calls at least once-a-week and sends money from his pay to care for the family."

That was good to hear, but, "Why doesn't he send for you and the children?"

"Because," she answered, "It takes five years to become an American citizen. But once he does, he can send for us."

The daughters were just babies. Probably too young to even remember their father. Sometimes I wonder how people can do the things they do, like leave a wife and family behind for some notion they believe to be freedom. Isn't taking care of your family more important? If you're single, you have only yourself to care for, but when you have a wife and children, then it's not just you anymore. I wondered how the freedom he had living in some one-room apartment, making a lonely living as a truck driver could be better than having found another way where they all might have gone together.

"You know," said Alfredo. "I stay here last year."

"Nice place."

Just from where I sat, I could see comfortable, stylish furniture; a modern TV; a stereo with dual cassette deck and speakers; and a table-top, artificial Christmas tree, trimmed with lights, bells and assorted ornaments that was playing versions of favorite, familiar carols.

A later inspection tour revealed toiletries you could only pay for in dollars; hot and cold running water; and toilets with lids on them. These people were not living in poor conditions.

"The mother used to house foreigners in exchange for dollars," mentioned Alfredo in passing. "She make more in a year than her husband did in *pesos*, but give it up."

"Why? Sounds like it was profitable."

"*Si,* but the government license too expensive. Every month you must renew. And you must keep records of who stay in your house. Too much."

Pointing over to the artificial tree, I asked, "I didn't know Fidel allowed the people to celebrate Christmas?"

"*Si,*" nodded Alfredo. "The first time since he take over country we can, and no' be thrown in jail."

"Mighty nice of your dictator. Why the change?"

"His health," nodded Alfredo and the ladies, as he was interpreting our conversation to them.

"Is he going to die soon?"

"No, but he getting old. That is why he allow Christmas and the Pope to visit next month. He even allow the Pope to say whatever he want, and Fidel say he no' take revenge on the people after Pope John Paul leave Cuba."

"So, Castro's trying to make amends," shaking my head.

"*Si.* We can now go to church and worship God freely. He even let us have Bibles. He fear his own mortality and is trying to make up for his sins, some say."

"Perhaps. Death, at some point, comes to all of us. It's one of the few things we all have in common."

Turning to the young woman whose husband was living in Miami, I asked, "Is there anything I can do for you since I'll be returning home in a few weeks?"

There was an exchange of words, Alfredo smiled. "She say you could marry her and take her wit' you."

"Excuse me?" My jaw dropped.

Pregnant pause may not be the most suitable phrase, but there was definitely an awkward silence in the room.

Her fiery eyes flared up and she looked at me with a mischievous smile.

"Well, that wasn't exactly what I had in mind," I tried to explain. "I thought maybe I could carry a letter or some package. Send photos or something that I could mail upon returning to the States."

"But if you marry her, then she can deliver them herself," prodded Alfredo, in a devilish grin.

No one upstages me. "It's like this Alfredo: We marry, and then I take her and the girls back to America. We part company, and she goes to Miami, where, surprise, they find husband and daddy in bed with another woman. No *problemo!* Because she's with her daughters on the next flight to California to be with her new husband, where she finds me with Jean. And then, I'm *really* going to have a lot of explaining to do. Not only to Jean but to my church. What do I say? 'Uh, just a few extra souvenirs I picked up in Cuba I forgot to tell you about.' Sorry. Think I'll pass."

The dark-haired beauty was sitting on the edge of her couch seat, her black coal eyes growing wide with excitement wondering what I was rattling off about.

"Alfredo, *que?*"

Alfredo shook his head. "It not possible," he informed her most diplomatically.

In the meantime, the mother had slipped out the back and went half a block down the street to a friend's place, making arrangements for our lodgings.

She returned, and I'm sure she and Alfredo were talking over the situation in Spanish, right in front of me.

Before I knew what was happening, I was asked if I wanted to take a look at a place to spend the night. *Oh, really?*, I thought, *smooth move.*

We left our bikes and gear and walked the distance to a house that was much the same as the one we had left: Tall, cathedral ceilings, tiled floors, large wooden rocking chairs and a Christmas tree complete with all the trimmings.

The couple and their two married daughters were just as charming as the family we had left. The father of the house was a retired Army captain named Pedro. A jolly, infectious, teddy-bear of a man with a gregarious laugh. He wanted to show me the upstairs.

"Well, come on," I said to Alfredo. "Let's get this over with."

"I already seen it."

"Oh? You must tell me how you managed to disappear so quickly, and why do I feel like I'm being set up?

The place was clean, leaning more to a foreigner's taste with scented soap and shampoo; toilet paper, a lid on the bowl, and lukewarm water in the shower.

There were a couple of bedrooms-- one with twin beds, the other more of a master suite with the bathroom in the middle. It even had a balcony for sitting and talking.

The place was great, I knew, and I couldn't really complain, but I had my heart set on decadent pampering, especially if I were going to have a day of rest.

Alfredo was in the kitchen with Pedro's wife when we came downstairs. It was question time. How much per night? Fifteen dollars for the both of us (minus five bucks for the contact) with a noon check-out. I still had a fancy resort in mind for the next day. The immediacy of those thoughts quickly eroded, though, when I spotted a can of Nestle's chocolate powdered drink mix on the kitchen counter. Like a magnet, I was drawn to it, embracing it like a cherished lover. How could I possibly help myself? We rode 80 miles, and I was starving.

Pedro's wife had a look of fear on her face concerning my actions. Words were exchanged with Alfredo who laughed, saying, "It is nothing. He is just in need of American products." They all shared in the humor.

"We could have our meals here if you want," said the Manipulator.

The Captain's wife nodded in agreement, telling Alfredo that she could cook me most anything I desired.

I would have killed for a couple of burgers with all the trimmings, but said I'd settle for a spaghetti dinner-- anything other than *congris* and *yucca.*

Adios, Hotel Alcon.

Once settled into our comfortable lodgings, Alfredo decided to check out a couple of things in town, while I took pleasure in a shave and shower. Dinner would be at 7:30, so we had plenty of time.

Upon stepping out of the shower, I slipped on the tile floor and instinctively grabbed the corner of the sink, breaking it in three pieces. "Damn!" I screamed to myself. "Not now." I felt like an idiot standing there with the sink hanging in my hands. Water was spewing out of the pipes, and onto the floor, as I wondered how I was ever going to explain this to the Captain. *What a great first impression this makes*, I thought. Will we now have to leave? Damn!-- This was not an added expense I was counting on. Where the hell was Alfredo? And oh, please, Lord, get me through this.

I cut the water off from the valves, laid the broken pieces on the floor, cleaned whatever mess there was, closed the bathroom door, dressed, and waited for my interpreter to return.

When he did, I explained I had a bit of an accident and showed him the results.

"Wow!"

"Is that all you have to say?"

He laughed nervously. "The last time I went cycling wit' one of my American friends, he need to use a bathroom, but wouldn't go outside, so we find someone's house and there he broke their sink and had to pay. It was an expensive shit."

"That isn't what I need to hear right now."

We thought of how best to handle the situation, and, just as we were being called for dinner, we did the deed.

"Wow!" said Pedro. Two wows. I was nervous.

Alfredo explained the situation in rapid Spanish. I felt as miserable as could be. "But I'm sorry...and yes, I'll pay for the damages, no *problemo*."

Pedro's only reaction was to laugh it off as a circumstance, shrugging his shoulders. "It happens," he said through Alfredo. "Do not think about it anymore. Other people have stayed and have broken things. They are paid for and replaced."

To show it was all right, he gave me a big bear hug and motioned for us to follow him downstairs. There, we were treated to a great dinner of spaghetti in a fine sauce that reminded me of my grandmother's cooking. We also had sliced tomatoes, potato and bean soup with kielbasa and plenty of bread and butter. For dessert, Pedro went out for ice cream bars, which we enjoyed, in the living room rocking chairs, listening to some of my Christmas and Classical music. I promised to make them copies the next day.

"The wife want to know what you want for breakfast?" said Alfredo, just before we were ready to turn in.

"Doesn't matter," I replied. "Coffee, juice, hot chocolate, bread. Whatever you want."

Yeah, I admit, I'm a fool many times over. We were treated like kings that night-- better than we would have been at a commercial hotel, and the price was right.

I'm sure glad God doesn't pay attention to me sometimes.

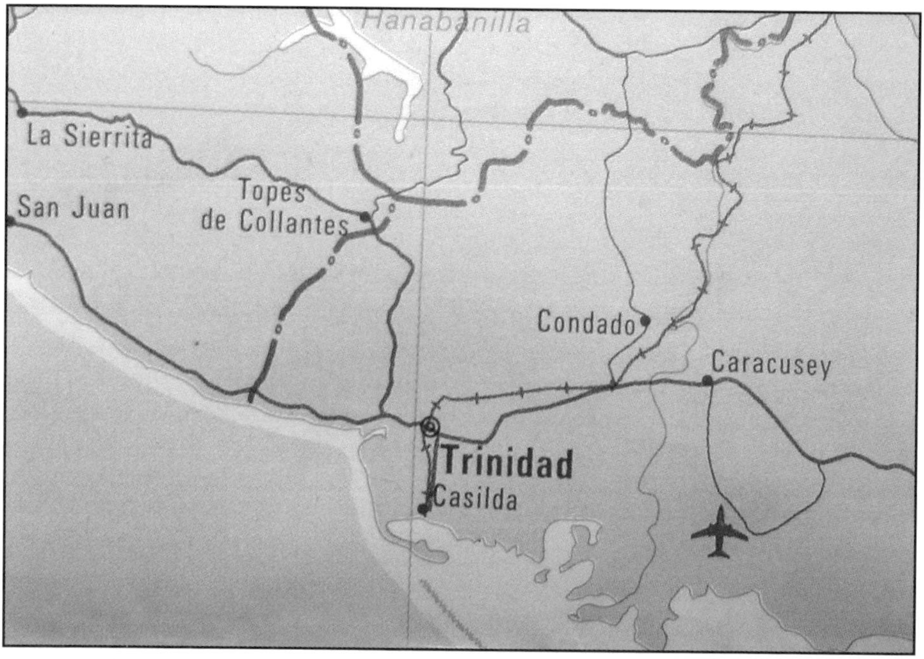

VEINTIUNO

21

REST DAY in TRINIDAD
DAY 13
DECEMBER 03, 1997

It was our second day of rest so far on the Tour, and perhaps our last until we returned to Havana. The best part was being able to sleep and not be awaken by the alarm clock. For us, that was 7:30am; going down to breakfast a half-hour later.

From our balcony, we could see a mosaic of tile roofs, patterned in layers. In spots, they glistened in the sun. Off to one side, workers were preparing a section, covering a gaping two-room sized hole.

Pedro's wife-- plump and jolly like her husband-- was fresh with smiles, waiting by a fully laid-out table of the simple breakfast items I requested the night before. We were served on elegant, family china and silverware, with cloth white napkins. I'm a light eater upon waking up, but the smell of fresh hot bread, freshly-squeezed orange juice, bananas, and hot chocolate with sweet milk made me want to fill up in spite of myself.

As Alfredo and I ate, we viewed the map of our route and itinerary.

"If we have no more rest days, and can average one hundred kilometers per day, I think we finish the Tour by next Friday," figured Alfredo, as he dipped his bread into his rich, black coffee.

"You think so," I asked, sipping my sweet milked, hot chocolate. "That would make up for all the time we lost."

"*Si.* We can do it."

We found our calculations quite amusing: The original schedule, if we began on time, called for us to finish by that date. Two days in one, extra miles... It all adds up.

By 9am, we were ready to set out with our bikes for the cobblestone streets of the ancient, sea coastal part of *Trinidad*-- a town more than twice as old as the united States. Christopher Columbus was just one of the more famous visitors, as he had walked in the same places we were treading.

Cycling through the time-worn streets, Alfredo pointed out, "You see the road we are on?"

"Pretty hard not to since we're cycling on it."

"This is the one we will be using during tomorrow's climb up the devil mountain."

Alfredo didn't have to remind me. The *Topes de Collantes* was ever-present, casting it's forever shadow across the town.

I was already dreading the work day. I'd been told too many times by the locals how God-awful steep that peak was to scale by motorized vehicle-- let alone by a man-powered bike. Yes, the visual effect did work on adding to my fears, which Satan, after all, loves to thrive on. There wasn't anywhere we could go in town without seeing it over our shoulders or having it stare us in the face. Images of *Fantasia's Night on Bald Mountain* danced in my head.

"I still say we take the coast to *Cienfuegos*," mentioned Alfredo for the umpteenth time.

"And how else can we reach the province of *Villa Clara?*" I umpteenth back.

"We lose a day because of it," he thrusted.

"And what happens to the unity?" I parried. "The bike is the thread that binds all the provinces together."

If I were smart and had forethought, I considered, I would have taken a different road out of *Sancti Spiritus*. But then I would have missed *Trinidad's* Old World charm and beauty. And we had had a blessed week of flat lands. A day of uphill work would renew our appreciation of the journey we'd come to thus far and what would lay ahead, I was certain.

I wanted to take in as much of the surroundings as possible, and, knowing our time was limited, Alfredo and I kept our concentration to a small, tight section of the historical district.

That town had tourist written all over it, so leave those *pesos* behind, because you'll be spending the dollars. We came across some craftsmen working their trade in front of a government-owned, controlled and operated store that sold their wares to foreigners. The prices were ridiculously high, and they cut short bargaining no matter

A Cuban craftsman. Trinidad, Cuba.

how much we wanted to. A set price was a set price, and there was just no getting around that rule.

Outside the store there were weavers of baskets and decorative animals, wood carvers and knife sharpeners, dress makers and bead threaders. Much of the cobblestoned area reminded me of Old Boston; the streets were similarly small and narrow, the vendors smiled and waved at us to enter their hundred-plus year old stores for a browse and a bargain.

In an open space between a couple of plaster-cracked buildings, a Cuban *salsa* band played native songs on various instruments as tourists passed by, tossing coins and bills into a small, handwoven basket. Empty beer cans, strung like Christmas ornaments, hung above their heads, rattling in the breeze. An old farmer passing by on his burro stopped to listen; the donkey was obviously not pleased with the music judging from the donation he left behind. Others, perhaps old *amigos,* waved to each other or stood nearby to reminisce about a familiar tune they tapped their feet to.

Heading down one narrow side-street, a Che Guevara T-shirt caught my eye through a barred window. Inside, two young *senoritas* sat with some of their inventory of clothing and jewelry. Being invited into the house, I saw that the front room acted as a storefront during the day. We perused the merchandise, finally choosing a Che and Cuban flag shirt-- with a string of beads thrown in for six dollars.

One of the women, Diley, a petite young lass, asked if we wanted to return to her place to see some clothes she made. Since it was a day of leisurely

Trinidad musicians playing to the crowd of tourists.

exploring, we decided to take her up on the offer. Walking the several blocks to her house, I kept thinking about Cinderella-- someone so beautiful who lived in filth and poverty. As with many of the women we'd met, I had a passing urge to marry her, just to better her situation. The added blessing would be that I think we'd fall in love with one another.

Once at Diley's, we were introduced to her parents, and offered a seat in the front room. Shortly, she brought out a few of her white, laced-knit vests and tops. The prices for such handmade craftsmanship were anywhere from three to ten dollars. I could have bought her out without a second thought. The problem would have been carrying the items. I settled for one vest for $10US that I felt Jean would like. My return home, after all, would be Christmas Eve.

This day of rest would also be a day of shopping for whatever little items I could carry with me. These would be the Christmas presents for that year.

Upon saying our good-byes, Alfredo and I walked around the corner, running into a horde of vendors ready to converge upon us. When they heard I spoke English, someone shouted, "*Americano*," and I was bombarded with clothes, jewelry, wood carvings, paintings, and anything else they could throw our way. Bartering was in their blood, and taking no for an answer was not.

"No, I'm sorry. I can't take anymore with me."

One woman held my half-empty knapsack. "You have plenty of room. We fill, you pay."

"I unloaded my stuff to make room," I tried to explain. "We are on bicycles.

Can't carry anymore."

"You have room for one more dress," said another woman. "Here. You buy from me."

"No," said another woman beside her. "I see him first, so he buy from me."

"That's very kind of you, but..."

"Who you kid?" laughed the woman in white lace. "You clothes no good. Her clothes cheap, mista'. I make mine."

"Who you call no good?" hissed Lady Purple. "You buy from others and say you make yourself."

"Well, that really doesn't matter to me..."

"You lie! I kill you for that!"

"*Madre de Dios!* Look!" I quickly turned the two women around to view a group of tourists exiting their bus into shopping heaven. The manna had arrived.

"Hey!" Screamed the women to the group. "We have nice clothes for you. Good price. You buy from us."

We quickly went our separate ways.

"Thanks for the help," I said to my laughing partner.

"I like to see how you do," he cackled.

I did, however, spot a bargain I couldn't resist-- one that I could easily carry and bring back to the States. Necklaces made from coffee beans, parts of trees, and other knick-knacks were selling 10 to a dollar. I purchased a rack of them to the delight of the vendor, who smiled while most helpfully, dumping the product into a bag faster than I could think of what I was doing.

On our way back to the Captain's house, we came across a courtyard with a flight of stone stairs, much in the same design as the Spanish Steps of Rome, low and wide.

"Hey," stopped Alfredo. "You go to the top and cycle down. I take picture."

It was a grand idea when mentioned, and I quickly agreed. It soon turned into a crowd-pleasing event.

"Hey, *amigo*, let us try. Okay?" asked the one who could speak the most English in the group of local men and teenage boys. Well, that's what these Tours are all about.

I changed positions with Alfredo, taking over camera duties, while he stayed off to the side as a sort of cheerleader-encourager. "You can do it!" he yelled from the bottom of the stairs. "Just make sure you ride in front of camera for good photo. And don't crash. Bike is expensive."

"Oh, that helps," I nodded. "Why don't you tell them the cost while you're at it?"

"Because then they fall for sure."

Some of the older group came down slowly, while the younger *muchachos* barreled down hard, making attempts to soar through the air on the last step.

The tourists that had been roaming around the marketplace found their way to us. Soon, many other cameras, and camcorders as well, joined the circus.

Just another lazy afternoon in sunny Cuba.

Once we finished taking photos and addresses of the cycling daredevils, Alfredo and I went through other parts of town.

We passed small crowds gathered at a side door, their ration coupons in hand for their portion of yogurt. Others were standing in line at the back of a truck where workers weighed sweet potatoes for sale. As in China, never would I see a supermarket of any size in Cuba. They just didn't exist, the people only knew a ration way of life.

As a boy, I grew up with Norman Rockwell's paintings (he lived just 90 minutes north over the border in Massachusetts), and a series he once did has always stuck with me. I was reminded of it when traveling through third world countries.

"It's a series of paintings called the *Four Freedoms*," I explained to my friend. "Freedom of Religion, Freedom of Speech, Freedom from Want, and Freedom from Fear. Those freedoms are what make America what she is."

"Do the Americans know them?" asked Alfredo.

"I don't know," I had to honestly answer. "Perhaps. Or perhaps they have to lose what our forefathers fought and died for in order to appreciate them."

Alfredo gave a silent, quiet nod, then added, "When people have too much they get lazy. When you hungry, you fight all the time."

"Someday, it may be that way with America."

As we made our way back to the house, we came across a group of men involved in a serious game of dominoes. Half of them were bare-chested, the other two, dressed. Skins verses shirts for the domino championship of the moment.

Alfredo and I watched them throwing down their black chips when their turn came, each toss became bolder and more aggressive. A moderator stood off to the side, so that none could cheat. They appeared to be playing for life or death.

"Why are they so serious over dominoes," I asked.

"Because dominoes is a serious game in Cuba," answered Alfredo in whispered tones.

"But what makes it so serious?"

"Money," nodded Alfredo.

Bam! went a domino playing piece that shook the other chips and table. We were given glaring looks.

"No make so much noise," whispered Alfredo. "It dangerous."

"Perhaps there should be a warning label on every box of dominoes that playing could be dangerous to one's health."

"Or the people watching the players," countered Alfredo.

"Well, it seems to be doing the job."

"What job is that?" asked my partner.

"Keeping them entertained, while the government keeps control of the country. It's like that in every nation."

One of the shirtless *senors* turned and yelled something to us in Spanish. Judging from the look on his face, I didn't need the interpretation.

"Come," said Alfredo, leading me away. "We have stayed long enough."

It was late afternoon by then, and although I wanted to do more exploring, I had other responsibilities, such as devoting a serious amount of time to my

An intense game of Dominoes.

journal and the promise of the previous night to record my Christmas and Bach music, not only for Pedro and his wife, but for the sex starved *senoras* whose house we first arrived at.

Captain Pedro didn't have a dual deck cassette recorder, but there was one across the street. For the rest of the afternoon, I combined my writing and recording among a gaggle of giggles. And among their quiet laughter, there was at least one set of goo-goo eyes from a married-with-children *senora* who was still intent on being an American bride.

"I think you be okay," said Alfredo. He left for our room across the street to do his own writing. I kept to myself, and, after a few hours, the work and the promise was complete. Just as I was ready to leave, the father of the house walked in with dreadfully perfect timing.

We sat in the living room, drinking coffee, while Luis' granddaughters watched a Spanish-styled Mr Rodgers Neighborhood. We tried to make conversation. To brook the language barrier, we used small, understandable words. Our conversation became part hand gestures, part charades. Whatever works to get through the ordeal.

"You," said Luis, pointing to me. He held his fists in the air like a boxer's and then rotating them in a circular motion. Then he spread them open and widened his arms.

I quickly caught on and pulled out the map of his country from my knapsack, placing the sections on the floor in front of him. From there, I traced the highlighted route from our starting point in *Maisi* to where we currently were: *Trinidad.*

His head shook in amazement.

"Me," he pointed to himself. "All Cuba." He waved his hand over the country.

"All Cuba?" I asked, repeating the gesture.

"*Si,*" he nodded with a smile.

"*Maisi?*"

"*Si.*" He nodded once again with authority.

"*Caleta Larga?*" I asked suspiciously.

"*Si.*" He smiled.

"*Si?*" My eyes widened.

"*Si.*" His teeth showed.

"*Maisi,*" he pointed out, shaking his head in disgust. "No." His hands made mountains. "Bad."

"*Si,*" I nodded. I knew all too well the steepness.

"*Caleta Larga,*" his eyes lit-up. "Good." His hands flattened out.

I clapped my hands. I finally found someone who knew the area. Where the hell was Alfredo when I need him?

"*Caleta Larga,*" I began. "*Permito? Governmenta?*"

He looked at me for a moment, trying to understand what I was trying to say, then the light bulb in his head lit.

"Ah! *Si! Si,*" his eyes grew. Then he pointed to the last town before *Caleta Larga*. "Military. *La Bajada*. Bad."

"*Si.*" I understood.

"Permit," said Luis. "*Pinar.*" He pointed to the last capital in the last province we would be traveling through: *Pinar del Rio*. That would be where we would have to get our government permission. *Pinar* was also where I had to get my visa extended before it expired in a little more than a week. I was literally on a race against time.

Dinner was about to be served, so I handed the music tapes to Luis' wife, thanked them for their hospitality, warmly apologized to the sex-starved *senora* for not being able to marry her, and quickly made my exit back to Pedro's house. There, the Captain and Alfredo were in the living room rocking chairs engaged in conversation.

"*Kebin!*" greeted an enthusiastic Pedro. "How you?"

"*Muy bien,* Pedro."

"You marry?" he bellowed, laughing.

"Don't you have anything better to talk about?" My eyes lowered toward my companion.

Alfredo threw up his hands in innocence. "What I do?"

Pedro, through Alfredo, mentioned that he bought a new sink-- pink-- for $20US, and would only add that cost to the overall bill, no charge for installation. To paraphrase Alfredo's other American friend, I had an expensive shower.

Christmas carols were playing away, near the three-foot high, artificial, decorated evergreen that stood off to a side of the large living room. A plastic, colorful *Feliz Navidad* sign hung on a wall just above with pictures of angels added.

While we were waiting to sup, Alfredo and I spoke with Pedro's wife in the kitchen as the Captain showered. I thought this would be a good time to Witness, since we were so near to Christmas. Personally, I've never been good at Witnessing. I just don't have the patience to spend years trying to convert someone. Either you know Jesus died and shed His blood for you, or you don't.

But for some reason, I wanted to reach this kind, tender-hearted woman, who took us in and made Alfredo and I feel as though we were home.

"Do you know what Christmas is all about?" I asked the woman, through Alfredo.

"No," she shook her head, as she stayed over the stove cooking tonight's meal. "It's a nice idea that Americans have for giving gifts to one another."

"That's because Someone who loved us gave you and me and everyone in the world a gift. Would you like to hear the story?"

"*Si*," she nodded.

I took out my King James Bible, opened to the Book of Luke, second chapter, and began, "A decree went out in all the land--"

"What a decree?" asked Alfredo.

"A law from the government." I answered, before he interpreted.

"--from Caesar Augustus, that all should be taxed--"

"What taxed?" He took a swig of his beer.

Although the question should not have amazed me, I just didn't know that many people who didn't have a healthy concept of the meaning of the cursed word. This was going to be a long story to get through, but I was determined to do my best.

"When the government takes your hard working money away from you without permission," I answered.

"Ah, government theft," belched Alfredo, his eyes lighting up. "We know about this. We fight." He gave a spirited explanation, and I could only wish I knew the language.

I continued with the story, as the wife cooked and listened. I got quite far with Joseph and Mary and the visit from the angel, until...

"How can virgin have baby without man? It impossible."

"You're suppose to interpret, not ask questions."

"*Si,* but no' can have baby without man. I think something left out."

"Look, God can do anything He wants to. He's God.

"*Si,* if you believe in such things."

Reading from the Good Book went by the wayside, as I laid it aside and recited the story in my own way.

"This virgin girl who never had sex with a man, had a baby who was God in the flesh named Jesus."

Alfredo interpreted through the sounds of laughter.

"He led the people to God His Father. He preached. He cured many people from sickness. But the political leaders didn't like Jesus, so they told lies about Him."

"I know this. American politicians tell lies about Fidel," nodded Alfredo, guzzling down his beer.

"I would hardly compare Castro to Christ."

"But politicians tell lies and people believe."

Alfredo with Captain Pedro and his wife standing by their first Christmas tree in nearly 40 years.

"Okay. Fine. Yes, you're right. Anyway, Jesus was put on trial. Found guilty. Nailed to a cross where He died. But, in three days, He rose from the dead, and lives today."

"He die, and come back to life?"

"Is there a problem with that?"

"Not if you believe in such fairy tales."

"Alfredo, didn't your grandmother, who believed, who had to be hidden during the revolution, tell you this story?"

"*Si.* When I was a child. But she was crazy."

"Alfredo, if you don't know that Jesus died for your sins, you will end up in Hell."

He took another drink of beer and kept quiet.

"Okay, look. Just interpret the story, and say that we celebrate Christmas to remember Jesus' birth, and at Easter in the Spring, we remember that He died for our sins."

Alfredo reluctantly did, without much enthusiasm. During this time, all I could think about was a verse from the Lord that said, "My words shall not return void." I just wanted to share the story of Jesus with this woman, no matter how convoluted it turned out.

I asked if she believed that the Lord died for her.

"No," she shook her head. "I do not even believe in God. But I like the idea of Christmas. The giving and the music. That is why I am celebrating. For that, and because Castro is allowing it for the first time in forty years."

I acknowledged her honesty, and said that even though she didn't believe in God, He believed, knew, and loved her. And I simply left it at that.

For dinner, Alfredo and I each feasted on a whole chicken-- killed, plucked, and served, all in a day. There were also generous helpings of rice with french-fried potatoes and salad. We devoured everything in sight.

"You eat so much," said Alfredo in amazement. "You will make yourself sick."

"I haven't eaten much in four days, and when it comes to good food, I don't care how sick I am. This might be the last great meal we have until Havana."

My stay in *Trinidad* was beyond any expectations I had. I would make it a point to fellowship with Pedro and his wife whenever I was back in the area, which I hoped was soon and often.

The next day was a workday, and an uphill one at that.

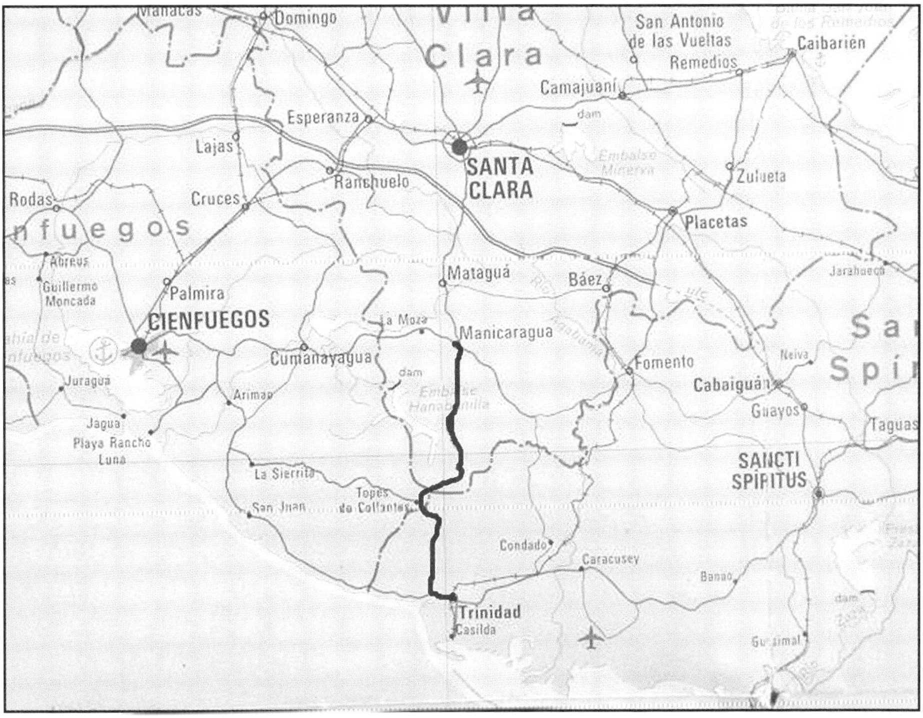

VEINTIDOS

22

TRINIDAD to MANICARAGUA
DAY 14
DECEMBER 04, 1997

DAILY DISTANCE :	**36 miles**	**or**	**60**	**kilometers**
TOTAL DISTANCE :	**685 miles**	**or**	**1141.7**	**kilometers**

"*Kebin!* Time to call de police!" laughed Pedro.

It wasn't exactly the way I wanted to be awaken at 5am, but it did get my attention.

Alfredo and I stumbled about dressing and packing our gear ever so slowly while Pedro added up the bill.

"We can still do the coast," mentioned Alfredo. "It no' too late."

I kept quiet. What was the point of arguing about "the bike being the needle to connect the country" again?

Regrettably and with great reluctance, we had to leave our comfortable surroundings to face the mammoth beast awaiting us just outside of town. Fortunately, we were sent off with a fine breakfast. During my China days, one of my coaches at the Olympic training center in Lake Placid, New York used to say, "A good cyclist knows how to pack his fuel," and we were packing it in pretty good.

The bill was what I had expected for such hospitality-- and a lot less than what we would have paid if I had had my way.

The breakdown, for both of us during the last two days, all in US dollars was: $30 for the room; $24 for the dinners; $6 for the full breakfasts; $2 for Alfredo's two beers; $20 for the new bathroom sink. Total amount...$82.

The Captain and his wife gave us a warm send-off, still shaking their heads at us for attempting that day's insanity.

Our journey began with a warm-up, three-mile stretch of flat road. It was quickly replaced by a demonic, torturous, all-day climb.

"This is definitely a Mineral King day," I huffed toward Alfredo, who was only a few feet from me.

"What is Mineral King day?" he huffed right along.

"Oh, just a little twenty-five mile uphill back where I live," I grunted and groaned in the lowest gear I had.

"Shit!" spat Alfredo. "You cycle it?"

"Not for a long time," I answered, quickly wiping away the salty sweat that was burning my eyes. "And I'm paying for it now. Don't Cuban engineers believe in building a road up a mountain in a circular pattern instead of straight up?"

"Why should they?" Alfredo pressed on, eyes focused. "The road only made for trucks. No one crazy to cycle it."

Now finishing the second week of the Tour, my body was conditioned to take the 60-80 daily miles we were putting in as well as the temperatures. But an uphill grind is an uphill grind-- and the only way to be in any shape for it is to train on uphill grinds. If you don't, then put your head down and pump. One pedal stroke after another. And get the mind games going. Song lyrics, made up or not, work for me.

Just put one foot in front of the other and soon you'll be walking 'cross the floor-or-or. Just put one foot in front of the other and soon you'll be walking out the door, is one of my stock supply from the animated 1970 film, *Santa Claus is Coming to Town.*

At least I had 24 gears to play with, and needed every one of them to get me through this beast. But Alfredo's bike was nothing more than a 10 speed, chrom-moly, 30 pound-plus bull that some tourist left him a couple of years before. Coupled with the 40 to 60 extra pounds of weight he was carrying, it's amazing he could do this climb at all, as we inched our way upward, side-by-side, a little piece at a time. He was a work-horse, a wunderkind, and I vowed that the next time I returned to Cuba, I was going to bring him a better, lighter, more technically advanced bike.

Big wheels keep on turning, proud Mary keeps on burning. Rollin', rollin',

Alfredo posing at the top of the *Topes de Collantes.*

rollin' up the hillside. Because what goes up, must come down. Spinning wheels, spinning 'round. Got all my troubles 'cause I didn't train. Ride a painted pony let the spinning wheels reign...

After a torturous hour and over 1000 feet of elevation gained, we heard a tractor approaching, going slightly faster than us, carrying a load of military personnel. As soon as it passed, Alfredo grabbed hold of the back end for a free ride to the top. Speeding to catch up, I followed suit, being encouraged by the soldiers. The easy assistance didn't last long; I lost my grip, watching the tractor of men and Alfredo pull away from me.

It was a dangerous stunt, I knew, but one born out of desperation. Being locked into the bike by the pedals, and with the constant uphill cadence of the tractor putting a strain on my wrist, if I were to slip, I could've been sucked under, being squashed like some giant cockroach. Alfredo was much more used to this mode of travel than I, and he-- too easily, for my tastes-- got up the road, to roughly 1800-feet. I met up with him during his rest break.

We continued onward at a snail's pace, an endless inch-at-a-time.

"We can turn back and go the other way," said Alfredo.

"What! And miss the fun of entering another province?"

Several hundred feet later, we heard the sound of another vehicle, a truck this time. It was slow-moving and groaning, as though it were carrying a heavy load, using every ounce of power it could to get to the top. Sweating, I wondered how a mechanical device could actually be moving slower than we were.

We waited, catching our breath, until the truck was in sight. Dump-truck sized with a cargo of workers, it neared us. We hopped on our bikes, peddling at a pace to parallel the freighter, grabbing hold of a corner on either side.

Again, I lost my grip after a few yards, nearly slipping off the bike. But Alfredo, the wonder horse, managed to hang on. I was ready to give up and console myself to the fact that it would be a tough day's work, but the people in back of the truck urged me on, cheering and waving their arms, motioning me to catch-up.

Knowing I could never peddle fast enough up the steep grade to meet the truck and the driver would never be foolish enough to stop unless he had some major breakdown meant I had to work fast.

I began to run with the bike alongside me. It was difficult at first in the cleats; like running on gravel. I actually began to get ever so close to the truck. The crowd was cheering me on, working up a wild-eyed, foaming frenzy as they watched my valiant effort.

Caught up in their excitement, and being so irritatingly close, I grabbed the bike, hoisting it over my shoulder, and began picking up the pace. There were cheers, laughter and shouts from both the men and women, and then...

The bike disappeared. Literally, a weight was lifted off my shoulders. As I was running past the truck in order to have enough time to jump back on the bike to gather momentum for another chance to latch on, one of the workers, in his excitement, decided to help me out by grabbing my baby from me, placing it in the truck to the delightful screams and laughter of the people, including Alfredo.

It struck me that if that truck got past us, there went a $20,000 two-wheel wonder. So I took off, full sprint in cleats, reaching the driver-- whose only focus was in getting to the top of the hill. Desperate, I jumped on the running board, managing somehow to grab the door handle before slipping off.

Catching my breath, I worked my way to the back of the truck, taking a seat with the much-excited group. Imagine what a little incentive can do for you!

Alfredo had been laughing so hard at my antics, he lost his grip and therefore his ride to the top-- which, after all that trouble, was no more than a half-mile; and it was a mere 300 feet before the road leveled off.

Here, it split three different ways, and an imposing edifice marked the fork like some concrete, totalitarian, Cuban demi-god. I got out, along with many of the other workers. While they scattered, I waited no more than 15 minutes for my partner to show.

The *Hotel Topes de Collantes* is a seven-story, several hundred-room palace that occupies several acres. The provinces of *Sancti Spiritus, Villa Clara*, and *Cienfuegos* divide the top of the mountain; the hotel was in the latter's province. Open year-round, the hotel has so many workers there's actually a village nearby to accommodate them all, so that they don't have to make the daily commute from *Trinidad*.

It would have been my choice to end the day there, but since we couldn't, I at least wanted to check out the scenery and gather some details for a future time when I could spend the night.

The hotel didn't spare on luxuries. It had an indoor pool, spa, gym, game room, two HBO channels, as well as American news piped in from Miami. Several trails from the hotel lead to fully-equipped cabins near jungled, private waterfalls. A regular room went for $33 per night; a two-room suite, $43; and an entire apartment (or cabin) was $50-- and it doesn't matter how many people occupy the room.

After getting my fix of creature comfort, capitalistic-esque culture, Alfredo and I set off for the expected downhill.

My philosophy has always been that, "You work the uphills, and pray for a good downhill." This prayer was not answered. Instead of a great, expected downhill, we were given a substituted, frustrating rollercoaster ride. The road dropped some 700 feet, only to climb 500 in return. Toward the bottom, it was an utter tease: Lose 100 feet, gain 100 feet, lose 100, gain 100.

During this up-and-down course, eagle-eyed Alfredo spotted a green guava tree growing amongst the fern. He pulled off the road, into the thick brush.

"This good for your diarrhea," advised the doctor.

I liked the fruit and still had a bit of the runs. So?

As I snacked on the fresh-from-the-tree fruit, I remembered how at one point in my life I had been doing so much cycling I'd wake up and find my fingers curled, ready to slip over the handlebars. I hate drugs, and won't take them unless absolutely necessary, so I thought I'd have to live with this problem. I shoved the worry of developing arthritis later on to the back of my mind, until someone told me that if I took a teaspoon of apple cider vinegar in an eight-ounce glass of water, my fingers would right themselves again within a few months. I thought this was the craziest thing, but I was willing to give it a try. After three weeks, I awoke one day, fingers straight, no pain. In fact, I had no pain in any of my joints, so continued with the remedy daily for the next 18 months, but then got lazy. But there has never been any joint discomfort of any kind for years, and I was still doing tours. The only thing I could figure out was that the apple cider vinegar acted as a meat tenderizer, so if I'm ever caught by cannibals, I'm going to taste great.

At the top of the *Topes*, an abundance of vivid green engulfed us. Mountains seemed to overlap with other ranges, and a river cut through the entire picture. We were in coffee bean country, and picked some ourselves for a fast jolt.

A group of young men-- about a dozen pickers who worked the mountain fields-- were making their way home, baskets of coffee beans and bedrolls slung over their shoulders. They looked tired and hungry, yet full of spirit as we waved to one another. They stopped to admire the bike and pose for photos.

Just before the final descent, Alfredo and I came across a magnificent, spiral waterfall, cascading over shale rock. Alfredo stripped down to his shorts for a quick swim in a spa-size pool of warm water on one of the upper levels. He motioned me to join him.

"This a good picture wit' the bike," he yelled.

I had to admit he was right, but getting to the spot was the problem. One bad move, one slip, and I'd be seriously injured from the fall. Up in no man's land there would be no help, no hospital for at least a day.

Coffee bean harvesters returning home after much time in the fields.

"Come on!," he continued yelling. "You can do it."

"You should try walking in high heels," I yelled back.

I finally maneuvered to his spot, taking photos of him in various positions with the bike. Then we reversed roles. And there went another hour-- enjoyably, yes; but it was gone.

For most of the day, the sun played peek-a-boo with the overcast sky, and as the afternoon drew on, I wanted to get off the mountain before a serious storm came our way. During **American Summits**, I had had enough experience with storms, bikes and mountains.

Near the bottom, a sculptured metal *Don Quixote* on horseback guarded a planter's field. Just as we began to drop the final thousand feet, the skies opened up with a downpour that separated Alfredo and I, making us scramble for shelter. He was nowhere to be seen as I dove inside a covered bus stop with a motorcyclist who tried to have a conversation with me, but it was hopeless.

When the rains cleared about a half-hour later, we parted ways. I reunited with Alfredo near the bottom.

When we finally reached the village of *Manicaragua*, we had put in a full day's work of 36 miles. Alfredo looked at my odometer, then tossed me a hard stare, pressing his lips hard. Keeping silent about the low miles, he went off to make arrangements for the night.

Manicaragua is another one of those forgotten towns that no one visits unless they had to. So, arriving in red-white-and-blue glory created more than

The bike and I in the midst of a cool, refreshing waterfall somewhere along the way to *Manicaragua.*

even the usual stir.

Approaching the only hotel in town, Alfredo did his spiel about the Tour and how we only had *pesos*.

The owner was cool. Not much in business, so we were given a room for 23 *pesos* ($1US). A cell of a room-- small, cramped quarters with no windows, the usual lumpy beds and cold water. But the price was right.

Again, we couldn't keep the bikes in our room, and even if we wanted to, I wondered where we could. Instead, the owner said there was a man a few doors down that had a place for bike storage, which he kept under lock and key. For 20 *pesos,* Alfredo brought them to the house, while I unloaded my gear and tried to relax.

But not for long. My partner came running back, bursting through the door. "A funeral procession is making their way down the main street to the cemetery."

"So? Haven't you seen a funeral procession before?"

"But no' so public like this," he yelled, hopping up and down. "Hurry! Get yo' camera. This a rarity."

A funeral procession along the main street of *Manicaragua.*

He was practically pushing me outside, so I took what I could and was out the door, not even bothering to change out of my uniform.

It was an incredibly large crowd for such a small town as they marched slowly toward the setting sun. Children carried wreaths of yellow chrysanthemums and a single, white sedan drove slowly through the crowd with the casket. The rest of the town watched from the sidelines; life, old and new, watching death pass. No music, no sound. A deathly silence all the way to the above ground graveyard.

At that point, I stood in respect, before making my way back to the hotel. One life is over, others continue.

Back at the room I was ready to take a shower, but the electricity went out.

The hotel's owner told everyone, "This is the town's night to go black. Cubans must unite and suffer for the good of the country."

Balls!

Since there was still some daylight left, I roamed around the area being the photo-journalist, while Alfredo scouted out a restaurant, bringing back a pitcher of fruit juice and thick, fatty, ham sandwiches topped with lettuce on a dry bun.

"What is this obsession you have with the swine?"

"Then no' eat it," answered Alfredo, as he pigged out on pork.

By now, word had reached the area that an American was in town. This was a wondrous event for the children as they stood at a respectable distance from me. Just far enough to run away if I came too close. Aside from breakfast in *Trinidad,*

I hadn't eaten. Now, all that was staring at me was the swine sandwiches. I tried to give the hungry looking children the meat, but they just ran off to a safe distance in laughter. I couldn't even give the pork to the pathetic-looking, emaciated dogs who ran away if I got too close, so I just began throwing it in the street, eating the bread and lettuce instead.

Watching me-- the crazy *Americano*, I presumed, made a young teenage girl laugh with delight, as she sat on a front porch across from the hotel. Hanging out with me the rest of the evening, she wanted to practice the only English sentence she knew, "What yo' name?"

I'd tell her, she'd repeat it, then a few moments later, we were back to, "What yo' name?"

It went on like this for the next few hours.

Her mother, Olga, a slim, plain woman, told Alfredo, "A friend of mine from America is in town. Would you like to meet her?"

"An American in this nowhere town?" I questioned Olga's statement. "This I've got to see."

Her name was Irene. A bit shorter than Olga, with fiery rust-colored hair done in a short cut that made her green eyes stand out. She cut an attractive figure for a young, mid-40s grandmother, and dressed way beyond the local code of tattered clothing.

Irene was born and raised in *Manicaragua*, but left with her first husband and a couple of their children nearly a decade before, settling in the Miami area. After divorcing, she went on to New Orleans with her second spouse. Once again divorced, she was here for a month with a four-year-old child, paying a visit to an older daughter and her family who refused to leave Cuba for a life of anything-you-want in America. Twice a year she did the trek, bringing her daughter and grandchildren gifts, toiletries, medicines, and twice a year she ended up leaving without them.

We stayed on the front porch of the hotel. As the sun set, our eyes began to adjust to the night. Olga, her daughter and some other children were hanging around us, but the only one that could understand what we were saying was Alfredo. Every so often, if we laughed about something, Olga wanted to know what we were talking about, so Irene interpreted.

"I've already been in town a week," said Irene, "And I've been bored the minute I arrived."

"Then what do you do to relieve yourself?" I smiled.

"Wouldn't you like to know?" she laughed. "Actually, there's a guy in town that has a car, so I pay him to be my chauffeur. He takes me to *Santa Clara* where I go to the nightclubs, drinking and partying."

"Sounds like a way to escape the boredom."

"The best way," smiled Irene. "Let's do it!"

"Do what?"

"Party in *Santa Clara* tonight."

I was bored, too, not wanting to write in my journal by flashlight, and rarely do I pass up an invitation to party. Alfredo was game as well.

We were still in our cycling clothes, grimy from the day's work. With the electricity off, our only option was an offer from Olga, who had a place where we could take a cold, refreshing shower.

Well, it wasn't quite a shower, but it was cold. I thought it was quite interesting how the family converted the outhouse into a bathing facility, with a steel pipe sticking through one side and a cork plugging the hole.

I was given a candle in a holder and told to watch where I stepped, to make sure the shithole was covered before I walked completely inside. The sound of pigs could be heard grunting and squealing in a corner of the backyard as I made my way to the box with my toiletries.

The inside was darker than Satan's soul. I shone the candlelight all around, fixing my bearings, but I was not sure if I were stepping on dirt or something else. I stripped down, remembered to breath through my mouth, unpopped the cork, and allowed the ice cold water to wash over me. I worked up a lather as quickly as I could, and was in and out as fast as possible. This was probably the first time I could recollect exiting a shower stall still smelling like shit. It was probably just the area I was in, but the pigs *did* sound happy to be near me.

Back inside, Irene returned to inform me that, "I couldn't find my driver to take us to *Santa Clara*. Perhaps he'll return soon."

Pointing to the house she was staying at, she said, "I'm going to put my daughter to bed and wait to see what happens."

In the meantime, Alfredo and I hadn't had much to eat, and were getting hungry. But with everything closed down, our chances for any food were slim to none-- until Olga invited us to her house a few blocks up the road for rice and beans.

I just couldn't seem to get away from *congris.* I was ready to return to chewing vitamin E tablets, but Olga was insistent, so we took her up on the offer, following her back to the *hacienda,* her daughter tagging on my arm.

At the simple framed house she shared with her daughter and older son-- like Irene's, her husband had abandoned the family years before-- we sat outside, eating by candlelight. The food was heated on a woodstove.

Olga sat opposite me, the daughter close to my right, the son on my left. I felt like a specimen under close observation. In the glow of the light, Olga's eyes seemed to dance with fire. She sat quietly, smoking a cigarette, keeping her focus on me.

What goes through their heads, I wondered. *Is it a real treat to have an authentic American to sup at your house? What do they see as they smile silently? Do I represent the outside world? A world of untold riches and wealth that they've only heard about, but will never experience? Did Jesus ever feel like a bug under a glass whenever He ate with people He met along His journeys?*

Olga only understood a few simple words of English, but somehow picked up on the conversation I was having with Alfredo, and through him, mentioned she was a Christian.

"And what makes you think that?" I probed.

"*La fe.*" Faith was her simple reply as she took another deep drag on her ever-present cigarette.

Her children laughed. Her son, knowing a bit of English, said, "Mama, she crazy," pointing to his head.

"Hey!" yelled Olga, slapping her son. She understood.

"Alfredo, interpret, " I asked. "And don't ad-lib."

He did as I asked-- I am not totally ignorant of the Spanish language-- as I explained why Jesus came down from Heaven to take on the humble appearance of a man; His Ministry; the resurrection; that Jesus loved her enough to die for her, so that when she dies, she will be with Him in Paradise.

Nodding in agreement, she repeated the word "Jesus" each time I mentioned His name. An eternal life with Jesus is the only thing this woman has to hang on to, I thought. Some kinship with the Lord who was born into lower poverty than she was.

When she gave me her address, I was determined to get a Spanish Bible to her so she could further her growth, even if it meant returning someday in the near future. I knew if I mailed it, the government might detour it to the burn pile.

When Alfredo and I were ready to return to Irene's place, I knew Olga wouldn't accept a straightforward offer of money, so I had Alfredo tell her that it would, "Make me very happy if you would do me the honour of being allowed to give you something in return for all that you have done for us."

Versing it that way seemed to work, as I was grateful for her hospitality and fellowship.

At Irene's place, a group of us sat around the front porch, drinking beer; Irene and I in our own little world.

"Sometimes I feel looked upon by these people I once grew up with," she confided in me. "I've known them all my life, but I no longer feel as though I'm one of them."

"They see you as someone who broke through some invisible, impossible barrier," I answered. "You went over the rainbow when you landed in America."

"I feel isolated, and I hate it."

Irene looked radiant in her pants outfit. All dressed up and no place to go, as she nervously tapped her feet on the well-worn out wood of the porch. She was smoking so much, I didn't know where one cigarette ended and the other began. She was ready to fly.

"Come on," she took my hand. "Let's take a walk."

We wandered off toward the center of town, to a park-like setting, complete with benches and some grassy turf. She handed me a piece of paper and a pen from her gold lame handbag, and said, "Write down your address and phone number."

"Ah," I laughed. "A woman of authority who doesn't beat around the bush."

After giving her the information, she announced boldly, "I'm going to call you when I return to New Orleans."

"Oh, really?"

"Yeah," she nodded. "I think I'll come and visit you for a while with my daughter."

I laughed, thinking about my small-town lifestyle and the gossipy rumors that would begin once she arrived.

"I'm not interested in that kind of involvement, Irene."

"Oh," she hissed, "that's what I hate about American men."

"What do you want out of life?" I asked. "What are you looking for?"

"Since my second marriage failed, all I want out of life now is to find a man I could live with. I think we could have some good times in and out of bed," she smiled, snuggling up to me on the park bench. "If it doesn't work out, then we can go our separate ways. I want to leave New Orleans, and California sounds great for me and my four-year-old daughter."

"Wow! Sounds like you have the whole thing figured out. Thanks for inviting me along for the ride."

"I'm laying myself on the line," she said, lighting another cigarette. "I don't like game playing."

"Great, because neither do I."

"In January. After the holidays," she nodded to herself. "That's when I'll move in with you."

She moved in closer to me once more, taking my arm and wrapping it around her silky clothed body.

"I'm going to be good for you," she smiled, placing her hand on my thigh. "The best lover you've ever had."

"That's quite a statement. Would love to find out if it's true or not." My eyes met hers, our lips ever so close to one another. "Unfortunately, Irene, what you want is not my style. I don't want a live-in love, but a lifetime lover. I want a wife, not a girlfriend."

She reeled from that kind of talk, like a vampire would to a crucifix. "You're crazy! I'm making you a great offer and you're turning it down? There are many men who would want what I'm giving you!"

The conversation came to an abrupt end when Irene stormed back to her place. By then, I was ready to call it a night in *Manicaragua* and move on to the next adventure.

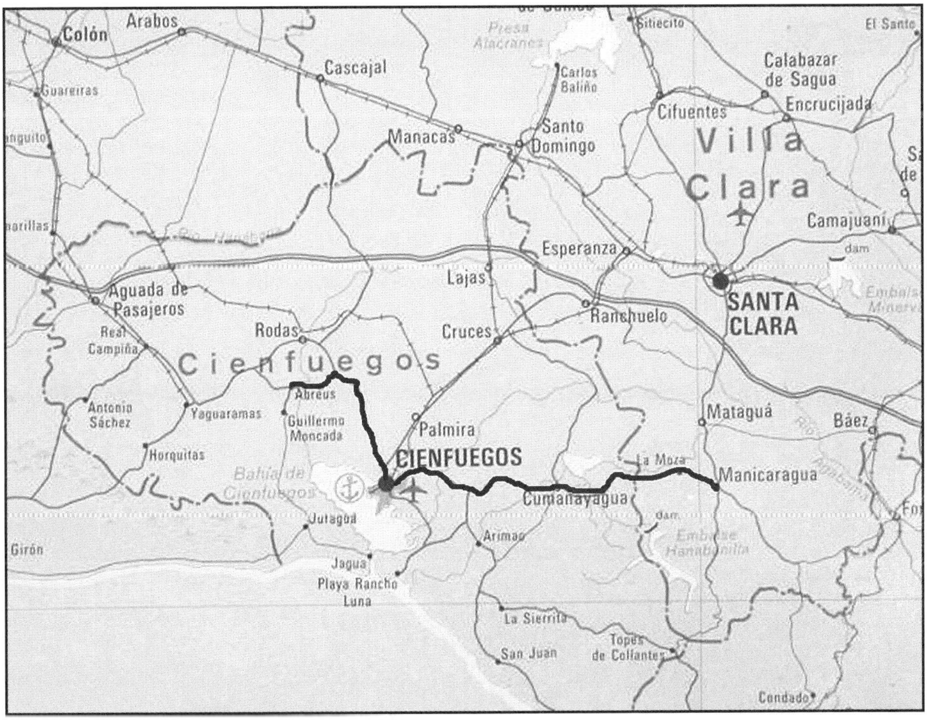

VEINTITRES

23

MANICARAGUA to ABREUS
DAY 15
DECEMBER 05, 1997

DAILY DISTANCE :	**63**	**miles or**	**105**	**kilometers**
TOTAL DISTANCE :	**748**	**miles or**	**1246.7**	**kilometers**

Disaster struck!

The runs returned full flow after a deceptive lapse. I was out of toilet paper, and trying to find some in that country was like looking for gold. I was down to either tearing blank sheets out of my journal-- a humbling experience, knowing what one's writing can be used for-- or using the paper *pesos*, trying to keep to the lower denominations. Excuse me, but do you have change for a twenty?

There was an abundance of the three-*peso* bills with Che Guevara's likeness embossed on it. I hated everytime I had to use them, apologizing under my breath. I hoped ol' Che would understand that, at times, it was a necessity.

"There goes Kevin, throwing his money away on shit."

On the usual empty stomachs, we left the tiny town of *Manicaragua* while it was still dark, heading west to *Cienfuegos*.

"Since we're not heading north to *Santa Clara*, we should have a good day for putting in the miles," I said to my enthusiastic partner.

"*Si*," smiled Alfredo, "We make up the time now."

The further west we headed, the longer it took the sun to reach us. The dark, early mornings were noticeably chilly, as Alfredo and I went from T-shirts to sweatshirts. In cycling, the legs get the workout, not the upper body. When the warm rays of the *sol* finally caught up to us, we'd have to momentarily stop to peel down.

On the route, we passed farmers plowing with their ox and cattle in the sugarcane fields, workers picking the harvest of the banana plantations. There were other men cutting grass by the side of the road, swinging their long, curved sickles back and forth in rhythmic unison. Cowboys roamed the land on horseback, waving as we went by on our own steeds.

During a brief afternoon stop in the town of *Cumanayagua*, we found a group of people gathered at a mobile PanAmerican store, buying products with US dollars.

"There," pointed Alfredo. "Perhaps this store will have the toilet paper you are looking for."

"Your lips to God's ears," I answered in disbelief. "We haven't come across any yet. Don't expect to now."

"Still, it is worth a try."

With hope and a prayer, I entered the guarded facility looking for gold.

Unfortunately, not a role was to be found. Not even facial tissue, or papertowels of any kind. That was the one thing I always found a shortage of in the Communist countries I've traveled through-- a complete line of paper products. And that was why I would've rather used paper *pesos* instead of blank sheets from my journal. *Pesos* I could always acquire. Blank paper for recording facts, memories, and incidents, I couldn't. Sorry, Che.

But with the frequent stops for a private moment and having nothing to clean with, I was in a *tight-ass* state, praying, "Lord, I know You're a God of miracles, and I need one in the form of a roll right now!"

Then it was time to move on.

By mid-afternoon, we had entered the metropolis of *Cienfuegos*, stopping briefly for some refreshments before changing our direction north.

It was another couple of hours of desolate road riding through overcast skies before we reached the small town of *Rodas*. Just as we came upon the office of the only hotel in town, a sudden downpour began.

"God is with us once again," I said to Alfredo. "Not only do we come across the only hotel in town, but we made it before we got soaking wet."

"*Si*. He good to us," he acknowledged.

The hotel was designed in two rows of side-by-side bungalows with a paved

Locals shop at the nearby Pan American store for USA products.

parking lot and grassy turf divider. Situated on a river, a short walk would take us to the dock, where a full-sized boat awaited passengers for a cruise along the banks. There was also a thatched-roof gazebo with a fully-serviced bar, and nearby was the hotel's restaurant, where a party was in full swing. It was a Friday, after all, and that was usually enough reason for the local natives to celebrate.

"These are workers who did more than their share of work," mentioned Alfredo. "They receive bonuses, and are allowed to come here with their families for the weekend."

"Very benevolent of your government to allow the dogs such creature comforts. Wouldn't it be better to pay the people in dollars and let them decide what they want to do?"

Alfredo gave me a frowned look. "What do you think this is? America?"

"Sorry," I shot back. "I forgot myself."

Speaking with the hotel manager, Alfredo informed me, "There may not be a room for us tonight. The hotel is full and there have been no cancellations."

"Do you want to wait a while?" I asked.

The rains had died down momentarily.

"I think we should go into town and get something to eat," said Alfredo. "We come back and see if hotel is still full."

We cycled the half-mile into town. There, we found the ubiquitous juice and ice cream and a crowd full of curious children, who stopped screaming and smearing each other with the sticky goo when I entered the building. They watched us from one end of the counter, we watched them. After a few moments, they ran outside in a herd to inspect the bike. This gave Alfredo and I-- and a grateful waitress-- a few minutes of relaxed peace and quiet.

After an hour's fill of the cafe's only two products, we returned to the hotel, where the manager announced to Alfredo, "All the bungalows are occupied for the entire weekend."

"'No where does the Son of Man have a place to rest His head,'" I mumbled under my breath.

"*Que?*"

"Jesus never had a problem finding a place to spend the night, so why should we?"

"Because we are not God," frowned Alfredo.

"But He promises to watch over His children."

"Only if you believe. And I no' His child."

"Not yet," I smiled. "But you're with me, so you receive the blessing as well."

"You crazy," scowled Alfredo, in a defensive mood. "We are in the middle of nowhere."

"Well, that's better than being nowhere at all."

I understood my friend completely. It took me years of humbled experiences to totally rely on the Lord for the basic needs. I just needed to give up trying to do everything myself, and allow the Lord to provide. Once I did, the miracles began, and I've been at peace ever since. In time, perhaps Alfredo would experience the same type of faith. It was a prayer of mine.

With the on and off rains and daylight nearing an end, we were running out of options-- until the manager told us of another hotel, in similar structure, about nine miles down the road in *Abreus*. "They may have rooms available," she said, shrugging her shoulders.

The next nine miles to *Abreus* was-- like most of the day-- in open country, with limited options on shelter. A darkening, overcast, thunderous sky loomed above us, and just as we hit the crossroads, the tempest came crashing down upon us once again. Before we became completely drenched, I spotted a covered bus stop toward which a horde of people in summer clothing were running full bore enmasse, pushing and shoving their way into the cramp quarters.

Picking up my pace, I rode full throttle toward the mark, jumping off the moving bike. I nearly hit those around me as I made my way inside.

I turned to congratulate Alfredo, but he was nowhere in sight.

For the next half-hour or so, I stood like a sardine, watching the sky do its best to drown our group. The water was slowly making its way toward us, rising to the ankles of those of us who were at ground level. Others bought dry time by standing on the benches.

When the rains subsided for the briefest of moments, I emerged with some of the more braver members of the group, looking around the area for my partner. Some hundred yards off, behind the bus stop, I saw him waving to me with a group of construction workers, under a gigantic concrete complex. Just as I got to them, the skies let loose once more and we were stranded another half-hour.

This time our detainment passed quickly. The workers welcomed me into their sheltered space with open arms, cheers and slaps on the back. An American was in their midst. Soon, the group surrounded the bike, giving a detailed inspection. When one of them accidentally pushed the button on my handlebars and the saddle shot straight up, they jumped back in surprised astonishment, nearly falling over themselves.

During my time with the group, Alfredo struck up a conversation with a young man about our age. With a trimmed moustache, he reminded me of Errol Flynn in his prime.

"*Kebin*," called out Alfredo. "Come here."

I left the construction workers to lust over the Beast.

"This man Carlos--"

"Charlie," he corrected, offering me his hand.

"Charlie," corrected Alfredo. "He say he know the hotel we look for. It is just three miles from here."

"Great! As soon as it stops raining perhaps he could point the way."

"He do better than that," smiled Alfredo. "He say he take us there himself."

"Oh, *gracias, amigo*," I nodded to Charlie. "Alfredo, tell him that isn't necessary. We don't wish to intrude."

"It no' problem," laughed Alfredo. "The land the hotel is on once belong to his family. They give it to the government, and Charlie help design and build the hotel for tourists. His entire family work there."

Charlie beamed with pride.

"*Gracias, amigo. Gracias.*"

"Funny, how it rain just as we arrive here," commented Alfredo. "If it no' rain, we no' find Charlie."

"Imagine that," I nodded. "Must be God."

"Perhaps," nodded my partner. "It is a coincidence."

There were plenty of bungalows available at the quaint, roadside resort. Built in a circular pattern, the centerpiece was a several-story tall, thatched-roof rotunda that served as the restaurant, dance hall, and for banquets and weddings. Nearby was a smaller, one-story replica that housed the bar and played piped-in *salsa* music. Still daylight, there was a substantial group of overweight, underdressed tourists cooling off with drinks.

Once the check-in process had been completed, Carlos escorted us to our 20 *peso*-a-night bungalow, showing us the detail and workmanship he put into the place along the way. It was set up as though each unit was a house unto itself, with its own walkway leading to the front door and a yard for children to play in. "Weekends are full," he said, through Alfredo, "You are very fortunate."

Each hut had its own theme. Ours was the circus, and the inside walls were painted with scenes of animals and acrobats. I felt as though I had invaded a child's bedroom, but we did have a place to rest our heads for the evening. Of course, it was only a one-bed accommodation, which meant this would be the second time during the Tour that Alfredo and I would be sleeping together. But, really, by then we had grown accustomed to one another.

Although the bungalow had plenty of room, Carlos said, "You cannot keep your bikes with you. They must be locked up in another area."

I stood straight, my wall of defense was up. Alfredo looked at me. I never had to say a word.

"Carlos," informed Alfredo, "*Kebin's* bicycle is the only one like it in the world. If something were to happen to it during the night unguarded..."

Charlie held up his hand. "I understand. I live next door with my family. You can keep the bikes there. It will be an honour."

Alfredo interpreted the situation. I agreed. What other choice did I really have?

As soon as the three of us approached the family homestead, the front door swung open, pouring out Charlie's parents and an assortment of brothers, sisters, husbands, wives and a large number of children.

By the hand gestures, I presumed Charlie was explaining to his family who Alfredo and I were and how we all came to meet up with one another.

The children gathered around the bike to inspect it as Charlie's siblings greeted my partner and I with handshakes and pats on the back. The mother offered us cold, refreshing water. Her bright smile and laughing eyes made us feel welcomed. While Carlos demonstrated some of the more advanced features of my bike to his nieces, nephews and siblings, the father showed Alfredo and I the land they farmed, as the last rays of the sun began to fade.

Before it got completely dark, Carlos stored the bikes in the barn, while we thanked his family for their kindness toward us. Our gracious host then escorted us back to the inn just as the final assault of thundershowers came crashing down upon us, remaining the rest of the evening.

"If it rain like this all day tomorrow," said Alfredo, "We agree to stay, okay?"

"I would never think of disagreeing," I countered.

The three of us headed to the outside bar, the huge grass canopy protecting us and the other hotel guests from the torrential rains. We ordered drinks and fellowshipped.

A truck stopped nearby and a pair of occupants emerged. Heading for the rear, they quickly retrieved a large pig, who began to put up such a magnificent fight, it got the attention of us all.

"It sounds like the pig no' want to be someone's dinner," yelled Alfredo above the soul-disturbing squeals of the swine.

"Guess he knows what he's in for," I shouted back.

The pig was thrashing about, trying to break free. It took both burly men to cart him off to the restaurant. Once he was subdued, some of the guests looked at one another giving nervous laughs while checking their own throats.

While the three of us were off in our own little corner of the bar, Carlos, through Alfredo, spoke about his life as a construction worker.

"It is something I am good at, and can provide for my family," replied the father of a boy and girl.

During the early 80s, when Carlos was in his late teens, he was drafted into the Army, "Where I served as an ambulance driver during the Angola Civil War. It was horrible, *amigo,*" he cried.

He'd finish one beer and begin another, stopping long enough to open the cap.

"I would have to pick up my dead and wounded countrymen. Many of them were my friends. I shed many tears."

Upon returning to Cuba, he couldn't handle the stress ...all the memories and the questions.

"Why?" he cried. "What was the war for? Why did we have to go? Why did we have to die? What was there to gain? What was the cause we were fighting for?"

Why? The most difficult question in the world to answer. How do you reach out to somewhere who's been looking for answers these last 15 years?

Through Alfredo, I said, "War is big business, my friend. Politicians make the wars. Corporations make the money. And we the people make no sense out of any of it."

"*Si, si,*" he acknowledged through tear-stained eyes.

"Since man was first created, he's been wanting to rule over other men. To gain power and land for himself. To conquer. It will never end until Jesus returns."

"Ah, *si,* Jesus," he nodded. "I pray sometimes."

"That's good. It helps. But most importantly, you must pray to God that He relieves the burden from your heart. Let the dead bury the dead, while you go on living for your wife and children who need you the most."

"*Si, si,*" he nodded, patting my shoulder.

"What did you do after the war?" I asked, trying to divert the conversation.

"I went to the Soviet Union for three months to study business. Someday, when the embargo ends, I will represent the people of this area as a buyer of goods and services."

"That's wonderful," I smiled, patting him on the back. "I pray you will have the chance to see it come true."

"*Si.* The embargo is choking my people," exclaimed Carlos. His voice rose; his hands formed a circle, as though he had a physical hold on someone. "This cursed embargo is choking my country."

"*Si,*" agreed Alfredo. "It is time for a change."

Catching himself, he looked at me, and began to calm down. "I am sorry, *amigo,*" he said, giving me a hug. "We are a passionate people who fight injustice. We Cubans do not hate America or Americans. We love you and your country. We care for you and want to be friends. When you return home, you will tell your people we love them?"

"Of course I will, my friend." I gave him a reassuring hand on his shoulder. "We, in America, love the Cubans. You will see. In this life, we will sit at the table of love together and fellowship with one another."

"I would like that very much," smiled Carlos.

"I would like to live long enough to see that myself," commented Alfredo.

"You must understand, my friend," continued Carlos. "We Cubans are a strong and proud people. We will not bow down to any government, no matter what they do to us."

"Many of my people in America would not want you to."

"The embargo keeps us hungry. Keeps us fighting," shouted Carlos as he punched the air with his fists.

"Many of us in America are embarrassed by what our leaders do. We have, through our technology and slavery to consumerism, become a slothful society, who fear the government. We like the way our lives are, and don't want them disturbed by anyone or anything."

"*Si*," agreed Carlos. "Jesse Helms no good. Clinton is a puppet. He say one thing, and do another."

"*Si,*" acknowledged Alfredo. "No' can trust Clinton."

"Someday, God will damn his soul to Hell, because he doesn't fear the Higher Authority he's under. So are the leaders, so goes the nation."

It was dark when we began to wind-up our conversation. Some of the other guests returned to their rooms. The rains continued. Insects darted in and out of the lights.

"A toast," I proposed, raising my glass of rum. Alfredo and Carlos did the same. "*Americano-Cubano, amigos!*"

"Ah! *Si!*" shouted Carlos with a smile. Even the bartender who listened in on most of our conversation, drank the toast with us. We downed the clear liquid in one shot, striking the counter with our glasses.

Before returning to his family, our new friend gave Alfredo and I warm, tight hugs. As he bade us farewell, I prayed for peace and contentment to enter his life. That he could find comfort in the love and arms of his wife and children.

At the restaurant, there wasn't much variety. *Congris* or pork or both. Beer or water or juice. You want dessert?... we'll give you some sugared swine.

This was the extent of the menu.

"Large selection," I mentioned to Alfredo. "First time you don't have to read the menu to me."

"*Si*," laughed my partner. "A big decision to make."

Food is food. It sustains you, gets you through. I took the usual rice and beans-- and a big plate of it, too-- thanking the Lord for His daily providence.

Tomorrow we would be entering the *Bay of Pigs*. A day I had been looking forward to nearly all my life.

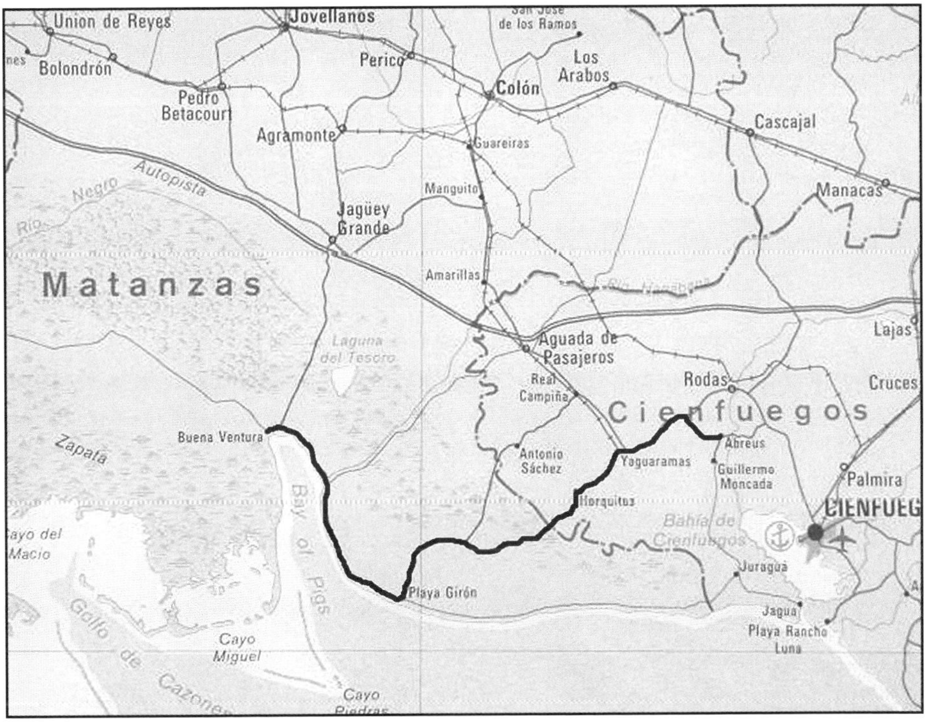

VEINTICUATRO

24

ABREUS to BUENA VENTURA
DAY 16
DECEMBER 06, 1997

DAILY DISTANCE : 62 miles or 103.3 kilometers
TOTAL DISTANCE : 810 miles or 1350 kilometers

We awoke to a dark fog. No rain. No day off.

Alfredo and I lethargically took our time and left at daybreak.

The morning was chilly, and we had to dress in layers once again. Upon check out, we passed the restaurant, outside of which Charlie's mother was working near the open barbecue pit, preparing breakfast for the other guests who had not yet risen.

At the monument to American Brigadier General, Henry Earl Reeve, who died in battle fighting the Spanish for Cuba's freedom during the War for Independence in the 1890s.

She held up a glass of fresh milk, offering us some.

"*Si.*" Another excuse to linger.

Within an hour from our departure point, between the tiny towns of *Yaguaramas* and *Horquitas*, we came across another lone monument by the side of an open stretch of road. Near a large field, it was dedicated to an American Brigadier General named Henry Earl Reeve, who, as the plaque read, "Shed his blood for Cuba during the War of Independence, 1876 against Spain."

The memorial, a stone platform, several yards long, had a flag pole on one end. Opposite, a stone pillar had been erected by Castro about ten years before.

"I'm surprised to see such a structure for an American. Especially one that is dedicated by Castro himself," I mentioned to Alfredo as I took some photos.

"*Si*," agreed my guide. "It is listed as a National Historical site of great value."

"So much for government propaganda on how our two countries are at constant war with one another. If we were, why would Castro spend money on such a fine memorial?"

"This man very famous in Cuba," stated Alfredo. "All Cuban children learn about him in school. During the war, the General lost part of his leg in a battle that was fought here. He ask his men to tie up his leg and put him back on his horse. They did not want to, but he order them to, and he go on fighting until he die."

"People helping people," I nodded. "Not only did he love his neighbor as himself, but he willingly laid down his life for his brother. Isn't it strange how in my own country, we have never heard of this man?"

"*Si,*" nodded Alfredo. "It is all in the perspective."

My lower bowels were still doing flip-flops and rumbling the warning signal to let me know I had just enough time to find a spot before exploding outward. I was continuing to tear blank sheets out of my journal or using the lower denomination *pesos*, literally crying out to God, "I need that miracle now! You're supposed to be a God of miracles. Where's that toilet paper?" Anything that looked like a store, I didn't hesitate to go in searching for gold.

Once we passed the border into the province of *Matanzas,* we became surrounded by the swampy marsh world of no man's land. There was not another soul to be seen, only the insistent sounds of birds and other unidentified animals in the jungle brush. The paved road was our only solid dividing line through the area. Being caught out there after nightfall would not be a wise decision, unless, of course, you enjoy being preyed upon.

The road was on a long, slow, gradual uphill slope, so slight that my altimeter hardly registered any figures. About midway from the border to the town of *Playa Giron*, we came across a group of people making coal from wood.

"Cubans in this area use it for heating their homes and cooking," mentioned Alfredo.

The place looked like an apocalypse in the midst of the jungle. Mounds of soot and smoke, thatched-roof huts, pieces of wood and straw laying about; the workers looked war-torn and ravaged. Off to one side, bags of charcoal were ready to be packed in hay and shipped via horse-drawn carriage to other towns nearby, who would then transfer them via truck to the rest of the country.

The workers' faces were well-worn. Some of the older ones had hunch-backed bodies caused by years of abuse carrying coal, while the younger workers were still bony and strong. All were covered in fine coal dust. Their clothes appeared to stick to themselves, their bodies were just as grimy. Two-story mounds of wooden logs covered by a layer of hay were being built. Off near a burnt area of coal dust, a little girl seemed happy and content eating slices of green oranges among a group of tired workers.

I asked, through Alfredo, "What did this type of work do to your lungs?"

They shrugged their shoulders, saying, "We feel no side effects. Most of us live into our seventies and eighties."

By lunch, Alfredo and I reached *Playa Giron*, the sight of the infamous *Bay of Pigs*. Growing up with the familiar monikers, Fidel Castro and John Kennedy, the name, *Bay of Pigs* had taken on, in my life, a sort of myth. Like *Xanadu, Shangri-la*, and *Valhalla*. Was the *Bay* real or a place made up by distant historians and storytellers? In nearly four decades of life, I have never known anyone who has ever been to the *Bay of Pigs*, much less Cuba for that matter. Entering the area, it brought an exhilaration and rapid heartbeat. The place was real, and I was here.

After ten days of open country travel, we were once again back on the coast-- if only for the day-- since veering inland from *Manzanillo*. The smell of salt and the sound of crashing waves always made the Piscean in me feel alive and rejuvenated.

The process of making charcoal: Preparing the wood, above...

...to bagging and shipping the final product, below.

In *Playa Giron* there was a museum erected to the *Bay of Pigs* invasion, and for two dollars you could buy a pass to view the memorabilia.

"We have made good time today," said Alfredo. "Let us take a tour of the museum."

Growing up with the American perspective of the *Bay of Pigs* invasion and the Cuban missile crisis, I thought it'd be interesting to get a Cuban's view of what took place.

Outside stood a war plane used in the mini-conflict. Alfredo didn't have to pay. He was acting as my guide-interpreter because no one on staff could speak English. We had the entire place to ourselves.

Unlike the museums I'm accustomed to in my country, the one Alfredo and I entered was nothing more than a cold concrete room. The walls were pale in color. The only thing that didn't make them look completely stark naked were the large, black and white photographs of the battle. See-through cabinets were strategically placed in a maze-like setting, many of them with cracked glass and chipped wood. Inside were showcased stark mementos of uniforms, canned food, buttons, glasses, handguns, swords... There was no creative style to the placement of the memorabilia. They were simply just there. Dropped and left.

We began our tour with some of the giant photographs lining one side of the wall, Alfredo interpreting the Spanish titles under each one.

"When Fidel take over the country in January, 1959, many countrymen escape to united States," began my guide. "There, they form an army with American government money, training to overthrow Castro."

The people in the photos had a stark reality to them. These loyal Cubans looked starved and ghost-like, as they prepared to defend their homeland against their exiled countrymen whom they felt betrayed Cuba.

"In January 1961, Castro take over all American businesses. Then United States ended diplomatic relations. In April, the exiles go from United States to Central America for more training. There, they get ready to invade Cuba. But Fidel, he know," smiled Alfredo.

"How?" I asked.

"Spies." replied Alfredo, nonchalantly.

"From where?" I questioned.

"All over." he answered off-the-cuff.

"Of course." I scoffed.

Continuing down the line, the photos grew more battle laden with tanks and ships in and around the *Bay.*

"The exiles chose the *Bay of Pigs*, because it is on the south coast of Cuba, and only a two-hour drive north to Havana. Once the *Bay* was captured, reinforcements could arrive, and that would be the end of Fidel."

"But of course, your beloved leader arrives just in time with the Cuban calvary."

"*Si!*" lit Alfredo. "Fidel lead the way in the tank."

"As seen in the miraculous photo. Amazing how some of these photographers can capture the moment."

A young *senorita* with her father and co-workers having a lunch of green oranges.

"Kennedy promised support once the exiles landed on the beach, but he no' keep his word."

"That's true," I agreed. "We at least learned that much in history. Kennedy was supposed to send air and sea cover, but backed-off at the last moment."

"*Si.* Many exiles were killed. Cubans love a good fight, but this was nothing for us. We kill them good."

If Kennedy had kept his word, he probably would have succeeded, and history would be different today, with Castro either dead or in exile somewhere.

"I love this next photo," I commented to Alfredo.

"*Si.* This most famous. All Cubans know it."

About the size of a very large movie poster, the black and white image shows Castro leaping off a moving tank during the heat of battle. The image clearly states that the beloved leader of his oppressed people was willing to fight and die, if necessary, with his comrades-in-arms.

"This one striking act permanently cemented Castro's image and his dictatorship," I noted to my guide. "And made Kennedy look like a fool."

"*Si,*" nodded Alfredo. "After this, the people follow Fidel to the death."

"But what happened to the exiled survivors?" I asked as we continued to head down memory lane.

"This," smiled Alfredo, pointing to a series of photos. "All the survivors were captured and brought to a camp for prisoners. Here, Fidel trade them back to United States for food and medical supplies for the Cuban children."

"Beautiful," I laughed, clapping my hands. "Castro becomes the benevolent dictator. The saviour."

"The people love him."

"Suffer the little ones to come unto me."

"They no' suffer," frowned my friend.

"Forget it. Bad humor. Guess the moral of the story is: Never trust a politician unless you have a secret back-up plan to get yourself out of the jam."

"The exiles never try again after that."

"Who could blame them?" I countered. "But let's not be too judgmental against Kennedy. The following year was the Cuban missile crisis, and I see nothing about that."

"There is nothing to tell," replied Alfredo.

"Yeah. Guess we should have just let the Russians point their little ol' nuclear missiles at us, huh?"

"America no' have right to tell Cuba what to do."

"And I agree... up to a point. But with Russia aiming their weapons of destruction at the United States, it showed an open act of defiance. Cuba, being so close, was merely a pawn to the Motherland."

"But you still no' have the right," he quipped.

"In this case we did," I shot back. "Do you honestly believe America could tolerate such insurrection? Castro may have grown some *cojonas* after the *Bay of Pigs* fiasco, but if Khrushchev didn't back off, we would've bombed Cuba off the face of the earth, and there goes World War Three. So, Fidel was pissed. Kennedy redeems himself. Score: tied."

"But Fidel still in power," smiled Alfredo.

"Yeah. And Kennedy's a martyred legend."

Between the museum tour, lunch at a nearby restaurant, and taking time out to gather our notes, we were at *Playa Giron* for nearly three hours. Before leaving, Alfredo pointed to a PanAmerican store across the street.

"They may have what you looking for," he quipped nonchalantly.

I had all but given up hope of my search for the elusive roll of toilet paper, but we were there and it was open, so what could a few extra moments mean?

The establishment had so many American products, I couldn't tell there was an embargo. Sifting through the well-stocked shelves, I again came up empty. Heading out the door, I decided to ask out of sheer desperation. The cashier smiled, stepped aside, and there, on the shelf behind her, sat a single roll, like some tissued Holy Grail.

My initial reaction was to jump for joy. Suppressing my emotions, I asked how much, knowing I would pay anything for that most valuable of valuables.

"Twenty-five cents. American money," she announced.

"Twenty-five cents!" I screamed. I knew that if I showed how badly I needed the product, the price could be raised, so I had to act as though I wasn't interested. "That's too much."

"That is the price," she stated bluntly.

The trade was made. I coveted the prize greedily, literally jumping for joy

At the *Bay of Pigs* museum in *Playa Giron*, where history gives a different point of view about the American invasion of 1961.

once outside.

"Hallelujah! Praise the Lord! Thank You, sweet Jesus!"

I kissed it. I fondled it. It wasn't exactly squeezably soft, but it was enough to get me through the rest of the Tour. I was so happy, I could've had a bowel movement right then and there. No more note paper or *pesos!* Che was happy.

"You see," laughed Alfredo. "I tell you we have toilet paper in Cuba. It just no' easy to find."

At this area called the *Bay of Pigs*, you'd never know a war went on some 35 years before. The only reminders were the museum and monuments along the coast which were inscribed with the names of the dead who fought beside their fearless leader.

Now it's a major tourist attraction, a playground for the rich foreigners who go zooming by in their newly-rented automobiles, wearing the latest fashions from Europe. Lifestyles of the filth and shameless who take scuba diving lessons off the coast, or sip champagne in nearby yachts.

Playa Giron located on the south end, *Buena Ventura* on the north and in between are 35 kilometers of virgin, white-sandy beaches. The water was a deep sea-green and the temperature of a warm bath. Paradise had emerged from destruction, the phoenix out of the ashes.

My only regret was the surety that once the embargo was lifted, the area would be one of the first to be commercialized. I would have loved to plunge myself into the raucous water, to feel the hot sun on my chest-- but there was no time. We had spent too much in one area and had to make up our miles if we intended to reach the opposite end before nightfall.

Within the last five miles, we came across several places to stay, but not for us. The first we came to was a campsite. For 11 pesos, we could have had a run-down shack on the beach. Alfredo always liked to look for cheap places in order to save money, and though I don't argue this point, it's always good for the ego to spend time pampering yourself in luxury every so often.

The campsite was full-- for 11 *pesos* a night, and this being a weekend, I could understand-- so we had no choice but to move on.

It was also getting cold and cloudy. We had been blessed with no rain showers, so far, which fueled my desire to swim in the *Bay of Pigs*.

Our next stop was a fancier hotel. But this one was only for Cubans-- Cubans who worked hard, did well, and did more than their share at their jobs: perks and bonuses.

"In my country," I explained to Alfredo, "Money is the incentive for hard work. The more you work, the more you earn, and the more you can have. Capitalism makes for a happier environment."

"I understand," he nodded. "This is why I work at odd jobs for dollars, because no' can live on what I earn in *pesos* from my job. I make my own bonus."

No amount of money in any type of currency would get us through those locked gates.

So we went onward a few more miles until we reached the duplicate resort town of *Buena Ventura-- Good Fortune*. It was a *deja-vu* of *Playa Giron*, in that there were the same type of shops and hotel arrangements.

A massive layout with individual, white stuccoed, bungalows, trimmed in red and green-- it was fitting for the time of year. The place was picture-perfect, with a kidney- shaped swimming pool and what was surely a soccer fan's idea of a perfectly-manicured playing field.

The place was called *Playa Larga*, and walking toward the courtyard, we spotted rows of shops and restaurants elegantly decorated with high-priced clothing and other expensive trinkets. American toiletries, wines and liquors. The place had enough to satisfy any tourist's appetite.

Upon entering the well-kept facility, I once again felt uneasy being near so many richly-dressed guests. I knew the price wasn't going to affect me, as the Tour had shown that prices were not expensive on the island, but just on the way we looked. The road rats had arrived. I certainly wouldn't want to be too close to me...

When you don't have a choice, you need to conduct your business ASAP and be on your way. The lobby was elegant and spacious. There was an eight-foot tall artificial Christmas tree trimmed in gold and red, and music played the appropriate carols that radiated feelings of warmth and charm. I was momentarily swept back to my New England childhood, to being back home in general.

At the front desk, a well-groomed young man, speaking excellent English, answered the usual questions...

"Were bungalows available?"

"Yes," he answered casually.

"Hot water for a shower?"

"Yes," was the business-like response.

"How much?"

"Twenty-nine per night," he yawned.

"So far, so good," I quipped. "Now, tell me something that'll really make me happy."

"Like what?"

"Like you have a phone or fax with a direct line to the United States."

"We have both," he answered in a flat tone.

"Bingo!"

What more could we want? We had reached Paradise by the end of the day and were ready to partake of its pleasures.

Alfredo pulled me aside. "This too much."

"You think we're going to find something in town?"

"Perhaps."

"Alfredo," I consoled with a pat on the shoulder. "I realize this is three month's pay for you, but it's a *Motel Six* to me."

He scratched his head, and was about to speak when I gave the clerk my passport, the money, and signed the deal.

Alfredo needed his identification book, plus the letter stating he was with me on a tour of Cuba. Without that seal of approval, he wouldn't be able to stay. And that would mean neither would I, because where he went, so did I. No matter how much Alfredo denied it, he loved the luxuries as much as I admitted I did.

The clerk rang for the steward, who took our room key and my backpack, and led us to our bungalow. Each unit had about 1000 square feet of space and was set apart from the others. All were identical in shape, size, and color. The buildings were surrounded by a concrete path, with a walkway leading up to the front door.

As we entered the two-room suite, I felt right at home. The living room consisted of four comfortable stuffed chairs, a color TV set, and enough room for our bikes-- without tripping over them! Even the front porch was spacious enough to easily sit outside and relax to the sounds of the nearby crashing waves while watching the setting sun on the horizon.

Down the hall was the tiled bathroom-- with soap, a lid on the toilet bowl, a roll of paper, and hot or cold running water all the time.

The bedroom had a pair of twin beds, firm and comfortable for a good night's sleep and with plenty of blankets to keep us warm. There was enough shelf space for a clothes horse and a safe deposit box for any valuables.

"Now this is what I like to see at the end of a work day," I announced with open arms to my partner.

"*Si*," agreed Alfredo. "When I do a tour with some American journalists, we sometimes stay at fancy hotels."

We still had enough daylight to hit the beach for some fun and photos.

The bellboy, through Alfredo, said I was the only American at the resort-- a rarity it seemed-- as I gave him a generous tip. Before leaving, he smiled, "The restaurant is open late. We have many fine foods, including *Cocorice*."

"What?"

"You know," stated Alfredo matter-of-factly. "*Cocorice.* You have it back in America."

"We do?"

"Of course. I have seen pictures of them. But it is too expensive. We find something else."

I had no idea what he was talking about, and wasn't particularly interested in finding out at that point. What was foremost on my mind were photo opportunities with what little daylight was left.

Saturday night at the *Bay of Pigs*. There was volleyball and horseback riding on the beach. Drinks were served nearby, in an outdoor, thatched-roof, gazebo bar. There was a full-time *masseur* at the ready when guests decided to emerge from the crystal-clear, bath-warm Caribbean.

Alfredo and I were swimming in tempered bath water. The sand felt cool between the toes.

"I know people who would envy me," I laughed to Alfredo. "And politicians who would love to arrest me."

"Come," said Alfredo. "We can walk out further. Better picture with the sunset in the background."

We walked at least a quarter mile out to sea, and still the water reached only to below the knees. We took photos of each other standing, sitting, splashing, and doing push-ups. The last rays of the sun gave us a spectacular light show, bursting the sky with reds, oranges, blues, yellows, pinks and purples. If I were to die at that moment, I wouldn't have known it.

Watching the sun dip toward the horizon, I commented to Alfredo, "You know what the worse thing about this moment is?"

"What?"

"Not having a woman to share it with."

"*Si,*" he sighed.

When the sun finally set below the horizon, it was with much effort to have to leave the warmth of the water for the chilly air. With a hurried pace, we returned to the bungalow. This is where we had to remember the location. Since all buildings were the same in shape, size and color, the potential was there to forget and walk into an embarrassing situation. Once inside our own unit, we changed into warmer clothing.

While finding a comfortable seat in the living room, it was a chance for me to play catch-up with my journal.

Alfredo went out on a bike run, saying, "I want to go the two kilometers into town to see about a place to eat."

"The restaurant will be fine," I called out. "Let's just enjoy ourselves. You do so much as it is."

"It okay," he assured me with a thumbs-up.

"But why, Alfredo? There's enough money."

Finally getting the chance to swim in the *Bay of Pigs*.

"*Si,* but the more you spend, the less for me afterwards."

"Is that what you think?" I laughed. "You don't have to worry. The money for you is back in Havana."

"It is?" he asked with a cocked head, and a quizzical look. "Where?"

"At your mother's house with the rest of my stuff. In case something should happen, I wanted to have your money in a safe spot. So now you don't have to worry and can relax."

His eyes went to the floor, as his feet did a slight shuffle. "Well," he mumbled, "I still go into town. We try to use our *pesos* first before the dollars."

I shook my head. "If it makes you happy."

About an hour later, he returned with two hot plates filled with fried fish fresh from the bay, rice, *yucca*, and salad. He also carried another wrapped package but wasn't divulging what it was for the moment. Alfredo the man-- always after a deal.

We devoured the food like a pair of hungry animals. Total cost: 20 *pesos* per plate. No way, I knew, could we get a price like that at the hotel's restaurant, since we would have to pay in dollars.

"You know, Alfredo, we're a lot alike. We always try to find the best deal. We try to figure out all the moves. We give of ourselves to others. Now, I know you were born in 1963, but when?"

"March fourth," he mumbled through his food.

"A Pisces," I laughed. "Just like me. Well, it shouldn't have surprised me. It figures."

Knowing that he didn't have that much money on him, I asked, "How did you manage to acquire this food?"

"I promise the woman who cook for us that I would return with the plates and you to pay."

"And she believed you?"

"Of course," he answered nonchalantly.

"Amazing," I shook my head.

When we returned from town, I went to the lobby to write out a letter to fax to Jean. There was a desk nearby the giant Christmas tree. And the sound and mood of the Christmas carols seemed to put me in the right frame of mind. Alfredo made himself comfortable in one of the overstuffed chairs.

I thought it would be easy to send the note, but it turned out to be a real hassle. Jean kept answering the phone, and I finally had to get on the line to tell her to get off. That's what I wanted to avoid: Once we began speaking to one another, I didn't ever want to cut her off.

"Is everything all right?" she asked quickly, knowing time and expense were valuable to me.

"Great. Alfredo and I are at the *Bay of Pigs*. Looks like we'll finish the Tour within the week."

"Everyone at the church asks if I've heard from you. They want to know where you are on the map. We've seen the reports on CNN and the regular news and they're still praying."

"Good. I can use it. Anything else while we're online?"

"The offer from Hollywood on *Nine Dragon* still stands at two million."

Silence on my part. Before leaving the country, negotiations were underway with many of the major Hollywood studios to finally begin filming my rags-to-riches life story during the **Great Wall of China** tour. Two million dollars was the current price for the rights to that story.

"Did you hear?" asked Jean, interrupting my thoughts.

"Yeah...yes, I did," I answered, rubbing my forehead. "The answer's still no. I'll see you in a couple of weeks."

She finally switched her machine on, and the fax went through. It cost $12US instead of the planned three, but it was still a small price to pay for peace of mind.

Before leaving the US, I had made up a four-foot long map of Cuba, highlighting the route, with a proposed itinerary, and hung it in the church hallway, so that the congregation could view the progress. They knew CNN was covering the event, and reports were coming in from other sources. Jean could fill them in the next day.

"Is everything all right back home?" asked Alfredo.

"Yeah," I mumbled. "Nothing like problems to keep you focused. Let's get out of here."

After the last of these more business-like needs were taken care of, Alfredo and I went to the impeccably tailored restaurant for chocolate ice cream and got a couple cans of cold Coca-Cola to take back to our rooms. We mixed the soda with the bottle of rum Alfredo had secretly purchased in town.

"If we can arrive in *Guines* before tomorrow night, we should make *Pinar* before your visa expire."

Judging by the map, it was going to be another long haul. We drank and contemplated the situation.

"It'd be nice to be able to spend another day here."

"*Si*," agreed Alfredo. "Perhaps next time you come to Cuba we can stay here longer."

I had found a jewel of a place just a two-hour drive south from Havana. That discovery alone should have made me feel at ease, but all I could think about was what I had facing me back home: Hollywood's stinking offer that gnawed at me like a bad ulcer.

Alfredo and I killed the bottle of rum as we viewed the map and traced how far we'd come in the last couple of weeks. Two-thirds complete and still going.

Saturday night in the *Bay of Pigs*. Can you believe it?!

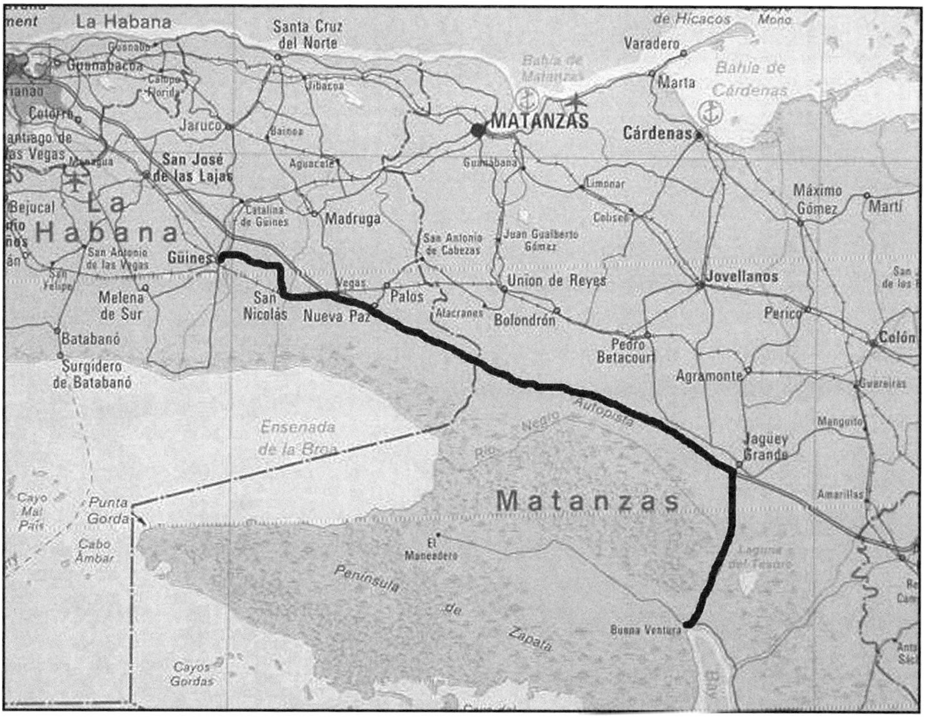

VEINTICINCO

25

BUENA VENTURA to GUINES
DAY 17
DECEMBER 07, 1997

DAILY DISTANCE : **85 miles or 141.7 kilometers**
TOTAL DISTANCE : **895 miles or 1491.7 kilometers**

When you're in wretched surroundings, you can't wait to rise and get on the road. However, when your environment is of supreme quality, you become paralyzed. So, it should go without saying that we found it difficult to move from our beach-front bungalow to face the chill of the day.

"So what if we sleep in another hour?" I protested.

"I know you," shot back Alfredo. "You say another hour and we no' leave

Alfredo outside our private, beach-front, *Bay of Pigs* bungalow. It cost no more than a night at a low-priced, American motel.

until lunch."

"So? Then we get our money's worth."

"I no' want to stay here. It was your idea."

"Balls! You wanted to be here just as much as I did. I'm just more of a man to admit it."

"We no' leave now, we cycle in dark later."

"You're such a taskmaster."

Reluctantly, we left our seacoast sanctuary, knowing we wouldn't reach the shore again until our very last day of the Tour. With the wind in our faces, it was another layered dressed day as the cold front made for a miserable outing.

Heading north toward *Jaguey Grande*, we were entering the land of the dreaded *cocorice.*

Since Alfredo made mention of this unusual creature, I tried to figure out what he meant. Cycling through the swampland of the *Matanzas* province, I was still at a loss of any real or mythical creation.

Alfredo stopped suddenly and began shouting, "*Kebin*, come quick and see the *cocorice!*"

I stopped half-heartily, somewhat curious.

Standing by the roadside, I peered through a fence and the grassy marsh and saw a couple of black boulders surrounded by water about a hundred yards off in the distance.

"There! do you see them?"

I couldn't say that I did. Perhaps if I knew what they were I could focus in on them. "Are they some type of bird?"

"No...No bird."

"Are they some kind of fish?"

Alfredo just gave me a blank look and slumped shoulders. "No!" he yelled in frustration. "They are those things right in front of you! Can you no' see?"

I was getting frustrated, and he getting frustrated at my frustration. "What? You mean those rocks?"

And then one of them moved, as the other turned toward us with its mouth wide open in an evil-looking grin.

"Holy shit! Crocodiles!" I jumped backwards.

"*Si*. That is what I have been trying to tell you," said Alfredo, matter-of-fact. "The area we are in is a reserve." And the reserve was some 30 miles in length.

"That is *not* what you've been trying to tell me! That is no where *near* what you've been trying to say!"

Although these two beauties were fenced off, I suddenly found myself being cautious where I stood and stepped.

"And what the hell happens when one of these ugly bastards escapes?" I yelled out of nervousness. "Or...worse. Some wild ones are still roaming about?"

"Then we try to cycle as fast as we can," advised Alfredo, with a smile as devious as the crocodiles.

That was an understatement. The stomach-churning fear reminded me of earlier incidents, as I thought what a horrendous time it would be for a bowel movement. Every huge, black rock seemed to have eyes, and squatting over one of them would probably not be a good idea. To date, I have yet to crap on a crock, nor was I about to offer up a rump roast to one of these creature's.

During our route, we came across a pair of cyclists. Rather, they came upon us on their five-speed road bikes, out for a training ride. Of course, their pace slowed down a bit, matching mine, while they studied my bike in great earnest. Or at least as best they could without crashing into one another.

"Er...gears. How many?" one of them asked.

"Twenty-four," I responded.

The other cyclist pointed to my frame. "Aluminum?"

"*Si*," I smiled. "And titanium. Wheels. Carbon fiber."

"Ah," they nodded. "*Si. Mucho dinero*."

"*Si*."

This was always an enjoyable way to pass the time on the road. I remind myself how blessed I was for being able to do something very few people ever have the chance to do.

"You race," I asked, noticing they were in cycling apparel like myself.

"*Si*," they nodded. "For here," they pointed to the ground, indicating the current province we were in.

"Photo," I asked, pointing to them, and forming an imaginary camera

With a couple of road racers in the swampland of *Matanzas.*

with my fingers.

"*Si*," they both nodded, and we pulled off to the side of the road.

While Alfredo was adjusting the camera, I kept an all around view of any roaming crocks. This down time also gave the cyclists a chance to really study my bike.

"How much?" asked one when he picked it up.

"Ten kilos," I answered.

"Same," he replied to his own bike. That may not be significant to some, but when viewing each other's bikes, one can tell the difference in tube size and tires. Road bikes are slim and trim. Mountain bikes are overweight.

"*Dinero?*," asked the other.

"Twenty thousand."

"Dollars?!" they both sung out in unison.

"*Si*." I nodded with a sigh. And the reason why mine weighs the same as theirs. The lower the weight, the higher the price tag.

There was only a single road through the marsh. After a while, we bid each other farewell, and they sprinted off. Mountain and road bikers were united by a pair of wheels.

Still further along, we came across a couple of boys getting ready with their make-shift harpoon guns to do a bit of swamp spear fishing. They were standing over each end of a submerged corrugated pipe that lay beneath the paved road, trying to lure some of the fish that were hiding inside.

One of the boys, about 15 and of stocky build, slipped on his snorkeling mask and went into the watery cave to chase the fish out one end, while his friend stood ready to fire his spear gun.

Alfredo and I watched with quiet interest to see what would happen.

"You know," whispered my partner, "the fish they are trying to catch for their dinner is indigenous to the area, and are not suppose to be hunted."

"Alfredo, when you're hungry, there's no such thing as an endangered species." And that's the plain, honest, simple truth. There are no rules in survival--except to survive.

After quite some time of poking and prodding from one end of the tunnel to the other, what finally emerged and was caught was a three-foot swamp snake. They looked disgusted and killed the snake for having scared their dinner away, but still, they would not be deterred, and were continuing the fight when we cycled away.

Back into the cold wind. I thought once we reached the town of *Jaguey Grande* and veered west, the gusts would work in our favor. But it seemed to change direction with us, remaining in our faces.

The town was just on the other side of the *Autopista,* the main highway that cuts through Cuba in an east-west direction. Food and drink vendors were serving a variety of people, and seeing nowhere else we could eat, we went for the usual pizzas and juice.

"Because today is Sunday," mentioned Alfredo as he munched on a pizza, "Cubans rest."

"So?"

"So, the highway no' have too many cars on it. We can gain many miles if we change course."

Once again, we pulled out the map and looked at the original route, which zigzagged us into and around the *Autopista*. I wanted to avoid the main highway for fear of getting hit by some crazy Cuban, but Alfredo had a point. The road was practically deserted. And it was a Sunday...

"If we change course," I said, "Chances are we won't find food or drink the rest of the day."

"Then we buy some now for later."

While Alfredo stuffed more pizzas into his side bags, I filled up not only my PentaPure water bottle, but my 75- ounce Camelbak as well.

The highway, with its posted *100 kilometers per hour* speed signs, was ours, save for a passing motorist or two, or a truck. Occasionally, we'd come upon horse-drawn carriages, and one father-son team had a truck-sized cart full of wood being pulled by a black Angus. Alfredo latched onto the back of the cart for fun.

"Hey," yelled Alfredo, smiling. "Take a picture."

I could actually walk faster than the old bull was going. I raced ahead to get ready for the shot.

To say the least, there was neither much excitement nor photo opportunities along the way. Our change of route was strictly for gaining miles and nothing more. The cold was still piercing through to the bone.

The similarity of each mile caused my mind to wander. I thought of Jean's voice the previous night during the fiasco fax transmission. I had done the nightly

Alfredo hitchin' a ride.

ritual of setting the photos of her and the girls beside whatever bed I happened to be sleeping in, in whatever place I was. That gave me some comfort, but now I could hear her voice echo in my mind, haunting my soul.

Home... So much to do when I returned. Interviews to give. Stories to tell. Phone calls, faxes, emails, and letters to answer. Christmas presents to get ready...

"Hey!" yelled Alfredo, cycling up beside me. "Where are you today? You mind no' on the job."

"I'm in Never Never Land."

"You like this ever since you call home last night."

"Oh? Is it that obvious?"

"*Si.* What is the problem?"

"I have two million of them."

"That a lot of problems," laughed my friend. "Good thing we have many miles to go to *Guines*."

Our concrete route took us through palm trees and plantations. Every so often a motorist would pass us and honk their horn with a wave. In Cuba, it's legal to travel on any and all roads by bicycle.

"You ever hear of Hollywood?"

"*Si.* Is place they make movies in your country."

"Right. And they want to make a movie about my life."

"You?" Alfredo looked over at me. "Why?"

"Sometimes I ask that myself."

I didn't know where to start. So many thoughts since the previous night's conversation with Jean were rumbling through my head that it was difficult to sort out.

"When I came back from China, I had become the first person to ride a bicycle on top of the Great Wall, covering about two thousand miles. What the general public liked about the story, was that I had made a dream come true, and it gave them hope to go after their own goals."

"So it make you famous, and now people love you."

"Correct. But it was more than that," I continued as we maintained our course along the *Autopista.* "It was an average guy doing an extraordinary thing. From being electrocuted as a child to conquering a wonder of the world, and ending up as a Cyclist of the Year. The story was so perfect, it was Hollywood-made. In fact, the script is written and ready to go. It's called *Nine Dragon.*"

"So why you no' happy?"

"Because the suits behind the desks have a formula for making films. It's called sex and car chases with some fiery explosions thrown in along the way. They don't understand that the public is getting tired of the crap being fed to them. They hunger for truth. Not a pile of fiction."

"You have sex on the Great Wall of China?" smiled my fiendish friend through his sunglasses.

"No. But according to some of the suits in Hollywood I did. With a Chinese girl. And then we got caught by the Red Army who chase me and the girl about a thousand miles through the countryside, until we somehow reach the end, falling into each other's arms surrounded by guns."

Alfredo laughed uproariously, nearly choking. "Hey, that a pretty good story. I will play you."

"Forget it. Ain't gonna happen."

"Why no'?"

"No one plays with my life that way."

"How much they want to pay you?"

"According to Jean last night, the offer still stands at two million, plus royalties on everything."

"And you turn it down?" Alfredo's mouth fell open. "For that kind of money, I will have sex with as many woman as they want to write for me to have."

"That's not the point," I shouted above the noise of a passing truck. The winds began to sting my cheeks, my lungs felt icy. "What good is the money if your life story becomes a lie? If I let them have their way, I'll still have to answer to God when I face Him."

"Only if you believe," reminded Alfredo.

"When are you gonna get it through your head!" I shouted, nearly swerving into my partner. "You can't play dumb with your soul, Alfredo. You are going to have to answer to the Lord, and if you die in your sins, you're screwed! Down you go to Hell."

"But what is big deal about accepting money? So they change your story a little."

"You call telling lies little? Nowadays, people believe what they see, not what you tell them. The money means nothing if I have to live with the lie. The suits in Hollywood have to understand they can't buy everyone off."

"They can buy me. I give them my life."

"*Hell, Hell, the gang's all here,*" I began to sing. "*Come on down and give us some cheer. I have sold my soul for a peso ...*"

"You crazy for turning down that money."

"And I'd be insane for accepting it. When are you ever going to learn that your soul; where you spend eternity, is more important than anything else the world has to offer?"

Almost at the end of the day, we were near *Nueva Paz*. Riding through, we saw there was no hotel in town.

"We have to go back or go on," said Alfredo.

"I don't like to retreat," I answered.

"This, I already know," quipped my partner.

Our only choice was to head for *Guines* where lodgings existed, even if it meant cycling in the dark. Fortunately, we had some daylight to spare.

We arrived at the only hotel in town just as a children's party was ending. Among the raucous, departing mob, Alfredo had words with the owner, and a few minutes later returned with the news, "We have a room for twenty *pesos*."

It was a below-the-basics room: no blankets, sheets, pillows, toiletries. It was a place to lay our heads, and I was so exhausted that as soon as we entered the room, I collapsed in bed. I couldn't stop shaking from the coldness of the day. Alfredo took a curtain from the window and covered me with it. I quickly fell asleep.

When I awoke a few hours later, we went out for something to eat. It was then Alfredo told me the woman who allowed us to spend the night owned the two-story motel. She said it was actually closed for repairs, and wouldn't have even been around except it was her son's birthday. We just happened to arrive at that perfect time. Once again, Providence was on our side.

"We do the work, and the Lord sees to our needs," I reminded my friend. "How many times is it going to take for God to show you that He wants to be your Comforter?"

"Maybe it is God," said Alfredo, avoiding my eyes.

More sauce less pizzas were all we could find for dinner, and as usual, they satisfied, but did not satiate. The bland food had become tasteless, but it sustained us, kept us going toward our goal.

We did find a *Rumbos*, another fast-food chain of the island. Each one carried different foodstuffs, but all items were paid in US dollars. There, I found mineral water and chocolate.

I was still having the shakes and couldn't get that dead cold feeling out of me.

Before retiring for the evening, I went to the hotel's front desk to place a call to Lucia Newman of CNN in Havana. I had promised that I would as we got closer to the capital.

"You know," informed Alfredo. "We only an hour's drive to Havana. We could leave our bikes here and catch a ride. Maybe do another interview."

"Yeah, right," I laughed. "We go back to Havana, you won't want to finish the Tour."

"No' true!" he stood up in defiance, his manhood challenged. "I finish Tour."

"Then we stay where we are."

"But you no' feel well. Good doctors in Havana."

"We stay!" I began to dial CNN's office.

"But we need to get visa extended."

"In *Pinar.* Now, shut-up."

It had been a long Tour for both of us, but we would soon be through in the next several days. This time next week we would be back in Havana, laughing and hugging and boasting of our accomplishments.

Lucia said the interview aired in the States just before Thanksgiving. "You're a hit! Especially in DC."

"That could be good or bad," I replied.

She didn't go into too much detail. The story went national-- plenty of stations picked up on it, it hit the wire service.

"So, where do we go from here?"

"Call me if you can. We'll probably wait and do a wrap-up when you return. When do you think that'll be?"

"I figure about a week."

"Good. Call me when you get in."

As I hung-up, I thought about the after effects. Whatever scenario, I could handle it; I'd been prepared since formulating this Tour. Would my government be crazy enough to arrest me upon my return for doing my job, for wanting peace and friendship?

"So?" asked Alfredo, jarring me back to the present. "What did Lucia say?"

"The story aired around the world."

"Even Cuba?" he stood up from his seat.

"Last I checked, Cuba still existed."

"I wonder if my family and friends saw me."

"Probably. I'm tired. Let's get out of here."

For the moment, all I had an interest in was rest. Two weeks before returning to the States was a long time away. Any looming problems, I knew, would have to be battled when they struck. My health was what needed to be dealt with now.

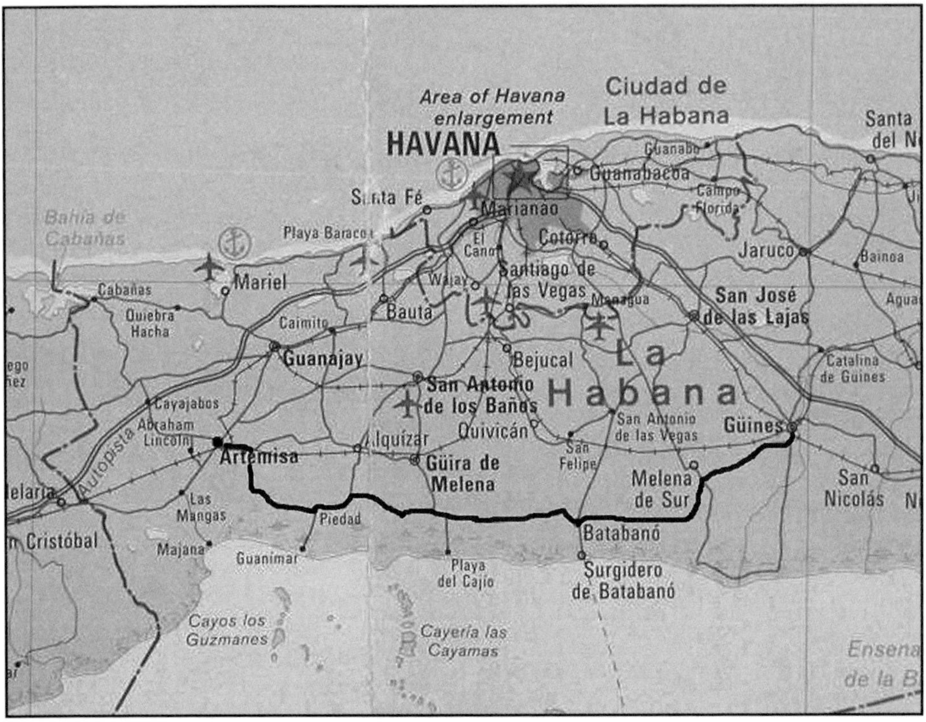

VEINTISEIS

26

GUINES to ARTEMISA
DAY 18
DECEMBER 08, 1997

DAILY DISTANCE :	**63 miles**	**or**	**105**	**kilometers**
TOTAL DISTANCE :	**958 miles**	**or**	**1596.7**	**kilometers**

When we awoke, the shakes and chills were still with me. I lay curled up beneath the curtain-blanket.

"The sooner we go, you get warm," advised my doctor.

"Fine. Then you get out of bed first," I quipped.

"But it take you longer to get ready."

"Look," I pleaded, "In another hour, the sun will be out, and it'll get warm. I just need to rest and conserve my energy. We'll get in our miles. Don't have a seizure."

When I finally did creak out of bed, Alfredo was already dressed and packing. I popped a couple of extra-strength painkillers into my cotton-dry mouth, downing them with a shot of the previous days water from my semi-moldy bottle. Too sick and tired from yesterday's *wind-in-your-face* miles, I didn't bother to rinse out my uniform, and now I was paying the price: damp, sweaty leftovers to place back on my body.

Alfredo was fairing much better, going about his business in a mechanical, methodical way.

"If we can hold out just a few days longer, we will finish the Tour by the end of the week," smiled Alfredo.

"Unless, of course, something goes wrong with the extension of my visa tomorrow," I reminded him.

His shoulders slumped. "We will know when we arrive in *Pinar*. For now, we stay with our schedule."

As I went about my routine in a slow, bleary-eyed, aching manner, Alfredo poured over the itinerary.

"Perhaps we have passed the cold front," he thought. "The next few days will be sunnier. Then we will have more cold fronts-- one after another until January. And then it will always be cold."

If this were true, then we really did want to finish the Tour by week's end. As for now, we had to dress in layers until the weather and our muscles had sufficiently warmed.

It was an either/or goal day, I realized. I was aiming for *Artemisa*-- what looked like a good-sized town, judging from the map. Finding a place for the night shouldn't be a problem there. But Alfredo wanted to crank out a few more miles further to *San Cristobal*, just over the *Pinar del Rio* border, another 40km away. That would then set us up for a capital arrival the next day, but another 80-mile plus day was certainly not on my itinerary.

We arrived in *Melena de Sur* for breakfast. A dusty-road, ramshackle, farmer town, it produced an abundance of the same character of life roaming its streets we had become accustomed to throughout our travels. Farmers and factory workers mingled and meshed with business-suited men and women, while traffic officers tried to get everyone moving along in a smooth and orderly fashion.

Once again, it was pizzas and juice.

"We should buy extra food for our journey," stated my ever-prudent partner.

"I agree, since it takes more time looking for something to eat, than actually digesting the stuff."

Coming into the land of coconuts, we happened upon a type of coconut-custard pie that many people bought slices of on their way to work. For 2 *pesos* a slice, it was quite a deal. And it had to be better than the bland bread dough we had been forced to eat.

One bite and it was. So I bought nearly an entire cake for Alfredo and I. It had a sweet, solid, creamy taste. The beige colored, nutmeged-topped delicacy was pleasing to the palate with just a tinge of rum added.

An old, overweight, unshaven Cuban wearing a bright yellow baseball cap with English lettering on it stood next to us in line. Most natives seemed to have a fascination with the united States and its products, but I laughed to myself at his choice of headgear. *Ugly Chap* is something I wouldn't want to be walking around wearing.

Other overweight men hung around the vending carts, smoking their morning *cohibas,* and drinking rum, the breakfast of Cuban champions!

We had just enough time to fill our fuel tanks and be on our way, disappearing into the countryside and the patchwork quilt of the farmer's fields.

The early morning observations were so often the same: people going to work, others preparing their vending booths, workers cutting the roadside grass with their machetes or plowing the fields with their ox and cattle, children going to school in their crisp, clean uniforms. So much activity happened during that period, when the day is cool and the time could be well-spent.

And so it was with us. We reached *Artemisa* by 1pm.

"Great!" I pulled off to the side. "I'm ready to call it a day." I slowly dismounted from the bike.

"Are you crazy?" Alfredo exclaimed. "We only do one hundred kilometers. We still have plenty of time before dark to cycle to *San Cristobal*."

"To hell with that." I slowly walked with my bike to work out the kinks in my legs.

"But it only an extra hour or two," he bounced up and down beside me. "We then make it to *Pinar* in less time."

"So we do another eighty-mile day like we did yesterday?" I snapped. "That'll make you happy?"

"*Si!*" he drooled.

"You're such a cycling masochist! I'm walking as if I'm on pins and needles, ready to drop a load because my intestines are rumbling. I'm tired. That's it."

"Fine." Alfredo walked off, then turned around to stick me with another piece of news. "But we have eighty-mile day tomorrow, and must arrive in *Pinar* early enough to take care of extension of visa."

"Fine!" I retorted. "But at least today I get to rest."

When we found a hotel that charged 20 *pesos* a night for the both of us, that settled the deal. We were staying.

The large, five-story hotel that sat on the corner of one of downtown *Artemisa's* major streets was of old, turn-of-the-century architecture, with huge cathedral ceilings. The building was once fancy apartments for Cuban elite before Castro took over. Now, they were less than ordinary, with paint-peeling walls, chipped furniture, and many occupants registered as Mr and Mrs Roach.

For less than one dollar, we had a suite that consisted of a living room with couch, tables and chairs; a kitchen area with sink; bathroom with fixtures; and two

Nothing like a good *cohiba* for breakfast.

bedrooms. It was as big as an average-size house. Our only problem was in getting the staff to turn on the water.

"The entire place is under renovations," explained the *senorita* who showed us to our room. "We do not have water to give," she sighed. "However, we can supply you with bed sheets and pillows. We're sorry for the inconvenience."

"Not at all," I reassured her. "It's quite all right. We'll get along just fine. *Gracias*."

Upon her exit, I turned to Alfredo, the handyman. "See what you can do about acquiring us some running water."

"*Si,*" he smiled, taking out a pair of vice-grips.

He went into the bathroom, turned on the main valve and-- *voila*-- running water.

"You're everything anyone could ever ask for."

During the check-in process, I had noticed a restaurant occupying a part of the ground floor, so as soon as we unpacked our gear and secured our bikes, we went to have lunch.

The establishment, done up in red and black, had a variety of choices on the menu-- *hamburguesas* being one of them.

"Hamburgers," I said in shock. "Am I dreaming?"

"No. No dream," answered Alfredo. "You want?"

Visions of fast food joints danced in my head, but I was slightly hesitant; my inner voice reminded me of past experiences thus far with any Cuban meat other than pork. My stomach and imagination won out. I gave the order.

From the outer appearance, it looked and was in the shape of a hamburger, but we know appearances can be deceiving. One bite revealed the true substance to be fried intestines-- from a cow, I could only hope.

My face practically in convulsions from the taste, I set the *burger* aside, sticking with the rice and beans and a couple of colas. Papaya pudding helped clear my taste buds. Alfredo kept on eating.

"How can you sit there and eat this crap?"

"I hungry," he mumbled.

"Animal!"

In the later part of the afternoon, we walked around the area. More filth and poverty. A man with a trailer, set on one of the street corners, had a small group of young men surround his 500-gallon tank of beer. They came for a cup of the brew, or brought their own jugs along to be filled for several *pesos.*

From out of no where, a cat ran across our path.

"Wow! Look at that," I shouted to Alfredo, as I pointed to the fast feline. "Do you realize during the entire time I've been in Cuba, with nearly a thousand miles of Tour under our bike wheels, that was the first cat I've seen?"

"Because Cubans eat cats," he stated nonchalantly.

I stopped dead in my tracks. "Just what did we have back at that restaurant?"

"Cat probably," he shot off.

"Shit!" I spat at the ground. "I need a drink."

"It no' big deal."

"Fish and chicken. Fish and chicken. That's all I'm going to eat so long as I'm in this country..."

"You make such a big deal of everything."

During our afternoon walk, we found a *cafe*-style side street restaurant that served spaghetti with sauce and cheese, just as the outside billboard mentioned.

"We're playing it safe for dinner tonight," I informed my garbage disposal partner. "Can't go bad with that? Just a nice, simple, filling, carbo-loaded dish."

It was difficult to describe just exactly what that dish was, but the spaghetti was overcooked mush. It all seemed to gel as one mass. At the *Artemisa* restaurant, I barely got through the meal. One bite for me and the surprise of a delightful meal was over. Because I was hungry, the rest of the meal was a forced, choked down battle. Alfredo just kept right on shoveling it through his mouth in blissful contentment. Perhaps it was the cheese that gave it its unique turpentine flavor. The sauce was more of a tomato soup. My Italian grandmother would be turning in her grave if she knew I subjected my taste buds to such a meal. "Ah! *Kevinooch!* My *bambino! Madon!* how could you?" she'd gasp. "Have I taught you nothing?"

During our mid-day constitutional, we also scoped out the local *Rapido*, with its variety of ice cream. There, we consoled our glands with after dinner vanilla-almond bars.

Before retiring for the evening, I stopped by the Catholic church across from the hotel out of curiosity. The place was lit up like a blazing Christmas ornament, and people were overflowing from the doors.

A communion service with young boys and girls dressed in their whites was in progress. The ceremony was in Spanish, but I knew the routine from my upbringing. It was all very Catholic in its pomp and circumstance, its statues and ornaments. But the rock music choir just didn't seem to cut it with the current surroundings. Mary and Joseph rocking to the beat of a different tune, as they looked from on high. Baby Jesus wrapped in swaddling clothes, swinging to jazz in the manger, while the priest appeared to be listening in a *Spiritual* swaying trance, grooving to the tunes.

Yeah, baby! Saints preserve us!

I only stayed a while, thinking about my own church family back home. Home...

But for the moment, I was facing an early morning 80-mile reality I was not looking forward to.

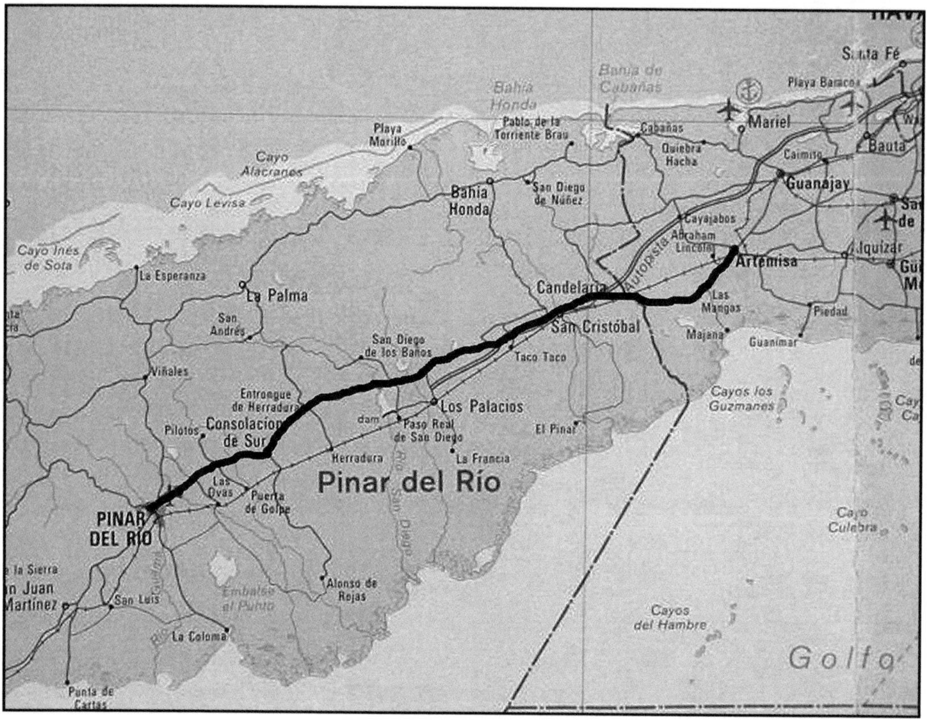

VEINTISIETE

27

ARTEMISA to PINAR DEL RIO
DAY 19
DECEMBER 09, 1997

DAILY DISTANCE :	**78**	**miles or**	**130**	**kilometers**
TOTAL DISTANCE :	**1036**	**miles or**	**1726.7**	**kilometers**

"We must arrive in *Pinar* in the early afternoon," informed a serious Alfredo, as we crawled out of our warm beds. "We must not stop too much for rest or photos."

"Strictly a work day, huh?" I fumbled around for the lightswitch in the still darkness of the early day.

"*Si.* If you want your visa extended before it expires tomorrow. If no' we will have to return to Havana."

"Sounds like incentive enough to me."

We dressed quickly, packed our bags, and headed down the two flights of stairs with our gear. Our half-day of work the previous day had greatly improved my stamina. Not even last night's spaghetti *a la tomaine* had any dire effect on my bowels, the bout of diarrhea ending once more.

"Will you look at this." I stopped to take in the full view, shaking my head in disbelief.

"*Si*," answered Alfredo, stopping alongside me. "I have told you. He is very popular in my country."

Standing like a sentinel on the side of the road was a sign with the name of the next town we were about to enter: *Abraham Lincoln*. Just behind the sign was a gigantic billboard announcing in big, bold, black, block letters: ***Abraham Lincoln***. Just below, scripted in bold, Commie red: ***Socialisimo!*** It was even underlined for emphasis.

"I give," I threw up my hands in exasperation. "You win! I'm a convert. Honest Abe was a good Socialist."

"What is the problem?" asked Alfredo, somewhat confused by my disgust. "Lincoln free the slaves and give so much to them."

"I've told you before. The Civil War wasn't an issue of slavery, but of tariffs and commerce. He sold out the South to pacify the North."

"*Si,*" agreed Alfredo. "And he give to the poor."

"He gave nothing to the poor, except more heartaches. Free the slaves? Fine. But educate them as well instead of allowing them from succeeding generation to feed off the breast of the government."

"All people deserve to be equal. To have the same."

"And where's the incentive to work and earn as much as you can? If you have the desire, the will and the brains to achieve all that you possibly can, is it right to have to share with those that do nothing?"

"This is nonsense," quipped Alfredo. "Lincoln do much for your people. He make everyone equal."

"And many of us have been paying the price ever since."

As we reached the town of *Candelaria,* just past the border of our last province, we stopped briefly for a bite to eat.

"If we return to the *Autopista* like we did two days ago, we will make up time," advised Alfredo while munching on a pizza. "The back roads no' good."

"I agree. It will give us more time in *Pinar*."

Changing course, we stayed on the main highway that severs the country in twain. About half-way to the capital of *Pinar*, we stopped along a roadside *Rumbos.*

Everything had to be paid for in US dollars. There was a bar that sold all manner of juices, sodas, water, coffee, and rum. There were T-shirts galore, and other touristy trinkets, like keychains and coasters and glasses in the form of Cuba, Che Guevara, or Ernest *Papa* Hemingway.

There was also an extensive line of Cuban tobacco products, most notably the infamous *cohiba* cigar. The distinguished, elderly gentleman who sold the product was quite knowledgeable in the art and manufacturing of Cuba's most infamous product.

"The tobacco is of the best quality," he smiled through his spectacles. "It's grown right here in the countryside of *Pinar*. The soil is the richest in all of Cuba."

He motioned with a wave of his arms, pointing to the hills on both sides of the highway.

"Just a single *cohiba* cost twelve-eighty. A box of twenty-five for three hundred and twenty dollars."

"That's an expensive smoke," I responded.

"*Si.* But a well-deserved memorable experience."

I thanked him for his time, and returned to where Alfredo was resting in the shade with a bottle of mineral water.

"If you are interested in *cohibas,* I have a contact back in Havana that can sell them to you much cheaper."

"It's a tempting offer," I answered my partner, taking a drink of my own water. "But I figure I'm already going to have problems with immigration when I return home. Finding a couple of boxes of *cohibas* on me would not help my already delicate situation."

Tossing the empty mineral water bottle in the trash can, I began to mount the Beast when I saw Alfredo retrieve the discarded receptacle.

"What are you doing?" I asked. "Don't you already have enough bottles to fill and carry?"

"I collect them for my daughter," he explained bashfully. "When we return to *Habana,* I fill them up again, and put different food colors inside for her to play with as a game."

There was an awkward silence between us, and he seemed somewhat embarrassed to tell me, adding, "It is just a game; something for her to do."

Yeah, I understood.

Being a weekday, the amount of traffic and smog along the *Autopista* was choking. Then there was the added fear of being knocked over the side or being sucked under a wheel by the force of a truck come screaming by at 100-plus kilometers per hour. The wind can knock your own wind out of you. The sudden rush could be fatal.

Alfredo had been right about the cold front passing. The next several days were bright and sunny. The main highway may have been great for making up the miles, and adding much valuable time to our schedule, but it also left us without shade-- except for the shading afforded by the occasional bridge, a moment's reprieve.

I stopped under one of these shady oasis and pulled out my journal. The notation I penned was in huge, flustered writing: somewhere mid-way to our day's goal, we had reached the 1000-mile mark. An exciting milestone for myself, but my counterpart had his eye on another figure of worthy prominence.

"Perhaps we will reach two thousand kilometers by the end of Tour. A first. Longest tour for me is twelve hundred."

Alfredo figured no one, no countryman had ever done 2000 kilometers or

A countryside cabbage patch.

more during a single tour, and that after ours was completed, the most anyone else could do of any significance would be to circumnavigate the island by bike. Even then would it matter? Since we were the first to complete one end to the other, going through every province, who cares who's the second.

"I think a Tour like this will never be done again."

"Perhaps. But there are others out there just as crazy and adventurous as we are."

Someone would try for the sheer joy of it, and it would be a first for them.

When we reached the outskirts of the capital by 2pm, we had, once again, put some killer miles behind us, but all the work thus far had finally paid off. The eight days we lost at the start of the Tour, from official foul-up in Havana, had been gained. According to my original itinerary, this was the day we were to arrive in *Pinar*, and, by the looks of it, we could actually end a day ahead of schedule. But first, we had some visa business to attend to. *Pronto!*

Just as we entered the city limits, we were surrounded by swarming, cycling teenagers. They approached from all directions, but seemed to come from nowhere.

"Hey mista! where yo' from?" they shouted, keeping pace with us, trying to slow us down-- or even, hopefully, to get us to stop.

"America." I looked neither left nor right.

"America! Oh, I want to talk to you!"

I bet they did, too, but Alfredo and I had no time to be hustled for a "very good room, very private." Eventually, they drifted off in search of new meat.

Sincc Alfredo conducted many cycling tours between Havana and *Pinar*, he knew the layout of the city. We had to deal with the government. We knew we would be bounced around. There was no time to waste, zigzagging through the city streets...

...until a cop pulled us over.

"Damn! What's the problem?"

"He say," interpreted Alfredo, as he was handing over his identification book to the foot soldier, "on his street we must walk our bikes, no' ride."

"Are you kidding me?!" I jumped.

The officer straightened his shoulders, looking at me through mirrored sunglasses. He stood a foot taller than my friend, who, at the moment, was slightly hunchbacked.

"*Kebin,* please," whispered Alfredo.

"Balls!" Getting in the officer's face, I asked, "Where's the signs for such an idiotic rule?"

"There are none," answered Alfredo. "You just have to know like the locals do."

"So now we're going to get a ticket for it?"

"It will be worse if you no' keep quiet."

"This is bogus."

I turned and walked away. Alfredo was right. If I kept shooting my mouth off, we'd probably end up in jail. End of visa. End of Tour. End of the end.

While the officer and Alfredo were in a heated discussion about why we were in his town, I kept a constant vigil on my watch. The seconds turned into precious wasted minutes. If we didn't get the extension on my visa before it expired the next day, I'd be in trouble once again. And I just couldn't afford to be-- not when we were so irritatingly close to finishing.

The officer's harsh tone made it clear he was demanding something. I saw Alfredo pull out the official document that explained why he was with me and what we were doing. It was such an agonizing slow process, I began to have marvelous thoughts of whacking this nit-wit over the head and being on our way. The worse part was that after the interrogation was over, the officer pointed to the guarded building we had to go for my visa.

Looking at him through steely eyes, I kept a tight lip and my fists to my sides.

"He say he no' like your uniform," answered Alfredo through downcast eyes.

"Tell him we have something in common."

Alfredo declined.

The place was military all the way, with a serious young stud of a boy in uniform, standing at full, starch-straight attention, rifle loaded and ready to be used. We couldn't get past him with our bikes, which had to be chained across the street.

Although I'd get nervous leaving my bike unattended for any length of time, I figured that no one would be brave enough to steal from us-- so nearby the child and his rifle.

The next hour saw us waiting, wheeling and dealing with the area's military unit. Many other Cubans were waiting to be seen; the tiny lobby was nearly overflowing.

Alfredo and I were shown into one of the offices ahead of the waiting group.

It wouldn't have anything to do with my star-and-stripes, American uniform, I wondered. Did I stand out that much?

Sitting across from two unsmiling officials, we went through the routine of showing them our papers and identification books, along with the soon-to-be expired visa. We pulled out the map of their country, the route clearly marked, and laid it out before them on the desk.

Alfredo explained what we were doing and why we were doing it. At least that's what I think he said.

They scratched their heads when viewing the sight, impressed by the scope of the route, the sheer magnitude of it.

Their faces cracked with laughter and said we were crazy (I know what *El Loco* means) for attempting such a feat. Then they had me wait outside in the oven-like foyer.

This lasted another half-hour. During that time, I had several dozen sets of eyes watch me. On occasion, they'd mumble to one another, yet never divert their gaze from me. We all sat and sweated, while another guard watched from a corner desk.

At one point, Alfredo came out with one of the officers, walking down the hall, then returning to the room. He didn't acknowledge me. The crowd I was waiting with began to mumble through the sides of their mouths once again.

When Alfredo came out of the office alone, his chin on his chest, his eyes avoiding mine, I felt my gut knot up in a burning twist.

"Okay, let's have it. Well?..."

"They say canno' extend visa."

"Oh?..." My tone went up like a rollercoaster.

"They say you have a host. We must go to Havana."

The knot tightened. "Freakin' government!"

A few of the people waiting nearby laughed, nodding their heads in agreement.

"So much for military intelligence," I spat. "Glad to see no one wants to take responsibility," I shouted to no one in particular. "Just pass it down the line."

Some of the waiting people nodded their heads and clapped their hands. Others shot short fists into the air. Alfredo didn't even try to stop me from rambling. He just walked outside. I stomped out after him.

"We must find a place to leave our bikes, and try to hitch a ride back to *Habana*."

"To hell with that idea--"

"We must!"

"We're not returning to Havana and that's final!"

"Then I canno' go any further with you."

"Then I'll go it alone from here."

"You will be arrested. *La Bajada* is well guarded."

"Then they can drag me back to Havana in chains. And won't that look good for CNN and the other reporters."

"The military say I will be in trouble."

We were near our bikes. Alfredo began unlocking them, pulling forcefully at the locks. I turned to see the young guard. He was still stone-cold silent.

"Alfredo, c'mon. All the military knows how to do is put fear into the people. That's the only way to control you. The Devil rules by fear; God by faith. Think! The Lord has brought us this far. If the visa was extended--"

"But it no'..."

"Fantasize! If it were, what's the next move?"

He looked away, his brow deeply lined.

I knew Alfredo. After all we'd been through during the Tour, I knew him as I knew myself. He was just as ambitious. He wanted to go to the end of this Tour as much or more so than I. We were, at best, two days away from finishing. He wasn't about to see me go it alone; I knew he'd never chance my getting through the guards at the last outpost and succeeding. He'd find a way. Of that, I didn't need faith to know.

He turned toward me, his face beaming with a smile. "If visa were extended, we then need permission to cycle last section from the Ministry of Environment."

We were on our way. There would be no more glorious side-trips as in *Pico Turquino*. We raced to our next destination.

At the Environmental Office, Alfredo spoke with the man in charge of the area in which we wanted to complete the Tour. A stocky man in his 40s, his dark features were accentuated by his military uniform.

The routine was performed as it had been a couple of hours before. The papers were handed over. The map was laid out before him on his desk.

Seeing the extent of our undertaking, he laughed with delight, tracing his finger along the highlighted line of the route from *Maisi* to our current stop, *Pinar del Rio*.

He said something to Alfredo, who answered, "*Si,*" and just shook his head in amazement.

We were crazy for attempting such a feat, but yes, he would give us permission. We had come too far to stop now, and out of respect for what we were trying to do, the officer waived the five dollar entrance fee.

It all sounded too good to be true, and that made me nervous. "Could we have the permission in writing with his signature on it?" I asked through Alfredo.

"That would not be necessary," he assured us. "I will place a call to the station in *La Bajada* and let them know of your arrival in a couple of days."

We had no choice. It certainly wouldn't be wise to push the issue.

Once outside, Alfredo lit up with a smile and a jump, clapping his hands for joy. "It is wonderful we can now do the last thirty-five miles without fear of being arrested."

Now I knew he would do whatever it'd take to overcome the last obstacle concerning my visa extension.

As we shook hands, the officer made one final suggestion. "You should change direction after *Guane*. The coastal road is bad. It would be better to stay inland until you reach the town of *El Cayuco*. From there it is only a single road to the end."

A *Pinar del Rio* mural. Pregnant women are very posh in Cuba.

Viewing the map ourselves, Alfredo and I estimated we had no more than 200 kilometers from *Pinar* to *Caleta Larga*; *El Cayuco* was the mid-way point. We had the goal figured out, and there was but one last hurdle to cross.

For my own part, I would have liked written permission from the officer for a smooth transition. If anything were to go wrong, it would be on the last day at *La Bajada*, during the last part. Regardless of how brave I may seem, I really do hate being placed under arrest. But I am a man of principle, and when injustice or foolishness is being committed, I must act upon those principles. Would to God I had no conscience. Life would be easier to handle, and sinfully fun to live.

With Alfredo's faith rejuvenated, he was ready to tackle the last governmental wall.

"Since you host is the Ministry of Sport, perhaps we can petition the local Sports Complex to help us."

He was fired up, ready to go with no holds barred. *Patria O Muerte, Venceremos! – Fatherland or Death, We Shall Conquer!*

We met with the second Director in charge of the towering sports complex of *Pinar del Rio* just before the 5pm closing. A handsome man with salt and pepper hair, he ushered us into his office with a wave of his arm and a humble bow to the waist.

When Alfredo showed him the map of our route, and our papers from his sister sports complex in Havana, he went into the situation concerning my visa.

“And, sir, my friend’s papers expire tomorrow. We are only two days from completing our task. If his visa is not extended for just a little while longer, we will lose everything we have worked so hard for.”

I wanted to applaud right then and there. Give that boy the golden Fidel award for Best Performance.

The second Director became so enveloped in our trials and tribulations, that he jumped straight up from his sitting position. Pounding his fist on the desk, he pointed a finger to the ceiling, announcing through Alfredo with great *gusto* that, “I will help in every way possible!”

Hallelujah! Praise the Lord and pass the plate!

When he calmed down, he began to view the visa. His eyes lit up.

“Ah! Look! You don’t have a tourist permit, my friend.” He showed us a three-digit code in one of the corners. “It shows you are in Cuba on the government’s behalf. That makes a big difference and the military at immigration should have known this,” he shouted, pounding the desk again.

His secretary was summoned and told to place a call to Havana-- in particular to someone in Jose Palaez’ office. When the call came through, words were exchanged. Then more in a heated tone. Then a fist pounded the poor desk once again, followed by the phone being slammed back into the receiver. The second Director cupped his head in his hands.

“He say no one in Palaez’ office want to take responsibility for extending your visa,” explained Alfredo.

“Military intelligence again,” I mumbled.

I began to silently pray. I knew-- *I knew*-- the Lord didn’t bring us this far to see us be cut off when we were so close. There had to be another way.

And then the miracle came when the phone rang in the outer room. The secretary answered, then came running into her boss’s office, speaking in rapid Spanish and nearly out of breath with excitement.

The animation from our friend’s face dropped like flat clay. He took a deep breath, patted his hair, wiped his sweaty palms on his trousers, took a seat, and with a trembled hand, picked up the phone.

The room became like a tomb as three sets of eyes focused on the phone and the gestures of the second Director. *Whoever that was on the other end,* I thought, *had to be special, extremely high up.*

Our new-found friend lit up with a radiant smile and a big *thumbs up* sign. When he hung up, he withdrew a piece of paper from his desk and wrote out a letter telling the military to overlook the date on my visa. He signed it in large, bold script. John Hancock couldn’t be more pleased.

Outside, Alfredo mopped his brow.

“I’m a bit confused as to what transpired,” I began. “Who was on the other end of that phone? God?”

“Close,” bowed Alfredo. His hands on his knees. “The man on the other line was none other than Ciro Perez. The very top man for every sport in Cuba. Only Fidel is higher.”

"I'm honoured."

"You should be. He take it upon himself to waive the extension on your visa. But we need to be in his office by eight o'clock Monday morning."

"That gives us three days to get back to Havana once the Tour is completed. Think that will be enough time?"

"More than enough," nodded Alfredo.

The Lord continued to be with us. I was totally prepared to go alone the next day, but prayed I wouldn't have to. Alfredo deserved to finish this Tour with me, I knew. Now, thanks to the higher powers and the Higher Power, we could.

Because the military and the local government knew we were in town, we decided to stay away from the private homes.

"Since we're so close to finishing, I don't want to get any family in trouble for housing us without a license, and we don't need the hassles."

"I agree," nodded my partner. "It best to stay at the *Hotel Pinar del Rio* no' far from here."

But the hustlers were still on us, even to the front steps of the hotel-- the largest and fanciest place in town. Alfredo once spent his honeymoon there.

"Hey mista, got a nice place for you," shouted out one young man as he ran across the street, before I could make the mistake of entering the hotel.

"I'm from the government," I replied.

He looked at me with a furrowed brow, his head tilted to the side. "Okay. Me understand. No problem." He ran off, disappearing in the darkness before he could be questioned.

So that's what works with these hawkers, I mused, entering the palatial structure. That was one trick I'd have to remember.

For $30US we had a fifth-floor room with a balcony and a view of the surrounding fields. HBO was playing American films, and the place had several restaurants surrounding a large swimming pool. Alfredo wasted no time in trying out the latter, as I relaxed in one of the lounge chairs with my notes and photos of my girls.

Looking at Jean, I said to myself, "It's almost over, Hon. I'll be home soon."

For dinner, we found a family dining facility called *El Mason* that served a great chicken breast with all the trimmings.

We were on our way. All we needed to do was keep focused a few more days and not let ol' Scratch get the better of us.

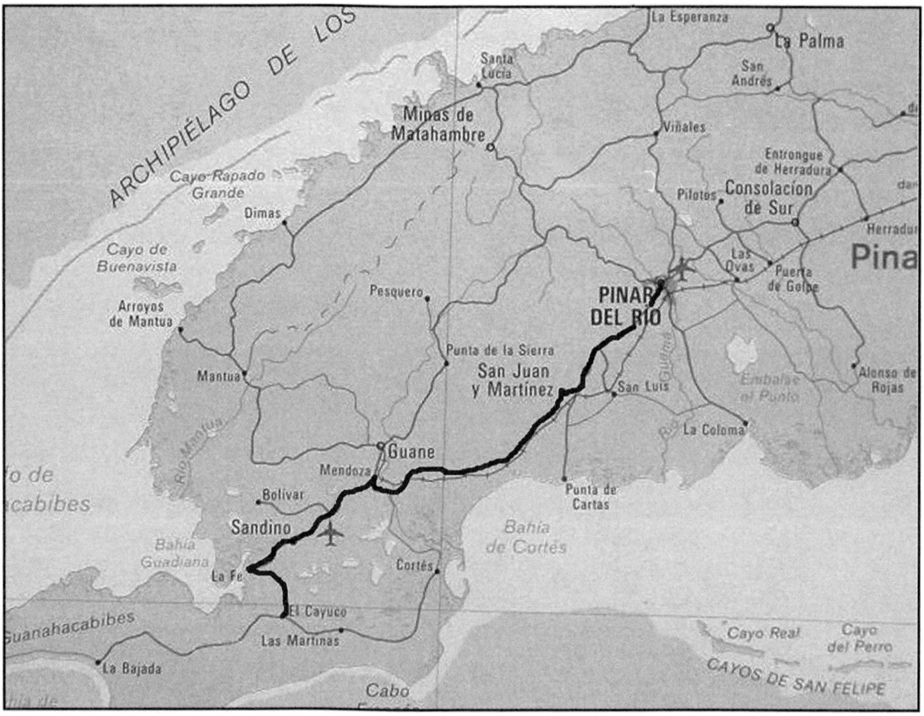

VEINTIOCHO

28

PINAR DEL RIO to EL CAYUCO
DAY 20
DECEMBER 10, 1997

DAILY DISTANCE :	**64**	**miles**	**or**	**106.7**	**kilometers**
TOTAL DISTANCE :	**1100**	**miles**	**or**	**1833.3**	**kilometers**

Cycling during the early dawn hours when the sun began to rise, casting its light upon the dew-soaked fields and plantations, brought joy and a new surge of energy to my soul. Because we were so close to finishing, I was experiencing *end-time* euphoria.

Waking from a comfortably warm sleep, tripping over gear on the way to changing into my uniform, and then finding the inner strength to get back on the bike is par for the course. But once you find the cadence, enter into the motion, the world around you begins to blossom like a perfectly-formed morning glory.

We were located deep in tobacco country. Passing by workers in a mist-covered field, seeing tobacco leaves hanging from the rafters of huge barns to dry-- it all added a surreal feeling to the immediate surroundings of the vast, lush, jungle greenery.

As we entered and became completely surrounded by the vaporous mist, I scared myself into believing that we'd never make it out, that we'd ride off into nowhere or another dimension. Perhaps, I mused, we'd become a part of some sort of cosmic, unnatural shift in time and space. Would we emerge from this valley of uncertainty and enter into another age? I love to scare myself sometimes. It gets the adrenaline flowing.

Alfredo, just a few bicycle lengths in front of me, seemed to evaporate into the mist. And the mind games continued until we put in about 30km without a stop.

"Hey, Alfredo, can you hear me? Are you out there?"

"*Si,*" came the voice out of the fog.

"When I was a boy, my parents and I went to the Virgin Islands. We flew over the Bermuda Triangle, and I thought for sure we'd disappear into another dimension."

I waited a few moments for some kind of a response from Alfredo. Hearing nothing, I became concerned.

"Alfredo, are you still with me, pal?"

"*Si,*" he answered somewhere in front of me.

"What's the problem?"

"I would like to disappear from this mist."

"We will when the sun breaks through," I encouraged him. "So, what's the plan for today?"

We hadn't really discussed it the previous night, nor during the time we were getting ready, so I figured now was as good as any.

"By the afternoon, we should arrive in *Sandino*," figured my partner. "It is a good size town. We will have no problem finding a room at the local hotel."

"But that would leave us with about seventy miles on the last day. I'd rather stay along the coast."

I could just make out his figure only a few feet away.

"*El Cayuco* is the only town left before the end. We will not find a place to stay there."

I had to laugh at my wheeler-dealer partner by reminding him that, "If we do our part in faith, the Lord will do His and that's to provide us with food and shelter."

"Sometimes you push things too far," he cautioned me.

Somewhere along the way, our roles switched.

"Also remember," cautioned Alfredo. "As we reach the coast, it will be more difficult to find food and water."

"Which were the same circumstances we had at the beginning of this Tour. We continue to *El Cayuco*."

For whatever was on his mind, Alfredo was just giving excuses. In over a

An early morning field worker.

thousand miles, how many times did we pass by coconut and banana plantations? Sugarcane and pineapple fields? Orange, mango, papaya, and guava orchards?

Since outside the town of *Santiago de Cuba*, we had all this and more at our disposal.

"Are you sure this is alright?" I'd ask Alfredo.

"Of course," he'd reply with a laugh. "It is the people's field. We can pick and eat all that we want."

"Just not something I can get used to," I'd tell him, shaking my head. "You do this in America, you get shot."

"Why? Is no' all for the people?"

"Only to those that work or can pay for it."

"That is not right," said my downcast friend.

"Neither is a Communist-Socialist way of life. It promotes laziness. We tried that in my own country about four hundred years ago when the Pilgrims arrived and the system didn't work. It allowed everyone to reap the benefits of the ones who did the actual work."

"But if no' provide for everyone, then people starve."

"Then they starve," I replied. "The Bible states that if a man doesn't work, neither shall he eat. That's the Law. It's fair. It's practical. And weeds out laziness."

We made great time, arriving in the tropical paradise town of *Sandino* by 12:30pm. Just in time for lunch. Alfredo found an abundance of pork sandwiches.

"God provides," laughed Alfredo.

"You're such a heathen."

I stayed with the healthier alternative of *banito* (fruit juice), biding my time until we reached our destination a few hours later.

In *Sandino*, there was an empty bus, parked off to the side. While I stayed at the juice stand, Alfredo decided to strike up a conversation with the driver who was waiting for his passengers. Several minutes later, he returned.

"The driver tell me he from Havana," smiled Alfredo. "He say he in the area with foreign tourists until Friday."

"Great. What's that to us?"

He helped himself to a *banito* and continued. "If we can return from *Caleta Larga* in time, he say he will take us back home for ten dollars each."

"Does that include our bikes and gear?"

"*Si*," nodded Alfredo, as he gulped down his juice.

"But can we make it back here before the deadline?"

"Is possible."

"You're learning."

Between *Sandino* and *El Cayuco* lay the one street village of *La Fe*-- Spanish for faith. Although the name wasn't an omen of encouragement to Alfredo, what did give him hope was the chance meeting of an elderly man who passed by when we took a break under the shade of a tree.

While I caught a few *Z's,* he and Alfredo struck up a conversation, which he filled me in on about a half-hour later when we were back on the road.

"The man say there is a hotel in *El Cayuco*, near the center of town," smiled my companion. "He say it would not be too difficult to find."

"*La Fa,* Alfredo. Just keep the faith going."

On the way to our destination, we came across a wooden shack of a stand near the side of a large plantation, where two women served sugarcane juice.

For a *peso*, you received two glasses of the cool, sweet, refreshing liquid that came straight from the stalk of the sugarcane.

The first time I tasted the nectar outside *Santiago de Cuba*, I was hooked. At least at this booth, a machine did the squeezing instead of my teeth. The light yellow liquid was easy on the stomach to digest, giving me a natural pick-me-up.

Almost immediately upon entering the community of *El Cayuco*, Alfredo began looking for the hotel, which, not surprisingly, sat in the center of town, the heart of where most of the activity among the people occurred.

Our presence was definitely made known. The uniform, the bike-- it all creates excitement. These people were near the edge of their known world, and I was an alien, a being from a magical country that they have only heard and dreamt about.

"I go look over the hotel," said Alfredo. Off he went while I was stuck

The process of making sugar cane juice, above...

...and where the extract ends up, below.

This look is achieved by a mixture of too much rum and a loathing suspicion of any and all foreigners.

in the public square.

A young man named Ariel decided to become my shadow, draining my energy beyond its reserves, scraping my patience raw. A motley crew of workers gathered around me, drinking their rum, engaging in the day's news. An old man who was white-washing a building spread more paint on himself than on the walls. Another man-- a real toad of a mongrel, couldn't keep from staring at me with his thirsty, blood-shot eyes. A mustachioed Cuban Peter Lorre, he didn't say a word, but turned to watch me wherever I went.

"Hey, *amigo,* you have a problem?"

The only reply being a silent, deadly stare. I took photos of the area, the people. I'd turn, and *wham!* There he'd be. So close to me, I'd have tripped over him.

"Can you talk? Are you deaf? No *comprehenda?*"

He stood motionless. His dead eyes unblinking. I took his photo, because his look was so unique that I could only suspect he acquired it over the years by drinking too much rum, and having a loathing suspicion of any and all foreigners.

But it was Ariel who was the real energy-sucking vampire. About ten years younger and two inches taller than myself, his skin the color of rich mahogany, Ariel was one of the first on the scene to greet me with an infectious grin and a constant nervous energy.

His questions were repetitious in his limited English, and it took a great deal of energy to understand what he was trying to say. What really sent me over the edge, though, was his constant tapping my shoulder, arm, or chest.

"Hey, hey, hey...um...hey...where from, where from... hey, hey," he'd ask, tapping my body the entire time.

"California," was my one-word answer. I tried to subtly maneuver away from his reach.

"Hey, hey, hey...um..." --tapping all the while-- "Hey...um, what you name?"

I'd mention it, he'd repeat it several times to get the full understanding, then ask where I lived again. Then he decided to broaden the scope of dialogue.

"Hey...hey, hey...um," --tap, tap, tap-- "Where, um...Mike Tyson," tap, "Scotti Pippen," tap, "Michael Jordan," tap, "Carl Lewis," tap, "live?" Tap.

When I answered the individual States, he stood momentarily dumbstruck (at least my body had a rest from his tapping). He then asked again, and I'd repeat my answers.

He screamed in frustration, raising his hands to his head as though he were trying to prevent a blood vessel from popping, and asked one more time.

"*America!*" I shot back. "*U-S-A!*"

He calmed down and smiled.

About this time, thank God, Alfredo reappeared.

"Do you wish to see the hotel?" he sighed.

"No smile? No joy? No hope? Should I ask?"

"It will do for the night," he answered low key.

I just didn't like the sound of that. At least seeing it for myself got me away from Ariel.

The hotel was right next to the plaza, about two flights up above a restaurant. By then, I was already used to the condemned surroundings and this one was no different. The place was empty, the stairs were questionable. I'd test each one before placing my full weight upon it. No bathroom --no furniture, for that matter. Just a large, open, empty, bug-filled room. The cost for us this evening would be 20 *pesos.*

Emerging from the death trap I found that Ariel and Alfredo were engaged in conversation. Or, more accurately, Ariel was doing the Cuban tap dance on my partner. These were the times when it was so good Alfredo and I could share the same experiences.

"He say he want to know what you do," asked Alfredo.

"You already know what I do," I shot back.

"I know, but he no' believe."

When Ariel finally succumbed to the notion that what I really did was ride a bicycle for a living, he grabbed my arm and dragged me to the town's sports complex across the street. Alfredo followed.

In passing, I mentioned to my comrade that, "Perhaps we should find ourselves a private house as soon as possible."

Within minutes of entering the house-converted sports building and signing the guest book, Alfredo slipped smoothly out the door, leaving me, once again, alone with the energy sucking vampire.

With a forced smile, I allowed Ariel to take me by the arm. Continuing to tap me on the chest, he showed me the gold medals he had won in basketball during the Friendship Games in Mexico a few years before. They were displayed in a glass case with other memorabilia and old, black-and-white photos of past athletes from another era.

"Hey, hey, hey...um," tap, tap. "How many you...um," he pointed to his medal in the display case, smiling.

"None," I answered, shaking my head.

He was actually immobile for several seconds, because he was performing two other functions: thinking and blinking. I could've escaped right then and there.

"No, um...hey, hey," tap, tap, tap. "How many?" He pointed to the display case again. "How many? How many?"

"None!" I yelled. "Zero! Zip! *Nada!*"

What the hell was taking Alfredo so long to get back? He was doing this to me on purpose, I just knew it.

"Me, good," he smiled, then went into the action movements of basketball, baseball, rowing, and boxing.

I nodded approvingly. "Great! Wonderful! Fantastic!"

"Hey, hey, hey...um," he continued tapping me nervously. "You...me... America," he smiled, obviously confident that I understood.

I didn't.

"America, I..." he held up his fists, dancing about like a boxer.

"*Si, si,*" I nodded impatiently.

"Tyson...Holyfield...*dinero*," he rubbed his fingers together. "Me, give you."

"Are you out of your stinkin' mind?"

As though I would be crazy enough to bring him to America so he could make lots of money boxing Tyson and Holyfield, sharing his winnings with me. Faith is one thing; fantasy another.

I hurried out of the complex, only to discover that not only was Alfredo missing, but my bike was as well. Momentary panic set in. My fists clenched by my sides. Gritting my teeth, I felt someone grab my arm from behind.

"What the hell do you want?" I screamed.

Ariel sighed with drooped shoulders. He was finally at a loss for words. His feelings hurt. I didn't care.

When I went across the street to take some more photos of the locals, Ariel grabbed me by the arm again. Pulling me to a corner of the plaza, he stripped off his shirt, motioning me to take pictures of him in his navy blue sweats, doing several boxing poses.

I looked to the sky. "Lord, I'm going to slaughter this lamb of yours. I thought You were suppose to give enough grace to be sufficient?" Ariel looked up to the sky with me.

Popping off several shots, some of the townspeople gathered to see the spectacle. Ariel was king for the day.

After what seemed like an eternity, Alfredo finally returned with one of the happy locals on my bike.

"Glad to see you had use for my bike."

A painter who paints more of himself than the actual work before him.

"He show me a house only a few blocks from here," replied Alfredo, as though that were excuse enough. "An old woman live there by herself. She have two rooms to rent."

"At what price?"

"Forty *pesos*!" Alfredo smiled with delight.

"No dollars?"

"No dollars," he repeated. "Good beds and hot water."

"I'm sold. Let's do it."

As I went to retrieve my backpack, three young girls approached Ariel. They stopped to talk, to check out the foreigners.

"I'm tired of putting on the happy face," I said. "Tell Ariel it was nice to meet him, but we have to leave."

"This will no' take long," said Alfredo.

"You haven't been with him as much as I have. I'm tired and I want to leave."

"Let's see what they want."

If you're unknown, you can pretty much be the way you want. You get into a scuffle with someone, it's forgotten after a period of time. But if you choose to be famous, you become a marked man. One incident, one momentary snap of being a real, honest, feeling individual, and that's what the ordinary people remember about you the rest of their lives. It stinks, but we made the choice to be known, therefore, we pay the price.

Introductions were made. The girls smiled. Two of them hung on each of my arms, while the third stood in front of me. All had flirtatious smiles on them.

Ariel turned to Alfredo, speaking their language.

"Ariel say he you friend, and offer you any one of these girls for you pleasure-- or all if you like." Ariel smiled like a generous pimp.

I shook my head, and asked what their ages were. At 11, 12, and 13, I was still older than them by one year of their combined total.

The girls smiled; one had a front tooth missing.

"In my country, 12 will get you 20-to-life."

"But we no' in America," returned my antagonizer.

"I have a girlfriend," I volleyed.

Alfredo relayed my answer, but the girls returned with shrugged shoulders, and wanted to see a picture of my woman.

I pulled the photo out of the top pocket of my knapsack. They studied Jean's picture, passing it between themselves.

"They say it no' matter to them. She no' here, and they are," interpreted Alfredo.

Ariel, the pimp, smiled. He pointed to the upper part of the hotel, inviting me to use the upstairs room.

I nodded, then turned to Alfredo.

"Let me explain why this sort of thing doesn't interest me. About twenty years ago, I wanted to marry my childhood sweetheart. We grew up together, our families were friends. She was it for me. I had my life all planned out. Began working after high school. Saved my money. Planned to marry her a few years later. Then six months before the big day, she informed me that she fell in love with another woman."

"She what...?" Alfredo's jaw dropped. "Shit!"

"It took years for me to get over that, but eventually I met another woman I could have spent my life with. She was a realist, I was a dreamer. Family and friends have always laughed at me for being a rainbow chaser, but when this woman joined them, it hurt even more. What really cut out my heart was when I found her in bed with another man."

"Fuck!" exclaimed Alfredo. "I kill for that."

"I have never been able to find a woman that could love me completely. Just the hand I was dealt with. So, my accomplishments become my heirs. Everything I have ever or will ever do in this life is for revenge. To get back at those who would destroy me with their laughter and hurtful words. Success has now become a drug. The power of fame more addicting and a far better aphrodisiac than sex. For the most part, relationships tend to get in the way."

I looked over at Ariel and the teeny-boppers before continuing with Alfredo. "Pray, that when this Tour is over, you don't end up like me."

As was to be expected, Ariel followed us to see where we were spending the night.

"Some town people say he crazy in the head," warned my partner.

"Probably too many knocks on the noggin'."

"*Si*," nodded Alfredo. "He no' good for nothing."

"That's cold, Alfredo. Don't misunderstand. I do realize what Ariel's going through. He's ambitious, full of energy. He finds it difficult to escape his environment. His living conditions are worse than my dogs. He can't fly after his dreams and desires as many of us can. No matter how hard he tries, how persistent, he'll always be stuck where he is. What am I supposed to do? Take him, and everyone else who wants to leave, out of the country?"

"It cost a Cuban two thousand American dollars for the proper papers and a passport," replied Alfredo.

"Probably why most of them take the raft approach. What choice do they have when the government makes it difficult, if not impossible to leave?"

The well-kept house was on a quiet side street. The plump, tiny old woman showed us in while Ariel waited outside with our bikes. Ushering us toward the back, she showed us the two spare rooms with firm, clean-sheeted beds. The *bano* (bathroom) was well kept with warm running water.

"There is only one drawback," mentioned Alfredo.

"Only one," I sarcastically asked.

"The old woman has no' license to house foreigners, and she afraid a neighbor will turn her into the police."

"We could find another place. I don't wish to cause her any unnecessary worry."

"She say it will be all right. She have other Americans from Miami in a back room."

"How big is this place anyway?"

"We just need to keep a low profile."

"Fine. No problem."

It was finally, joyously, time to say our good-byes to Ariel. A most difficult task, I know, but it had to be done. For some reason, he took it quite casually, walking off with a smile and a hearty wave, as Alfredo brought our bikes around the enclosed back yard. The old woman wanted no one to see any evidence that we were staying with her.

Food was the next problem. Because Ariel had detained us for so much of our time, the local PanAmerican store was closed. While pondering our options, we met the Cuban-Americans from Miami-- a mother-daughter team and their boyfriends, all husky and dressed as though they were about to burst from their two-sizes-too-small outfits.

"We're going to *Sandino*. There's a restaurant that's quite good," smiled the mother who was competing for age category with her daughter.

"Perhaps we could hitch a ride with you?" I asked.

"Oh," cooed the mother. "I don't think our driver would have room to fit all of us."

I bit my tongue.

"However," she smiled, "We will be returning about nine. He could take you then, if you'd like."

"I appreciate the offer. We'll be fine."

After a much-needed shower and change of clothes, Alfredo and I were on the front porch discussing our food options when who should appear, dressed all in white, but Ariel.

"I thought nightmares were supposed to appear in black, not white." I shot Alfredo a look of despair.

The old woman came out gibbering in Spanish.

"She want you to come back in before someone see you," laughed Alfredo.

"And what about you?"

"I okay. I Cuban."

"So you keep reminding me. Tell her, I hate to burst her paranoid world, but by now, the entire town knows I'm here and where I'm staying."

Alfredo did. She threw her hands up in the air.

"*Madre de Dios!*" she wailed, retreating back inside.

Alfredo laughed. "She say she have to get her Rosary and pray to the Saints."

"So, I either have to stay inside the house with a frightened old woman, or be outside with a twitchy, tappy shadow. These are my choices?"

"Come. Let us go to the restaurant."

We left. Ariel following close behind. At least I didn't have to keep him on a leash. And I presumed he was housebroken.

At the one-and-only restaurant in town, we found they had run out of food. Alfredo did manage to buy a bag of *congris* from them. This prompted Ariel to invite us back to his family's house.

"No! Absolutely not! *Nada!*"

Alfredo was insistent. And I was hungry...

"This will be a fun experience," Alfredo said. "I like situations like this."

"You're a masochist," I replied, having no choice but to follow-- he was the one holding the bag.

The center of town was well-lit, but as we moved away and down a few side streets, it became increasingly dark. Soon, I couldn't see a step in front of me. Used to such conditions, Alfredo had no problem following Ariel. But I kept tripping along.

We seemed to enter a shanty-town environment. The houses were slapped together with whatever boards and plywood happened to be available. One dwelling nearly directly across the street from Ariel's place, had an alien spaceship effect to it: it was all lit up inside, yet you could see the streaks of light pouring out from every crack and knothole. I was waiting for some ETs to step out, or, better, for the house to convert to a flying saucer and take off.

The only light emitting from Ariel's tiny house was the faint glow from the old black-and-white TV, in front of which sat an elderly gentleman watching some Cuban cowboy show. Other than that there were no other lights in the house.

"Ariel say his family is so poor they canno' afford a single bulb," interpreted Alfredo.

"Why?" I asked. "How much can a bulb cost in Cuba?"

With the magnificent
Ariel Camejo Bostamante.

"Plenty, since you have to pay for them in American dollars, and there are not very many of them in this part of the country."

There was no running water, no cooking facilities, and the place seemed as though it could blow over in the first good storm. Aside from the elderly man, there was Ariel's mother, sister, and a couple of brothers. They had never had an American-- or any other foreigner, for that matter-- in their humble abode.

They all crept closer toward me in the glow of the television light to stare at my features. Only the old man was more interested in his program than me. Ariel's chest seemed to grow, as he sat straight, smiling.

The mother took the *congris* to the back kitchen, where she placed it in a pan with some bits of fish, heating it over a tiny candle.

The furniture was wood and iron. There were no cushions of any kind, no comfort. The floor was a pile of wood on stilts. *Who knew*, I wondered, *what crawled through the cracks at night when all were asleep.*

"This another good experience for you," quipped Alfredo, as he scratched his head, trying to look away.

"Why haven't I killed you yet?"

"Because you need me."

"I knew there was a reason."

Our supply of food was probably the most that family had seen in quite sometime. Yet they lovingly and happily prepared it for us, never asking any for themselves.

The meal had a burnt, lukewarm taste to it. The family sat around, staring expectantly at me with smiles. After a few bites even the mighty Alfredo, who could stomach anything, dropped his fork in his plate, letting his mouth hang full of food.

As for myself, I couldn't handle the scene anymore. The last straw had been broken, and I was near tears. In my Italian upbringing, I was not taught that you ate in front of someone who had nothing. That was inconceivable. I excused myself and left them the food. Better for me to go hungry a night.

Not more than a hundred yards or so from the house, my shadow caught up with me, insisting he walk back to the house I was staying at. We didn't speak a word, but once at the old woman's house, Ariel said, "Friend," shook my hand and gave me a big hug. He crept back into the night.

Lord, how I felt for him and what kind of life he must think I had in America. I imagined that whatever he thought was still much better than the only life he knew. His dreams would remain forever with him. Unexplored.

When Alfredo returned to the house, the old woman asked if we had found anything to eat. Shaking our heads, she mentioned to Alfredo that, "I have some food in the house and would be happy to cook you a meal if you would like."

"*Si,*" we both said. "*Gracias.*"

Within a half-hour, we had ourselves a large dish of rice with chopped snails in a delicate herb sauce. We devoured it completely.

I wanted to kiss her, but she'd probably go running off to find her Rosaries again. I did ask, through Alfredo, what I could do for her as a way to say thank-you.

"She ask if you could pay her two dollars, so that she could buy some toiletries."

I gave her five, but she pushed three back into my hand. I tried to refuse, but she said two was more than enough to buy what she needed.

"My God, Alfredo, the Tour's going to be over tomorrow. After all this time. Can you believe it?"

"*Si,*" he smiled. "Another day. The final push."

"*Si.* The final push."

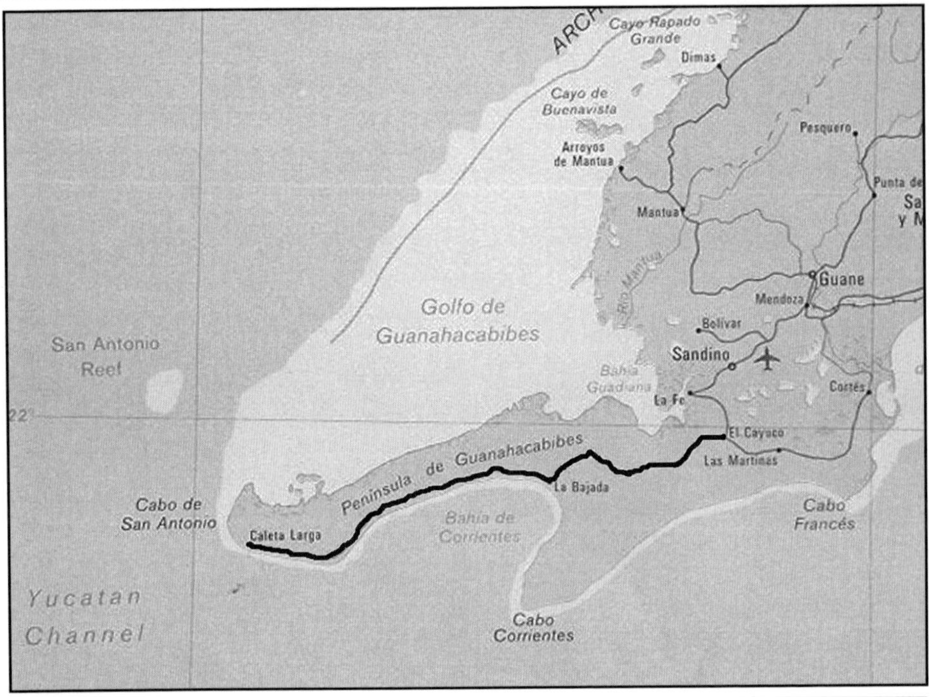

VEINTINUEVE

29

EL CAYUCO to CALETA LARGA
DAY 21
DECEMBER 11, 1997

DAILY DISTANCE : 58 miles or 96.7 kilometers
TOTAL DISTANCE : 1158 miles or 1930 kilometers

We overslept an hour, and were punished for it. Ariel showed up at the door to see us off. Dressed in his slightly soiled white jacket and pants, he greeted us with a radiant, full white-tooth smile that was repulsive and out-of-place to someone who hates rising so early in the morning. I returned his smile with a growl.

After filling all our available water containers at the old woman's place for the last part of our journey, we bid farewell. The three of us walked around the corner where we found a couple of vendors along the main street.

Not only was this the last day, but we were venturing into uncharted, uncivilized, remote territory. To be caught without food and water would be foolhardy and suicidal.

Our breakfast consisted of fried *yucca* and *banito*. I naturally paid for three helpings without even the thought of asking our uninvited guest. When Ariel shook his head in refusal, I ignored the gesture and shoved the food and drink into his hands. He smiled, bowed slightly and ate.

Like a dog, he swallowed the food whole before Alfredo and I had the first bite of our breakfast down. I bought him more and he did it again.

"You are one hungry mutt," I commented.

He asked Alfredo to translate, which my partner did, only it came out as, "He amazed by your appetite."

Ariel smiled and nodded at me. That's a good boy. Here, have another *yucca*.

When we were about to leave, he said, through Alfredo, "I am going to miss you." We shook hands, and then he engulfed me in his arms.

The sunrise seemed more glorious than usual, the day more radiant, the colors more vibrant.

"Can you believe this, Alfredo?" I laughed. "The last day. Did you ever think we'd see it?"

"Sometime I think we no' have a chance, but now I think we do."

"All the way, *Cubano*."

"*Si, Americano*."

The fresh air washed over our faces, brushing through our clothes, as we followed the coast once more. Twenty-five kilometers later, we entered lush, tropical, jungle territory-- and came upon the first guard station.

"Lions and tigers and bears, oh my!"

"What are you saying?" asked Alfredo. "There are no lions, tigers and bears in Cuba."

"How about flying monkeys?" I asked, looking around the green canopy, where even sunlight couldn't get through.

"This has been a long tour for you. It is good we are ending today."

The guard, a mere boy, sat on a metal folding chair by the side of the road, waiting to check someone's papers, probably for the sheer excitement it would afford the boredom he must have faced daily.

The procedure didn't take long. I handed over my passport; Alfredo his papers. The two of them spoke in their native tongue, and we were allowed to pass.

"That was a bit too easy," I commented to Alfredo, as we mounted our bikes and continued on.

"That was nothing," he jerked his head sideways. "The real pass to get through is up ahead. There is where the problems will begin for us."

"'*We're off to see the Wizard...*,'" I began to sing.

"Now it is wizards? I do not know about you sometimes."

Just 10km further, we came upon the military outpost on the *Bahia de*

Alfredo with the first border guard checking our papers.

Corrientes-- a horseshoe-shaped land mass-- the Caribbean's waves crashing against the coastal town of *La Bajada*.

We were literally at the end of the road, as it formed a T. Just a few yards from the shore we were stopped by the main gate. A boy with an AK-47 stood beside his guard booth in a slack position. He promptly came to attention once he saw us approach. He shot straight up, as though he had just received an enema, his trusted rifle in the defensive position. I supposed from the attitude he had, he didn't get to see many people all decked out in red, white and blue.

A couple of bare chested boy soldiers were washing some of their clothes in a bucket near the aquamarine-colored outpost building. They, too, stood at attention upon first seeing us, one of them running inside, presumably to get his commanding officer.

Just beyond the gate, the road was laid out before us horizontally. If we were to turn left and continue for about ten miles, we would come across Cuba's last tourist resort. Turning right was *Caleta Larga* and our destiny some three dozen miles away.

A few of the soldier boys, now dressed, came out to greet us fully armed. They surrounded us, and the spokesman talked with Alfredo.

"They no' believe we are doing a Tour," said Alfredo. "They want to see all our papers."

We handed over whatever we had-- our stamped documents, passport, identification books-- everything. I noticed a shadowy figure peering out at us from a window. I couldn't make out his looks, but presumed he was the man in charge.

Once all our papers were collected, the soldiers, save for the border guard, retreated to their outpost building, while we waited in the sun.

We had arrived here from *El Cayuco* within two hours, thinking we could call it quits by noon, but that was just a fantasy to believe things will go smoothly when dealing with government officials, especially the military.

After a long, solitary hour passed, the *Commandante* of the *La Bajada* station came out with some of his armed *muchachos* to speak with Alfredo. He looked upon me with contempt when passing by. Tall, dark featured, beady-eyed, big-nosed and mustachioed, he barked words of intimidation to my partner, throwing all our paperwork back in his face.

Alfredo cautiously, humbly, picked up the papers, while Commander Cockroach looked down with a devilish smile.

"He say we no' have proper permission," stated Alfredo.

"Tell him to go play with himself. We have permission."

"I think he rather shoot you instead," cautioned my partner. "They no' like Americans."

"Really? I hadn't noticed."

The young guard and other uniformed boys held their shiny Commie rifles tight, ready for the mildest of incidents to occur. Their steely eyes were fixed on my uniform and bike. The colors were obviously not to their liking. I smiled.

"Did you explain to the Chief here that we received permission from the top man in *Pinar?*"

"*Si,* but he no' believe."

"I'll get myself arrested before I give up the last three dozen miles of this Tour," I gritted through clenched teeth. "We better come to some agreement soon."

"*Si, si,*" said Alfredo, tapping his fingers to his lips. He was focused on the waves of the sea, but his mind was racing for some sort of solution.

"Ask the Chief here what we need to do to cross the border? Remember, Alfredo, we need to practice the art of gentle pushing. Make our agenda known."

Alfredo once again explained our situation to the commander.

"He say, we would have to call his superior, who would have to call the *Commandante* of this area at *Pinar*."

"Great! Let's do it!"

"Only one problem," said Alfredo. "No telephone at this outpost. Just a radio."

"I don't suppose this cockroach will make the call?"

"No," answered Alfredo.

The *Commandante* smiled that particular smile that one would love to slap off. I continued to hold my ground.

"What needs to be done?"

"I must cycle back a half mile or so to the nearest telephone and make the call."

"Then let's get this show on the road."

Alfredo unloaded his gear with me. While he was away, I found a spot to rest and catch up on my journal under a shady palm tree. I watched other men and women and some children on bicycles come and go past the gate. Other tourists as well could easily enter when showing their passports if they were going to the resort.

I observed a couple of young men string their catch of the day. It was enough to feed their family for a while. They offered me a couple of fish to take along, but I politely declined.

About 40 minutes had passed when Alfredo returned with the good news that he had made contact with the superior in *Pinar*, who would, in turn, radio the *Commandante* for us to continue on our way. It must have worked, too, because a few moments later, a gruff-looking Cockroach emerged from his quarters, angrily ordering the gate to be raised. He reluctantly allowed us to fill our water containers.

By then, some two hours had passed since we first arrived. So much for an early day finish.

Turning right after the gate, we immediately came upon *La Bajada*. Not more than a couple dozen concrete homes lined along the coast on the single road. Painted in pastel colors, they extended no more than a quarter-mile before coming to a sudden end. Fittingly, just a few yards farther, the pavement turned to dirt. There, we were able to turn loose.

At last! Dirt! Home turf to a mountain bike instead of the endless miles of pavement we've had to endure these last few weeks. Civilization left behind, the jungle engulfing us into her fold. All the work and the bureaucracy was behind us; we were completely free to roam. To feel the wind in our faces, the smell of salt through our nostrils, and the dirt spinning off our rear wheels.

I christened this 36-mile section of road the *Lost World Trail*, because of the habitat, complete with giant iguanas the size of Komodo dragons, king-sized rats larger than my dogs, wild horses and pigs roaming about the hills.

Jungles formed a barrier between us and the waters of the Caribbean, but when they opened up at times, inviting us to explore and have a look, we found a rugged coastline complete with white sandy beaches. Rarely had I found a Paradise so private. Rarely were the conditions so perfect for cycling. I laughed at the thought of how the cursed environmentalists would love to slap restrictions all over this place if they could. This area was a mountain biker's dream come true. I was back in my element. No pavement. No vehicles. All dirt.

The Beast seemed happy, too, picking up the pace somewhat. That was what it was made for, and I suspected that it was having as good a time as I was. It took over 1100 miles of work to finally arrive at this moment of the last 36. I wanted to take in this *Lost World* and all the natural beauty it had to offer.

A giant iguana or brown, hairy rat would often shriek from the bushes and dash across our path.

"Damn!" I screamed, nearly falling off the bike as I tried to prevent myself from slamming into one of them. "Did you see the size of those things."

"*Si,*" smiled Alfredo. "A meal for an entire family."

"Which ones? The iguanas or rats?"

"Both," he laughed. "We Cubans like variety."

"That would be some serious road kill."

Going the last 35 miles surrounded by utter desolation
on the newly christened, *Lost World Trail.*

Iguanas didn't seem to bother me as much as those big, ol' hairy king rats showing their claws and teeth.

When the area opened up to flat, short brush, I watched horses run wild and free. Reacting and interacting with one another in near ballet formation. Their nostrils flared, their mouths foamed, their manes and tails thrashed about their sweaty bodies. Such a graceful beauty, such power and movement to it all. And I saw what were perhaps the most fortunate pigs on the entire island. To think that some actually lived out their existence without the threat of being eaten by man, nor thoughts of a glazed apple stuffed in their mouth being surrounded by honeyed pineapple.

Since we were left to ourselves, I was grateful that our water containers were full and we had sufficient food to last us the day. But what of the next?

"It doesn't look like we'll be able to keep to our original plan of being in and out of this area in one day," I mentioned to Alfredo as we cycled along.

"*Si,*" he agreed. "We may have to spend the night at the lighthouse and return in the morning. But we may no' have enough provisions to last us until tomorrow."

"*La fe,* Alfredo. Faith. If nothing else, we can make it back to *La Bajada* on sheer will and perseverance."

About six miles to the end, we came upon a scene straight out of *Deliverance.* In a small clearing within the jungle were a couple of make-shift homes, made from scraps of metal and wood. A group of men, filthy and scrappy looking, were working on a truck in their yard.

Alfredo (at right) nearly camouflaged by the jungle of the *Lost World Trail.*

"Perhaps we can get a ride out of here," said Alfredo.

As I refilled our water bottles, Alfredo struck up a conversation. He returned a short while later with a smile on his face and a lightness to his step.

"They say they will leave here about seven in the morning when their truck is fixed."

"Where are they going?"

"To *Pinar.*"

"Really," my voice raised an octave. "Praise God!"

"*Si,*" agreed Alfredo. "It is good news to hear."

"Tell them we'll be here on time."

"I already have," smiled my partner.

The skies were getting black on the horizon. A mid-afternoon storm was brewing; the sooner we finished, the better off we'd be. About three miles of the final push, drops began, followed by an all-out downpour.

Alfredo was nowhere to be seen, and since I was already soaked, why bother to stop? The ground became like sandy mud; my tires wiped the wet grains of earth all over the bike and myself. Puddles the size of small ponds filled the dips in the road. I had no choice but to go through them, getting even more wet and muddy. I was back to being a boy again, ignoring my mother's shouts to come in out of the rain. *Don't matter now,* I smiled, *'cause mama ain't around to spank me when it's over.*

Whether you call it *Cabo San Antonio* or *Caleta Larga*, it still means Alfredo and I reached the westernmost point on the island, and the end of the **Tour de Cuba** on December 11, 1997, after 1158 miles in 21 days from the lighthouse at *Maisi.*

The bike and I were soaked through and through. She squeaked and I sloshed. I began cursing the weather, the situation, the *La Bajada* guards who kept us waiting most of the morning.

And where was that blasted lighthouse? That Holy Grail I had been setting my sights on for the last three weeks-- ever since my encounter with its first cousin in *Maisi?*

The road wound its way through the jungle, zigzagging left and right. The effect made me feel as though I still had forever to go, and my old chant began to kick in: *This won't last forever, this won't last forever...*

"*'Doctor Foster went to Glochester in a shower of rain. He stepped in a puddle right up to his middle, and never went back there again...'* "

It had been my first song in a public appearance at the age of three, and never more did it fit than now.

Rounding another corner, the jungle seemed to open its arms, parting like the Red Sea. And there it was, like a tower of strength, appearing so out of place, so isolated. She stood tall, proud, and alone like a beacon should. What a beautiful sight.

A group of people in a nearby house called out to me, motioning me to come inside. It was a welcomed invitation which I gladly accepted. With the last of my energy, I walked me and the Beast to them. Exhausted, I slipped off my soaked backpack and sank into one of their overstuffed, leather chairs.

Five strapping young men, two healthy-looking women, and a baby boy made up the group that kept vigil over the last lighthouse on the westernmost part of the island nation. Through simple words and hand gestures, we made ourselves understood.

They asked where I had come from.

"*Maisi*."

They mumbled the town's name among themselves, scratching and shaking their heads in disbelief. Perking up a bit, I took out my slightly wet section map of their country, placing the pieces on the desk, so they could see the extensiveness of the Tour for themselves. Whispers of shock and surprise echoed through them.

One young man asked, "*Dias?*"

"*Veinti-uno*."

Not long after I arrived, the rains stopped. A herd of goats emerged as the sun came out. I looked about the place, feeling warmed by the sun, and noticed many maps hanging on the walls-- nautical charts, timetables-- as well as radio equipment. This handful of men and the two *senoritas,* monitored the weather in the area, and any storms or something of significance to report, they radioed the military in *La Bajada*. The men shared a room with four sets of bunkbeds, while the women slept in another part of the building. There was also a full-scale bathroom and kitchen.

The bathroom was especially tempting. I was soaked and sanded completely through, and wanted to shower and change. But not until after the photo ceremony.

Within a half-hour, Alfredo arrived, looking a lot dryer and cleaner than I was. He had taken refuge in the thickness of the jungle.

Endings are not what you think they'll be. Throughout the Tour, Alfredo was always a mile or two ahead. I never had to wait or stop for him, so, naturally, I thought he would arrive first on this day. Never did I imagine it would turn out like this...

No matter the situation, six years after first envisioning the event, the Tour was finished. A done deal. Another accomplishment from the shelf of dreams was transferred forever to the rack of reality. And it almost didn't come to pass without the intervention of the Lord and His unknowing servant, Alfredo.

"We did it!" smiled Alfredo with a hug. "We have done what no one else has ever done in all of Cuba. I wish I had some rum."

"Yeah, we did it, *amigo*. We did it."

"Why you no' happy?"

"Oh, I am...I am," I said, looking out to the horizon. "I'm just blank right now. I need time to take it all in."

Rest and relaxation were placed on hold while trying to finish off the little odds and ends. Now that the sun was out and shining there was work to be done. I

Posing in front of the westernmost lighthouse called *Roncali*.

surveyed the area for the final photos.

Since there was another military station just on the other side of the lighthouse, a couple of the young men went to speak with the officer in charge. Knowing how paranoid the military was, they would probably have to go through some lengthy chain of command to get a simple answer on whether we could photograph the lighthouse or not.

"I think we should forgo the military formalities and take as many photos as we can before we get run off."

"I think this a good idea," nodded Alfredo.

The area came to a point that jutted out to the vast, open sea. The waves crashed just below the stone cliffs, and a path led down to the beach. It was Paradise once again, and I was thankful we were able to spend at least a night.

Once again, Alfredo made mention that, "Although most maps name this place *Caleta Larga*, the locals call it *Cabo San Antonio*."

"Why?" I asked, snapping some scenic shots.

"No one seem to know exactly."

On our way to the lighthouse, we met the keeper, doing some repairs of the building nearby. As he looked down from his position on the ladder, our presence, and my costume nearly made him topple.

"*Hola!*" he shouted to us with a wave.

"*Hola!*" we shouted back up to him.

Visitors were a rare sight, as he came down to give us a warm and friendly greeting of sweaty handshakes and slaps on the back.

We noticed the beacon had a name on it called *Roncali,* and through Alfredo, the keeper, announced, "*Si,* it is named after an 18th century Spanish military officer. The lighthouse itself was built in 1848, and is the second oldest in the country, after the one in Havana."

With the lighthouse as the perfect backdrop, I shot a roll full of combos with the Beast: Me, Alfredo, some of the group we first met, Alfredo and I, the keeper and I, the keeper and Alfredo.

There wasn't much to look at in terms of scenery. A crystal blue sea on three directions from the point. The sun sinking lower with each passing moment, as a light breeze washed over us.

"Alone like this, out in the middle of nowhere, is when I feel close to God," I said to Alfredo as we watched the sky go from a blue to a rainbow of colors.

"It is peaceful out here, away from Havana," commented Alfredo. "It is my first time out here, but I feel good."

"For some reason I'm not even sure why, I do these Tours to get a sense of myself. To seek God's face."

The sound of the waves crashing against the shore, thundered below us.

"In the blink of an eye in the measure of time, I'll be on my deathbed, and will have barely scratched the surface of my understanding of this world, and the life given me."

"It seem like only yesterday we begin this Tour," said Alfredo. "And now it over."

"Just as the sun sets, a new day will dawn. A new adventure for both of us will begin."

"I must go and pay a visit to the officer in charge to see if we can stay the night," said Alfredo as he rose. "I am sure it will be all right. It just a courtesy call."

"Yeah. Good idea."

As he left, I stayed transfixed on the setting sun, watching the sky go from a light blue to a cobalt, the oranges, yellows, reds, pinks and purples giving off their last brilliant colors before going completely dark.

I could imagine myself living in an area like this. Peace. Solitude. Warm sunshine. Swimming naked with my wife, if I had one. Entertaining one another with our love-making and conversation. Laughing. Holding. Touching. Rearing a family. Planting a garden and catching our dinner off the coast. Going into *Pinar* every month or so to stock up on staple supplies and delights. The civilized world would become a thing of the past. Taxes would be a memory. Paradise...

But how long would it take before going insane with too much of *the good life?*

"It okay," announced Alfredo upon his return and bringing me back to reality. "We can stay."

I began to understand the military's paranoia about this area and why it was so well-guarded.

One of the meteorologists, speaking through Alfredo, mentioned that, "A man came cycling through here a couple of years ago. Once at the lighthouse, he took a side road toward the northern point. A boat was waiting nearby to take him to Florida. We still have and use the steel-framed bike he left behind."

"If the government would just ease up on the people and not want so much

Where the sun sets on the last point in Cuba.

control over them, perhaps there wouldn't be so many trying to escape to a better way of life," I commented. "If you're given the freedom to leave whenever you want, you'd stay, because, really, deep down, who hates their country enough to leave it forever? Have you ever heard of Americans trying to escape?"

"Is true," said Alfredo. "I stay if I could go."

Alfredo and I were invited to spend the night at the group home the meteorologists shared with one another. After a much-needed shower, I was relaxing on the front porch. Making notes and watching the sunset, it occurred to me that it was my mother's 69th birthday.

Alfredo mentioned this to the group, who said, "We could call her in the States through a relay hook-up."

"*Gracias,*" I nodded. "But I don't have her phone number. In any event, she is probably freezing where she is, and if I were to tell her how warm I am, she'd yell at me. It's not the kind of ending I want."

They laughed at the remark, nodding their heads.

I watched the sun rest on the last point in Cuba, just as I observed it rise three weeks earlier at its first juncture in *Maisi.* The first and the last, the Alpha and the Omega, the beginning and the end.

I counted the many blessings God had given me throughout the Tour and my life. He is my Forever Friend who teaches me compassion for those less fortunate by giving it to me. Who shows me mercy for the unmerciful by having mercy on me. Who gives me patience by being patient with me. Who fills me with

His love when I have no desire to be loved because He took on the form of a man and became Love in order to understand me. He never allows me to stray too far off the track even when I want Him to leave me alone. And I thank Him continually for not listening to such a childish fool, because I know, in reality, I don't even deserve an acknowledgement from Him.

Our meal for that night was *congris*.

I smiled and nodded. "*Gracias,*" I said to the *senorita* who served us. I had two generous helpings, along with some rum one of the men had in his quarters.

The Tour was over. We were in a laughing, singing, joyous mood in a shack of a building with our new *amigos*. The waves crashed against the shore, topped by a burnt-red evening sky. Tomorrow we would begin the final journey back to Havana. Cycling history had been made in Cuba and Alfredo was sitting proud and drunk to be a part of it.

I was in the most remote, most uncivilized, most beautiful part of the world.

Americanos-Cubanos, Amigos!

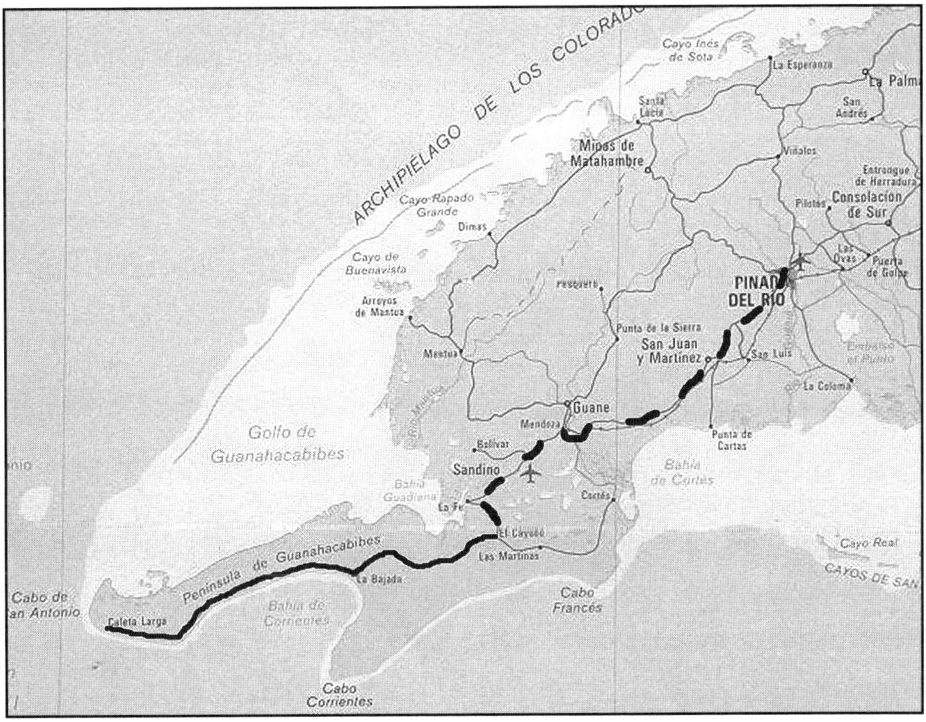

TREINTA

30

CALETA LARGA to EL CAYUCO
DAY 22
DECEMBER 12, 1997

DAILY DISTANCE : 57 miles or 95 kilometers
TOTAL DISTANCE : 1215 miles or 2025 kilometers

EL CAYUCO to PINAR DEL RIO (by truck)
MI/KM? Who cares!

It was still dark when the alarm on my Avocet Vertech watch woke us from a restful sleep. On the opposite end of the island, it would already be daylight in *Maisi*.

We had at least an hour's wait for the first rays to show.

Some of the men were still asleep in the bunk-filled room as Alfredo and I carefully made our way to our clothes and gear. My cleat-styled shoes were still wet from the previous day's storm, but since we were only going six miles to meet up with our ride back to *El Cayuco*, cycling on the clipless pedals with ordinary sneakers wouldn't be much of a problem.

Stepping out into the main living room, I noticed an eerie luminous glow from the desk radio. It crackled and whizzed; faint voices could be heard coming through, possibly from ships out to sea. One of the men was on shift. He gave us a hearty smile, and an enthusiastic thumbs-up sign.

By the time we dressed, packed and filled our water bottles, there was enough light to see the dry, sandy road that stretched out before us like some giant garden snake.

"We must leave soon, if we are to hitch a ride to *Pinar*," said Alfredo, as he packed the last of his bags.

"I'm already out the door," I said, piling the last of my belongings into my knapsack.

The other occupants of the building were still asleep, so we were only able to thank the individual for his generosity.

"You return," he smiled and point to the ground.

"*Si*," I nodded. "*Gracias*."

We made it in plenty of time before the 7am deadline. The only problem was, there were no men and no truck. My gut went back into a knot-- with the feeling of a sharp knife added to it. This was a bad sign, I knew, though I wanted to be optimistic.

"Are they in the area somewhere?" I asked Alfredo, who was looking around himself. "Please!...pretty please with sugarcane on top."

Alfredo found a couple of workers. Words were exchanged and then he reported back to me.

"They say the men in the truck decided to leave last night instead of this morning."

"Would another truck be by this way again?"

"They no' say. Maybe in a week."

"A week!" My voice rose, the nearby jungle birds shrieked. "I just don't understand that kind of thinking. We were just six miles away," I began to rant and rave. "Ten stinking kilometers! They couldn't think to stop by and ask if we wanted a ride?"

"It is only about fifty miles back to *El Cayuco*," informed Alfredo. "We can do it."

"With no food and little water?"

Alfredo's eyes were cast downward, his feet kicking some sand around. Anything to avoid me.

"At least out of *Maisi*, we had vitamin E tablets to chew on," I informed Alfredo. "We don't even have that."

"But the day is still cool. The sun no' on us yet."

"Yeah, and when it does, we're toast," I shot back. "I can't maintain the speed and energy of yesterday. Without fuel at some point, I'm going to burn out. And so will you!"

"I be okay. Come, let us leave."

We mounted our bikes and headed toward *La Bajada*.

"When are you going to learn you're not a machine?" I yelled from behind. "Or are you? Come to think of it, since this Tour began I've never seen you bleed."

"I no' think of such things. I just cycle."

"Alfredo Rodriquez, the six million *peso* man."

Since I was forced into the situation, I figured I may as well enjoy my surroundings. Who knew when or if I would ever be in this *Lost World* Paradise again? We had the day to ourselves; and there was no particular goal or distance to attain. A truck would not be passing by our way as we were at the end of the road. At best, though, we might find one in *La Bajada*.

It was an all-day affair. I took the next six hours to do 36 miles. I would cycle a mile or two, and then walk the bike another mile. Anything to conserve my energy and strength. To stretch the muscles.

Alfredo fell into his own pace of going a couple of miles ahead and then resting on the beach or under some shaded palm.

I watched the king rats and giant iguanas dash across the road in front of my path, always too fast to get a good photo of them. It was as if they were playing a game with me to alleviate the routine boredom of their lives. They'd rustle in the nearby bushes, shriek and shrill, and then dart out to the other side. Sometimes I'd hear them up ahead, and make my own weird sounds. I'd throw pebbles where I thought they were, just to see them run and skirt around. Wild horses and pigs ran and roamed the open fields of palm, coconut and papaya trees.

At one point when Alfredo and I actually did meet up with one another, we came to a house where an elderly man gave us water and fresh papaya from one of his nearby trees. We dove into them. The juices flowed down our hands, arms and necks to our chests.

Another man engaged Alfredo in conversation about what every Cuban wanted to know when meeting us: What were we doing? Where were we going? The numerous questions about the bike. It bores the hell out of you after so many weeks.

His companion was a woman who did nothing more than stare at me through dark-circled eyes. Her emaciated frame, tattered clothes, and black feet betrayed a harsh life. For all I knew, this woman could've been younger than me, yet she looked so old. Even the men had nothing more than frayed clothes; their shoes were worn to the point that their sockless feet showed through. They live in Paradise surroundings, I mused, yet there's a price to be paid, and that's extreme poverty.

They all seemed to live together in that little house nestled in the jungle on that remote coast of Cuba.

With Alfredo continuing to maintain a pace well ahead of me, I stopped a few miles down the road, where the jungle opened up and gave an inviting glimpse of the beach. Knowing this would be my last time, I made another detour.

The small, white-capped waves rolled along the shore-- a shore whose pure, unspoiled white-sandy beaches were unmarked by man.

Since the opportunity presented itself, and this, I knew, would be the last chance before heading back to Havana, I stripped off my shoes and clothes, walking freely, wonderfully, and uninhibitedly naked along the coast. I marvelled at the many different seashells I came across. There were sand dollars, and conch shells. Shells of pink and yellow and silver. Shells that twisted and turned and rolled and curled. Shells the size of a pinkie and as large as an adult fist.

I carried what I could as souvenirs. I laid spread-eagle on the beach, and swam in the warm waters. I imagined that that was what Heaven was like. Free. Peaceful. Unburdened.

Of course, reality had to come at some point, and for us that was at 1pm, when our tires touched the single paved road of *La Bajada*. It was time to act civilized, Alfredo and I facing the military boys and their AK-47's. The gate was raised, allowing us to pass through once more.The beady-eyed, mustachioed Commander came out with a smile and open arms.

"Did we miss something while we were gone?" I asked Alfredo. "Or does the *Commandante* have a twin?"

The two men spoke in their native tongue. The Commander would point at me from time to time, and Alfredo would look over at me and laugh. This had to be good.

"The *Commandante* say he surprised to see us return," smiled Alfredo, as he began to clue me in on what was happening. "He say, he thought you were my American contact helping me escape Cuba with a boat at the end."

"Tell him the boat didn't show up," I smiled.

"You always ask for trouble," frowned Alfredo.

The two of them exchanged words about how things went, and if some type of vehicle would be passing toward *El Cayuco* or farther. The officer pointed to a group of people who had been waiting since the early morning for a truck, but, he added casually, "Who know, if any, would show?"

"Oh well," shrugged Alfredo. "I like all types of situations. This is good."

"I can't wait to hear how this is good that we still have another twenty miles to go before we find any kind of a truck."

"I only need ten more kilometers to have 2000. And then that will be my longest tour," he smiled.

The Tour had already far surpassed anything he or anyone else had ever done, but he just had to get past that 2000-kilometer milestone mark.

I was just pissed that we had to do another 21 miles. "You and your stinking goals," I said, to which he just smiled and sang a happy Spanish ballad.

Just beyond the 2000-kilometer mark, I had run out of fuel, including the reserve tank. Half a papaya and a bottle of water can only go so far. I wondered how I would ever be able to make the last 15 miles to *El Cayuco* when we were in no man's land?

It was then I heard someone shout, "*Hola!*"

Alfredo was just up ahead, waiting to see what I would do. Nearby, a father,

Alfredo leaving the single street town of *La Bajada*.

who was working on some reeds with his two sons, saw me crawl by on my bike. We met at the gate. I held out my bottle. "*Agua?*"

"*Si,*" he nodded, and invited me in. Alfredo followed.

I was just so weak that I needed to sit down and rest. The man, dressed in old Army fatigues, spoke with Alfredo.

"Where did you come from?"

"*Cabo San Antonio,*" answered Alfredo.

"Without food or water?" his eyes grew large.

"*Si,*" nodded my friend.

"You are lucky the sun did not get you."

The wife, dressed in a tank top and shorts, brought us the water, and some freshly-baked sesame seed cocoa bars. I ate them like a hungry animal. We stayed an hour resting, regaining our strength.

We took photos, and showed our hosts the bike. That seemed to interest the bare-chested boys, who laughed and fought over who was going to be the first to touch it. The father laughed, grabbed a hand from each son and placed them both on the bike's frame at the same time.

We thanked them for their help. Trying to give them some money was a bit of a problem. I handed a 20-*peso* bill to the man, and he pushed it back to me.

"*Senor, por favor.*"

This time I placed it in his shirt pocket. He let it stay.

They were a Godsend and a lifesaver, and I only wished I could do more.

Now that we were refreshed and he had passed his personal goal of

With a local family near *La Bajada.*

2000-kilometers, Alfredo set his sights on another prize...

"If we can be back in *El Cayuco* by five o'clock before the local PanAmerican store close, I could buy an ice, cold beer."

"With such a lofty goal, don't let me stop you."

I gave the blessing. He was out of sight.

Within 90 minutes, we were back in *El Cayuco*. The rest and sesame seed cocoa bars gave me the energy I needed.

After spending that time on the road in blissful thoughts of catching a ride to *Pinar del Rio* and eating hot dogs at the nearby *Rapido*, it occurred to me that perhaps we would be stuck in town. That would mean a tedious torture from Ariel, who would know we were back. I was sure that he'd seek me out and haunt my soul.

Although I had arrived just past the 5pm curfew, the PanAmerican store was still open, a horde of people standing in line.

I found Alfredo sitting at the curb quenching his thirst on a cold brewski.

"It is the town's night to go without power," he casually mentioned between guzzles.

As it had happened in *Manicaragua,* the government chose that day and that town to turn off the juice. And I was really looking forward to a shower and a chance to play catch up on my notes, too.

"Great! What else can go wrong?"

"Oh, Ariel is looking for you," smiled Alfredo.

"Thanks, *amigo*. I'll remember you for this."

Figuring Ariel would try looking for me in the PanAm store, I stole out of sight in the shop next door.

It didn't last long before a familiar, smiling, ugly mug came peering in, discovering me. He reminded me of my dogs when I try to hide from them. They'd check every room in the house, becoming nervous and jittery with each passing one until I'd been caught. Then their tails would wag with delight as they tried to jump into my arms and smother me with kisses.

It wasn't that extreme with Ariel, but I still asked, "Why Lord? Am I being punished for something?"

I wanted to cry.

Fortunately, it didn't last long. Once again, Ariel used me as a poking board, peppering me with questions in his limited English. I tried my best to answer. Alfredo was having none of that nonsense, staying far away from us, drinking his beer.

"Just walk away from him," he shouted out to me.

"You don't think I've tried?" I shouted back.

"Aw, he crazy in the head."

Only when we were at an exhausted end, would Ariel speak to Alfredo, communicating what he wanted to tell me.

"He say he want you to sponsor him to America, so he can make lots of money in sports," Alfredo interpreted, shaking his head. "Now he want to be a professional cyclist." Alfredo nonchalantly walked off to enjoy the last of his brew.

Ariel stood there, beaming with delight, knowing that his message had finally gotten across to me. But how could I explain that he'd be better off as a punching bag for Tyson? There's hardly any money to be made in professional cycling, and it was rare that you could make anything at all in adventuring. And I'm considered to be in the cream of the crop.

I was given a momentary chance to escape when Alfredo called me over to say the PanAmerican store was about to close, so it was the last chance to get what I wanted. Ariel, my puppy dog, followed.

While my partner purchased another beer to soothe his thirst, I bought a liter of Coca-Cola to take with me to the old woman's house, where I planned to spend tonight. I also picked up a soda for our attached guest, but just as we stepped outside, Alfredo's peripheral vision spotted a truck and ran off to it.

Ariel continued poking and jabbing and explaining how he needed enough money for America where he'd pay me back.

Before reaching my wit's end and wasting a liter of soda on his head, Alfredo called out, "*Kebin,* come! The truck is going to *Pinar*."

Oh, thank You, Sweet Jesus, I thought, *for those wonderful miracles You provide.*

Ariel stuck with me like glue, and I actually thought he'd climb into the truck with us. Alfredo loaded the bikes and gear into the back.

Other people would be joining us, and as I reached the rear tail, my eyes came into contact with a familiar pair of black military boots, and olive green shabby pants.

"Oh, no...no...please," I prayed, looking up to a smiling pair of beady black eyes that belonged to the *La Bajada* Commander. "You bastard! How did you get here?" I screamed. "Alfredo, ask him!"

He did. The answer: "This truck came from the resort on the other side of *La Bajada*. The *Commandante* have a weekend pass to *Pinar*, so he hitch a ride."

"Stuck with you all the way to *Pinar*," I shook my head in disbelief. "Thank You, Lord." He couldn't understand a word. And that stupid, shit grin look on his face...

Saying good-bye to Ariel, he motioned with his hands for me to write, then gave me a big hug. Since I no longer had use for the liter of Coke, I turned it over to Ariel and his family.

We drove off. The last sight I had of Ariel was of him with his arms in the air in victory, a big smile spread across his face.

"You know," said Alfredo, "he crazy in the head. He want to be everything, then don't know what he want."

Yeah, I understood. A shelf full of dreams and a discontented shelf of realities. Wasn't it that way not so long ago with me?

The back of the truck was as greasy and grungy as it was on our first ride out of Havana to *Holguin*. And like that memorable journey, we were once again stuck inside another tractor tire. Could it have been any different?

For as long as I could, I watched the sunset turn the sky into colors of yellow, red, orange, pink, blue, mixing and swirling them into pastels. *No artist could ever copy the Master Painter*, I thought.

Alfredo was already making time with a lovely *senorita*.

"...I jus' finish the longest bicycle tour in history of Cuba. Over 2000 kilometers." He smiled with satisfaction.

I smiled to myself. He should be satisfied. He had earned the bragging rights.

For 40 *pesos* and two hours of bump and grind, we reached the capital of the province. There, we were met by young vultures out for the tourist dollars.

"Hey, mista', where you from?"

"Hey, mista', have nice room for you."

"Hey, mista', have anything you want."

Some went away when being yelled at, but one stuck with us, following us no matter how many times I had to tell him to go away. He wanted our dollars bad, and was not about to let us out of his sight.

"Hey, kid, I'm from the government," I said.

"Okay. Me go with you and see."

"Listen, you cocky little buzzard, I don't need your help."

He wanted to know where we were going to stay, and knew of a "very nice place for--"

"--fifteen dollars," I countered.

"Oh, you know the place," he smiled.

"We were in *Pinar* only two days ago and have a place," said Alfredo. When he wanted to know, my partner blurted out, "*The Hotel Globo*."

Smooth move, I thought. We knew where it was, and had checked it out before leaving town the first time. We figured on staying there upon our return.

Approaching the front desk, Alfredo asked for a room for the night. The clerk looked up, but his eyes were focused on what was behind us: the kid.

"No rooms," he mumbled, bowing his head back to the newspaper on the counter. "Hotel all full."

Another bold-faced lie: It was a monstrous building, occupying the entire corner. We challenged the man's statement, but it was a no-go. He wouldn't give us a room for the night.

I turned around to glare at the kid who gave me a toothy smile. "I know a good place, mista. Only--"

"--only you're pissing me off."

"All hotels in *Pinar* full. Me know good place."

Alfredo took me aside, out of earshot from the kid. "So long as he is with us, we will get nowhere with the hotels. Best to let him have his way."

"To hell with that," I shot back. "The game's not over yet. But let's go along with him for now."

"All right, punk," I said. "Lead the way."

"Okay, mista'," he smiled, rubbing his hands together. "I show you good place. You like." He jumped on his bike.

Alfredo followed close behind, while I trailed. At one point, I dashed down a side street where I saw a lit up vacancy sign that read: *William and Mary's Hotel.*

"Do you have a room for rent?" I asked quickly. I didn't want to be discovered missing.

"Yes," answered a thin, mustachioed William.

"How much?"

"Ten dollars," answered his curvacious wife, Mary.

"Sold."

The deal was done by the time Alfredo and his shadow did some back-tracking and found me.

The kid's lips were locked so tight over what I did, that he spoke to the owners. "These two with me. I want my share of the money."

"What you talk about?" answered William. "He come here and make deal by himself. No cut for you."

The young hustler threw his bike to the ground, and began cursing in his native tongue to William. At least, I presumed it was cursing, judging by the flushed cheeks of his wife, Mary.

William told him to get lost, "before I kick your chicken little ass up and down this street."

As we all entered the couple's establishment, we could still hear the kid cursing down the street.

"Sometimes," whispered Alfredo, "you balls so big, I am surprised they can fit into your bicycle tights."

"I don't like to be hustled all the time, that's all."

The room was adequate. The double bed took up the entire space. Just outside the room was a foyer.

"Looks like we are sleeping together again," mentioned Alfredo.

"Aren't you used to it by now?"

"*Si.* Only, I have slept more times with you than with any other woman... including my wife."

After a hot shower and change of clothes, we left the house, only to be greeted by a horde of vultures just outside the front door. Our hustler friend among them. I seriously thought we would be getting into a rumble. And I didn't even have so much as a knife on me.

"Hey, mista', we know a good place to eat," taunted our hustling hawker.

"How much do you get if you show us?" I volleyed.

"Half what you spend," he smiled. I looked Heavenward.

If I had wanted a fine meal, I'd return to the *El Mason*, but right then, hot dogs and chips were on my mind. My nose and our uninvited guests made a beeline to the *Rapido* around the corner.

After dinner, Alfredo and I walked the streets. The night air was cool. It was good to stretch the legs.

On the main avenue, we came across a department store. Other people were window shopping, admiring the computers, housewares, and most importantly the brand new, three-speed bikes for 125 *pesos*, or roughly five dollars.

"That's an unbelievable price," I commented to Alfredo about the blue beauties.

"*Si*," nodded Alfredo, "but there is a special reason why they are so inexpensive. All the merchandise in this store is only for Cubans who work hard and do more than their share at their jobs. If the boss like what they do, he give them a coupon of merit to buy what they want."

"Even the computers, telephones, TV's--"

"-- anything. Right now, if I want to buy this bike, I canno'. Even if I want to pay in dollars."

"It doesn't seem right. At least to my way of thinking of how I was raised."

"But it make the people more productive in working for the government. It give them the incentive to buy the things they want. It make them feel special when other people don't have and they do."

"Someday, my friend, when the embargo's over, it's going to be a very different Cuba indeed."

"*Si.* I think it will be more fair then."

"*Si*."

I was looking forward to returning to Havana sometime tomorrow. We had been away long enough.

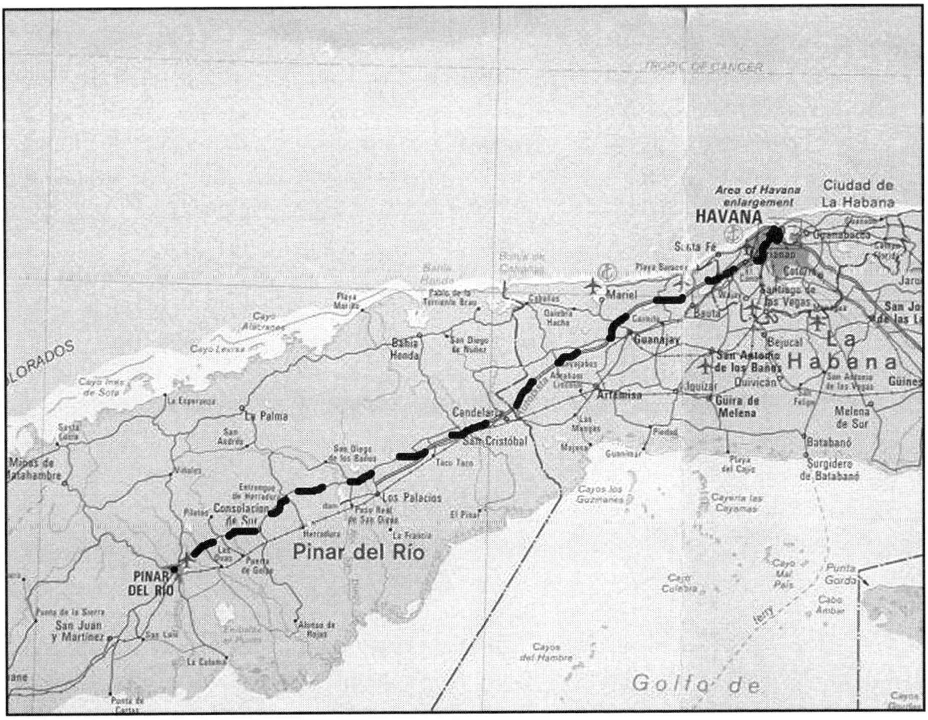

TREINTAIUNO

31

PINAR DEL RIO to HAVANA
DAY 23
DECEMBER 13, 1997

We bolted out of bed to the sight of daylight and the aroma of freshly-brewed coffee-- a rarity-- and momentarily forgot we didn't have a schedule to keep, other than hitching a ride back to Havana.

Just outside our bedroom, in the small foyer, we sat on wicker chairs, drinking java with William. His wife, Mary, offered slices of oranges. Music from the Beatles played over their stereo system.

"We love Americans and anything American," smiled William. "Where, in America, are you from?"

"California," I answered.

"Oh!" William's eyes lit up like saucers. He jumped out of his seat, and raced to a dresser in the hallway where he pulled out an envelope. "My English, no' so good," he began. He pulled out some photos from the envelope. "My friend from California. Alameda. You know?"

"*Si*. I am familiar with the place."

Alfredo and I viewed the photos of a blonde-haired young man. There were different poses: the young man, the young man with William, the young man with Mary, the young man with William and Mary. All smiles and laughter.

"He stay with us when in Cuba."

During the next two hours, William spoke about many of the unjust and unfair conditions Cubans face on a daily basis. While he talked, Alfredo translated, and I listened. A couple of the more bizarre incidents to occur between the friendly, loving couple involved Americans.

"Some rich American friends invited my wife and I to a fancy resort outside *Pinar*," began William. "It cost thirty-five dollars a night. They were taking care of the cost."

He took a long drag of his cigarette, then continued through Alfredo. Mary was listening nearby while doing the days laundry.

"When we arrive at the resort, we were asked to leave, because the place was only for foreigners."

"But your American friends were paying for it," I said.

"*Si!* Even if we were rich Cubans and could afford it ourselves, we still could not stay."

"That's pretty bad discrimination," I protested.

"*Si*," said Alfredo. "I would have the same problem on this Tour if I did not have official papers saying I am with you and signed by my sports division."

"So much for what Fidel thinks of his own people," I quipped. "Don't you get tired of being second-class citizens in your own country?"

"*Si*," they nodded. "But for now there is not much we can do about it," answered Alfredo.

"To be fair," I stated, "we have discrimination in my country as well. What usually remedies that is how much green you carry on you. What you're worth. Sadly, the dollar is god in the united States."

"As it is here," smiled Alfredo. "Fidel say we are a Socialist-Capitalist nation."

"Balls!" I laughed. "That's like saying I'm a Satanic Christian. There's no such thing. And it's a Maxim of Law, whether you or Castro want to admit it or not, that one cannot serve two masters. You already prove that with the *peso* and the dollar. Which do you want more?"

"The dollar," answered Alfredo.

"Why?"

"Because it is better. Can buy more things."

"Exactly. One master is greater than the other."

"It will take time," continued William through Alfredo, "before the people see justice. Perhaps when Fidel is gone, it will begin. Did you know Cubans are not allowed to have foreigners in their own private cars?"

"Really," I asked, taken aback. "Why not?"

"Because you take money away from government-owned taxicab drivers," answered William, his voice rising. "Even if we no' charge foreigners. I have American woman friend in my car. I take her around *Pinar* when she here. One day, police officer stop me, and ask why I have foreigner in my car. I tell him she my girlfriend. I even put my arm around her and give her kiss on cheek, but he no' believe, and give me one hundred *peso* ticket."

"Wow! That seems a bit steep."

"*Si.* It is to teach Cubans a lesson."

"What's it going to take," I asked Alfredo and William, "for Cubans to get tired of the tyranny and fight back?"

"Who know?" they shrugged.

"How about if Castro pulls the plug on the dollar?" I suggested. "Cubans can no longer have dollars. If you do, you will be arrested."

Alfredo laughed, then interpreted what I said to William and Mary who also joined in the laughter.

"Impossible," said Alfredo. "Fidel would never do such a thing."

"Why not?" I asked in mocked innocence.

"Because the people would kill him."

"Exactly!" I jumped an octave. "By his own hand, Castro has given his people a taste of Capitalism. If he were to take the dollars away now, how much power would he have over the people who supposedly love him?"

"None," shook Alfredo and William.

"The people would love him to death."

"*Si,*" they nodded and laughed. "*Si.*"

By 10am, Alfredo and I were packed and ready to leave. With a smile and a wave to our new friends, we mounted our bikes, heading for the highway out of town. We stopped at a place for some juice and bread, as neither one of us knew how long we'd have to wait for a truck going our way.

We cycled perhaps a mile, past the check point.

"The drivers try to avoid the check points," informed Alfredo. "If they have to pick up people near the police or military, they no' get to keep all the money."

"Just another side effect to Capitalism."

So we rode beyond the point, to where a side road intersected it, thereby bettering our odds on catching a ride. All a matter of geometry, I figured.

On the *Autopista,* people waited off to the side and flashed money to show they could pay. Sometimes it worked, sometimes not. Alfredo tried it for a while with browns and greens. The paper *pesos* that Cubans have range in different colors for different denominations. The singles are brown, the threes are green, the fives are purple, the tens are a pink-red, the twenties are blue. Both the color being flashed and how much of it there is often determines how far you'll get.

I understood the principle of greed and what effects it could produce. The rules of the game are standard throughout the world, so I handed Alfredo a fistful of

With *pesos* in hand, Alfredo hitches us a ride back to Havana...

The *pesos* do the job, and we are on our way home!

The building of a tobacco barn in progress,
somewhere in the province of *Pinar del Rio*.

blue bills and let him flash to his heart's content. Within a half-hour, we had ourselves a truck that took us as far as *Candelaria* for 10 *pesos*.

During the two-hour, open-aired ride, we picked-up other cyclists, and even a pair of honeymooners. We passed thatched-roofed farmhouses and banana plantations. Farmers were sorting through grain along the highway's edge, and a new barn was being built for drying tobacco leaves.

Dropped off just outside the town, we waited another hour under a shaded bridge along with other people and hordes of vendors trying to sell their food. It was pizzas and *refresco* for lunch while waiting for another truck. We found one that took us the last 60 kilometers to Havana for 20 *pesos*, dropping us off within a mile of Alfredo's home.

We returned with 60 *pesos* still in my pocket. A close financial situation, but as usual, Alfredo was right. I only had to cash $100US for the Tour.

Family and neighbors came running out to greet us, smiling and laughing with open arms. Their Alfredo had returned home safely, and for his reward he received hugs, kisses and handshakes of congratulations.

When we were able to enter his family's apartment, tales of the Tour were spoken, the map of the route was laid out before everyone that filtered in and out.

"*Kebin* and I sleep together three times in the same bed." Alfredo smiled. Those around him responded with raised eyebrows. His chest swelled, his face radiated like a cherub. He had accomplished something of great significance in cycling. He should reap the rewards, I thought. He deserved every one of them and much more. My only prayer for him now was that this current success wouldn't be as addicting for him as it was with me after China.

Since the previous night when we were catching a truck out of *El Cayuco*, everyone within range heard Alfredo's talk of the Tour de Cuba-- the immensity of it, the making of cycling history.

"I would like to do a big cycling event every two to three years," said Alfredo in a private moment. "But I know I will never do another tour on so grand a scale as what we have gone through."

"Perhaps," I answered. "But what fond memories you will retain for the rest of your life."

We'd come full circle. It was 4pm. The same time as when we left Havana on November 19th.

Out of the houseful of well-wishing guests, was a petite girl standing off to the side. She had doe eyes, full lips, a tiny nose and skin as smooth, hard, tight and chestnut brown as I'd seen in a long time.

We were introduced by Alfredo's knock-out blonde sister, Dania. Kenia was her name. It was as exotic as she was. I melted when gazing upon her.

"Er, *Kebin...teatro*...er, you like?" asked Dania.

I had to think a moment what she was asking. "Ah, *si, si, teatro. Si.*" Yes, I enjoyed the theatre very much.

"Er, you...er, Kenia..." Dania and I looked at each other a moment, spellbound. Kenia's eyes were downcast. Dania shook her head in frustration. "Alfredo!"

In a moment, big brother was beside us. Dania rattled off what she wanted to say to me. Alfredo interpreted.

"Kenia want you to take her to the theatre," he casually answered, then walked away.

"What a minute," I shouted. "Come back here."

"What is the matter?" He asked in disbelief.

"Don't drop a bomb like that on me. What good would I be watching a bunch of Spanish actors?"

"It would be a new experience for you," he smiled. "A good situation."

"Forget that. I want to party. Let Kenia go with someone else."

The girls were watching us with furrowed brows, trying to understand what we were talking about. Alfredo smiled at them, then took me by the arm to a corner of the room.

"Kenia recently broke up with her boyfriend, so she awkward right now. No' hurt her feelings."

"Don't do that to me. That's not my problem."

"So what? You canno' go out with her once?"

"Fine. Let's all go out and make a night of it."

"I canno'."

"Why not?"

"I tired. Long Tour. Me rest."

"You're such a coward. C'mon, be a new experience for you. A new situation."

"I know someone else who will go with you as interpreter," smiled Alfredo. "I go get."

Before I could answer, he left the room of people, heading down the hall to his bedroom.

"Here," he said, a moment later. "This best interpreter I know. Help me many times."

He handed me his English-Spanish dictionary.

"Balls! Don't stick me like this."

"Look at her," said the matchmaker, turning me toward the prize. "Is she no' pretty?"

Kenia looked at me with those round, moist eyes and smiled shyly. I sighed. I've always been a sucker for a pair of mesmerizing windows to the soul. And I am adventurous...

"What's the play?" I mumbled.

"*The Gentleman*," said Alfredo. "By Moliere."

"Great. A French play in Spanish. Good thing I know the story. But Kenia knows as much English as I do Spanish. How are we supposed to get through the rest of the evening?"

"Chaperone," smiled my friend, patting the dictionary.

Showering and changing into a clean pair of clothes brought a song to my lips. It felt good to be dressed up and going out for an evening of entertainment once again. I still couldn't talk Alfredo into going along.

Kenia arrived in a cream-colored dress that went well next to her brown skin. My heartbeat increased by several bpm's. I needed a shot of rum; and Alfredo's brother Alberto offered me two shots to calm my shaking hands and erratic breathing.

This was going to be one incredible night to get through. Kenia was silent during our taxi ride to the theatre, and I wasn't in the mood to pull the chaperone out of my pocket.

A massive crowd of people stood outside the closed door to the theatre. All of them were holding the same gold-lettered invitation that Kenia had.

I remembered my days at the *American Academy of Dramatic Arts*, where I got free tickets to Broadway and Off-Broadway shows. This was the same set-up, with the crowd waiting. I wondered if we were going to get in. There was no problem with the paying public to enter.

When someone from management came out to announce the show for tonight was booked, I asked, "Are there any tickets for sale?" Since the cost was in *pesos* that amounted to 50 cents, what harm could there be in asking?

"No," said the young man. "All booked."

"Hey, *amigo,* dollar?" I showed him a ten spot.

"Okay," he nodded. "Me ask."

Kenia and I waited several awkward minutes until the tuxedoed gent returned.

"Sorry," he shook his head. "All out."

I actually had a plan B. I had thought that after the performance, we'd do the nightclub thing.

Taking Kenia's hand, we walked around the corner to the $150US a night *Melina Cohiba*, where, on the ground floor, was a bar-restaurant called, *The Habana Club.*

A bouncer stood at the front door, blocking my path to enter. I said, "*Americano.*" And he quickly stepped aside. There was no problem allowing Kenia in as she was with me.

Walking up the short flight of gold-carpeted stairs, the foyer had an eight-foot tall Christmas tree and a sweet, smiling hostess. Inside, the area opened up to full view: Decorated with life-sized cardboard cut-outs of some famous Cubans and an American named Hemingway, the main floor had a restored Harley motorcycle and a '57 Chevy convertible in which one could sit and have their photo taken. An airplane hung from the ceiling, and there was a dance floor, where live bands played in between the prerecorded American rock-'n'-roll. There was plenty of room for tables and chairs in a sunken eating area and a fully stocked bar that curved around one side of the establishment, loaded with the finest international liquors I'd seen in a long time. The place was clean and capitalistic.

The staff spoke English, and I immediately headed for the bar, nearly jumping for joy when my eagle eyes spotted a bottle of *Drambuie.* The sweet aroma filtered up to my nostrils, the taste went down the throat like liquid gold.

Kenia ordered a cream liquor, and Joel the bartender allowed me to run a tab.

As we headed toward the tables near the stage, we were stopped by a young man.

"I'm sorry, sir, but the tables are reserved for those who intend to eat. If you are going to drink, you must stay at the bar." He began to show me the way back.

I side-stepped him. "Alright, pal. No problem. What's your name?" I offered him my hand.

"Julian," he smiled, taking my hand in his.

"Okay, Julian. What kind of food do you have here?"

"Only the best," he gave a toothy smile.

I laughed. "Let's see a menu."

He grabbed one from a passing waitress. My eyes nearly popped when I spotted such items as: spaghetti, *nachos*, hamburgers, cheeseburgers, chickenburgers, club sandwiches, banana splits.

"How's the burgers here?" I inquired.

"The best," answered Julian in a flat, cock-sure tone.

I laughed. "I've been in Cuba five weeks, and haven't had much success with your beef."

"I understand. But this beef is the best. Our food is flown in from Miami daily, and if you don't like it, the meal will be free. But if you like it, you have to pay double." We both laughed. I ordered.

After Julian showed us to a stage front table, Kenia and I pored over the menus.

"Me," she pointed to herself. Then she pointed to the ground and held up her index finger.

"First time?" I held up my index finger.

"*Si,*" she nodded, looking downward.

I patted her hand. "We are going to have a good time," I smiled. "*Bene.*"

"*Si,*" she smiled, looking at me. "Good...time."

Between looking up certain catch words in the dictionary, plus the added help of paper and pen, I discovered that Kenia was 20-years-old, living with her mother just a few doors down from Alfredo and his family, going to acting school for a life in the *theatro*, and like me, a Pisces.

Her smile was devilish, her eyes seductive, her spirit intoxicating. Coupled with the atmosphere, the music, the drink, I was hooked. And I melted.

Martha, our waitress, was a short, spunky, spitfire of a girl, bouncy and bubbly with a perfect smile. Julian was correct about the food: I would've paid the double fee, but he laughed it off. "So long as you return for more."

"That, I can promise you, my friend."

Scanning the room, I noticed a large number of gray-haired older men (other Americans?) and the young women they were seated with. I wondered if I was viewing myself in the future. *If I don't marry soon*, I thought, *I could end up like them: someone who tries to make himself believe he's still young by copulating with granddaughter-age women.*

About 10pm, the stage was lit for a fashion show. We had center seats, close to the designer, and watched the male and female models careen about in a controlled, rehearsed pattern. They were all as perfect-looking as models generally appear, flashing the latest styles to come out of Havana. Kenia knew a couple of the male models from some of her acting classes. She sat straight up, turning to speak to me quite excitingly, momentarily forgetting I didn't know her language. She held her hand to her lips, laughing shyly when she realized her mistake.

This, I thought, digesting the glamor, was definitely better than trying to stay awake in an attempt to follow a 17th century French play in Spanish.

About 11pm the show ended. We took a taxi back to the apartment buildings and said good-night. I watched her climb the stairs to her place before leaving.

The evening set me back some $35US, but, oh, how it felt wonderfully, lustfully good for the soul.

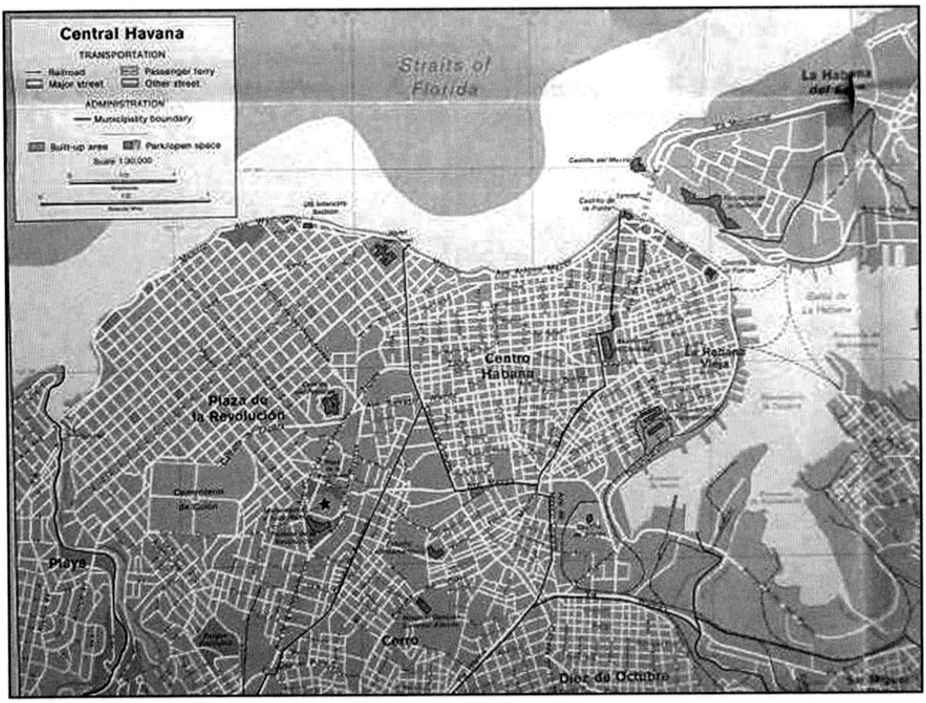

TREINTAIDOS

32

HAVANA, CUBA
DECEMBER 14-21, 1997

8am Monday came early. Too early it seemed. The weekend went by in a party blitz. Alfredo had a sparkle in his eye and was full of energy. I tried to maintain the appearance.

We were sitting outside the office of Ciro Perez, the man in charge of every sport in Cuba, the one who allowed the extension on my visa via phone in order that we could finish the Tour. Havana was in the midst of preparing for the Pope's arrival the next month. Posters and flyers hung everywhere, in the streets and in offices.

A short while before, we were greeted at the front entrance by Alberto, after a five-week absence.

"How did the Tour go?" he asked, smiling, sincerely offering me his hand.

I looked at him a moment with pressed lips, letting his hand stand erect in mid-air before taking it. "Fine," was my curt reply.

"Did anyone from Jose Palaez' office contact you after that first meeting?"

"No. I thought that was your department?"

"No," his tone changed to one of mild seriousness. "I only acted as interpreter."

Enjoying the cool breeze of the fan inside the outer office, Alberto asked to see my visa.

"I heard you had problems with the military in *Maisi?*"

I shifted in my seat. "None that were not taken care of the next day. Now that the Tour is over, what arrangements need to be made for an appointment with your president?"

He continued to glance at my document. Without looking up, he replied, "It would be best if you handled those arrangements yourself."

"And how could I do that, Alberto?"

"I would not know. Getting arrested did not help the matter. I see your visa has the CO2 code on it."

I let the meeting with Castro drop for the time being, but achievers do not give up on the first negative response.

"Does the code make me special?" I tensely smiled.

"It means you have a courtesy visa that needs the extension approved by the Foreign Minister. It is a slight matter to handle. I will be happy to take care of it."

By late morning at least one problem was solved. When we shook hands good-bye, Alberto finally gave me his number to call him if I should need any other assistance. He was going to make a wonderful politician someday, I imagined.

There was still the matter of the meeting and the gifts I had brought along for Castro-- perfectly wrapped in tune with the season. One package contained assorted baseball memorabilia from the '40s, '50s, and '60s, while the other was a King James, large print, red-lettered Bible in English and Spanish. Getting caught with this in Cuba, I knew, would be a serious offense-- probably moreso since it was intended for the leader of the country. Not even Alfredo knew what was in the second package. I figured it was safer for him that way.

Ever since I made the decision to present Castro with a Bible, it caused a stir with the people I came into contact with.

When buying the Holy Book, for instance, the saleswoman asked, "And what name would you like stamped on it." The name was placed on free with the purchase.

With so many people milling about nearby in the store, I didn't want to create a scene, so I asked to write it down. Handing me a slip of paper, I produced the name.

She looked at it wide-eyed. "Is this who I think it is?" she asked in a quivering voice, her smile disappearing.

"Yes."

"Well, praise God! Hallelujah! He needs to be saved just like the rest of us, even moreso."

"Yes, yes, I know. You're absolutely right," I said in whispered tones, as some of the people nearby became mildly curious as to what was going on at the counter. "Could we just keep this between ourselves?"

"Why? This is magnificent! You're actually going to present this to him? I want to pray for you. What's your name?"

I wanted to run out the store. When she handed the piece of paper to the high-school kid assistant to emboss the Book, his voice rose an octave. "Fidel Castro? Far out!"

Hearing that, people came forward with sincere kindness mixed with comments of well wishes and prayers. Whenever I try to do something good in secret, the Lord always makes it known at some point, instead of leaving well enough alone and allowing people to think I'm the devil.

The congregation at my church had a part in the process as well. When Castro and the Bible were mentioned one Sunday during service, I made a general invitation to all that this would be their opportunity to speak, through the Bible, to the Cuban dictator. Whatever he may be in the eyes of the world, he's still a God-created being.

During the next month, members of the church told or wrote me about particular verses, which, I highlighted in both the English and Spanish text. If Castro received the Bible, and casually flipped through it, his eyes would at least focus on some important messages that people were trying to tell him.

"If you have the chance to meet Castro," advised my pastor, "you should try to convey to him that his salvation and where he's going to spend eternity is most important."

"I agree. He doesn't understand God's love. He still has time to change."

"If he does accept Jesus Christ as his Saviour, it would have profound effects on the country and his people."

"Amen."

With the gifts in hand, and virtually no chance to present them to Castro, I was at a loss as to what to do. I began to pray; I'd let God handle the situation.

Later, when Alfredo and I were returning to his place, we came to a modestly dressed, gray-haired woman sitting on one of the steps of the front entrance to the apartment building.

Alfredo's eyes lit up. "I think we have found the miracle to present Fidel with your gifts."

He began to converse with the woman in their native tongue, as she didn't know English. Words went back and forth; there were hand gestures. Then a car came by to pick her up. When she was gone from sight, Alfredo explained what had occurred.

"Did you know who that woman was?" he smiled.

"Does it look like I do?"

"That was Fidel's personal secretary."

"And I'm standing right here and you didn't tell me!"

He brushed off my irritation with a wave of his hand. "Even if I tell you, what could you do?"

"Charm her into a meeting with the boss."

"It no' work. But she did tell me that if you write a letter of personal introduction, and bring your gifts to the headquarters at the *Plaza de la Revolution*, she say she see Fidel receive them. Your God work good, no?"

"*Si*," I nodded. "It's probably as close as I'm ever gonna get."

"If you do soon," added my friend, "could be you meet with Fidel, or maybe he send letter of thanks."

"It's worth a try."

As we began to walk back to his apartment, I asked, "What do you think the chances are of meeting a man who has all the qualities I need to realize a successful Tour? Who also happens to have a neighbor that lives in the same apartment unit as he does, who's the personal secretary of the leader of the country, in a city of two million?"

"It is a coincidence, I admit," shrugged Alfredo.

"Interesting choice of words, Alfredo. Coincidence means to *co-incide*. To fit perfectly. And that's what the Lord does when His will is carried out by His servants."

"I do not know. It is all too religious for me."

When the letter was written to my satisfaction, we took the gifts the several blocks to the well-guarded fortress. Armed military was thick in the area where the seat of power stood.

We casually walked right up the front steps, entered the building, and saw the man at the desk. He had us fill out some forms as to the contents of the packages. "Baseball memorabilia," we wrote. Period. Then we produced our individual identifications for the officer to copy down.

With nothing more to do, we left with a hope and a prayer.

In the last few days of my stay in Cuba, I heard nothing from Castro or his office, but continued in faith that all went well. The Law states that God's Word will not return void. Someday, the results may be known.

Just after the party weekend, I spoke with Lucia Newman about doing a follow up story, but the higher-ups back in Atlanta, Georgia weren't interested. The first piece ran several times in Cuba and the States to good reaction; Rudy, the cameraman, even said it was a hit, but that it had played out, and so it was onto something else. That's showbiz!

However, Lucia did say, "Stop by the offices sometime during the week to take a look at a copy of the interview." Taking her up on the offer, Alfredo and I went to the *Hotel Libre*.

It was a good piece, I thought, running about three minutes-- and for a half-hour program, that's long. Watching it on one of their office monitors, it showed Alfredo and I cycling through the streets of Havana; the interview part in the courtyard of the *Hotel National*, where we spoke about the embargo-- that enough was enough; our meeting with the people and being surrounded by the children; others trying out the bike, and Lucia on the Beast herself. Rudy had performed a nice edit, cutting out the part where I grabbed the petite reporter just before she fell. In between the interview were shots of me on my last two Tours, atop the Great Wall of China and at 17,200 feet on Alaska's Mount McKinley.

With Cable News Network's Havana Bureau Chief Princess, Lucia Newman and soundman, Tony Valdez after the tour.

"Not bad, huh, Kev?" said Rudy, smiling.

"Great editing, but you left out the part where Lucia and I get friendly toward the end."

While we were laughing over the memory, princess Lucia and her soundman, Tony Valdez walked in.

"Hey! Did I hear someone talk about me?" laughed Lucia.

"Congratulations, you two," smiled Tony, as he shook both our hands. "That was an incredible Tour you did."

"Absolutely," agreed Lucia. "It got a lot of mileage over the wire service."

"What were your impressions of the country and the people," asked Tony, "now that you've just finished the longest cycling tour in Cuba's history?"

Giving the question a moment's thought, I paused for reflection. "Aside from the extreme filth and poverty I've witnessed," I began, "the Cuban people are so warm, friendly, and giving, that it makes the American government's embargo look like a ridiculous act of revenge."

"Right on!" said Rudy. "Exactly. I felt the same way when I first arrived in this country. I love these people!"

Tony and Lucia nodded in agreement.

After taking some keepsake photos, and all around well wishing, they reminded me that if I was ever back this way to look them up.

Tony added, "You have friends here now, Kev."

True. I had made many new *amigos.*

When there was a free night in the schedule, Alfredo asked, "do you wish to attend a baseball game? It only cost a *peso* to see."

Since the stadium was nearby, why not? After all, baseball is another one of Cuba's pastimes; some of the best ball players come from that country.

The game was between the *Holguins* and the home team, the *Industrials* (who won). We arrived about half-way through the game. The largest stadium in the country, it could seat 50,000 people. That night, there wasn't much of a crowd. In any case, in a Communist country, all seats to an event cost the same, so it's a first-come, first-serve attitude.

For our four-cent ticket, our seats were front row behind third base, where I felt I might get the best photo shots. We settled into our wooden chairs.

No one else was taking photos, so the camera was a dead giveaway that I was a tourist. Some of the people around us spoke in whispered tones. "*Americano*," was the buzz word.

When Alfredo and I actually did speak to one another in my tongue, a few of the more beer drinking men shouted, "Okay, *Americano*," giving me full missing tooth smiles and big thumbs-up signs. Word spread like wildfire through the crowd, as they pointed and gawked at me.

A young boy came up to us, speaking Spanish. Alfredo did the unwanted honours of interpreting. "He ask if you want to buy his baseball?" he quipped.

"Now what would I do with a dirty, grimy ball?"

"Souvenir," he shrugged, drinking a swill of beer.

The boy asked through Alfredo, "If I get some signatures, would he be interested in buying it then?"

"Maybe," I shrugged. "Why doesn't he--"

Before I could finish my thought, he ran off toward the *Industrials* dugout, handing over the ball to the players. A few minutes later, he came back with three autographs.

Alfredo looked them over. "Hey, the kid got you some pretty good names. Two of them are Cuba's batting champions for the years 1996 and '97. This other one, Lazeros Vargas, is a double Olympic gold medalist in 1992 and '96 games."

The boy smiled, holding out his hand.

"All right!" I threw my hands up in frustration. "I give. How much?"

The boy asked for one dollar.

"That's all? For a signature ball?"

"For that, he can see twenty-three more baseball games, and get many more balls," laughed Alfredo.

I handed him the money. As soon as the single dollar was in his hand, he did a victory tap dance for the crowd of on-lookers, screaming with wide-eyed, toothy joy. He showed his friends how much the stupid American paid for his, made in Cuba, baseball.

Soon, a horde of other children came to sell me their balls. Alfredo chased them away as the crowd laughed.

Alfredo pointed out that number seven, Juan Padillo, also of the *Industrials*, was another double gold Olympic medalist.

"You should try to get his signature after the game."

"All right," I shook my head in defeat. "I'll play the fan. May as well make tonight's experience complete."

My escort took me around back where the players would emerge. Already a crowd of people had gathered. These were some of the biggest names in Cuban baseball. They emerged in plain, ragged clothes, and some of them went home riding their bicycles, while others walked. The bigger stars like Vargas and Padillo were given their own house and 1970s automobiles by Fidel, as well as other perks. These were the best years of their lives, and when it was over there wouldn't be much to show for it: Their top pay was roughly $11US per month.

"Any one of them could be instant millionaires if they left Cuba, but they no' go," said Alfredo.

Those who did leave their island home for America found instant wealth. "When Fidel die," said Alfredo, "some of them may return upon retirement and buy the village where they were born."

When Padillo finally emerged, still dressed in his outfit, Alfredo talked with the gate keeper, mentioning I was a famous cyclist who wanted to get Juan's autograph. The young man went to Padillo, who was on the pay phone, and made mention of who we were. Juan looked over at us, and gave the nod. We were allowed access past the gate, away from the crowd.

He was very generous after completing a call to his wife, signing a clear side of the ball and happily taking some photos with me for posterity before shaking hands and driving off.

During the week, Alfredo and I settled our financial account. He had no idea what the amount for his services were going to be. No matter what I intended to give him, it would never be enough for all he had done for me in bringing this Tour to a success.

I began with giving my friend several hundred dollars worth of bike supplies I didn't have a need for and didn't want to carry back home. They included a pair of $200US sunglasses, and an extra $100US altimeter-bicycle computer. Toward the end of my stay, he figured out a fair price to pay his mother for her hospitality toward me.

"And what have you figured for yourself?"

"I do not know," he shrugged. "The Tour was the greatest cycling experience of my life. In terms of dollars, you decide what you think is fair."

I handed him a stack of bills. "Will this do?"

His eyes were as big as the wad I presented to him. He took the gift with a shaky hand, and began to count.

With the signed ball and Cuban baseball great, Juan Padillo, a two-time Olympic gold medalist during the 1992 (Barcelona, Spain) and 1996 (Atlanta, Georgia, USA) Games, after the *Industrials* win against the *Holguins.*

"*Madre de Dios*," he cracked, dropping to his bed. "This is...this is...nearly two years pay for me."

"I wish it could be more."

"If it were, I may have died from shock. *Gracias,* my friend. *Gracias.*" He stuck the money in a desk drawer.

"You back five days and you no' call me?" screamed Carmen. Her lips pressed tight. Her eyes moist.

I knew I should've called her when I was back in town. It was, of course, just a matter of time before she found out. I ran into her near the *Hotel Morro* with Alfredo.

"Carmen, baby, I've been meaning to, I swear."

"You lie!" She cut me off. "How many girlfriends you find?" she asked to the point.

I professed to be shocked. "Carmen, I'm surprised you could even think that of me. I was just too busy and too tired to notice."

She gave me a disapproving, narrow-eyed nod. "You come here, see me... tomorrow. I want you. You call."

"I'll try, really, I will."

"I know you," she nodded, tight-lipped. "*El Zorro*."

I smiled to myself at the thought of being a fox. As a child, *The Mark of Zorro* was one of my favorite swashbuckling films, and the main reason I took up the Old World art of fencing. I never thought I'd ever hear me be called by that name.

The next day Alfredo rode by while I was setting up a timer shot of me in uniform with my bike, viewing the Che Guevara Army Defense building. He had a smile on his face, and a place he wanted to go. We were on our way.

A few days before, while eating hot dogs at a nearby *Rapido*, Alfredo struck up a conversation with a curvaceous young beauty named Thais (pronounced Tice, as in rice). With long brown hair, green eyes, full lips, and a perfect white-toothed smile that matched her sweet personality, one could not help but be drawn to her spirit. A flirt, like myself, Alfredo somehow managed to shift from our table to hers, thereby striking up a friendly conversation.

"I just cycled longest bicycle tour in history of Cuba," he began. I stayed to myself.

Somehow, within the next couple of hours, I moved to their table. We learned Thais was a musician who played the piano and another instrument called a *Guiro*. It's a type of fruit Cubans use as a medicine with a hard shell like a gourd, where a hole is cut out on one side, scraped clean, and the opposite side has carved notches for different sound effects. She was a singer in a local band called *Tropical Havana*. Aged 21, she was divorced with a two-year-old son. A perfect match for Alfredo and his two year old daughter, I mused.

Before leaving, he managed to acquire her address and phone number with plans to meet later on in the week where she worked during the day: entertaining tourists across the harbor.

On this second to last day before departing for home, we headed across the harbor bridge in a cyclebus-- it is, quite literally, a bus for bicycles. From the outside, it looks like any other bus one might see in any country, except for the fact that bicycles are hanging on hooks all around it's perimeter. Inside, there are no seats. Passengers stand. If there aren't many people, as it was with us at this time, then bikes are permitted to be carried on board.

It was at the historic fort where we met up with Thais and her band playing for the tourists. From a quarter mile away, I could see a full-bodied figure in a hot, red cherry dress. Getting closer, Thais recognized us with a nod and a surprised laugh,

The ever beautiful and enticing, *Thais*.

obviously thinking she'd never see us again.

I took photos, we listened and danced to the sounds of the *calypso* music. Soon, the session was over and the band packed their instruments away.

"While we are here," said Alfredo, "We should cycle to the other side of the fort."

"Why," I asked, changing the film in my camera. "What's so important that's over there?"

"A gigantic Jesus," he smiled. "Good photos."

When Thais decided to join us, Alfredo beamed with pleasure, as his chest swelled with pride. We had lunch in a park-like setting beneath the five story statue of Jesus that shaded us from the afternoon sun and overlooked Havana. The Lord was positioned blessing the city of Havana and perhaps the country as well. Manicured lawns, tables and benches surrounded Jesus. Senior citizens fed birds, while young lovers held close to one another under the Saviour. One could view the skyline that stretched for miles. The old part of Havana, with its capital building was in the foreground. The new and improved part of the city, with its 20-story People's Tower in the heart of the *Plaza de la Revolution* could be seen miles away.

The three of us spent a lazy afternoon in good, "getting to know you" conversation, with much laughter in between. Somehow, I found myself making party plans with Thais for the evening.

Donning a festive mood with Thais' band, *Tropical Havana*.

When we departed for our respective places, Alfredo informed me that, "you are having dinner tonight with Carmen."

"Oh, really? I don't recall making such plans?"

"She say to let you know," was his reply.

"We're going out with Thais tonight, remember?"

"I no' go," informed Alfredo, as we began cycling across the harbor bridge back into the city. "I stay home."

"Why? Let's go have some fun."

"I think you have better fun with Carmen," laughed Alfredo. "She say she want you. Cook special meal for you."

"Yeah," I quipped. "Bet I know what dessert will be...*Carmel Carmen a la mode*, spread out on a white linen sheet. No thanks. There's only a couple days left and I plan on partying up to the last moment.

Amazingly, in a city as large as Havana, Thais only lived some ten blocks from Alfredo. After an easy walk that took no time at all, I was knocking at the sixth floor apartment door. Her mother, not more than a decade older than I, answered smiling, allowing me to enter.

Thais was a goddess in a navy skirt and burgundy bodice topped by a navy jacket. Her long brown hair flowed about her shoulders, and her green eyes sparkled.

"Why is it, that just as I'm ready to leave a place or a party, I meet someone I want to spend all my time with?"

"*Que?*" Her smile melted me.

Jesus Christ above Havana.

The skyline of Old Havana as seen from the statue of Jesus across the harbor.

“Nothing,” I answered, shaking my head. “You,” I pointed, then pressed my fingers to my lips. “Beautiful.”

Aside from Thais’s mother, there were also her elderly grandmother and two-year-old son Nelson, who hid behind mama’s skirt.

The routine by then was to go to the *Habana Club*, where a reserved table in front waited for me. My main man Julian was at the front door to greet us, and spunky Martha served as our waitress.

There was all-night drinking and dancing and laughing, then a taxi ride back to her place where we stayed in the foyer, conversing in a minimum number of words with the help of my substitute guide, Alfredo’s English-Spanish dictionary. Soon, the birds were beginning to sing; the sun, rise. We forced ourselves to part with the promise of seeing each other again in the afternoon.

Five hours later, we found ourselves together again, exploring parts of the city, taking the last of the photos.

Toward the end of our day, we sat across a table at the *Rapido* where we first met earlier in the week. The inevitable parting arrived, and Thais cried tears of loneliness, saying in her limited English, “this... best time me have... *anno.*”

“All year?” My jaw dropped.

“*Si,*” she nodded through her tears. “You,” she pointed. “Me,” she pointed to herself. “Tonight?” She brought her two index fingers together, then cupped her hands in prayer, tilted her head and rested on them.

If there was ever a woman I wanted to have in my bed, it was the erotically beautiful and enticing Thais. She is what wet dreams are made of. Even though every fiber of my being wanted to be inside close to her, I just couldn’t. It was, after all, my last night in Cuba. Spending only a single night with this voluptuous woman, would be masochistic torture I didn’t need. Also...

“I...Alfredo...go out tonight.”

Alfredo promised he’d go out with me and party on my last night in his country. I couldn’t go back on my word no matter how bad I wanted to. Thais began to cry again.

A bud of mine who ended up visiting the island and came back to the States with a Cuban born wife, told me, “Kev, you’ll want to leave as soon as you get there, and toward the end you’ll find it difficult to pull yourself away.”

I remember responding with a laugh and a mock *know-it-all* attitude, replying, “when the time arrives, I’ll be more than ready to leave.” How wrong I was.

“Okay,” sniffled Thais. “Me understand. I...miss you.”

She placed her hands over her left breast. Thank God I was leaving the country. I *really* needed to get out.

“Me, have something to remember?”

“*Si,*” I nodded, “*Que?*”

She pointed to my T-shirt.

“*Si?*” I touched my navy blue shirt.

“*Si.*”

I looked around the *cafe*. The rest of the customers were in their own little world. It was an unusual request, and since there was no time to return to Alfredo's place, I literally stood up and gave her the shirt off my back.

She laughed with delight, cupping her hands over her mouth while looking around at the people nearby. "You cwazy, *Kebin*, you cwazy!"

I carried a light jacket in my knapsack, and put that on. Walking slowly back to the foyer of her building, we held each other arm in arm until the dreadful time came to part.

It was difficult, awkward and cumbersome, but when it finally happened, she stepped into the elevator and was gone in the blink of an eye. A forgotten dream upon waking up.

Back at Alfredo's place, I went through the usual shave and shower ritual, while my friend and his brother, Alberto did the same. Their sister Dania, feeling somewhat left out, slinked up to me, purring, "*Kebin*, me go, too?"

"*Si,* Dania! You be my date."

"Okay," she smiled. Before going off to prepare, she asked, "Eh, *Kebin*... Kenia go, too?"

"*Si, si,*" I nodded. "Kenia, too."

She ran off to inform her friend of the party plans.

By 11pm the five of us arrived at the Club. Julian was ready for us with a table down in front, where a nine-piece band was playing a spicy number.

"Great spot, Julian." I tipped him some green.

"Only for the best customer of the week," he smiled.

The place was packed to a standing crowd; the stage filled with dancers. Martha came by with a hug and kiss.

"Martha, my love! My last night here wouldn't be the same without you." More green exchanged hands.

"Tonight, you have two women?" She mockingly scolded me. "When will you find time for me?"

"If only there was time to find."

When my friends were seated, I headed for the bar. Omar, another bartender, kept the *Drambuie* flowing.

"Keep the tab running, Omar."

"*Si, senior*," laughed the husky hustler.

When I arrived at our table, Alfredo and Alberto sat like a pair of bumps on a log. Expressionless. Arms folded across their chests. Dania and Kenia were the opposite, tapping their feet and hands to the beat of the music. That was signal enough for me.

Grabbing Kenia by the hand, we did some hot, body-close dancing, wrapped up in our own world among the other dancers on stage. It obviously got to Dania: she jumped out of her seat and onto the dance floor, spinning me around to try me out for herself.

My bike never looked so good as it did with *Thais*.

"Dania," I said in mocked shock. "I didn't know you were so forward."

"*Si*." She held me close to her. "Me want, too."

"Then who am I to argue?"

During the exercise, I worked up a sweat. Taking off my jacket, I threw it toward our table, and Alfredo made the quick catch. I reveled in my American flag T-shirt, spinning around the stage like an ice-skater, all to the howls and claps, cheers and standing ovations of the audience. At times, both Kenia and Dania would join me in dance, grinding both sides of my body with theirs. Dirty-dancing, Cuban style-- I wondered how far we could take the act before getting ourselves thrown out for such an indecent display.

"Ah, my friend, you are a wildman on the dance floor," laughed Omar, shaking my hand vigorously between rounds.

Alfredo and Alberto continued to sit somberly in their chairs, drinking their beers and snacking on the food that was continuously served.

"C'mon, boys," I said, sitting between them, my arms wrapped about their shoulders. "We're making enough noise to wake the dead. It's the last night. We're supposed to be having fun. Remember?"

"We are," answered Alfredo, taking a sip of his beer.

"Oh, yeah, I can see that." I grabbed the beer from him, looking at the can. "And why are you drinking this cheap stuff when you can have whatever you want?"

"Because I like it," he replied, taking his drink back from me.

"Couldn't you at least use a glass?"

"But why be wasteful?"

I just shook my head.

"You beautiful dancer," said Alberto. "Me like to watch." He, too, drank the same canned beer as his brother.

"You having fun like your brother, Alberto?"

"Is okay," nodded Alberto. "Me no' use to such a place. It all so big and fancy. I like, though."

"Good. I'm glad."

"Come," said Dania and Kenia, as they each grabbed an arm. "Let's dance more."

We were off and dancing.

We closed the nightclub down. The staff provided everyone at our table with fancy place settings, showing many colorful cars from the '50s along with some *Habana Club* mini-posters.

The entire bill, with all the tipping, came to some $60US. In the States, it'd be at least five times that amount.

Hugs and kisses were exchanged. It was nearly 3am when we returned home.

After two nights with little sleep, I was beginning to feel the effects. I thought that perhaps I could pass out for a few hours before going to the airport. Alfredo and Alberto were already comatose, but Kenia and Dania still had enough energy to bump and grind, wanting to spend every moment they could with me. So we hung out together, keeping the noise level down.

By 5am, Alfredo helped me carry the fully-loaded bike bag to the taxi, where we stuffed it in the back trunk, strapping it down with bungee-cords.

As Alfredo and I were about to leave the apartment, Kenia and Dania made their way to me.

"We go...airport," said Dania.

"Wouldn't you rather go to bed instead?"

"No bed," she replied. "We go."

The girls were out the door and in the taxi before I had a chance to protest. Women!

Alfredo and I shook hands and hugged.

"You have been a great friend to me," I said. "I couldn't have done this Tour without you."

"*Gracias,* my friend," replied Alfredo. "You return. We travel somemore."

"*Si,*" I nodded. "I will."

Before climbing in the back seat between the girls, I turned to my friend one last time with a *thumbs up* sign.

"*Cubanos-Americanos, amigos?*"

"*Si,*" he smiled. "*Americanos-Cubanos, amigos.*"

As we began to drive off in the darkness, Alfredo raised his right fist in victory.

During our drive to the Josi Marti airport, Dania gave me a worried, frightened look. She wrapped her arms around mine, placing her head on my shoulder. She announced in her limited English, "Please, no go!"

I took a deep breath and kissed the top of her head. I turned and did the same with Kenia, who was in the same position as Dania was on my other shoulder. I was nearly tempted to tell the driver to turn around.

When we finally arrived at the airport, the driver went to the wrong terminal and was stopped by a police officer-- and given a 20 *peso* ticket, because he was a private individual carrying an American. I remembered the story William told me in *Pinar.*

The officer gave me a narrow-eyed, tight-lipped look over. I returned the gesture, adding, "You, are a butthead!"

I paid the driver his ten dollar fee plus the added 20 *pesos* for the unjustified ticket he received. He smiled, shook my hand vigorously and thanked me profusely.

Dania and Kenia escorted me inside with my gear. Staying a while in awkward silence, Dania said, "You come back, soon."

"*Si, si,*" I nodded. "I promise."

They sent me off with hugs and kisses. "We will miss you," they said one last time, and left.

Six weeks had passed like a dream, a vapor. The sky was gray, though sunlight was breaking through. It took a couple of hours to jump through the hoops before boarding the plane. Military personnel armed with rifles watched the foreigners' every move.

Once on the plane bound for Canada, I thought I could finally sleep, but the next party was about to get underway; the rum and Coke beginning to flow like a river. A no-frills flight-- but a great party atmosphere.

I thought if I were any older, the Tour would've killed me. It was going to be good to get home to a more quiet, slower way-of-life...

But until that happened...

C'mon! Get that rum and Coke going, dance those aisles, and let the party begin!

EPILOGO

KAWEAH COMMONWEALTH, CALIFORNIA REPUBLIC 2003

Sitting in front of the computer, in the still quietness of the night, I reflect upon the fact that two things have occurred today. It's exactly six years to the day Alfredo and I finished the **Tour de Cuba** at *Caleta Larga*, and it's my mother's 75th birthday.

Six years. I marvel at the swiftness. In the fraction of a blink of an eye in the span of time, another dream became reality, being replaced by many fond memories.

The evenings are getting cooler now, as they were upon arriving in Toronto that day in 1997. Going from warm, sunny temperatures to the freezing, bitterly cold Arctic winds in a few hours woke me with a jolt, but when I cleared Canadian customs and stepped through the doors to a throng of waiting people, I noticed the airport decorated with the sights and sounds of Christmas, and I began to warm once again.

People were in a hurry, going to and fro, this way and that. A woman passed by me and became startled. "Oh, excuse me," she cried. "You look so much like Che Guevara in that beret." That was a first for me.

A man ran by, trying to make a connecting flight when he bumped into a fur-coated, classy looking high-society woman who cursed the Lord's name. That made me wince, and suddenly made her look dark and ugly.

The first thing I did upon arriving in Toronto was to place a phone call to an anxious Jean.

"Thank God you're out of Cuba. Now I can stop praying."

"Whoa! Not so fast. I still have to get through US Immigration." It was good to hear her voice again.

"I think you've given me more gray hairs," she moaned.

"Great! You know it's my favorite color on a woman."

"When can I expect you back?"

"If you don't hear from me in a couple of days, you'll know what happened."

"Wonderful," she quipped. "Thank you for those words of encouragement. What jails should I start calling?"

We laughed and talked at least the next hour. Ending was still somewhat difficult to do, but I held on to the hope that I would be seeing her within 24-hours: Christmas Eve.

Viewing the airline schedule, I discovered I could do an early connecting flight, thus saving me a day of waiting. Passing through the metal doors of US Customs, I filled out a Declared Value card, as the female officer began reading me the riot act concerning my recent off-shore excursion.

"Do you have any statement or permission from the Treasury Department or other US government office allowing you to go to Cuba?" she asked, oh, so sternly.

"Didn't know I needed one." I smiled.

"Don't be taking an attitude with me!" she snapped.

"Look, baby, you've been up all night and I've been awake the last three days, and I'm not about to argue on whether or not I'm a *US* citizen. Now, we're both tired. It's Christmas. And arresting me would swamp you with paperwork, so just say what you have to say, and let me get on the plane."

She shot straight out of her chair so fast it made other Americans take notice.

Placing a "closed" sign at her booth, she barked, "Follow me to the back. We want to have words with you."

Several yards away was the US Immigration Office. Inside, was a bald, bespeckled, middle-aged man at one of the desks. I waited outside while the promotion-hungry wench went in to have words with her superior. A few moments later, they both emerged to speak with me.

Bracing myself for the verbal fight, I found just the opposite with this quiet spirit; this easy-going man, who asked the usual, straight-forward questions.

"How long were you in Cuba?"

"Six weeks."

"For what purpose?"

"Peace and friendship."

"Hey, I like that answer," he smiled. "Never heard that one before. Do you have any government papers giving you permission to go to Cuba?"

"Sure," I answered, sifting through my briefcase. "I have a letter from the Cuban Interest Office in DC."

"No. I meant from our government."

"Oh. Being that I'm an American, and raised in a country that promotes individual thinking and freedom of life, liberty and the pursuit of happiness, I never thought about asking Uncle Sam to go where I pleased."

"That's good...that's good," he nodded. "I can accept that. You're the cyclist, right?"

"Yeah. Got some great publicity out of the Tour."

"Yeah...right. I remember seeing you on TV."

He viewed the letter from the Cuban Interest Office, then handed it to the smiling assistant, saying, "Make a copy of this, his passport, and Declared Value slip, and send him on his way."

Her mouth hung open for a moment before clamping shut. She gave me a steely-eyed death look, which made me believe I'd be in a different situation if she were in charge.

When she had retreated behind the glass cage, the superior turned to me with a smile and asked, "So...how was Cuba?"

I broke into a donkey grin. "Great! Love the people, the weather. Can't wait to return. You should check it out someday."

He laughed and repeated, "Yeah...someday."

"I suppose you'll be sending that paperwork off to DC, huh?"

"That's where it usually goes."

"It's cool, man. The FBI already knows where I live. We've had words before. Probably have a good-size file on me by now."

The Fed boys had stopped by a couple of years before to talk with me regarding some info they had. Seems someone saw me hanging out for a while with Timothy McViegh of the Oklahoma City bombing fame, but that's a whole 'nother story in itself... None of it was true, but still made for an interesting afternoon with the boys.

After a few moments, the unsmiling lass returned, slapping the passport back in my hand, and sent me on my way; pouting when I offered her a "Merry Christmas."

To this day there has never been a problem with my country over going to Cuba.

On the flight to LA, I slept off and on, ate and drank. The in-house movie was *Conspiracy Theory*. I laughed at the irony. It was good to be going home.

When I touched down in Los Angeles, the first thing I did upon getting my touring van out of the parking garage was to hit the fast food restaurants in the order I came to them. It was Burger King for burgers and onion rings, McDonald's for fish filets and fries, Wendy's for a smooth, chocolate frostie, and Taco Bell later on in the evening for Gorditas, a seven-layered burrito, and tostada. My appetite was satisfied, not to mention that I showed no prejudice toward any single fast food competitor.

So many letters, phone messages, emails, and faxes bombarded me upon my return that it took a week to get through them all. But none of that yet: It was Christmas Eve. No time to rest, for Cuban gifts had to be wrapped and ready to be placed under the tree. It was strange how it didn't feel like any particular holiday was upon us. Maybe it was that I had just returned or that I never had time to adjust to the Christmas atmosphere, but the span between Thanksgiving to New Year's Eve wasn't at all Spirit-filled. I think I was just mentally and physically exhausted, and running on reserve energy until the holidays ended.

After the parties, there were slides to develop, speeches to make, letters to answer, and interviews to give. Almost immediately, I began to receive passionate letters from the many women I had met throughout the Tour. All in Spanish, they required an interpreter for me to handle them. They spoke about loving me, about settling down, about being able to satisfy me. All the usual surface stuff, but nothing solid and lasting. Eventually, the letters stopped arriving.

Irene made good her word to call me in hopes of moving Westward, but my position still stood: no one-night stands and living together unless married. That produced a fast click of the receiver.

And then there was Ariel, who wrote to plead, beg, and finally demand I send him the needed money for his release from Cuba to America, where he could make his fortune as a sports star.

Not too many changes happened while I was away, but one significant factor hit me like a jolt upon my return was the news of the death of Klein's marketing and public relations manager, Phyllis McCullough, from cancer.

Phyllis' personality was always bubbly, bouncy, and positive. When my own manager, Charlie Litsky, died of a heart attack at age 33 during the **American Summits** negotiations, I was left high and dry-- and in the business of entertainment, you can't represent yourself and expect any kind of a deal to work.

Publicity had already come out about the Tour, sponsors were signed, preparations made-- but there was still the matter of the bike to be used. Some scrambling needed to be done, *pronto!* I was at a loss, calling companies, trying to handle the deals myself, but it was all futile. I was seriously contemplating going to the local Wal-Mart and purchasing a couple of Huffy's when one of the writers for *Bicycling* magazine called for an update. With Charlie's death, **American Summits** was in danger of being cancelled. He suggested I call Phyllis at Klein Bicycles.

I did.

She responded with what I would learn was her usual enthusiasm, and within a month we had ourselves a showpiece. Phyllis was just as much an entertainer as I was. We worked well together, so the Cuba Tour was a natural.

Back in 1995, I knew she had cancer. We talked about it. She was always so positive the treatments were going well, everything would be fine. We spoke just before I left for Cuba, and it was still the same cheerful lines, but my gut had its doubts.

Now she was gone. Like Charlie. And I took a good look at myself, asking, *Why do I need to continue in a field where those closest to me are dead or dying, and where I'm just scraping by on nickels and dimes?*

I'll always have the memories. As the old man on the front porch rocking chair, the children will pass by my place, turn to their friends, and boast how, "that's the guy who rode a bicycle two thousand miles on top of the Great Wall of China, and did all fifty State highpoints, and went to Cuba when our government said we couldn't."

It's those future generations that will do the boasting for me; that'll relive the times of today, while I hang on to the realities of the day-to-day survival of what it took to get the job done. Of the weariness I felt to not fail those who believed in me. Who believed that perhaps, possibly, dreams could come true if one were persistent, determined, and bold enough to achieve.

I announced to the press I was ready to retire from my life as a cyclist-adventurer, concentrating more on returning to my long-detoured acting career, and being more involved in the film version of my life story, *9 Dragon*. During the long Tour, I had some great ideas for the script that I couldn't wait to set down on paper.

What more could I do in cycling? How much further did I need to prove myself? I had done tours that boggled the public's imagination; they would probably never be repeated in my lifetime-- or anyone else's, for that matter. I entered the '90s as an unknown factory worker, and by the end of the century as the dawn of a new millennia approached, I was leaving with a life far beyond anything I could have ever possibly realized. I had arrived at a time when the word *mountain bike* was just a question mark to the general public and within a dozen years, showed that it was a piece of machinery you could take anywhere. Sure, there were plenty of cycling adventures I contemplated, other countries to explore, the chances to place a bicycle where none had ever been. But it was time to enter into a new phase...

The call came two weeks into the New Year of 1998.

"Say, Kev, how'd you like an all-expense paid trip to North Korea?" said the potential sponsor.

No...no! I was retired. That's it. No more. I had developed a reputation as a person for getting the impossible done. Sure, I had cycled through Communist countries. But North Korea? Well...it had been one of those wish-list tours after China...but no. *No!*

"I'm retired...really...yes, for sure. I really, really am...North Korea, huh? Fully paid, did you say?"

Eventually, the numbness and tingly feeling in my hands faded away, returning to normal with no side effects to speak of, no noticed nerve damage. I constantly thank God for my continued health, and that He is ever-present, watching over me.

There were the offers of writing the book of this Tour, as it was with the first two, and I actually began with a couple hundred pages, but then the stronger pull of *9D* and Hollywood kept enticing me, calling me back. Negotiations are still ongoing, and I still can't agree on certain terms with the money people, but eventually I am hopeful that a deal will work out one day for the good of all. I continue to take it a step at a time.

Shortly after the final Tour of my illustrious career, I spent the next several years immersing myself in charitable work within my church and community, pretty much devoting the majority of my waking hours to helping those less fortune.

When the new millennia approached, I finally broke down to my sponsor's persistent pleas, and went ahead with a website of my life and adventures, never thinking anyone would really be interested in living through someone else. Once again, I was wrong, when the site made it's debut on my birthday and over the years have heard from a great many of the fans who were encouraged by my travel writings that it made me want to return to writing this book.

Pope John Paul II did arrive in Havana exactly a month after my departure. He spent a week visiting as many of the major cities as his six-day schedule allowed. He was greeted by millions wherever he went, and Castro stayed by his side the entire time, looking quite different in a business suit, rather than his familiar military dress greens. Somehow, he looked changed-- old and tired, the weight of mortality resting upon his shoulders. *Did he have the Bible with him during the Pope's visit*, I wondered?

By March that same year, Hollywood celebrities showed up by the planeload to have their fun in the sun, and were covered by a score of media. Between the three events, Cuba was getting some mighty fair publicity that was making it look like the happening place to be. As of this writing, over 100,000 Americans travel to the "jewel of the Caribbean" on an annual basis.

Florida is out, I think, and Cuba is in as the next Spring Break vacation hot spot. For about $1000US, including round trip airfare from Toronto to Havana, you could live like kings and queens for a couple of weeks.

Of the many college co-eds I've spoken with since returning from the **Tour de Cuba**, many are just itchin' and eager to see for themselves what they're missing out on. I encourage this, because it's up to us, our generation, and future ones like us to move forward into the next decade, century and millennium.

Boys and girls, you must, *must* stand up and have your say. Speak your minds. Enough is enough with this embargo. It's idiotic and childish. The warmth of the climate only outdoes the warmth and hospitality of the people.

And if you've learned anything new after reading this book, you should know enough not to be afraid. Only fear will keep you from seeing and going after whatever strikes your imagination and curiosity. Do you chose to explore or exist in a bubble? Do you want to live in fear or by faith?

It's up to us-- *We the People*-- to tell those we vote into office that we've had enough. If you, we ought to say to our government, "won't open the barrier and end this embargo, then we will."Cuba is known as the key to the Caribbean, and it's giving that key to us, inviting us with open arms (and don't forget to bring those lovely dollars, *amigos*) and smiles. Take the opportunity. It's yours, because building hate upon succeeding generations is not healthy. Everyone loses out.

Remember the Babe wrapped in swaddling clothes, lying in a manger. He grew to be a Man, teaching us how to love one another as well as when to pick up the sword and fight. He showed us how to die while still loving His enemies.

And Who spoke these words written in the Book of Leviticus 25:10, commanding His servant Moses to...

...proclaim liberty throughout all the land...

Because when the last light of your life begins to fade, I hope and pray you can smile, hold your head up high, and know you did the best you could with what your Creator had given you. Then pack those bags full of memories and experiences, because you're going Home.

But until that glorious day arrives, it's up to us, and only us, to move forward, never back.

I wish all of you reading this the very best of God's blessings. Let His peace be upon your hearts.

To dare to dream the dream of dreams
is to dare to live your life.
I have dared to live, to seek God's face,
against the world's abundant strife.
I have dared to look another way.
I have dared to live another life.

Well, Lord, where do we dream from here?.....

MERRY CHRISTMAS from KAWEAH COUNTRY
December 11, 2003

THE FAQ'S ON TOURING CUBA

So...now that you've read the book, you're just itchin' to get down to the jewel of the Caribbean and have some fun in the sun. But where exactly do you begin, so that it could be smooth cycling for you?

Since the debut of my website, I have received many questions regarding how to get around the island nation on the basic, bare necessities. How can one do a tour similar to what I've done, or at least attempt shorter versions of the **Tour de Cuba**?

Below are some answers to the most frequent questions. By no means is the list complete, but it is a start to get you going. If you happen to think of something to ask that I didn't answer, drop me a line at: **www.kevin-foster.com**, and I can add it to the growing list.

In the meantime, I hope and pray the answers below will help get you, the budding adventurist, started on your first steps toward breaking the unnecessary US embargo toward a nation of people that are as warm and friendly as their weather. And when you finally do arrive in Cuba, and perhaps even meet some of the people mentioned in the book, tell them Kevin says, *"Hola!"*

HOW DO I GET STARTED?

The single, biggest question I receive from everyone who writes to me wanting to travel to Cuba. This question in itself can be an entire book (as a matter of fact, it just was), but let's try to take the question apart and go in a somewhat, organized, step-by-step manner...

WHEN IS THE BEST TIME TO GO TO CUBA?

Between November to April. After that, the island gets hot and humid to where no one, including Cubans, want to do anything but stay indoors. September and October is the hurricane season, so what's left?...November thru April.

WHERE'S THE BEST PLACE TO LEAVE FROM?

Unless you're going with an organized group (for educational, scientific or humanitarian purposes), and you're an American, you only have a few choices: Mexico, Canada, or somewhere in the Caribbean like Nassau or the Bahamas. Let's look at the pros and cons of each...

MEXICO...

The weight limit on *Mexicana* Airlines is 66 pounds, tops! After that you will be paying about $2.50-3.00 per pound. Then there's the problem of the baggage itself. My sources have told me that if the Mexican government needs the plane space to send whatever to Cuba, you may be asked to leave your baggage behind and just bring along whatever you can carry. I couldn't take that chance, so I went to...

CANADA...

The weight limit on *Cubana* Airlines is 44 pounds (or roughly 20 kilos). After that the price goes up to about the same amount per pound as *Mexicana* Airlines, but at least you're assured that what you take you can keep with you, and if you make the call to the man in charge of the per person weight limit and tell him you're doing a bicycle tour of his country, he may just double your weight limit to 88 pounds as he did with me. The contact info for this is...

General Manager, *Cubana* Airlines, 4 Place Ville Marie, Suite 405, Montreal, Quebec, Canada H3B 2E7. Phone Number: 514-871-1222 Fax Number: 514-871-1227.

The GM will probably want you to fax him something in writing to let him know your itinerary, and even when you arrive at the terminal, so make sure you have a copy of the letter you send, because the GM may forget to tell his people that he gave you the double weight.

IMPORTANT!!!...

The day before leaving Cuba, make sure you have your 88 pound (or 40 kilos) weight limit, else you will be charged before you can leave the country. The man to check on this is located in Havana, and the info is...

General Manager, Marketing & Sales, *Cubana* Airlines, 64th 23rd Street, Havana 10400 Cuba.. Phone & Fax Number: 537-334631.

ALSO IMPORTANT!!!...

Remember to have $15.00 (and this price can change at a glance, so check what the outgoing price will be when you land in Havana) US dollars on hand when ready to board the plane. This is the all-important export tax.

NASSAU OR JAMAICA...

Another possibility, and I've heard nothing but good things mentioned from those people who have traveled from these countries, so it's worth looking into.

WHAT WOULD YOU SUGGEST?

Canada is my winning choice, and here's why...

Unless you don't mind cycling grueling miles in triple digit heat and humidity, you'll be like me and head to Cuba between November thru April. The winter months are really the best time of year to travel to Cuba, because even though it's our snowy season, the temperatures South of the Border are roughly 90-degrees Fahrenheit during the day; 75-degrees Fahrenheit at night.

And no humidity!

So, again, why Canada for the departure? Because prices for flights South in the winter are stratospheric. But who really wants to fly North in the winter?... Now you're catching on. A flight South would have cost me about $700.00 round trip, but my flight to Toronto, Canada in the winter was roughly $200.00 round trip (and don't forget to add an extra $100.00 round trip for your bike to the overall cost), so the decision was made for me by my wallet. Flights out of Toronto, Canada to Havana leave every Sunday, and take five hours of no-frills to reach the sunny island.

WILL I NEED A VISA? AND SHOULD I BRING MY PASSPORT?

YES TO BOTH!

Even if you were going to Canada or Mexico or anywhere else outside the united States, it's always a good idea to bring along your passport. For Cuba, the government won't stamp your passport, because they don't want Americans getting into trouble when returning home, but you'll still need to show it to them, both entering and exiting their country. Also...

As an American, you'll need an entry and exit visa that can be obtained (usually free of charge) by the Cuban Interest Office in Washington, DC. Once you know the exact dates of your itinerary, make the call. Don't wait until the last minute! You'll probably have to fax your itinerary to the Cultural Exchange office, and then have the visa mailed to your home. The contact info for this is...

Cultural Exchange, Cuban Interest Office, 2630 16th Street NW, Washington DC 20009, Phone Number: 202-797-8518 (or 8519), Fax Number: 202-797-8521.

HOW DO I GET A PLANE TICKET TO CUBA?

One of two ways I can think of, and that would be either to go through a Canadian or Mexican travel agency, such as *Magna* in Toronto, Canada (905-761-1380), or secure a plane ticket on your own. With a travel agency, you'll be charged about $300.00 more than what you can get the ticket for on your own; the reason being is that you're an American and are somewhat limited, because you can't use an American credit card to charge your flight.

Do you have friends in Canada or Mexico that can get the plane ticket for you, and then you reimburse them? Or you can call one of the Canadian banks (say near the Toronto airport) and have them send you a debit card for whatever amount you want to give them (usually $500 or $1000), and use that to charge your airline ticket by dealing directly with *Cubana* Airlines in Montreal (or Mexico City). Believe me, a $200 round trip ticket to Havana purchased by you is a lot cheaper than spending $500 for the same fare when bought by the tourist agent.

WHERE DO I GO WHEN I FIRST ARRIVE IN HAVANA?

Your flight to Cuba will first take you to the beach resort town of *Veradero*, where you'll have a layover. Then it'll be onto Havana. You'll arrive about nightfall, and the check in process will take time. Once that's over with, and you head outside, you'll be bombarded by a horde of people wanting to help take your luggage, offer you all kinds of services for your all important dollars. To not act like a tourist, but rather someone who knows their way around, find a cab (private ones have their own cars; government taxis are yellow and black). Both private and government ones take dollars, but with private ones, you can make a deal, whereas with the government ones they have a set price per mile. The cost of a private taxi from the airport into Havana will be at or around $10 US dollars. Any more than that is thievery.

WHERE'S A GOOD PLACE TO STAY IN HAVANA?

Are we talking inexpensive as opposed to outrageous? If you're only going to be hanging out in Havana a couple of days in order to get situated, then ask your driver to take you to the *Hotel Morro* or the *Hotel Lincoln*. Both are around the same in price. About $24 USD for a single; $28 USD for double occupancy, per night, in the low-season (April 16th-December 14th), and $32 USD for a single; $38 USD for double occupancy, per night, in the high season (December 15th-April 15th). Places like the *Hotel Libre, Hotel National*, or *Cohiba Molina* are $150.00 USD per night, and all it is, is more attractive surroundings.

AND REMEMBER...

Once you arrive in Havana, *EVERYTHING IS IN US DOLLARS!*

BUT WHY WAIT?...

Why wait until you arrive in Havana to find a hotel to check in, when you can fax the *Hotel Morro* in advance and make a reservation. Their number is: 537-333907.

You can also use the good old fashioned internet as well.

ANOTHER GOOD PLACE TO STAY...

Want something a bit more private than the commercial hotel? My *amigo*, Raul Sarmienta, a retired journalist, has opened up his home near the *Plaza de la Revolution* to all guests. You can get a room with a double bed, private bath, hot & cold running water, and air conditioning all for $30USD per night, which is about what you'll be paying at one of the other hotels mentioned above. Smaller rooms go for $20 USD per night. The staff speaks English and he even has email service, so you can pop off some fast notes to friends and family. Check out Raul's place on his website at...

www.geocities.com/vedadohabana or drop him an email at: **vedadohabana@yahoo.com.** He loves to hear from people, and making reservations will be easy enough to handle. And check out Raul's bike links while you're on his site. Don't forget to tell him Kevin says, *Hola!*

WHAT'S NEXT AFTER CHECKING IN?

Flick on HBO or CNN and chill out. Relax. Take a walk along the *Malecon* or around Havana itself... Okay, since we're talking about the next day upon arrival, my perspective comes from the *Hotel Morro's* point of view.

THE MOST IMPORTANT PIECE OF INFO YOU'LL WANT...

Why wait until you arrive in Havana? Write a letter, send a fax, or call the man that saved me and the **Tour de Cuba**...Alfredo Rodriguez Martinez! You can usually find him helping out other tourists at the *Morro*, and he'll be happy to offer whatever assistance he can to you. He is the man! He knows everyone; has plenty of contacts. He's the best to have, and the best to have around. What more can I say about my *amigo*? I love him like a brother! And remember... tip him well for helping you. He only makes $12 US dollars a month! My favorite person to have on a tour can be reach at...

Mr Alfredo Rodriguez Martinez, Calle 37 Nro 140 Apto 12, Plaza, Ciudad Habana, Codigo Postal 10600, Cuba. Fax Number (*Hotel Libre*): 537-333141. Fax Number (*Hotel Morro*): 537-333907. Home Phone Number (after 6pm EST): 537-814304.

WHERE CAN I FIND ROAD MAPS OF CUBA?

Seriously? The best maps come from our CIA and the US Defense Mapping Agency (800-362-6289) out of Maryland. You can get any map of any place, any country on earth for about $20-25 dollars per section. I've been getting my maps at the USDMA since the Great Wall of China, and they've been a wonderful asset. Just give them a call and ask for what you want. The map of Cuba is in one sheet, 3 x 4 feet, and has a serial number stamped in the back corner that reads: PB92-928347. The map shows the roads, towns and railways of the entire country, as well as the streets of Havana. This will at least get you started. When you arrive in Havana, you'll need about a day or two to gather some supplies as well as other little odds and ends. You can find street and road maps of Cuba while in Havana. I've seen Alfredo's and they're very good quality.

WHERE CAN I CHANGE DOLLARS INTO PESOS?

Before heading out on your intended route, you'll need to get some pesos to use in the country. REMEMBER...there are TWO DIFFERENT KINDS OF PESOS!!! The ones the Cubans use at 23 pesos to 1 US dollar, and the foreign pesos for the tourists at 1 peso to 1 US dollar. You want the ones the natives use. From the *Hotel Morro*, go directly across the street, facing west, where you'll see a giant marketplace where vendors set up their wares. The place is alive with activity, and you'll be hounded to buy everything from them, especially the infamous *cohiba* cigars. Forget all that. In a corner of the marketplace, you'll come across a white, trailer building made of aluminum that will be guarded by two armed, uniformed men. This is where you can change your dollars into the native pesos, but don't buy too much. Start with $10, which will give you 230 pesos. That will get you around Havana for a good week on their food and drinks. When you're ready to leave the city and head out on tour, then change more dollars. Most of the time, you'll be paying in dollars (remember to bring small amounts like 1's and 5's). If you stay at someone's house, you'll want to pay in dollars to help them buy little household things like soap, light bulbs, etc... at their local Pan American store.

WHERE CAN I GET A GOOD BURGER, FRIES AND COKE?

The *Molina Cohiba!* Face it. We're American and are in love with our junk food. We need it like a fix, and there's nothing wrong with that, because after awhile you're going to get tired of rice and beans. Think of rewarding yourself with a good burger with all the trimmings after your tour is over and you're back in Havana. Once again, from the *Hotel Morro*, facing the market place across the street, take a left toward the *Malecon* (the Caribbean) and walk two short blocks. At the corner you'll come to the area's Pan American store. You'll know it by the fence and barbed wire, and all the people hanging outside asking you for some loose change. In this store, you can find almost anything American. It's a giant grocery store. Treat yourself on a daily basis if you want, but don't forget you pay in dollars.

From the Pan American store, take a left and head east (opposite the marketplace) and walk several blocks until you come across the skyscraper-tall, glass-encased, *Hotel Molina Cohiba* (there is absolutely no way you can miss this building). At the base of this massive complex is the *Habana Club* where, for about $5 US dollars, you can get a big, beefy, juicy thick burger smothered in fries and all the other trimmings, along with a cold Coca-Cola. Most of the meat in Cuba is either pig or cat, but the food (as well as the drinks) from the *Habana Club* is flown in daily from Miami (don't ask me how with the embargo going on, I didn't want to know). And while you're enjoying your meal, stay and watch the singers and dancers, and work off the meal by joining in for some bumping and grinding yourself.

HOW DO I START MY TOUR FURTHER FROM HAVANA?

Most bicycle tourists will begin in Havana and head either east or west, doing some sort of loop. However, if you're like me, and want to begin at one specific point to another, then you'll need to find other means of transportation. There are several...

THE PLANE...

You can make arrangements to fly to one of Cuba's other major cities such as *Pinar del Rio* or *Santiago de Cuba* from Havana. No waiting around. Just purchase a ticket for you and your bike for about $100 US dollars and get on board. American money really does talk in Cuba.

THE TRAIN...

Same situation as the plane only cheaper (but still in US dollars). However, the train only goes as far as *Santiago de Cuba* or *Guantanamo* and then you're on your own. For schedules to both trains and planes, check with someone at the *Hotel Morro* or ask Alfredo.

THE TRUCK...

The one I like the best. It's the most adventurous and by far, the cheapest, because you can pay in pesos! The best place to find a ride to where you want to go is the truck depot at the edge of town. Ask for directions to where this is. All the trucks from around the country come to this spot to refuel before heading home. The difference in, say, going to *Santiago de Cuba* by truck ($10 in 230 pesos), is a lot cheaper than taking the plane ($100 USD), or train ($50 USD more or less). It's all in the cost factor.

HOW DO I KNOW WHICH TRUCK IS GOING WHERE I WANT?

Ah! Here's the fun part...being able to read Cuban license plates. Unlike our own method in which you know what State the vehicle is from by simply reading the name on the plate, Cuba is set up a little differently. They go by codes, and you have to know how to read them. Every Province in Cuba (there are 14 of them total) is represented by a single letter on ordinary motorcars, with trucks having the letter **Z** following the Province letter. Thus, if you saw a truck where the first two letters on the plate read: **UZ**, you'd know by the chart below that it was from the town of *Santiago de Cuba,* and can plan your tour accordingly. When different Provinces have the same first letter in common, other letters are substituted. Here are the following codes to getting around Cuba by way of thumb and peso...

H ... *Havana city* (a Province unto itself)
B ... *Havana county*
O ... *Holguin*
P ... *Pinar del Rio*
M ... *Matanzas*
V ... *Villa Clara*
C ... *Camaguey*
A ... *Ciego de Avila*
F ... *Cienfuegos*
T ... *Las Tunas*
S ... *Sancti Spiritus*
U ... *Santiago de Cuba*
G ... *Granma*
N ... *Guantanamo*

ONCE ON TOUR, WHERE CAN I SPEND THE NIGHT?

In every town Alfredo and I came to, we never had a problem finding a place to rest our heads (and weary bodies). The Cuban people are just wonderful, in that they really do love to visit and fellowship with Americans. Alfredo and I would arrive in a town and ask passersby where we could spend the night. Someone always knew of a local house where we either paid in pesos or a few dollars to help our host buy some products he or she could only purchase in dollars, such as toilet paper, soap or light bulbs.

Of course, about every four days or so, I needed to bask in Western-styled hedonism (which drove Alfredo crazy, spending all that unnecessary money), so instead of spending the night with the natives, I opted to cut the day short (around 2pm or so), and go resort hunting, which amounted to no more than $30 US dollars. Normally, this would cost us ten times the amount in the States. Believe me, you'll enjoy these little diversions of pleasure every few days. Not having to deal with cold showers and lights out at 10pm will recharge your batteries. If you go to the Bay of

Pigs area, the entire place is one giant resort along the coast, and a great (and cheaper) alternative to expensive Havana.

WHAT PROBLEMS WILL I FACE AT THE EXTREME ENDS OF THE ISLAND?

Plenty! Getting arrested being one of them. If you think or are planning on cycling either end of the island as I had done, be prepared to be stopped by guards and ready to show some sort of official government permission to do what you want to do. That's why having a host in Cuba can be very helpful in obtaining the papers you need to get the job done. Cuba's highest natural point, *Pico Turquino*, outside *Santiago de Cuba* is also on the list of needing special permission to climb. BE PREPARED!!!

Okay, that's the scoop as far as I can think off the top of my head. If you have any other questions I've missed, email me and I'll include them on my website in a special section.

Now get out there and have some fun!!!

ABOUT THE AUTHOR

Since his electrocution and return from death in 1968, Kevin has devoted his life to turning his dreams into reality. At age 16, he became a professional actor, and worked steadily for the next decade in theatre, both On and Off Broadway in New York, as well as in film. Training in his choosen profession consisted of: *The American Academy of Dramatic Arts; The Actor's Studio; The HB Studio;* and with *Stella Adler*, all in New York City.

Kevin grew up in and around the tough ghetto area known as *The North End* of Waterbury, Connecticut, where he learned to fight and discipline himself in the Old World art of fencing, becoming a street-smart survivalist which helped in his role as a world-class adventurer.

In 1989, Kevin burst onto the national scene when he broke the near-impossible **Guinness World Record** of traveling the entire length of the New York Subway system in 26 hours, 21 minutes, 08 seconds. A year later, he followed up that accomplishment with becoming the first and only person to ride a bicycle, from one end to the other, atop the **Great Wall of China**, covering some 2000 miles, and earning the **1990 Cyclist of the Year** award over his friend, 3-time *Tour de France* champion, Greg LeMond. Needless to say, Kevin took a serious detour from his acting career.

The 90s became one rollercoaster ride after another for Kevin when he followed up the *"last, greatest cycling adventure on the face of the earth"* with the **American Summits** tour of placing a full scale mountain bike atop the highest natural point in each of the 50 united States, and the tip-to-tip, 1158-mile, **Tour de Cuba**, the longest bicycle trek in that nation's history.

Mr. Foster has also been honoured with entries in: **Who's Who in the World**; **Who's Who in America**; and **Outstanding Intellectuals of the 21st Century**.

When not traveling throughout the world turning dreams into realities, Kevin spends his time presenting slide shows and giving motivational talks of his adventures to the various schools, colleges, and corporations in the united States. He also keeps busy around his homestead and community in the tiny hamlet of Kaweah Commonwealth, located at the base of the Sequoia National Park in central California.

Known as **Captain America** (because of his love of the red, white and blue; stars 'n' stripes) by millions of schoolchildren around the world, Kevin can be reached through his official website at: **www.kevin-foster.com**, and actually tries to answer most of his fan mail when time permits.

Still single, this is his first book about his third adventure.

Visit Kevin Foster's Official Website at...

www.kevin-foster.com

or

www.kevinfoster.us

to read about his other adventures or
to find out the latest dreams Kevin is pursuing
or to just drop him an email to say, Hola!

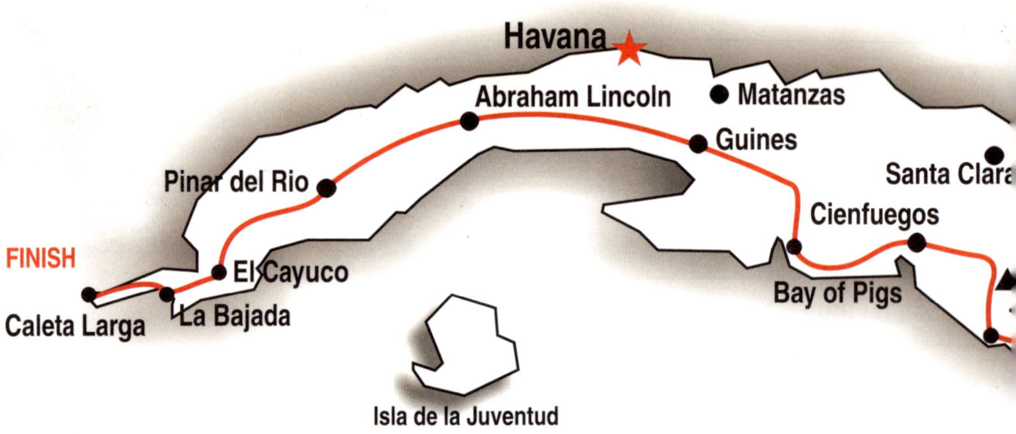

The Tour de Cuba
Start Date: November 21, 1997 at Maisi
Finish Date: December 11, 1997 at Caleta Larga
21 Days - 1158 Total Miles Point to Point